MW00527860

WOMEN'S BODIES IN CLASSICAL GREEK SCIENCE

Women's Bodies in Classical Greek Science

by

LESLEY DEAN-JONES

CLARENDON PRESS · OXFORD
1994

Oxford University Press, Walton Street, Oxford OX2 6DP
Oxford New York Toronto
Delhi Bombay Calcutta Madras Karachi
Petaling Jaya Singapore Hong Kong Tokyo
Nairobi Dar es Salaam Cape Town
Melbourne Auckland
and associated companies in
Berlin Ibadan

Oxford is a trade mark of Oxford University Press

Published in the United States
by Oxford University Press, New York

British Library Cataloguing in Publication Data
Data available
ISBN 0-19-814767-8

Library of Congress Cataloging in Publication Data
Dean-Jones, Lesley.
Women's bodies in ancient Greek science/by Lesley Dean-Jones.
Includes bibliographical references and index.
1. Gynecology—Greece—History. 2. Obstetrics—Greece—History
3. Menstruation—Social aspects—Greece—History. Title.
RG59.D43 1993   618'.0938–dc 20   92–21079
ISBN 0-19-814767-8

Set by Create Publishing Services Ltd, Bath, Avon
Printed in Great Britain by
Bookcraft (Bath) Ltd
Midsomer Norton, Avon

for **D.E.D.-J.**

PREFACE

The germ of this study was a seminar paper I wrote for G. E. R. Lloyd in the spring of 1982 when he was a visiting professor at Stanford University. The original topic of the paper was the statement made in Aristotle's *De Insomniis* that a menstruating woman would stain any mirror she looked at with a bloody cloud. I wondered how the Greeks envisaged the mechanisms in a woman's body that could cause this phenomenon and what other powers, for good or evil, they attributed to a menstruant. Research in the literature of the Classical period showed that while 'scientific' writers (primarily the Hippocratics and Aristotle) articulated detailed and subtle models of the female body using menstruation as their chief explanandum, other genres were completely silent on the topic. This was not the case for later periods of antiquity. In the Hellenistic and Roman periods the presence of menstruants in certain circumstances was acknowledged in a variety of ways (including the *De Insomniis* passage, which I eventually concluded, for a variety of reasons, had been interpolated into Aristotle's text at a later date), but the importance of menstruation in the medical definition of a woman's body declined.

Initially I intended to trace the development of this inverse relationship from the Classical to the Roman period, but the wealth of the material from the Classical era alone caused me to limit the time period of my study. Even so, within the compass of the fifth and fourth centuries I detected the beginning of the shift in the differences between Aristotle's theories and those of the earlier Hippocratics. The major part of this book, then, is an account and a comparison of Hippocratic and Aristotelian theories on the physiology, pathology, and reproductive processes of women. The Introduction provides all the background to medicine and the position of women in

Classical Greece that a general reader will need to set the theories in context. The Conclusion draws on recent anthropological work to suggest a reason why menstruation should be almost absolutely ignored in the general literature of the period when it was so integral to the physical definition of woman in scientific theory.

At all stages of this study (from term paper to dissertation to book) I have received help from many quarters. Financial support was provided by a Graduate Fellowship in the Department of Classics at Stanford University, a Mellon Fellowship from the Center for Population Studies at Stanford University, a Whiting Fellowship from Stanford University, a Rachel and Ben Vaughn Fellowship from the Department of Classics at the University of Texas at Austin, a Summer Research Grant, a Summer Research Award and a Faculty Research Fellowship from the University Research Institute of the University of Texas at Austin, and a Recent Recipient's Fellowship from the American Council of Learned Societies.

Many, many friends and colleagues have given me intellectual stimulus in constructive criticism, helpful suggestions, useful references, and unflagging encouragement. G. E. R. Lloyd was an exacting but supportive critic from the earliest stages of this study to its incarnation as a doctoral thesis and has continued to offer valuable assistance in its further development into a book. I had the great good fortune to be able to work under Jack Winkler during my time at Stanford. His rigorous philological scholarship combined with his capacity to present the most familiar text in a completely original light was a wonderful exemplar, and his enthusiasm for my project was a constant source of moral as well as professional support. Although my subject was outside his area of specialization, Michael H. Jameson gave me much valuable assistance, particularly in his comments on rural life in modern Greece, which suggested many fruitful possibilities. Ann Ellis Hanson, Helen King, and John Scarborough have all given generously of their time to read large parts of the manuscript, and I have benefited greatly from their comments and suggestions, based as they were on their deep knowledge of the field. Among others who have given time to reading and commenting on various parts of the manuscript are Judith Evans Grubbs, Christopher A. Faraone, Helene Foley, Michael Gagarin, Mary Louise Gill, Maud Gleason, David Halperin, R. J. Hankinson, Sally Humphreys, David Konstan, Dirk Obbink, Paula Perlman, and Wesley Smith.

Parts of the book have been presented as papers at the annual convention of the American Philological Association, the Institute for the Medical Humanities at the University of Texas Medical Branch at Galveston, the Center for the Study of Science in Society at Virginia Polytechnic Institute and State University, the Graduate Center of the City University of New York, the Columbia University Seminar on Women and Society, the Mary J. Pearl Lecture in Ancient Classical Studies at Sweet Briar College, Virginia, and at colloquia in the Classics departments of Stanford University, Texas A & M University, and the University of Texas at Austin. I am grateful for all the questions and suggestions I received from the varied audiences at these institutions. My study has benefited immensely from the interest and criticism of all these individuals. Any errors of fact or judgement which remain are my own responsibility. I should also like to acknowledge the encouragement, patience, and constructive questioning I have received from the editors of Oxford University Press, in particular Hilary O'Shea and Leofranc Holford-Strevens.

Finally, I would like to thank David, who has supported me in every way possible in my bringing this book to completion. I am indeed fortunate that he belies so conspicuously Dr Johnson's comment that 'A man is in general better pleased when he has a good dinner upon his table than when his wife talks Greek.'

L.D.-J.

Austin, Texas
October 1991

CONTENTS

Texts and Translations   xii
Abbreviations   xiii

INTRODUCTION: CONTEXTS AND SOURCES   1

1. FEMALE ANATOMY AND PHYSIOLOGY   41

2. FEMALE PATHOLOGY   110

3. THE FEMALE'S ROLE IN REPRODUCTION   148

CONCLUSION   225

References   255
General Index   277
Index Locorum   282

TEXTS AND TRANSLATIONS

Here listed are editions and translations to which reference is made by the name of the editor or translator.

Texts

Joly	Robert Joly, *Hippocrate XIII* (Paris, 1978)
Jones	W. H. S. Jones, *Hippocrates*, 4 vols. (Cambridge, Mass., 1923–31)
Littré	Émile Littré, *Œuvres complètes d'Hippocrate*, 10 vols. (Paris, 1839–61; repr. Amsterdam, 1961–2)
Louis	Pierre Louis, *Aristote: Histoire des animaux*, 3 vols. (Paris, 1964–9)
Peck	A. L. Peck, *Aristotle: Parts of Animals, Generation of Animals, History of Animals*, 4 vols. (Cambridge, Mass., 1937–70)

Translations

Barnes	Jonathan Barnes (ed.), *The Complete Works of Aristotle* (Princeton, NJ, 1984)
Chadwick–Mann	J. Chadwick and W. N. Mann, *Hippocratic Writings* (Oxford, 1950)

I have generally used the Littré text for the Hippocratic Corpus (references after citations are to volume, page, and line number). The text for Aristotle's biological works is Peck's, except for Books 7–10 of *HA*, which is Louis's.

In the interests of objectivity I have used existing translations where available. For the Hippocratics I have used primarily Chadwick–Mann, and Jones for treatises which they do not include. Translations of *Genit.* and *Nat. Puer.* are those of Lonie 1981. I have also used the excerpts from the gynaecological works translated in Hanson 1975 and Lefkowitz 1981. Other translations from the Corpus are my own. The translations from Aristotle's biology are mainly those of Peck. Translations of *HA* Books 7–10 are from Barnes.

ABBREVIATIONS

The abbreviations of ancient works are those used in *A Greek–English Lexicon*, ed. H. G. Liddell, R. Scott, and H. S. Jones, 9th edn. with suppl. (Oxford, 1968). The abbreviations of modern journals are those used in *L'Année philologique*. Below is a list of abbreviations used in this book which are not to be found in either of those publications.

AJOG	*American Journal of Obstetrics and Gynecology*
ARW	*Archiv für Religionswissenschaft*
CMG	*Corpus Medicorum Graecorum*
DK	H. Diels and W. Kranz (eds.), *Die Fragmente der Vorsokratiker* (Zurich, 1967)
IJP	*International Journal of Psychology*
JASO	*Journal of the Anthropological Society of Oxford*
LSAM	F. Sokolowski, *Lois sacrées de l'Asie mineure* (Paris, 1955)
LSCG	F. Sokolowski, *Lois sacrées des cités grecques* (Paris, 1969)
LSCG suppl.	F. Sokolowski, *Lois sacrées des cités grecques*, supplement (Paris, 1969)
MLR	*Monthly Labor Review*
PRAI	*Proceedings of the Royal Anthropological Institute*
RE	*Real-Encyclopädie der classischen Altertumswissenschaft*
SAMPh	*Society for Ancient Medicine and Pharmacy*
Ut. Diss.	*De uteri dissectione. Corpus Medicorum Graecorum*, v. 2.1, ed. Diethard Nickel (Berlin, 1971)

Introduction: Contexts and Sources

Until the last decade very little research had been done on ancient views of female physiology. That it is now a focus of considerable scholarly activity[1] is due to a new intellectual perspective on ancient science and a growth of interest in the study of women in antiquity. Seemingly bizarre theories based on erroneous observations are no longer scoffed at as bad science or distilled in the hope of discovering a kernel of truth to be identified as the theory's true contribution to Western science. Instead, they are recognized as intellectual products capable of providing insight into how the ancients interacted with their world. The recognition that women were an important part of this world has latterly blossomed into an acknowledgement that half of the ancients were women. That this acknowledgement appeared late in Classical scholarship is not surprising because few works by women survived late antiquity. Theories of female physiology, however, presumably received some input from women, so scientific texts concerned with women's bodies could be doubly useful in revealing both how men in antiquity regarded women and how women regarded themselves.

CULTURAL RELATIVISM IN SCIENTIFIC THEORY

Earlier in this century scholars were concerned to detail where ancient medicine had made progress towards modern theories.[2] They were interested more in pointing out where early medicine could be seen to be right, or nearly right, rather than in investigating where and why it seemed absolutely wrong. In pursuance of this aim

[1] e.g. Grensemann 1982; Lloyd 1983, 58–111, 168–82; Campese–Manuli–Sissa 1983; Gourevitch 1984; King 1985; Rousselle 1988. See essay review of current research on the topic, Hanson 1989.

[2] e.g. Pohlenz 1938; W. H. S. Jones 1946; Bourgey 1953; Singer 1957.

they each bestowed most attention on those treatises they considered the most rational. The gynaecology did not fall into this category for any of them. Recent work on ancient medicine has taken a different direction. It attempts to illustrate the patterns of thought which guided the Greeks' perception of the physical world in their emergent science. Interest now lies not so much in determining the extent to which the Greeks laid the basis of rational Western medicine as in ascertaining in what way their rational medicine was shaped by the ideologies of their own society and how it functioned within that society. In this respect, the occasions on which the Greeks appear to us to be correct in matters concerning female anatomy and physiology are uninteresting in and of themselves, but the mistaken conclusions they arrive at in spite of their genuine attempts at empirical observation and rationality can be very revealing of societal assumptions about women's bodies which are elsewhere taken for granted.

Prior to scientific or rational medicine, a society expresses its attitude towards the female body, as it does towards other phenomena of the natural world, in myths, superstitions, and folk remedies. A scientific approach to the phenomena dispenses with supernatural causation, and attempts to explain events as the result of natural forces in the world which can be observed and understood by humans. Cultural assumptions play a part in shaping the scientific explanation of an event, and this can result in theories which seem to us as fantastic as the mythological conjectures they were meant to replace. For example, the author of a fifth-century treatise on epilepsy dispenses with divine displeasure as the cause of the disease and develops instead a detailed physiological account in which an excess of phlegm from the brain traps air in the veins of the thorax causing a loss of consciousness and convulsive movements.[3] One of the main occasions for onsets of the attack, he claims, is a change in wind direction.[4] Attributing epileptic seizures to meteorological phenomena may seem to us only one step removed from attributing them to Poseidon's anger, but to the farming and seafaring Greeks who spent most of their life out of doors, the wind was one of the most readily identifiable powerful agents of change in all aspects of nature, and it was not perverse to claim its influence stretched as far as the human body.[5] Nevertheless, unlike theories

---

[3] *Morb. Sacr.* 7 (vi. 372. 4–374. 20).   [4] Ibid. II (vi. 380. 20–382. 1).
[5] Cf. *Aër.* 1 (ii. 12. 9–14).

which cite supernatural intervention or magical powers as an explanation for events, scientific theories are open (in theory at least) to proof or rebuttal from observable phenomena, so the acceptance of fantastic new scientific theories, even if they do validate cultural assumptions, seems harder to explain than the acceptance of unverifiable entrenched myths. Cultural assumptions, however, shape not only scientific explanations, but also the very perceptions of observers within the culture. Because they expected a change of wind to cause certain types of events in human life, Greeks would note whenever an epileptic seizure did coincide with a change of wind and would explain the coincidence as cause and effect.[6] If the wind changed direction without the expected seizure taking place, a Greek observer might still think they had perceived a seizure or credit its non-occurrence to preventive factors. Similarly, if a seizure took place in the absence of a change of wind, a Greek observer might claim that there must have been an imperceptible shift in wind direction or that the seizure had been precipitated by other factors. Such flaws beset even the comparatively refined methods of modern science;[7] it is not surprising that we see them in the early stages of scientific explanation. This is not to say that no scientific theory is better than any other, nor that there is no progress (an explanation of epileptic seizures based on brain lesions accounts for more phenomena and has a better success rate in treatment than does an explanation based on humoral pathology), but no scientific theory is entirely objective and we should not be surprised that, generally, scientific theory conforms to rather than challenges social ideologies.

Because of this 'culture-bound' aspect of science it has been claimed that contemporary observations of rare syndromes which appear to conform to ancient medical reports are entirely irrelevant since they arise from a different theoretical system.[8] However, while

---

[6] They held the same belief about the ruining of wine and the dimming of heavenly bodies, see *Morb. Sacr.* 13 (vi. 384. 22–386. 4).

[7] For example, at the beginning of this century a belief in social Darwinism led to well-documented statistical 'proof' of a correlation between 'inferior' races and social classes and low IQ scores, see Gould 1981, 146–233. For a general account of observation and scientific error, see Rostand 1960; Beattie 1984, 1–5.

[8] e.g. Joly 1966, 42 n. 3, 43 n. 2; King 1989, n. 12. Thivel 1981, 23, says we should not assimilate ancient and modern hypotheses but should look for a correspondence between experience and theory for indications of the scientific spirit. This means we must make some assumptions about what the ancients' experiences were, which will be based unavoidably on our own notions of what 'really' happens.

medical theory may be culturally bound, physiology is not. Different
theories on reproduction have never served as a contraceptive. Even
Lévi-Strauss conceded that cultural relativism did not encompass
anatomy and physiology *per se*.[9] If our culture observes a physiological phenomenon, it is possible that it does in fact exist and that the
Greeks also observed it. And if we claim that it is the 'mistakes' of the
ancient physicians that are illuminating and important, we should try
to ascertain where it is that they make the mistakes. We do not doubt
that the female *katamēnia* (literally, 'monthly coming-downs') they
describe are the phenomenon of menstruation, so we do not feel it
necessary to look for a cultural reason to explain why they believed
women bled at fairly regular intervals, we only seek to explain why
they should interpret this fact as they did. Ancient theories which
described as common biological events which are extremely rare in
our culture, could simply have been elaborated from the ancients'
theories of normal physiology without any actual observation of the
rare phenomenon in question, but it is also possible that the accom-
modation of a few observations of rare syndromes in their physiological model led to a heightened expectation and thus a more frequent
perception of these events, even though the rare syndromes were no
more common then than now.[10] Therefore, while I am not primarily
interested in the foreshadowing of modern medicine in ancient texts, I
note modern physiological observations when they seem applicable
to ancient descriptions of physiological phenomena.[11]

EARLY GREEK SCIENCE

Greek scientific thinking began in Ionia (the coast of modern Turkey)
in the sixth century BC.[12] Over the course of the next century individuals from all over the Greek world developed theories

[9] Lévi-Strauss 1976, 303–5, 331–2. He emphasizes that cultural assumptions can
affect observations but that among 'hard sciences' observation and induction can lead
to knowledge universally applicable. MacCormack 1980, 2, says that medicine as a
cultural code may be accessible because cultures have the same matrix to work from.
[10] Conversely, rare syndromes which are not easily accommodated in our theories
of normal physiology may be under-reported.
[11] A rapprochement between modern physicians and historians of medicine was
recently urged in Riddle 1985, pp. xxii–xxiv.
[12] For a discussion of the 'Ionian Revolution' and the general development of
Presocratic philosophy, see Guthrie 1962; 1965; Lloyd 1970, 1–23; Hussey 1972;
Kirk–Raven–Schofield 1983.

explaining the universe in naturalistic terms, but no treatise from this Presocratic period of philosophy has survived intact. The study of the earliest rational theories in Greek thought is dependent upon comments, quotations, and compilations made in later periods of antiquity. These fragments suggest that the main concerns of the Presocratics were cosmological and meteorological, but there is clear evidence that they were also interested in the conception and development of humans, both as a species and as individuals, and that sexual differentiation was one of the problems they examined.[13] Female physiology, therefore, was a subject for scientific speculation before medicine established itself as an independent discipline from philosophy,[14] but the nature of our evidence on the subject makes it impossible to develop a connected account of pre-medical theories. Scattered remarks by the Presocratics, however, can suggest the origin of some of the later theories on women's bodies.

HIPPOCRATIC MEDICINE

Composition of the Corpus

About the middle of the fifth century BC, philosophy began to turn gradually from consideration of the composition and organization of the external world to questions of human moral and ethical values. Cosmological and ontological theories (including some on sexual differentiation) still held a place in later philosophical systems, but extended investigation into the various aspects of human physiology became the province of medicine. At the head of this medical tradition, contemporaneous with Socrates, stands the figure of Hippocrates.

Unlike Socrates, Hippocrates probably did commit at least some of his teaching to writing, but from all of the sixty or so treatises which have come down to us under the rubric of the Hippocratic Corpus we do not know which, if any, were actually written by

[13] e.g. Epicharmus, DK 23 B 59; Alcmaeon, DK 24 B 3; Parmenides, DK 28 B 17, 18; Empedocles, DK 31 B 57–67; Diogenes, DK 64 B 6, 9; Democritus, DK 68 B 122a, 148.
[14] For a discussion of the problem of the relationship of medicine and philosophy, see W. H. S. Jones 1946; Edelstein 1967, 349–66; Lloyd 1979, 32–49; Longrigg 1989.

him.[15] The Corpus is a collection of medical treatises probably assembled sometime in the third or second century BC at Alexandria.[16] Although there is disagreement over the date of some of the individual treatises, the collection as a whole can be dated broadly, by considerations of style and anatomical and pharmaceutical knowledge, to the second half of the fifth century BC and the first half of the fourth, with a few treatises falling considerably later. Not all the authors represented in the Corpus, therefore, are contemporaries one with another. Nor, although the works are generally written in Ionic dialect, should they be assumed to have the same provenance. Ionia (the birthplace and home of Hippocrates) was doubtless the place where medical knowledge was first committed to writing in the fifth century, but the Greek tendency to apportion dialect to genre would be sufficient to explain why all subsequent medical writers continued to use Ionic, even when writing in completely different parts of the Greek world.[17] The content of the collection is also diverse, comprising professional monographs, notebooks of case histories, compilations of aphorisms, treatises on internal medicine and surgery, and works aimed at gaining the confidence of the general public. The various treatises within the Corpus, therefore, have no strong unity in time and place (apart from Classical Greece), form, purpose, or audience. It is also a mistake to assume that the Hippocratic Corpus enshrines a single medical doctrine; there is no agreement, for instance, on the number of vital fluids, the humours, in the human body or what they are. Even the most admired theoretical treatises, which have all been attributed to Hippocrates himself at some time (*VM, Morb. Sacr., Aër., Nat. Hom.*), show no obvious unifying doctrine.[18]

[15] This was at one time the burning question of Hippocratic scholarship and *VM* the most widely agreed upon answer, but although individual scholars continue to suggest candidates for Hippocrates' authorship (e.g. Smith 1979: *Salubr.*; Mansfeld 1980: *Aër.*), the issue has generally fallen into abeyance.

[16] Smith 1979, 199–204. For an alternative theory that the Corpus was generated in Hippocrates' personal library on Cos, see Kühn 1956; Diller 1959.

[17] Although Hippocrates actually came from Doric-speaking Cos, he probably originally wrote in Ionic, since this was at that time the normal dialect of prose. However, in the later period Attic replaced Ionic in all genres except that of medical writing. In his edition Littré multiplied and exaggerated the Ionicisms of the manuscripts to reflect what he believed to have been the original dialect of the treatises; the Ionic dialect is not as pronounced in recent editions because modern editors retain only those Ionicisms found in the manuscripts.

[18] For an excellent discussion on the composition of the Hippocratic Corpus, see Thivel 1981, 17–151.

Interplay of Theory and Observation

For the most part, the Hippocratic authors, even the most theoretical of them, seem to have been practising physicians and to have written their treatises with an eye to improving therapy and increasing custom rather than with a purely academic interest in increasing and improving knowledge.[19] Medical theories differed from contemporary theories in other areas of natural science, such as astronomy and geography, in that their hypotheses could not remain speculative but were expected to be applied with some measure of success.[20] Accordingly, the Hippocratics were among the first Greek scientists to try to make close observation rather than abstract reasoning the foundation of their theories.[21] In some ways they were spectacularly successful at this; the detailed compilation of symptoms in the *Epid.* and the knowledge that was accumulated on bonesetting in the surgical works are still an object of admiration among physicians today.[22] However, in most cases not only, as today, did theory precede and shape observation (the case histories of the *Epid.* were compiled on the theory that there were certain 'critical days' during the course of any illness), but observations, even correct observations, were made in an *ad hoc* manner during the course of their clinical experience rather than as part of deliberate investigation or experimentation.[23] These observations were adduced almost exclusively when they were thought to corroborate favoured theories with no acknowledgement (or perhaps realization) that this did not equate with disproving rival theories. Conversely, the Hippocratics rarely take into account empirical data that could con-

[19] e.g. *Nat. Hom.* is one of the treatises in the collection most concerned with theory for its own sake, but in its description of the course of the blood vessels it includes directions for the best spots for venesection in certain conditions (*Nat. Hom.* ii (vi. 58. 1–60. 19)).

[20] Cf. *VM* 1 (i. 572. 5–8); *de Arte* 5 (vi. 8. 3–6); *Prog.* 1 (ii. 110. 1–8).

[21] For a fuller account of the Hippocratic achievements and shortcomings in the development of the empirical method, see Lloyd 1979, 126–225.

[22] e.g. Withington 1928, p. xiv. The Hippocratic observation that a certain deformation of the fingertips signifies lung disease has been confirmed by modern research with no more knowledge as to why this should be so than the Hippocratics had. The syndrome is still called 'Hippocratic fingers', see Majno 1975, 170–1.

[23] Though the concept of performing experiments to prove a point does surface in the Corpus at various points, e.g. freezing and thawing water to show that the 'sweetest part' is lost, and that therefore drinking melted snow or ice is harmful (*Aër.* 8 (ii. 36. 9–16)). See von Staden 1975, 178–9, for references to the debate over how far the Hippocratic idea of experimentation reached.

8 *Introduction*

tradict their theses. As Lloyd says of their methodology: 'the gap between stated ideal and actual practice was often wide'.[24] Furthermore, in the course of their clinical experience, most ancient physicians would encounter surface rather than deep structures of the body. Although some surgical procedures are described in the Corpus (e.g. incising the nose to remove polypi, draining the thorax of pus),[25] they do not involve opening up the body. Surgery may also have been restricted to specialists, as *Jusj.* (iv. 630. 11–12) suggests: 'I will not cut, even for the stone, but I will leave such procedures to the practitioners of that craft.'[26] On those occasions when a physician did see inside the body (e.g. through a severe wound), the necessity for immediate intervention would prevent leisurely study. Apart from one brief remark, the Hippocratics do not seem to have considered the possibility of dissecting or examining dead animals and extrapolating their findings to the human body.[27]

Such methodological flaws and omissions were perpetrated not simply because the Hippocratics were unreflective, but because there was not yet established a body of scientific principles with which their methods and results had to accord. The Hippocratics were concerned with the relationship and interaction between the human microcosm and the macrocosm of Nature,[28] and a personal predilection towards one philosophical system or another might help to shape a physician's theories,[29] but in most Hippocratic treatises the effective treatment of the human body is the author's prime concern, as *VM* 20 (i. 620. 14–622. 3) asserts it should be, and this was conducive to unsystematized eclecticism. Philosophical principles such as the powers of the hot and the cold and the importance of number are applied, but there are no detailed cosmological, epistemological, ontological, or metaphysical systems sustained or elaborated which could act as parameters to make the Hippocratics re-examine the data or methods behind their theories.

[24] Lloyd 1979, 168. [25] *Morb.* 2. 36, 47 (vii. 52. 15–21, 70. 4–72. 5).
[26] οὐ τεμέω δὲ οὐδὲ μὴν λιθιῶντας, ἐκχωρήσω δὲ ἐργάτησιν ἀνδράσι πρήξιος τῆσδε.
[27] *Morb. Sacr.* 11 (vi. 382. 6–11) suggests dissecting a goat's brain to prove epilepsy is caused by phlegm. Galen (*Anatom. Admin.* 2. 1) says that Asclepiad families trained their sons in dissection, but evidence of systematic dissection does not appear until the Hellenistic period.
[28] e.g. *Aër.* 2 (ii. 14. 1–19); *Vict.* 1. 2 (vi. 470. 8–13).
[29] e.g. *Alim.* was written by an adherent of Heraclitus, *Flat.* by a follower of Diogenes of Apollonia. See W. H. S. Jones 1946, 25.

Cos and Cnidos

Since the edition of Foës in 1595, attempts have been made to identify two distinct schools in the Corpus: the Cnidian and the Coan. Various sets of criteria have been put forward by scholars to differentiate one from the other, but it is very difficult to isolate any treatise that sticks hard and fast to any one of these sets of differentiae. Consequently, while nobody denies that there were medical establishments on both Cos and Cnidos, and that certain traditions may have developed at each place under the auspices of individual teachers, it is now generally agreed that, in the Hippocratic period at least, both 'schools' were working within the same tradition with no sharp difference of approach to medicine as that which developed later between Empiricists and Dogmatists.[30] In fact, the dichotomy between Coan and Cnidian medicine seems to have been invented during later antiquity, in part to explain and justify the contemporary rivalry of Empiricists and Dogmatists; but even so, no ancient source identifies any extant Hippocratic treatise as Cnidian. Traits which were originally given the label 'Cnidian' in antiquity can indeed be identified throughout the Corpus, but often in treatises which were accepted as the work of a physician associated with Cos. Therefore, rather than treat these traits as the different approach of a rival school, it seems more correct to identify them as the earliest layers of a rational medicine which became increasingly elaborated and refined. Even if it is possible, through such criteria as asyndeton, style of exposition, or preferred particles, to identify the provenance of a particular treatise as Cnidos, it would not necessarily be any more incompatible with a 'Coan' treatise than two 'Coan' treatises by different authors would be between themselves.[31]

Therefore, in spite of various discrepancies, the majority of the

---

[30] During the Hellenistic period in Alexandria two schools developed with competing attitudes to the practice of medicine. The Empiricists believed that therapy should be based simply on experience of what had been successful in previous similar cases. The Dogmatists argued that therapy should be prescribed from an understanding of the causes of the disease.

[31] For a more detailed account of the derivation of the Cos/Cnidos distinction and its repercussions on the subsequent study of medicine, see Smith 1979; Lonie 1978 (a reversal of his earlier view); Thivel 1981; Joly 1983. Jouanna 1983, 129–48, and Mansfeld 1983 are among those who still argue for a significant distinction between Coan and Cnidian medicine. Grensemann, who began his study of the gynaecology on the premise that it was the clearest example of Cnidian medicine, has backed away from this claim without repudiating it altogether, see Grensemann 1987, 7.

treatises in the Corpus can be regarded as belonging to a single tradition. They all attempt to explain bodily functions and malfunctions as the result of natural causes which can be understood and explained without having to invoke supernatural intervention. Though we may consider some of the physical causes they cite to be basically imaginary, they were attempts at dispensing with both divine displeasure to account for diseases and with magical remedies to cure them. They used observations of the human body in disease and in health and analogy with more familiar and visible processes in the external world to support their theories; in general the Hippocratics did not dissect or experiment to further their knowledge. In addition to these general similarities, most of the treatises in the Corpus do subscribe to some form of a humoral theory, though there is no agreement on the number or composition of humours.[32]

Hippocratic Gynaecological Texts

The amount of interest in the female body within this tradition is illustrated by the fact that of the sixty or so treatises in the Corpus, ten are gynaecological in nature (*Nat. Mul., Mul.* 1-2, *Steril., Genit., Nat. Puer., Virg., Superf., Septim./Oct.,* and *Foet. Exsect.*), and some of these are probably the earliest surviving treatises of the Corpus; in fact they may be the earliest connected Greek prose we possess. Hermann Grensemann argues on the basis of asyndeton, particles, vocabulary, and the simple form of the humoral theory that *Nat. Mul.* was composed around or slightly earlier than 450 BC.[33] Most of the chapters of *Nat. Mul.* were later incorporated into *Mul.* 1-2 and *Steril.*[34] Further considerations of style, vocabulary, and aetiology suggest that the remaining chapters of *Mul.* 1-2 and *Steril.* contain material by at least two more authors dating from the middle to the end of the fifth

---

[32] *Nat. Hom.* criticizes particularly those theories which claim humans are formed from only one humour and those which claim that man is formed not from elements which can be readily identified in the human body but from such substances as earth, air, fire, and water. Neither of these theories is exemplified in any treatise in the Corpus, but *Anon. Lond.* 20. 25 ff. attributes the latter to Philistion, a physician of the Sicilian rather than the Hippocratic 'school'.

[33] Grensemann 1975, 195-202.

[34] The opening words of *Steril.* show that the author considered it to be a continuation of *Mul.* 1-2.

century.[35] The treatises may have grown by the process of accretion, or they may have been compiled and edited by the author of the latest sections or a later editor. In either case, although *Mul.* 1–2 and *Steril.* are the work of more than one author, it did not prevent the physicians of antiquity from viewing the gynaecological theory they contained (and obviously, therefore, that contained in *Nat. Mul.* as well) as a unity. It is true that those sections identified as early on stylistic grounds seem to have a less elaborate humoral theory than those identified as later, and that the later sections are in general more concerned with theory and less with therapy than the earlier, but the interweaving of the sections in the treatises shows that their differences were considered to be complementary rather than adversative (though they may contain latent contradictions). Unless there is evidence to the contrary, therefore, it is assumed that a statement made in one part of the treatises would be accepted by the authors of the other parts as well. For example, *Mul.* 1. 1 describes the process of menstruation. This is echoed explicitly nowhere else in the treatises, but the description of female symptoms, diseases, and therapy throughout *Nat. Mul.*, *Mul.* 1–2, and *Steril.* is compatible with this theory, and since no other is put forward[36] we may assume that each of the authors would have concurred in it. The more complex aetiology of symptoms in the later sections need not be taken as superseding the earlier sections since they are connected with more complex, not the same, forms of disease.[37]

The treatise *Nat. Puer.* follows *Genit.* in all the manuscripts, and the final sentence of *Genit.* makes it clear that *Nat. Puer.* is a direct continuation of the treatise by the same author. In *Genit.* 4 (vii. 476. 16) and *Nat. Puer.* 15 (vii. 496. 9–10) the author says he will explain in his *Diseases of Women* why women become ill when their menses are suppressed. The reference appears to be to *Mul.* 1. 2–5. Furthermore, the author of the later sections of *Mul.* 1–2 and *Steril.* refers

[35] Several treatises in the Corpus could be the work of more than one author, see Lloyd 1975, 180–1. Grensemann 1975 and 1982 divides *Nat. Mul.*, *Mul.* 1–2 and *Steril.* between authors A (earliest), B, and C (latest). It may be that we have the work of more than one author in each of these chronological levels, but if so they cannot be identified, as Grensemann tries to do for A in Grensemann 1987, by simply noting differences in descriptions of symptoms and treatment. This may be the sign of a different physician, but it may also signify the same physician confronted with a different condition, see L. A. Jones 1989.

[36] But cf. pp. 59–60 below on a possible discrepancy with a theory of menstruation put forward in *Genit.*

[37] See L. A. Jones 1989.

to a work he has written under the title of *On the Nature of the Child at Birth* (*Mul.* I. 1, 44, 73 (viii. 10. 7–8, 102. 5–6, 152. 22–154 .1)) in a context which corresponds to passages in *Nat. Puer.* 21 and 30. The same author also says he has written a treatise *On the Diseases of Young Girls* (*Mul.* I. 2 (viii. 22. 1–2)) in which he discusses the flow of menses through the anus. Such a passage does not occur in *Virg.* as we have it now, but there is reason to believe that we have only a fragment of a longer treatise,[38] and the reference may be to a missing portion, though it is possible that it is referring to a completely different treatise altogether. However that may be, the *Virg.* we have is compatible with the theory of female physiology in *Nat. Mul.*, *Mul.* 1–2, *Steril.*, *Genit.*, and *Nat. Puer.*

Superf. and *Foet. Exsect.* deal only briefly with the specialized subjects which give them their titles, and in the main they reiterate material in *Mul.* 1–2 and *Steril.* in shortened form. The use of Aeginetan weights and measures in *Superf.* suggests that it could be even earlier than *Nat. Mul.*[39] *Septim./Oct.* cannot be so closely associated by content with the main body of the gynaecology, but by a tradition upheld by Grensemann it is ascribed to Polybos, the son-in-law of Hippocrates, and is therefore to be dated to *c.*400 BC.[40] *Septim./Oct.* covers much of the same ground as *Genit.* and *Nat. Puer.*, but disagrees on some points with these treatises. Even so, the two treatises can be seen to emanate from the same Hippocratic tradition. In view of these connections, Hippocratic gynaecology will be treated as a unity. Those points at which individual treatises seem to depart from the dominant model will be indicated and discussed in the text.

In addition to the exclusively gynaecological works, women are mentioned in other Hippocratic treatises, most importantly in the seven books of the *Epid.*—compilations of descriptions of endemic and epidemic diseases as well as individual case histories. While the general treatises are not so homogeneous as the gynaecology, they share many of the same assumptions where women are concerned

[38] Bourgey 1953, 55; Kudlien 1968, 329; Manuli 1983, 202 n. 17.
[39] These were used at Cnidos only up until 480 BC, when it entered the Delian League and reverted to Attic measures, see Thivel 1981, 94.
[40] Grensemann 1968, 47–60. The manuscript tradition preserves *Septim./Oct.* as two separate treatises, but since Littré they have been recognized as belonging to the same work. Recent editions by Grensemann and Joly, however, have disagreed over how they are to be combined. I find Grensemann's ordering of chapters most logical, but for convenience I will continue to cite chapters by Littré's numbering.

and are invaluable in having men as a gender control to throw into relief what is peculiarly female.

THE SICILIAN 'SCHOOL' AND DIOCLES OF CARYSTOS

The Hippocratic treatises, then, are my primary medical sources for the Classical period of Greek science. There were non-Hippocratic physicians writing at this time, notably those of the Sicilian 'school', Acron and Philistion. This school, which originated in the Empedoclean and Pythagorean philosophical traditions, shows initially little concern with empiricism, basing its physiology on the four elements and breath (*pneuma*), rather than the humours, and including more number theory than did the Hippocratics. Only fragments, however, of these writings have survived. Diocles of Carystos seems to have attempted a synthesis between the Hippocratic and the Sicilian 'schools', but again, although his fragments are more extensive than those of any other exponent of the Sicilian 'school', no complete treatise has survived.[41] Such fragments as we possess, however, do not demonstrate that the Sicilian 'school' subscribed to radically different notions of the female body than those we find in the Hippocratics.

ARISTOTLE'S BIOLOGY

Composition of the Corpus

The core of Aristotle's biological canon comprises, in probable chronological order of inception, *HA, PA,* and *GA. HA* is a collection of data about many varieties of animals and consciously avoids

[41] Jaeger 1938 argued that Diocles was a younger contemporary of Arist. partly on the basis that Philistion is associated with Plato and that his visit to the Academy would have been the most likely time for Diocles to learn about Sicilian medicine. He attributes similarities in Diocles' and Arist.'s writings (certain expressions, theoretical elements such as *pneuma*, etc.) to the influence of the latter on the former. There is no clear evidence that the influence has to have been in this direction, however, and in the absence of such it seems preferable to retain the traditional dating of Diocles as a slightly older contemporary of Arist. This assessment agrees with that of von Staden 1989, 44–6. In so far as he is not squarely in the Hippocratic tradition, it may be significant that Diocles wrote in Attic rather than Ionic dialect. For the fragments of the Sicilian 'school' see Wellmann 1901.

any theorizing; *PA* explains the reasons behind the anatomy and physiology of the various species which *HA* describes; and *GA* explains the process by which animal species reproduce and maintain the same anatomy and physiology over successive generations.[42] There are no separate treatises or books of Aristotle dealing with the female.

Any sexual differences are dealt with in the biological works as they arise, though for obvious reasons these tend to be concentrated in *GA* and sections of the other works dealing with reproduction.

The biological works, like all the extant works of Aristotle, were never intended to be published in the form that has come down to us.[43] They are lecture notes and as such contain many ellipses, abrupt transitions, repetitions, afterthoughts, etc. Their unpolished nature allowed many spurious passages to be interpolated and transmitted in the genuine works, but because the body of the text is known to be by one original thinker (unlike the Hippocratic Corpus), the spurious passages can be isolated with some certainty, though there is not yet a full consensus on what is and what is not genuinely Aristotelian. Book 7 of *HA*, which deals extensively with human reproduction, was once considered highly suspect but is now generally accepted as a genuine work of Aristotle's.[44] Book 10 of the same work also deals with human reproduction, but it flatly contradicts one of the most characteristic of Aristotelian doctrines: that the woman does not contribute seed to the conception of a new individual. Although he began writing *HA* relatively early in his career, Aristotle added to it throughout his life, and as he never fully revised any of his esoteric works, it would not be surprising if some theories which he rejected in his later writings were retained in the early parts of treatises. However, the theory of female seed, which (in the biological works accepted as genuine) Aristotle argues vehemently *against*, is found nowhere else in the Aristotelian canon[45] and jars with his funda-

---

[42] Pellegrin 1986, 143–58, suggests an alternative to this traditional account of the different purposes of the biological treatises. He argues that *HA* deals with the material cause, *PA* with the formal and final, and *GA* with the efficient. In this case *HA* is as much a philosophical undertaking as the (logically) later treatises.

[43] See Lloyd 1968, 9–18. The extant works of Arist. are therefore called the 'esoteric' works.

[44] Louis 1964–9, i, pp. vii–xi.

[45] Though there is a possible reference at *PA* 689ª11–12, 'The same applies to the catamenia in females, and the part where they emit the semen' (τὸν αὐτὸν δὲ τρόπον καὶ ἐν τοῖς θήλεσι τά τε καταμήνια, καὶ ᾗ προίενται τὴν γονήν). Peck has recorded Platt's suggested emendation to, 'and *if* they emit any seed' (καὶ εἰ προίενταί τινα γονήν), but this still seems to me an unAristotelian remark.

mental dichotomy between form and matter, which in the process of reproduction he equates with male and female respectively. Moreover, some of the objections Aristotle raises to female seed in his later works are answered in *HA* 10, which argues against its being part of his earlier work. It is true that the book displays an overall sympathy with Aristotle's biology, but it also shows a marked interest in pathology and clinical matters not evidenced elsewhere in those works. I have therefore classed it as the work of a later Hippocratic doctor writing under the influence of Aristotle.[46] Aristotle's smaller biological treatises, *MA*, *IA*, and *PN*, are of less importance to my thesis, though reference will be made to them from time to time.[47]

Interplay of Theory and Observation

In 1961, when compiling *Principles of Animal Taxonomy*, G. G. Simpson gave voice to a view of Aristotle as biologist which had evolved with the advent of modern science when he declared that 'the study of Aristotle increases ignorance',[48] and despite the recognition by many scholars of a biological bias in Aristotle's philosophy,[49] the biological works have until recently remained comparatively neglected. The reawakening interest in Aristotle's philosophy of Nature was motivated primarily by a desire to reach new insights on the fundamental issues in the principles and method in the rest of his philosophy, the notions of cause, substance, teleology, etc., which permeate all his work.[50]

The nature of Aristotelian studies has led to more detailed investigation of the interplay of theory and observation in his treatises than in those of the Hippocratics, an investigation made easier by the fact that Aristotle had greater self-awareness as a researcher and original thinker and was more concerned to document and follow a prescribed method. This method generally began with a survey of

---

[46] This concurs to a large extent with the assessment of Louis 1964–9, iii 147–55. Louis edits *HA* 10 under the title *On Sterility* (ὑπὲρ τοῦ μὴ γεννᾶν). Balme 1985 argues for Aristotelian authorship of *HA* 10. For his particular arguments against Hippocratic authorship, see 193–4.

[47] For a more detailed description of the composition of Arist.'s biology, see Byl 1980.

[48] Quoted in Grene 1972, 395.

[49] e.g. D'A. W. Thompson 1913; Le Blond 1935.

[50] e.g. Balme 1961, 1962, 1965, 1980; Düring 1969; Preus 1975; Kullmann 1979; Byl 1980; Gotthelf 1985; Gotthelf–Lennox 1987.

previously held authoritative opinions, or *endoxa*, showing what should be retained from them and why. His aim in this procedure is to show where it is that he departs from earlier theories, not to indicate that he is in complete agreement with any of them. He finds reasons for disagreeing in empirical observations and in his own conception of the forces at work in Nature.[51] In his classic paper on Aristotle's scientific method, G. E. L. Owen claimed that the unexamined *phainomena* (encompassing initially both empirical observations and *endoxa*) provided a conceptual framework for Aristotle, by philosophical examination of which he could arrive at incontrovertible *phainomena* that would give him a sure foundation from which to elaborate his own hypotheses.[52] Since then a variety of positions have been adopted by a series of scholars. Two recent books (Morsink 1982 and Boylan 1983) take Owen as a reference point and reach basically opposite conclusions. Morsink, through a consideration of the argumentation in *GA*, argues that Aristotle does not believe that dialectic with earlier theories confirms the *archai* ('principles') of biology as a priori truths, but rather that it establishes empirical hypotheses which are themselves open to dialectical refutation.[53] Boylan is more supportive of Owen's view, believing that Aristotle considered the *archai* of biology to be a priori truths established by induction from experience and subjected to negative verification by dialectic in order to function as tools in analysis, rather than hypotheses subject to further verification themselves.[54] In either case, Aristotle did not hold the *archai* of biology to be self-evident. He was aware that various traditional theories could adduce competing evidence and he believed that the best theory was one which could explain the most facts or 'saved the *phainomena*'.

In order to gather as many *phainomena* as possible, Aristotle kept a record of his own and others' observations of animals in their native habitat and performed dissection on many different species.[55] Much of this produced impressive results—for example, in detailing insect anatomy and the respiratory system. Though he never dis-

[51] But cf. Lloyd 1968, 74–6, on how cultural assumptions vitiated Arist.'s in many ways excellent account of the vascular system.

[52] Owen 1967, 175.   [53] Morsink 1982, 179.

[54] Boylan 1983, 26, 241, though he shows on 141–217 that Arist. does not always follow this method.

[55] Preus 1975, 41, estimates that Arist. dissected about 50 animals, from bees to elephants.

sected a human cadaver, Aristotle had some notion of a *scala
naturae* which led him to apply to the human body knowledge
gained from other mammals;[56] in so doing, he could examine and
describe at his leisure the physiology of a healthy animal (healthy
before death at least). In the extant treatises Aristotle evinces no
particular interest in pathology *per se*. At *GA* 747ª4–23, he lists three
traditional methods of diagnosis for infertility which he accepts as
valid.[57] He is more interested, however, in his theories of congenital
deformities which could give these tests their effectiveness than in the
possible advent of disease in the body. At *GA* 746ᵇ31–5 he says,
'Some of these deformities are curable, some are not; those, however, who have become deformed during the original constitution of
the embryo, have a special tendency to remain infertile throughout.'[58] This suggests he would be less likely than a practising physician to shape his model to be amenable to human intervention and
attractive to customers. In many ways, therefore, Aristotle's
methodology was superior to the Hippocratics'; he was more
systematic in surveying the evidence and readier to challenge
cultural assumptions it did not support.

The *phainomena* to be saved, however, were not limited to empirical observations made on discontinuous problems or events. A
theory concerning the function of an organ in a certain type of
animal had not only to be consistent with the theory put forward
about the rest of that animal's body but also to be subsumable
under theories about the anatomy and physiology of all forms of
life. It also had to cohere with general ontological and metaphysical principles which Aristotle believed governed all existence.

[56] At *HA* 494ᵇ20–5, Arist. remarks that the internal parts of humans are for the
most part unknown and must be inferred from those of other animals. The animals he
took to approximate humans most closely were those in his grouping 'Viviparous
Quadrupeds', which very nearly coincides with our class Mammalia. The relationship of *eidos* ('species') to *genos* ('genus') in Arist.'s system (with the exception of
some methodological passages) is very vague. *GA* 736ᵇ2–5 says that during the early
stages of embryonic development animal foetuses look similar and only become
recognizable as different species as they approach their completion. It seems unlikely, however, that Arist. ever thought of any two species as having a common
ancestor, see Lloyd 1961; Balme 1962; Lennox 1980; Lang 1983.

[57] They are: dropping semen into water (fertile semen sinks because it has been
properly concocted); inserting a pessary in a woman's vagina (in a fertile woman it
will be smelled on her breath because the passages in her body are unobstructed); and
rubbing a colour on the eyes (in a fertile woman the colour will appear in her saliva
because semen is drawn in from the eyes).

[58] γίνεται δὲ τὰ μὲν ἰατὰ τὰ δ' ἀνίατα τῶν τοιούτων, μάλιστα δὲ διατελοῦσιν
ἄγονα ⟨τὰ⟩ κατὰ τὴν πρώτην σύστασιν τοιαῦτα γενόμενα.

18 Introduction

This is not to say that Aristotle ever consciously went against the dictum which he enunciated at *GA* 760ᵇ30–3:

This, then, appears to be the state of affairs with regard to the generation of bees, so far as theory can take us, supplemented by what are thought to be the facts about their behaviour. But the facts have not been sufficiently ascertained; and if at any future time they are ascertained, then credence must be given to the direct evidence of the senses more than to theories,— and to theories too, provided that the results which they show agree with what is observed.⁵⁹

But, as with all researchers, Aristotle's observations were to a large extent constrained by the theories he held, even where his theories were highly original and idiosyncratic rather than culturally sanctioned. He could not always recognize when there was an empirical datum contradicting a firmly held tenet (e.g. although he dissected and described the heart, he believed that it had only three cavities, probably because he believed that the heart of the higher animals had to have a central cavity⁶⁰). At other times, rather than admit that an empirical datum did contravene a theory to which he was deeply committed, Aristotle devised elaborate explanations to meet the challenge (e.g. his belief that 'animals which are constituted most in accordance with nature'⁶¹ touch the ground at only two or four points when they move leads him to assert that snakes move by touching the ground at four points, one either side of the head and one either side of the tail, and that the bends in a snake's body are the result, not the cause, of its movement⁶²).

Because Aristotle was interested in increasing the theoretical knowledge of physiology and anatomy rather than in the clinical application of knowledge, his researches were much more complete and systematic than the Hippocratics', attempting to take into account all the facts and hypotheses on a subject. He also subsumed biology under the same methodological, epistemological, meta-physical, and ontological laws as held elsewhere in his philosophy. His theories had to cohere to wider scientific principles which made

⁵⁹ ἐκ μὲν οὖν τοῦ λόγου τὰ περὶ τὴν γένεσιν τῶν μελιττῶν τοῦτον ἔχειν φαίνεται τὸν τρόπον, καὶ ἐκ τῶν συμβαίνειν δοκούντων περὶ αὐτάς. οὐ μὴν εἴληπταί γε τὰ συμβαίνοντα ἱκανῶς, ἀλλ᾽ ἐάν ποτε ληφθῇ, τότε τῇ αἰσθήσει μᾶλλον τῶν λόγων πιστευτέον, καὶ τοῖς λόγοις, ἐὰν ὁμολογούμενα δεικνύωσι τοῖς φαινομένοις.
⁶⁰ *PA* 666ᵇ21–4.
⁶¹ τὰ μάλιστα συνεστηκότα κατὰ φύσιν, i.e. his 'blooded' category.
⁶² *IA* 707ᵇ5–28.

his proofs more rigorous than those of the Hippocratics, but adherence to these very principles led him to make unwarranted assumptions which they avoided.

RELATIONSHIP OF THE HIPPOCRATIC AND ARISTOTELIAN CORPORA

Aristotle's biological works were written in the second half of the fourth century, later than the majority of Hippocratic works and probably slightly later than Diocles' *floruit*, and in many cases Aristotle can be seen as having been influenced to some extent by the Sicilian 'school' and arguing against the prevailing Hippocratic view.[63] It is difficult to know whether Aristotle is attacking general theories governing the practice of contemporary physicians or particular treatises, but on occasion the parallels between Aristotle's arguments and the arguments of Hippocratic works which are still extant suggest that Aristotle was answering specific treatises. The clearest evidence of Aristotle's knowledge of a Hippocratic treatise is his attack on the theory of pangenesis as expressed in *Genit.*, but there is other testimony to an immediate knowledge of Hippocratic doctrines. For example, the strange statement at *Morb.* 2. 8 (vii. 16. 11–12), 'The brain lies more to the front of the head than the back',[64] is echoed at *PA* 656ᵇ13, 'For the back [of the head] does not contain [any] brain'.[65] Preus cites other examples of Hippocratic influence and remarks, 'Many more parallels and related passages between Aristotle's biological works and the Hippocratic texts could surely be found by someone willing to look for them.'[66] This illustrates that although Aristotle was writing later than the period of the composition of the Hippocratic treatises, and although he was not primarily concerned with pathology and therapy, many of his con-

[63] In view of the important role of *pneuma* in Arist.'s physiology, it is unfortunate that we have only fragments from Sicilian medicine with which to compare him.
[64] ὁ ἐγκέφαλος ἐς τὸ πρόσω μᾶλλον κεῖται τῆς κεφαλῆς ἢ ἐς τοὔπισθεν.
[65] τὸ γὰρ ὄπισθεν [sc. τῆς κεφαλῆς] οὐκ ἔχει ἐγκέφαλον, cf. *HA* 491ᵃ34, 494ᵇ33.
[66] Preus 1975, 26–8; 1983. Cf. Morsink 1982, p. v. For the contrary view, that Arist. never knew any Hippocratic treatises and was simply arguing against views that were generally current in his society, see Fredrich 1899, 78. At present this view has fallen out of favour, but it should be noted that it was supported by no less a scholar than David Balme, who believed that the medical treatises were much later than is normally assumed (personal communication). However, Grensemann's painstaking lexical study (Grensemann 1975) makes it impossible that the gynaecology at least could be post-Aristotelian.

cerns were the same and he considered the Hippocratics part of the rational tradition with which he could have a meaningful dialogue. The two Corpora can be seen to be in opposition on many points. To investigate what these differences are and why they should have arisen is one of the aims of this book. From the foregoing brief survey it is obvious that the reasons for the differences are multifarious. The Hippocratics and Aristotle had different aims in formulating their theories, different methods in developing and proving them, and different philosophical contexts in which to set them. Moreover, although Hippocratic medicine continued to be practised throughout the fourth century, the society in which Aristotle conceived and elaborated his philosophy was beginning to develop away from the strictly gender-dichotomized world of the earlier Classical period (roughly the beginning of the fifth century to 323 BC) in which the Hippocratic gynaecological treatises were written. Women's legal, social, and economic activities gradually began to expand in the Hellenistic period (c.323 BC to roughly the end of the first century BC).[67] It is difficult to judge the extent to which the attitudes that enabled this to take place had begun to develop by the mid-fourth century, so we cannot know whether the development of these attitudes had any influence on Aristotle.[68] But for whatever reason, the Aristotelian theory of female physiology displaced the traditional Hippocratic view even among practising physicians in the less gender-dichotomized world of the Hellenistic and Roman periods.[69]

LATER SCIENTIFIC SOURCES

The differences between the society of the Hippocratics and that of Aristotle are not nearly so marked as those between the society of

---

[67] See Pomeroy 1975, 120–48; 1984. It is true that we have more information on the position of women in Egypt than anywhere else for the Hellenistic period, and that in many ways special circumstances obtained there. But Pomeroy 1984 shows that women's increased freedom in Egypt can be mirrored elsewhere, e.g. in education, 59–72.

[68] It is clear that he disagreed with Pl.'s claim in *Rep.* that there was no difference between the souls of men and women, but it is not clear that Pl.'s opinion on this matter was influential even in the Academy, or, for that matter, with Pl. himself.

[69] See Scarborough 1983 on the connection between Hippocratic and Aristotelian pharmacology.

the Classical period and Hellenistic and Roman societies.[70] In the
later periods the competence of women continued to expand, and
throughout these periods it was the Aristotelian rather than the
Hippocratic model of female physiology which was adopted by the
leading medical practitioners, in part because his model was better
adapted to the changing role of women in society.

Admittedly, the
Aristotelian model used scientific theory to argue for the natural
subordination of women to men in a way that had not been done
before, but those modern researchers anxious to expose the misogyny of Aristotle have failed to account for the fact that the elaboration and establishment of his model took place during a period in
which women were being admitted into more and more activities—
including the profession of medicine.[71] I do not intend in this study
to investigate the history of Aristotle's theories in detail beyond the
author's own writings, but I will be referring to later authors so I
include a brief note on some of the more important of the later
medical sources.

Alexandrian Medicine and Herophilus

In the two centuries following the death of Alexander the Great in
323 BC, the focus of scientific activity shifted from Greece to Egypt,
which was ruled by a Greek dynasty founded by one of Alexander's
generals, Ptolemy. Ptolemy's son, Ptolemy II, founded a literary
academy, the Museion (literally, 'a temple to the Muses') and
Library, in his capital at Alexandria. Here were gathered together
the most accurate versions of every existing written work, and new
works in literature, science, and scholarship were promoted. It is to
this library that we owe the preservation of most of the Greek literature we now possess, but ironically the medical works which originated in the period when the Museion and Library flourished have
been lost. As with the Presocratics and Sicilians, for those doctors
who were active between Aristotle and the physicians at Rome we

[70] Roman society has a history stretching back several centuries before the Hellenistic period, but its dominance in the Mediterranean was not established until the 1st
c. BC, and so the appellation will be used in this book for the period following the
Hellenistic.
[71] The story of Hagnodike studying under Herophilus is probably apocryphal, see
King 1986, but there is other evidence to suggest that in the later periods of antiquity
there were a number of female physicians in addition to midwives (who always had a
role to play in the treatment of women), see pp. 31–3 below.

have to rely on chance scraps of papyrus and second-hand reports in later writers. The loss is all the greater because, although Hellenistic medicine was heavily influenced by both the Hippocratics and Aristotle, the practice of dissecting—perhaps even of vivisecting—human beings which was introduced at this period led to great advances in anatomy and physiology. Now for the first time physicians were able to look inside human bodies and see what was there.[72]

There are two great figures in medicine from this period: Herophilus (often given the honorific title 'Father of Anatomy') and Erasistratus (similarly referred to as 'Father of Physiology').[73] Herophilus wrote at least one treatise solely concerned with gynaecology and in his treatise on anatomy paid a great deal of attention to the female reproductive organs. He had been trained in the Hippocratic tradition by Praxagoras, but his biological theories show a strong influence of Aristotelian concepts, particularly in the relation of the male to the female. Erasistratus is not an important figure in ancient gynaecology.

Roman Medicine and Celsus

During the two centuries from the Hippocratics to Herophilus, Rome had nothing comparable to show in the way of scientific medicine. Treatment for disease was still a matter for folk medicine, and the Roman ideal of self-sufficiency was reflected in the handbooks that every head of household or farm manager possessed to tell him how to deal with any illnesses or accidents that might befall those under his care. These handbooks might contain recipes for remedies that were no more fanciful or less efficacious than those in the Hippocratic Corpus, but side by side with these remedies were directions for magical treatments using charms and incantations.[74] Nor was it the business of those using or compiling these handbooks to systematize their anatomical or physiological assumptions. At the end of the third century BC the first professional Greek doctor arrived in Rome,[75] and although they were always viewed with

---

[72] See von Staden 1989, 139–53, on the controversy over whether or not the Alexandrians vivisected.

[73] It has been suggested that Erasistratus practised at Antioch rather than Alexandria, but the evidence for this view is minimal; see von Staden 1989, 47.

[74] See Jackson 1988, 9–11.

[75] Traditionally Archagathus of Laconia in 219 BC, see Majno 1975, 339–41.

suspicion by some of the more traditional Romans, Greek physicians quickly became popular and successful. The earliest text to show the success of Greek medicine at Rome is that of Celsus in the first century AD. He was an encyclopaedist who wrote on many subjects such as philosophy and agriculture, but the eight books of his *De Medicina* are all that survive. His work is derivative rather than the result of original research, theorizing, or practice, and was written in Latin to make the tradition of Greek medicine more accessible to Romans. In furtherance of this aim it incorporates some contemporary Roman beliefs and practices. References to female physiology are scattered throughout the eight books but are concentrated mainly in Book 3.

Another encyclopaedist of the first century AD, Pliny the Elder, compiled a *Natural History* in 37 books. These contain a great many medical references, and although most of them are from the Greek and Roman folk tradition, some are culled from Greek scientific sources.

Soranus and Methodism

Significant original works in scientific medicine continued to be written in Greek. Soranus was born at Ephesus, a major medical centre in Ionia, trained at Alexandria, and practised in Rome at the end of the first and beginning of the second centuries AD. He wrote many books on different medical subjects, all in Greek. The only work which survives, however, is his *Gynaecology*[76] in four books which deals not only with female physiology, pathology, conception, pregnancy, and parturition, but also with the care of the newborn infant and young child. Soranus is the greatest exponent of the Methodist school. Like the Empiricists, Methodists did not believe it was necessary to develop numerous and elaborate theories in order to cure a patient, but like the Dogmatists they believed it was necessary to have some guiding

[76] This is preserved in only one Greek manuscript. Caelius Aurelianus in the 5th c. AD adapted much of Soranus into Latin, and Muscio in the 6th c. made a Latin epitome of Soranus' advice to midwives (because, he says, he knows of no midwife who can read Greek). These Latin versions have been used by editors of Soranus to identify and supplement what is authentically Soranus' work, so although he originally wrote in Greek, Soranus may occasionally be quoted in Latin.

system, a method, in the treatment of similar illnesses. They classified diseases into three basic bodily states: relaxed, constricted and mixed. Having identified a disease as exemplifying one of these states, a Methodist would administer treatment which he thought would bring about the opposite state in the part of the body that needed treatment.[77] This generalized theory of disease held for both sexes, so Methodists tended to use the same therapy on women as they did on men, even for complaints we would consider specifically gynaecological. Soranus' gynaecological therapies are humane and sympathetic and his work was extremely popular throughout antiquity among midwives and those who treated women frequently.

Galen

Galen was born in another Ionian medical centre, Pergamum. He was active—very active—in Rome in the second half of the second century AD. We have more works from the hand of Galen than from any other single author of antiquity. References to female problems and patients occur throughout his work, but his only specifically gynaecological treatise is *Ut. Diss.*, though he also wrote an embryological treatise, *Foet. Form.*, and a treatise on reproduction, *Sem.* Galen was thoroughly versed in the works of the Hippocratics (we know that he wrote commentaries on various Hippocratic treatises, some of which treatises still survive and some of which have otherwise been lost), Aristotle, and the Hellenistic physicians. Galen's interest in Aristotelian philosophy for its own sake meant that Aristotle exerted a greater influence on his theories than he had done on Herophilus or other physicians. Galen considered himself to be continuing the Dogmatic strand of the ancient medical tradition (though he traced the tradition back to Hippocrates rather than the Alexandrians) and to be refining and proving earlier theories rather than constructing a radically new system; but the extent and quality of his understanding of the tradition led to his system superseding all earlier writings until the Renaissance, when texts of Hippocrates independent of Galen again became available.

---

[77] See Frede 1982.

Continuity of Tradition and Theory

With a few exceptions (e.g. the early Sicilian 'school', Rufus, and Aretaeus[78]) the chronological development of ancient medicine coincides with a geographical shift in the centre of medical activity from Ionia to Athens, then to Alexandria, and finally to Rome. As medicine is to a large extent culturally bound like other literary products we should expect this geographical shift to be reflected in the theories propounded by the various physicians. However, Ionia, Athens, and Alexandria were all part of a self-conscious Greek culture which exported itself over the Mediterranean from the eighth century BC and deliberately tried to preserve its heritage. Eastern and Egyptian traditions and thought may have had some influence on medical theories, but only so far as they were incorporated into the Greek culture in which the scientific texts were produced. The greatest sociological factor operating for change in the Greek scientific view of the female body was the development of women's social role over time. This is not so true for the Roman period. Roman culture had different concerns from Greek over male/female relations, some of which Greek medicine could not accommodate. To be accepted by the indigenous population, medical writers trained in the Greek tradition had to assimilate certain Roman cultural preconceptions, hence there is a greater disjunction in some aspects of ancient gynaecology between the Hellenistic and the Roman period than between others.

The medical compendia of late antiquity—(i.e. those of Oribasius, Aetius of Amida, and Paul of Aegina (all Greek), and of

---

[78] Rufus of Ephesus was a younger contemporary of Soranus who chose to return to his native city to practise medicine after his training in Alexandria. He dissected and commented on the reproductive organs and foetuses of monkeys (see Burguière–Gourevitch–Malinas 1988, pp. xxxvii–xxxviii). Aretaeus was active around the same time as Galen. He wrote several treatises, and discusses women's diseases in his books on acute and chronic diseases. He was a follower of Archigenes, who had in turn been strongly influenced by the Pneumatic school that had developed from Sicilian medicine. Galen was sharply critical of Archigenes, but makes no mention of Aretaeus, which would lead us to the conclusion that Aretaeus wrote after Galen, except for the fact that Aretaeus makes no mention of Galen's work either. It is hard to believe that a physician writing after Galen could ignore him completely, so it would seem that they were fairly close contemporaries who chose to ignore each other and were able to do so because they were living in different parts of the Graeco-Roman world (Aretaeus lived in Cappadocia) and wrote in different traditions.

Vindician and Theodore Priscian (both Latin)[79]—develop little original theory and their primary interest for this study is their preservation of the scattered remarks and theories of earlier writers on gynaecology in the ancient world.

THE MALE BIAS OF CLASSICAL TEXTS

Much of the early activity in women's studies in Classics centred on a reinterpretation of the depiction of women in the canonical texts of epic, tragedy, oratory, etc. The overwhelming majority of these texts, and all those from the Classical period, are male-authored and they purvey male images of women's emotions, capacities, and daily lives rather than the realities. Of course, male authors also use images of men's emotions, capacities, and daily lives the better to serve the purpose of their compositions, but most authors, and particularly those in the agonistic society of ancient Greece, write in the hope of striking a sympathetic chord with their audience. Since the audience of the extant texts from Classical Greece was also almost exclusively male, we can assume that the images of men in the extant texts do mirror the male social consciousness of the reality of their nature and lives. We cannot say categorically that male authors never questioned women on how far their actual experiences were reflected in the imaged norm, but no such inquiries would be needed to produce the images we have in most literary compositions. Woman is defined as what man is not, either confrontationally or complementarily; all a male author needs is an image of himself as a man to project this. Moreover, he can distort or leave vague the day-to-day activities of women's lives because he does not rely on the approbation of a female audience for success.

THE INCORPORATION OF WOMEN'S TESTIMONY IN THE GYNAECOLOGICAL TEXTS

There is no indication that the gynaecological texts of the fifth and fourth centuries are exceptions in being male-authored, but they are

[79] Oribasius, Aetius, Vindician, and Theodore Priscian had their floruits respectively under the emperors Julian, AD 361–3, Justinian, AD 527–65, Valentinian, AD 364–75, and Gratian, AD 375–83; Paul of Aegina wrote in the 7th c. AD. Further study of these works *in toto* might reveal Christian influence on the later interpretation of ancient theories, even when the authors themselves are pagan.

unique in that they contain privileged information obtainable only from women, were directed at a female clientele, and show some glimpses of the intimate life of women.[80] This has given rise to a debate over the extent to which male scientific theories (based, it is claimed, on gender-role ideologies) incorporated or challenged the theories of the female oral tradition (derived, it is claimed, from women's unmediated experiences).[81] However, even if the model of the female body in the female oral tradition originated directly from women's testimony, it is a mistake to assume that it was not itself based on gender-role ideology. Women would have personal experience of their body as complete rather than as a body suffering from the negation or deprivation of things male, but the importance to society as a whole of the production of offspring would lead them to regard their prime role as childbearing and -rearing, and so to define their bodies as potential mothers. Such a model would conform to socially accepted gender roles, though the significance of the model would be entirely different for men (focusing on what women could not do) and for women (focusing on what they could). Similarly, although the scientific theories may have displaced the traditional therapies, the treatment offered to women on the basis of the new theories must have been acceptable to them and have squared with their view of their own physiology. Despite the fact that cultural concepts of the female body are relayed to us through male authors, the more positive interpretations that can be put on the model at times show through.

[80] This last aspect of the medical texts will not be a factor in the present study, but the sort of material which shows that the texts reflect the reality rather than the socialized norm of women's lives is typified in two case histories. At *Epid.* 4. 26 (v. 170. 8–17) a doctor is called to attend the niece of a certain Temenes. He comments, 'If she had a child, I do not know' (εἰ δὲ καὶ εἶχέ τι νήπιον, οὐκ οἶδα). This implies that while the situation was too delicate to inquire further, the doctor thought it was conceivable that a young unmarried girl might give birth and be protected by her family, not sold into slavery as the Solonic law allowed. Again, at *Epid.* 5. 50 (v. 236. 11–20) a twenty-year-old *parthenos*, who is described as beautiful (καλή), is struck on the head while playing with some friends and has to be taken back to her own home. This shows that not all Greek women were married at fourteen and that they sometimes left their homes for reasons other than religious festivals.

[81] With regard to the Hippocratics, two recent studies have come to diametrically opposed conclusions on this matter. Rousselle 1988 believes that they took over the female tradition wholesale. Manuli 1983, on the other hand, believes that the Hippocratic authors paid little or no attention to women's subjective experience in elaborating their explanations of the female body. Lloyd 1983, 62–86, 168–200, argues that the truth lies somewhere between the two: the Hippocratics were starting to develop a critical approach to traditional assumptions but still relied on female experience in framing their own theories, though they may have distrusted it.

The apparent, egregious errors in detailing a woman's physical experiences are not a sign of the dismissal of female testimony in ancient scientific theory. It would seem possible to disprove many ancient theories about the male body from the subjective experience of men, yet male authors held to them. The Hippocratics, for example, claimed that a weakness of voice could be cured only by a varicose vein in one of the testicles,[82] and that most men could predict whether they would engender males or females by noting which testicle dropped first at puberty.[83] Aristotle believed that after puberty some men could produce milk.[84] It is not impossible, therefore, that in relating their experiences to men, women endorsed erroneous notions about the female body.

Men do not seem to have suspected that women gave each other different information from that they gave men. References to women learning from women in the literature of the period, even where they are hostile, do not say that women pass on wrong information, or that it is information deliberately hidden from men, merely that the transmission of it to women is performed by other women.[85] *Genit.* 5 (vii. 476. 17–20) states that if a woman does not want to conceive she can cause the seed from both partners to run out after intercourse, but that if she does want to conceive the seed will not run out but will remain in her womb. It would seem that any sexually experienced woman would object that not only had she no control over whether or not the seed remained inside, but also that there was no observable difference in the amounts of semen which flowed from her after fruitful or barren intercourse. Yet in *Nat. Puer.* 13 (vii. 490. 5–7) the author claims that a young girl had heard 'the sort of thing women say to each other—that when a woman is going to conceive, the seed remains inside her and does not fall out'.[86] There is, therefore, no difference between the 'facts' ancient male scientists learned from women and those on which the traditional theories of the female body were founded.

Nor do the scientific theories necessarily differ from traditional

---

[82] *Epid.* 2. 5. 1 (v. 128. 3–5).   [83] Ibid. 6. 4. 21 (v. 312. 10–11).
[84] *HA* 522ª19–20.
[85] The education and treatment of women by women is variously evaluated in the ancient sources. For positive assessments see Chariton 2. 8. 4–11. 6; Ar. *Eccl.* 526–50. For negative assessments, see Semon. 90–1; Eur. *Andr.* 930–53. The major criticism is that it brings about loss of innocence, see Hanson 1990, 309.
[86] ὁκοῖα αἱ γυναῖκες λέγουσι πρὸς ἀλλήλας· ἐπὴν γυνὴ μέλλῃ λήψεσθαι ἐν γαστρί, οὐκ ἐξέρχεται ἡ γονή, ἀλλ' ἔνδον μένει.

ideas about female physiology in their underlying assumptions. The syndrome reported by the author of *Virg.*—the epileptic fits and strange visions of adolescent girls which often resulted in attempted suicide—was already accepted as a common occurrence among unmarried girls before the medical theory was elaborated. The Hippocratic theory accepted the cultural belief that the passage to womanhood was a difficult one; it explained the origin of the disease as an accumulation of blood in the lungs which could be released by having the girl married and deflowered. The traditional remedy of making an offering to Artemis was directed at the realm of the divine, assuming that an unseen mechanism beyond the human sphere had caused the disease. This remedy had its own logic (Artemis was the goddess associated with female puberty and its attendant difficulties),[87] but it did not have the same link between cause and effect, observable in principle if not in practice, which the Hippocratic theory had. The difference between Hippocratic gynaecology and traditional belief lay in the type of explanation given for phenomena rather than in the facts or assumptions on which each was based. Similarly, Aristotle holds that an *endoxon* with which all men agree is beyond challenge,[88] and, rather than argue them away, he offers explanations for assumptions which we would consider obviously mistaken. For example, it was believed that menstruation was controlled by the moon because the moon was female. Although he knew of instances to contradict the belief, Aristotle accepted that the moon controlled menstruation, but attributed it to women being more susceptible to changes of temperature caused by the lunar phases.[89] Observations and assumptions that we would consider fanciful, therefore, were included in the oral tradition as well as in scientific theories, and do not preclude the use of female testimony in formulating these theories.

There is also positive evidence to suggest that information from wise-women was taken into consideration in scientific accounts of the female body. *Praec.* 2 (ix. 254. 4–5) instructs a doctor not to despise asking questions among lay people if it would be beneficial for therapy, and it seems that the Hippocratics thought this method particularly fruitful in the treatment of women, the lay practitioners

[87] For an excellent discussion of this issue, see King 1983.
[88] *NE* 1172^{b}36–1173^{a}1. However, where traditional assumptions could not be brought into conformity with his theories he rejected them without compunction.
[89] *HA* 582^{a}34–^{b}3; *GA* 738^{a}17–22.

being mainly wise-women. The gynaecology incorporates more elements of folk practice, such as a wider materia medica and more
attendant ritual in diagnoses and cures,[90] than other sections of the
Corpus. An acceptance of more general female testimony is suggested at *Septim./Oct.* 4 (vii. 440. 14–442. 1) where the author says it
is necessary to believe women when they talk about giving birth 'for
they would not be persuaded in word or deed that they do not know
what occurs inside their own bodies',[91] and *Epid.* 6. 8. 10 (v. 348. 3–5)
tells of a patient who knew what was going on in her illness by her
own inner sense. Sometimes, it is true, the Hippocratic doctor casts
doubt on the reliability of a woman's statements, as at *Epid.* 4. 6 (v.
146. 9–12) where the author questions the truth of a woman's statement that she had aborted a twenty-day-old male foetus before the
abortion he was called in to attend. *Mul.* 1. 62 (viii. 126. 4–19)
implies that the Hippocratics felt that it was part of their role to
educate women on their monthly courses rather than vice versa. The
author does not advise simply asking a woman if her menses are
excessive; this is a judgement the doctor himself must make after
eliciting other information from the patient because, the author
explains, women often do not know what is happening in their
bodies before they are fairly advanced in age. But several passages
make it clear that ignorance of the body is not restricted to women.
VM 2 (i. 572. 21–574. 2) says: 'it were no easy matter for common
people to discover for themselves the nature of their own diseases
and the causes why they get worse or get better',[92] and *de Arte* 11 (vi.
20. 7–9) complains that diagnosis 'is made more difficult by the fact
that the symptoms which patients with internal diseases describe to

[90] Riddle 1987, 39 n. 32, suggests 'many, if not most, of the drug references' of
Hippocratic pharmacology are derived from the gynaecology. Lloyd 1987, 251 n.
127, 252 n. 128, in giving examples of drugs and dosage in the Hippocratic Corpus,
takes most of them from the gynaecology. Von Staden 1992 discusses the fact that the
gynaecological treatises are the only texts in the Hippocratic Corpus to advocate the
use of human or animal excrement. *Mul.* 1. 11 (viii. 42. 9–16) uses a ritual-like
procedure with menstrual rags to diagnose bilious or phlegmatic menses. *Mul.* 1. 23
(viii. 62. 12–18) ties a procedure for promoting conception to the position of the sun in
the sky. *Steril.* 214 (viii. 414. 17–19) says that if a woman belches after drinking the
milk of a woman who is suckling a boy she will become pregnant, cf. Hanson 1991.

[91] οὐ γὰρ ἂν πεισθείησαν οὔτ' ἔργῳ οὔτε λόγῳ, ἀλλ' ὅτι γνῶναι τὸ ἐν τοῖσι
σώμασιν αὐτέων γινόμενον. Though his additional remark that it is possible that
there were women who thought otherwise suggests that the author was still a little
ambivalent on how far to trust women's testimony.

[92] αὐτοὺς μὲν οὖν τὰ σφέων αὐτέων παθήματα καταμαθεῖν, ὡς γίνεται καὶ
παύεται καὶ δι' οἵας προφάσιας αὔξεταί τε καὶ φθίνει, δημότας ἐόντας οὐ
ῥηίδιον.

their physicians are based on guesses about a possible cause rather than knowledge about it'.[93] Surveying earlier *endoxa* was an integral part of Aristotle's method, and like the author of *Praec.*, Aristotle considered it worth while to consult the experience of laymen as well as specialists.[94] Aristotle sometimes identifies his sources, but often does not. A name notably absent from the *endoxa* is that of Plato, though it is obvious that he was a pervasive influence throughout Aristotle's works. The absence of references to the opinions of women, therefore, should not be taken to signify that Aristotle rejected them out of hand, and there is no reason to suppose that he did not avail himself of the experience of wise-women in matters of female physiology, though he would incorporate less of their expertise into his theories than did the Hippocratics since it was largely therapeutical. His identification of the clitoris rather than the vagina as the area in which women feel pleasure during intercourse strongly suggests that he did number women among his informants.[95]

WOMEN AS PHYSICIANS

It is possible that in Classical Greece in some cases the figure of the doctor and the female informant could be one and the same. Plato, at *Rep.* 454 D 2, uses the example of a female physician as proof that there is no difference between the quality of male and female souls without any indication that he is citing a hypothetical example, and there is an inscription of the fourth or third century BC honouring the midwife and doctor Phanostrate.[96] While it is difficult to imagine female doctors treating male patients in antiquity, there is no reason to assume that they were trained in or practised a different type of

---

[93] καὶ γὰρ δὴ καὶ ἃ πειρῶνται οἱ τὰ ἀφανέα νοσέοντες ἀπαγγέλλειν περὶ τῶν νοσημάτων τοῖσι θεραπεύουσιν, δοξάζοντες μᾶλλον ἢ εἰδότες ἀπαγγέλλουσιν.

[94] Though Arist. did not feel bound to accept everything the layman told him. At *GA* 759^{a}25–^{b}1 he dismisses (correctly) the statement of beekeepers that bees reproduce by fetching their young from elsewhere, but he is mistaken at *GA* 720^{b}33–5 when he refuses to accept fishermen's accounts of the hectocotylization of the octopus's tentacle during intercourse (but cf. *HA* 524^{a}3–9, 541^{b}1–12, 544^{a}12–15, where he shows more doubt on the subject).

[95] *GA* 728^{a}32–4, see pp. 79–80 below; Dean-Jones 1992, 83–7.

[96] Pomeroy 1978; *IG* II/III (2), 6873; Kudlien 1979, 88–9; Krug 1985, 195–7. Cf. Benedum in *RE* Suppl. 14, cols. 48–9, for an inscription of the late Hellenistic period honouring Antiochis of Tlos for her experience in medicine. I am indebted to an unpublished paper by Ann Hanson for this reference.

gynaecology from their male counterparts. In *Jusj.* (iv. 628. 6–630.
2) there is a clause which reads: 'I will regard the children [of my
teacher] as equal to male siblings, and teach them this science, if
they desire to learn it, without fee or contract.'⁹⁷ The wording of the
commitment, to treat all the teacher's children as male siblings,
suggests that daughters of the teacher were also eligible for instruction in medicine. If the commitment was to be understood as
referring simply to the sons of the teacher it would be more natural
to substitute υἱεῖς for γένος and to omit ἄρρεσι. If it does encompass daughters as well as sons, it shows that women could receive
medical training in the same scientific tradition as men.

Hyginus tells the apocryphal tale of Hagnodike, the supposed
first female physician of antiquity.⁹⁸ The story claims that before the
time of Herophilus the Athenians did not even have midwives (*ob-
stetrices*). This cannot be true, but it is possible that in the early fifth
century the Greeks (or the Athenians) did not have female physicians and that at some time during the Classical period a law was
passed allowing women to practise as doctors. The story would then
have developed as an *aition* for this law. Originally, the story goes,
the Athenians had not allowed any women to practise medicine, and
many women suffering from gynaecological ailments were dying
rather than allowing a male doctor to attend to them. Hagnodike
masqueraded as a male and studied medicine under Herophilus in
Alexandria. On returning to Athens she practised gynaecology, still
disguised as a man, and disclosed her true sex only to those female
patients unwilling to have a male doctor examine them. Her practice became so successful that other doctors accused her of seducing
her patients, whereupon Hagnodike lifted her cloak and revealed
that this was impossible. The Athenians were then going to prose-
cute her for breaking the law forbidding women to practise medicine, until the women of Athens accused them of not caring about
their wives' welfare. The Athenians agreed that this objection was
just and changed the law to allow women to practise medicine. The

⁹⁷ καὶ γένος τὸ ἐξ ὡὐτέου ἀδελφοῖς ἴσον ἐπικρινέειν ἄρρεσι, καὶ διδάξειν
τὴν τέχνην ταύτην, ἢν χρηίζωσι μανθάνειν, ἄνευ μισθοῦ καὶ ξυγγραφῆς. The
translation is my own literal rendering. Others automatically translate γένος as
'sons' rather than 'children' and ἀδελφοῖς ... ἄρρεσι as 'brothers' rather than 'male
siblings'. The emphasis on the importance of training for the medical career from an
early age (παιδομαθίη) in *Lex* 2–3 (iv. 638. 11–640. 12) suggests that the ranks of
physicians were replenished primarily from doctors' children.
⁹⁸ Hyg. *Fab.* 274. 10–13. see Bonner 1920; Pomeroy 1977; Most 1981; King 1986
(who shows conclusively that the story is invented); von Staden 1989, 38–41, 61.

story argues for the treatment of women by women, not because they
have different or superior knowledge (Hagnodike was supposed to
have learned what she knew from Herophilus, not from her own
experience or any other woman), but because of a woman's natural
modesty.

The medical compendianists of Late Antiquity and the Byzantine
period attribute much gynaecological material to female authors,
and there exist two treatises entitled *Diseases of Women* attributed
to female authors: Cleopatra in the Hellenistic period and Metrodora in the fifth century AD. Given the expanded role women played
in Alexandrian scholarship, it is not unlikely such women did
exist:[99] However, when Aetius attributes several chapters on
gynaecological matters to Aspasia, the famous companion of Pericles in the fifth century BC, it is probable the attribution is apocryphal, though the work could be by a later Aspasia who was equated
with Pericles' Aspasia because the latter was the only woman re-
nowned for her intelligence during the time of Hippocrates. Aspasia
was the focus of so much praise and criticism during her lifetime and
immediately afterwards that had she written such a treatise it is
unlikely that no mention would have been made of it until the sixth
century AD. Accordingly, while there is a basis for believing women
practised scientific medicine in the fifth and fourth centuries BC, there
is no evidence that a woman wrote any of the extant treatises.

WOMEN'S PREFERENCES IN MEDICAL CARE

Despite the modesty Hyginus imputes to women and the possibility
of their being attended by female physicians as well as traditional
wise-women, it would seem the male doctors who wrote the treatises
were called to attend female patients. *Medic.* I (ix. 206. 4–10) says
that doctors must behave judiciously because they come into contact
with women and young girls, and *Jusj.* (iv. 630. 14–15) has a doctor
swear he will keep himself free from all wrongdoing, including not
abusing his position 'to indulge in sexual contacts with the bodies of
women or of men, whether they be freemen or slaves',[100] showing

[99] For Cleopatra, see Diels 1906, 23–4; for Metrodora, see del Guerra 1953. For
the role of women in Alexandrian scholarship, see Pomeroy 1984, 61.
[100] ἀφροδισίων ἔργων ἐπί τε γυναικείων σωμάτων καὶ ἀνδρῴων,
ἐλευθέρων τε καὶ δούλων.

that in general it was expected that doctors would come into intimate contact with free-born women. Moreover, *Decent.* 12 (ix. 238. 19–240. 4), while dealing extensively with the way in which a doctor should sit, dress, and conduct himself when entering the home of a patient, never deals with the problem of how to act when confronted with a female patient—a situation which might be thought to pose particular problems if there was widespread resistance to male doctors treating women.[101] Such passages as these indicate that a Hippocratic doctor did expect to have a number of women among his clients.

In the seven books of *Epid.*, however, there are twice as many male as female case histories. One author comments that women fall ill less often than men, but the proportion of case histories could suggest that women tended to avail themselves of traditional medicine at the hands of wise-women rather than seek the advice of physicians who were generally male.[102] They might also have recourse to temple medicine.[103] When a doctor does attend a female patient he usually refers to her by her relationship to a man, presumably the head of household who had summoned him. A third of the women in the case histories are suffering from complications arising in some stage of childbearing, perhaps reflecting the occasion on which the men of the household insisted on involving themselves in the question of a woman's treatment. Most of the births described by Hippocratic authors are abnormal in some way, but *Mul.* 1. 34 (viii. 78. 16–80. 5) gives a brief description of the progression of normal parturition. Such descriptions may be rare because uncomplicated births were left in the hands of midwives or women of the household,

[101] An alternative interpretation of this passage could be that some doctors treated women so rarely that this author did not consider the contingency of attending a female patient. However, while it seems likely that Hippocratic doctors saw fewer female patients than male, we have no reason to believe such an event was particularly rare.

[102] The nurse's speech at Eur. *Hipp.* 293–6, 'If you are ill with one of the unmentionable troubles [ἀπορρήτων κακῶν], these women here will help put your malady [νόσον] to rights. But if your trouble can be told to men, speak so that this case can be referred to doctors' (see Barrett 1964, n. ad loc.), could be taken to signify that gynaecological complaints would ordinarily be taken to other women rather than male physicians. But it could equally well signify that if Phaedra is suffering mental anguish over some socially unacceptable desire (which is in fact the case) she should unburden herself to women, but that if her suffering has a physical origin for which she could not be blamed she should seek the specialized knowledge of a trained physician.

[103] Throughout antiquity women make more dedications to Asclepius than men do, McClees 1920, 17–22, cited in Pomeroy 1975, 84 n. 21.

who were presumed to know what to do through having given birth themselves.[104] Even when a male doctor was supervising a difficult birth, a woman often delivered the child and severed the umbilical cord.[105] The balance of the evidence, then, suggests that women continued to have recourse to traditional medicine over Hippocratic physicians more often than men did. Men may have chosen the wise-woman or Asclepius over the Hippocratic physician as well, but women would have had the extra incentives of modesty and feminine sympathy.

For even if traditional medicine was no more correct than the Hippocratic in data and assumptions of the female body, ancient women may have felt that men could not understand or sympathize with their exclusively female experiences, and this may have led them to rely more on the diagnoses and therapies of wise-women. In cases of normal pregnancies and uncomplicated childbirth this may have been a fair enough assessment, but it could not be stipulated or expected that a wise-woman should have personally suffered every gynaecological disease in the way that it could be required of a midwife that she should herself have given birth. In matters of pathology a wise-woman was simply a receptacle of received wisdom which could be assimilated by a male as easily as by a female. The existence and continuity of a traditional medicine for women side by side with the scientific medicine, therefore, need not imply that the Hippocratic gynaecology was less effective or compassionate or less informed by female experience. It would merely illustrate an understandable female prejudice.

MALE ACCESS TO WOMEN'S BODIES

The new scientific theories, therefore, incorporated a great deal of the oral tradition that circulated among women concerning their own bodies. But one of the claims of the new theorists was that they based their theories on empirical evidence rather than unsupported beliefs. The question then arises, how much opportunity did male scientists of the Classical period have to investigate the female body first-hand.

It has been claimed both that Hippocratic doctors were always dependent upon second-hand information relayed to them by a

[104] Pl. *Tht.* 149 B.   [105] *Mul.* I. 46, 68 (viii. 106. 7, 144. 22–4).

woman who had been examined either by herself under their instructions or by a trained midwife acting as an intermediary, and conversely that women never examined themselves but were examined either by a midwife or the doctor himself.[106] When specific instructions are given on the point it could be either the doctor (*Nat. Mul.* 6 (vii. 320. 1)), a female assistant (*Mul.* 1. 21 (viii. 60. 16–17)), or the patient herself (*Steril.* 213 (viii. 408. 16–17)) who performed the inspection. However, in most cases the imperative to inspect is in the form of an infinitive, and as such could signify a command either in the second person (in which case it would be directed at the reader of the text, i.e. the doctor) or the third. The use of participles of both masculine and feminine genders in the instructions accompanying the inspection shows that it was assumed that sometimes the inspection would be carried out by a man, the doctor, and sometimes by a woman. The feminine participles are usually in the middle (reflexive) voice, indicating that the patient performed the action herself. There is little evidence that a third person was routinely involved in examinations, so the least common scenario would seem to be that in which a female assistant acted as an intermediary.[107] It is highly probable that different doctors and different patients had different sensibilities about this matter which resulted in different individual patterns of behaviour, but some Hippocratic doctors would have had the opportunity to examine intimately several women's bodies.

Since he was not a practising physician, Aristotle would have had access to fewer women's bodies than the Hippocratics; he was probably restricted to those of his own household—his wife, concubine, and slaves—and even then, without the therapeutical motives of the Hippocratics, he may not have subjected them to intimate examinations. However, Aristotle had an advantage in that his methodology included the dissection of animals, so he was able to study at his leisure the inside of healthy female bodies, albeit non-human, rather than being restricted to observing the surface symptoms of pathological conditions which had to be treated as soon as possible.

[106] Rousselle 1980, 1091–2; Manuli 1980, 396–7. Lloyd 1983, 70–81, discusses the issue and shows that there is evidence for all three procedures.

[107] Examples of masculine participles indicating doctor performed examination: *Mul.* 1. 19, 60, 64 (viii. 58. 11, 120. 8–9, 132. 11–13). Examples of feminine participles indicating woman performed examination herself: *Mul.* 1. 13, 40, 59 (viii. 52. 1, 98. 1, 118. 3)

WOMEN'S ACCEPTANCE OF SCIENTIFIC THEORIES

Their desire to rationalize therapy as far as possible led the Hippocratics to redefine some of the traditional notions of female physiology, and their specialized access to the bodies of women would have given such challenges authority even among women, but at very many points the assumptions of their culture had a constraining influence which prevented them from going far beyond the accepted wisdom of their day. Moreover, as there was alternative medical care to which women could turn if the Hippocratic theories diverged too much from the image they had of their own bodies, the gynaecological treatises had to be consistent with female beliefs. The models of the female body in the Hippocratic Corpus are the product and the common property of society, women as well as men. Aristotle inherited the same traditions concerning the female body as did the Hippocratics, but although he too was bound to a great extent by his cultural assumptions, he was more concerned that his explanation of the male/female dichotomy conformed to the basic tenets of his view of the universe, which in many ways departed from traditional modes of thought. Nor was he writing for an audience that included women. His view of women's bodies, therefore, is less representative of traditional Greek beliefs than the Hippocratic model.

Rousselle contends that while women's views of their own bodies were respected in the Hippocratics, they were dismissed by physicians of later antiquity in preference for male views owing to the influence of Aristotle.[108] Manuli sees a confirmation of patriarchal attitudes from the Hippocratics continuing through Aristotle down to the sympathetic theories of Soranus.[109] Both interpretations consider Aristotle to be particularly unsympathetic to women, and in this they are seconded by Horowitz and Saïd, who both present Aristotle's theories as the direct result of an actively misogynistic ideology.[110] Clark considers Horowitz's arguments so compelling that he reverses the favourable judgement he had previously passed on Aristotle's attitude to women.[111] However, it is unlikely that Aristotle's theories would have become as dominant in medical practice as they did if they had simply purveyed male animosities.

[108] Rousselle 1980; 1988, 24–46.
[109] Manuli 1980; 1983.
[110] Horowitz 1976; Saïd 1983.
[111] Clark 1975, 206–11; 1982.

Women must have acquiesced in the model to the extent of providing data to support it and acceding to therapy based upon it, but this need not mean that women were relinquishing a positive for a negative image. Men might cite the Aristotelian model to prove that women were their natural inferiors and as such subject to male rule; but women could cite it to argue that they were in fact more like men than had previously been allowed, and that they were therefore capable of fulfilling many roles hitherto restricted to men. Of course, there is no definite proof that Aristotle's model was used in this way, but we should be wary of assuming that women in antiquity were so abject as to defer to a male interpretation of their bodies in which they could perceive no advantage for themselves.

The experience of our own society shows that many women readily accept concepts about themselves which from a male point of view seem derogatory. It is only comparatively recently that women in significant numbers have begun to challenge these concepts and to argue that their acceptance of them is the result of social conditioning, which operates for the benefit of the male members of society in supporting traditional gender roles that exclude women from the centres of power and knowledge in the public sphere. The benefits women think they receive in the private sphere from the distinction between gender roles based on biology, it is argued, are illusory or insignificant. But to claim that generation after generation of women has lived with bodies they believed were inferior and/or disgusting and has accepted the male view of their physiology without realizing that they were being exploited, is to deprive most women that have ever lived of pride and intelligence. The benefits of being the 'weaker sex' may seem to contemporary women to be illusory—and if they are being forced on an individual that rejects them, they surely are—but in our culture women partake in the same (originally male) education as men, and the growth of the media has resulted in both genders experiencing society more and more from a single vantage point—the public, articulated perspective developed in the male realm. In the same way, anthropological researchers (male and female) studying cultures from the supposedly objective standpoint of an outsider receive their information primarily from one section of a society—the male.[112] But women in a dichotomized society do not necessarily share the same perspective as men. The advantages accruing from being female in a dichotomized society,

[112] Ardener 1975.

which seem illusory to those who share the traditional male perspective because they are unimportant in the public sphere, are as real as the male advantages when viewed from a female perspective which believes that the home is society proper and men's public activities a necessary but less significant adjunct. Ardener reports that when approached with questions which men in the same society had answered, women 'giggle when young, snort when old, reject the question, laugh at the topic and the like. The male members of a society frequently see the ethnographer's difficulties as simply a caricature of their own daily case.'[113] Such behaviour implies the women saw such questions as unimportant and marginal to their own lives, and were not impressed that men thought otherwise.

If the female realm had been the one to develop an articulate discourse about society and its organization it would surely have valorized and empowered the sphere of the home and the role of the homemaker; the male who had to leave the family dwelling place each day to provide for the home would have been viewed as marginal to society; social sanctions would operate to ensure that a man handed over his wages to the homemaker; men would fear the displeasure of their wives; caricatures would develop of men helpless in the techniques, economics, and psychology of running a home, and a man's view on most aspects of the organization of this society (including his interpretation of his role) would be considered irrelevant.[114] I am not arguing that gender-based social roles are a 'good thing', that they have to exist inevitably, or that many women have not been the victims of economic and physical abuse as the result of the empowering of the male sphere. But I do not believe that the articulated social view that woman is inferior to man and the female role subordinate to the male has been the rationale guiding the majority of women who fulfilled their expected gender roles, or that the traditional female view of women's role in society was always a compensatory illusion which deceived undiscerning women into being exploited.

Therefore, while it is not to be denied that the male-authored gynaecological texts of antiquity constructed a female body that evolved from and validated the social position of the female, and while it is highly probable that women of the period helped to shape

[113] Ibid. 2.
[114] It will be seen that many elements in this model are current in contemporary society.

and concurred in this construct,[115] it does not follow that women in antiquity were an abject oppressed section of society. Men may have thought that they had validated the inferior social position of women, but women may have been more concerned with what they themselves felt and believed than with the opinions of a section of society marginal to their daily lives. In developing their theories of female physiology, male authors who espoused scientific principles would have had to turn frequently to women for their data, and their images would have had to be ratified to some extent by women. This was not the case in other forms of literary production. It is possible that the significance of the model within female society is reflected in the male texts and that a study of scientific concepts of women's bodies in Greek science will give us some insight into women's consciousness of themselves in antiquity.

[115] Cf. Redfield 1977, 149.

I

Female Anatomy and Physiology

CULTURAL CONSTRUCTION OF SEXUAL
DIFFERENTIATION

In most cultures an individual is ascribed to one sex or another at birth on the evidence of external genitalia, and this categorization is taken to predict his or her physical and mental development and capabilities, which in turn support the differentiation between the sexes in the home, the workplace, religion, the law—even in hairstyles and dress. There is an obvious correlation between genitalia and an individual's role in the propagation of the species, but no culture considers this difference in external genitalia in and of itself sufficient to justify the complete separation of male and female roles in society. Rather, cultures support this division by claiming that there are other, less apparent, physical, mental, and emotional traits which naturally differentiate the sexes. The traits that a culture decides are typical of a male or a female form the construct of that sex in that society. These stereotypes are often contradicted by individuals. Taking our own culture as an example, a woman can be more muscular or more aggressive than many men, a man can be smaller and more gentle than many women.[1] However, these challenges to the cultural constructs of male and female are neutralized by claiming that they are exceptions to a natural law.[2]

[1] That men are naturally stronger than women would probably be the gender-distinction belief to win the widest consensus in our culture, but even this belief is not shared by all cultures, see R. C. Bailey 1989, 686, on the Efe of Central Africa.

[2] During the 19th c. many people still believed intelligence to be an exclusively male attribute. In 1879 the French scholar Le Bon (whose work on crowd psychology is still widely respected) stated: 'Without doubt there exist some distinguished women, very superior to the average man, but they are as exceptional as the birth of any monstrosity, as, for example, of a gorilla with two heads.' He believed that recent work in craniometry, demonstrating that the average woman had a smaller head and therefore a smaller brain than the average man, proved scientifically that she was also less intelligent. He failed to take into account the fact that the average woman is

The belief in a natural law of the disjunction of the sexes often finds its initial expression in mythology or religion, as in the derivation of Eve from Adam's rib. And although, as a society develops, this mythological expression may appear allegorical at best, the deeply implanted cultural belief that men and women are radically different can condition the interpretation of empirical evidence so that science, in its turn, supports the belief that perceived differences between men and women are a result of biology rather than social conditioning.[3]

SEXUAL DIFFERENTIATION IN GREEK MYTH

In ancient Greece the polarization of sexual roles was far more marked than in our own society and consequently there was a stronger need to sever the male from the female. This disjunction was expressed in Greek myth by the separate origins of the sexes. In *Op.* 60–95 and *Th.* 570–616 Hesiod portrays humanity as consisting originally of one sex—the male. In the Judaeo-Christian tradition also, and in the myths of many other cultures, man makes his appearance before woman, but when the latter does appear she is usually derived in some way from the male body, signifying that she shares an origin with man, even if she is ultimately subordinate to him.[4] In the Greek mythological account, however, the first woman (traditionally called Pandora) is derived from an origin unconnected with man. She was supposedly moulded out of clay and given to man as a punishment by the gods.[5] This myth makes woman in-

smaller than the average man overall, and that large men with large heads were not always more intelligent than smaller representatives of the male sex, see Gould 1982, 152–9.

[3] Hence the misinterpretation of the data on XYY males which led to the supposed discovery of a gene for aggression on the Y chromosome, see Gould 1981, 143–5; Fausto-Sterling 1985, 150–3. I do not wish to argue that it has been scientifically proven that all supposed male and female behavioural patterns are socially rather than biologically conditioned, or that there can be no biologically determined differences between men and women apart from their reproductive roles. However, I do believe that to date all attempts at accounting biologically for supposed male/female dichotomies have proved, at best, inconclusive.

[4] See S. Thompson 1955–8, i. 210.

[5] See West 1978, 155–72. For a discussion of the mythological separation of the sexes, see Vernant 1983, 127–75. Loraux 1981, 75–117, gives a more detailed exposition of the misogyny of Hes. and Semon. in characterizing woman as a separate species

herently different from man in the very material of her body.[6] The
differences in her body structure are taken for granted, implied in the
simple descriptions 'like a modest virgin' (*Th.* 572, παρθένῳ
αἰδοίη ἴκελον) and 'the lovely figure of a virgin' (*Op.* 63, παρ-
θενικῆς καλὸν εἶδος). This is the case in most myths of women's
origins; they assume that the differences between the sexes are self-
evident and do not bother to be explicit in describing the physical
differences which distinguish the first woman from the pre-existing
man or men.

SEXUAL DIFFERENTIATION IN PRE-SOCRATIC PHILOSOPHY

After the beginnings of natural philosophy in Ionia in the sixth
century BC mythology was no longer universally accepted as giving
a true explanation of the world, and so, as in our own society,
science assumed the task of bolstering the traditional dichotomy
between men and women.[7] However, while the Classical Greeks
could observe the difference in external genitalia and typical secondary sexual characteristics, they did not dissect the human body and
so had only a vague understanding of the internal reproductive
organs; nor, obviously, could they have had any knowledge of
genetics or endocrinology. The strict biological polarization of the
sexes, therefore, was more dependent on external sexual characteristics than it is in our own society. But, as today, many bodies would
have been annoyingly recalcitrant in conforming to the culturally
determined sexual norm, so the archetype of the male or female body
could not be substantiated by referring simply to the actual bodies
that men and women possessed. The cultural paradigm of masculinity and femininity had to be supported by demonstrating that
typical male or female observable characteristics (both genitalia

from man. King 1985, 15–27, argues that woman is portrayed as standing outside the
'gods/men/beasts matrix' and as pushing the lot of man from the pole of the gods
towards that of the beasts.

[6] In *Op.* 176 Hes. describes the present race of men as being created by Zeus from
iron. In *Th.*513 the epithet used to describe the first woman, 'manufactured'
(πλαστήν), differentiates her from the naturally born men, though *Th.* does not
discuss the origin of mankind.

[7] Though it should be clearly understood that 'science' holds a more assured
institutionalized position in our society than it did in the ancient world.

and the less constant differences of body shape and behaviour) were evidence of a more perfectly male or female invisible nature (*physis*). Once the cultural archetype was shown to be grounded in nature, a man or woman who deviated from this norm could be viewed as aberrant—lacking in something essentially masculine or feminine—rather than as a challenge to what it was to be male or female, and the traditional polarization of the sexual roles could claim a scientific foundation.

According to Aristotle (*Metaph.* 986^{a}23–^{b}5), the Pythagoreans linked the male to the right and the good (among other things), and the female to the left and the bad, and at *PA* 670^{b}17-22 he links the right to the hot and the left to the cold. Right and left were valued as positive and negative respectively in Greek thought, and so, generally, were hot and cold (though since they were relative terms the valuation was not so absolute; it was possible for something to be too hot in a way that it was not possible for something to be too right). It is not clear what evidence the Pythagoreans put forward to support their views. They may have been based on pure metaphysical reasoning from cultural values rather than supported by any empirical observation.[8] In Pythagorean philosophy men were also associated with the limited/unity and women with the unlimited/plurality, a theory which could have had only a metaphysical foundation.

Parmenides also associated women with the left. He claimed female foetuses were formed on the left of the womb (DK 28 B 17). This is theoretically provable by empirical investigation, though it is doubtful that any of his contemporaries thought to put the theory to the test.[9] However, contrary to the Pythagoreans, Parmenides claimed that women were hotter than men (*PA* 648^{a}29–30). Empedocles reverts to the Sicilian tradition of Pythagoras and asserts that women were colder than men (DK 62 B 65) and that this explained why men were darker, hairier, and more powerful (DK 62 B 67). Aristotle comments that it is surprising that there is dispute over whether women were hotter or colder than men because 'the hot and the cold ... are the most distinct of things which affect our senses'.[10] But the Presocratics were not necessarily claiming that the

---

[8] But cf. Crawfurd 1915, 1331, where it is claimed that the Pythagoreans believed that menstruation proved women had less dense bodies. I have been unable to find a reference to confirm this.

[9] But cf. *GA* 764^{a}33–7.

[10] *PA* 648^{a}34, τὸ θερμὸν καὶ τὸ ψυχρὸν ... ἡμῖν ἐναργέστατα τῶν περὶ τὴν αἴσθησιν.

temperature differences were perceptible on touching the surface of the body. Aristotle says explicitly that Parmenides argued that the proof that women were hotter lay in their menstrual flow. Blood was identified as 'hot', so the fact that women had so much of it that they could afford to (or had to) lose so much showed that they had more blood than men and therefore were hotter. Empedocles, says Aristotle, argued the opposite (τοὐναντίον). Aristotle does not elaborate, but presumably Empedocles argued that since women did lose so much blood they must be colder than men.[11] For the Presocratics, therefore, the major difference in male and female *physis* was the discrepancy in the heat of their bodies, and the prime empirical evidence for this was menstrual blood. The mechanisms the Presocratics devised to explain the production of this blood and its relation to the typical female secondary sexual characteristics are lost owing to the fragmentary nature of our evidence, but it is clear that from the earliest times Greek science, in accounting for the difference between male and female bodies, focused on physiological processes rather than structure.

THE OBSCURATION OF SEXUAL DIFFERENTIATION
BEFORE PUBERTY IN THE HIPPOCRATICS AND ARISTOTLE

That there was a difference between normal male and female body temperatures continued to be an article of scientific belief throughout the Classical period, but there was no consensus among the Hippocratics as to whether women were hotter or colder, or to what their temperature differences should be attributed. *Mul.* I. I (viii. 12. 21) states simply that women are hotter because 'a woman has hotter blood' (θερμότερον γὰρ τὸ αἷμα ἔχει ἡ γυνή). *Nat. Puer.* 15 (vii. 494. 22–3) says that the womb is heated by menstrual blood and in turn heats the rest of the body only when the blood is trapped for longer than usual. A test to determine the sex of an unborn child at *Steril.* 216 (viii. 416. 20–3) implies that the female was thought to be colder than the male. The test states that if cakes made from the milk of the expectant mother burn, the child is a boy; if they collapse (διαχανῇ) it is a girl. *Vict.* I. 34 (vi. 512. 13–19) says that women are colder than men because they purge the heat from

---

[11] This argument was still a point of contention in Plut. *Mor.* 650F–651F. See King 1985, 130–3; Hanson 1990, 332.

their bodies once a month. However, while the Hippocratic gynaecologists, in describing female physiology, include references to women being either hot or cold, they seem to have done so primarily from traditional considerations; temperature does not play a large explanatory role in their system.[12] The one aspect of female physiology on which all Hippocratics were agreed was that women were moist in comparison to men.[13] It was this excess of moistness rather than any excess or deficiency of heat which caused women to differ radically from men. The evidence of their moist *physis* was the menstrual flow. Aristotle follows the Sicilian tradition set by Pythagoras and Empedocles and asserts that the fundamental difference between male and female *physis* is that the female is colder than the male. Again, the main proof of this difference in *physis* is the periodical evacuation of menstrual blood.

The obvious corollary of this is that while both the Hippocratics and Aristotle argued that sexual differentiation occurred in the early stages of conception, both believed that in children the difference was of little account and did not become apparent until puberty. The Hippocratic treatises frequently fail to indicate the sex of young children,[14] and a similar homology underlies Aristotle's statement that a woman's body is like a boy's.[15] *Genit.* 2 (vii. 472. 16–474. 4) says that the passages in children's bodies are too narrow to allow the agitation of the fluids which will differentiate the sexes among adults. At *GA* 737^{b}11 Aristotle says that conception is not complete until the foetus is differentiated as either male or female, and at *GA* 716^{a}27–31 he locates this differentiation in the specifically male and female parts, which infants possess at birth. How-

[12] Hence (*contra* Hanson 1990, 332) 'cooling off' women did not undercut the importance of menstruation for the Hippocratics; a woman's temperature was extraneous to their main theory.

[13] So, after describing the test with the cakes, *Steril.* 216 continues to say that if a woman's milk coagulates on exposure to flame she is carrying a boy, but if it liquefies, a girl.

[14] Children identified as the daughter (θυγάτηρ or ἡ παῖς) or son (υἱός or ὁ παῖς) of an individual automatically have their sex specified, but often a patient is referred to with the neuter word for child, *paidion* (e.g. *Epid.* 5. 39, 93, 97 (v. 230. 21–23, 254. 13–14, 256. 9–12)), in which case it is impossible to tell the sex of the child unless it is indicated by a word such as 'male' (ἄρσην—as for the second patient of *Epid.* 4. 19 (v. 156. 4–15); the sex of the first *paidion* is not indicated), or reference is made to genitalia (e.g. the reference to testicles in *Epid.* 7. 52, 106 (v. 420. 14, 456. 14–17)). *Hebd.* 5 (viii. 636. 21–2) defines a *paidion* as a child aged 0–7 and a *pais* as aged 7–14, but it should be noted that *pais* and *paidion* can also mean 'slave', and it is possible, though unlikely, that *paides* and *paidia* in cases where age is not specified could be adult.

[15] *GA* 728^{a}17.

ever, at *GA* 765ᵇ35–766ᵇ10 he says that Nature gives male and female their own instrument (ὄργανον) simultaneously with its secretions and abilities, and that these secretions and abilities are related to their instruments in the same way as the ability to see is related to the eye. An animal cannot see without an eye and an 'eye' that cannot see is an eye in name only. Obviously, new-born boys and girls, while differentiated in genitalia, do not have generative abilities and secretions. They possess both the tools and their powers potentially. The receptacles and residues, and therefore their sexual *physis*, are not fully developed until puberty (*GA* 728ᵇ22–32).[16] According to Aristotle, at puberty a man's body changes more drastically than a woman's; until then the two sexes are very similar. Once puberty is passed, however, the female body is marked as differing in many aspects from the male. The most striking observable development in the female body at puberty—menarche—is explained by both the Hippocratics and Aristotle as the manifestation of the hitherto concealed female nature.

MENARCHE AND DEFLORATION ACCORDING TO THE
HIPPOCRATICS AND ARISTOTLE

In Greek society both sexes were thought to experience physiological changes at puberty, but while these changes marked the beginning of an extended period of adolescence for boys prior to their assuming all the duties of citizens, girls were thought capable of fulfilling the roles of adult women in marriage and motherhood often as young as 14, the age at which a girl's body was expected to produce menstrual blood.[17] Menstruation begins when the amount of body fat to total body weight reaches a certain ratio, and reaching this ratio at a young age is dependent to a large extent on good nutrition.[18] Even in the nine-

[16] For a discussion of how sexual differentiation comes about at conception, see pp. 192–3 below.

[17] Amundsen–Diers 1969. King 1983 has demonstrated how a young girl was thought to be in danger if she hovered too long in the liminal stage between childhood and adulthood, and how generally it was thought best to shorten the time between menarche and pregnancy as much as possible. But see above, Introduction n. 80, for evidence in the Hippocratic Corpus that it may have been common for women to have remained unmarried throughout adolescence, though the ideal may still have been to marry at menarche.

[18] See Asso 1983, 16, 148. Both Plut. (*Lyc.* 14) and Xen. (*Const. Lac.* 1. 3) comment that Greeks habitually fed women less well than men.

teenth century the average age of menarche in Western Europe and America was nearer 18, so it is unlikely that many young girls in ancient Greece did start to menstruate at 14. However, the Greeks viewed the advent of menstrual blood outside the body as the end, not the beginning, of puberty. If menarche had not occurred at the socially accepted age of puberty it was assumed, not that the girl's body was not yet sufficiently mature to produce blood, but that the blood had been produced and was sealed within her body.

Virg. says that a woman's menstrual difficulties begin, if she is not married, around the age of marriage (ὥρη γάμου (viii. 466. 11)), or puberty, or a little later (τῇ ἥβῃ ἢ ὀλίγον ὕστερον (viii. 468. 23–470. 1). These difficulties coincide with the descent of the menses to the womb.[19] The author explains that there is more blood flowing around the body at this period of a girl's life on account of food and growth (τὰ σιτία καὶ τὴν αὔξησιν (viii. 466. 16)), but he does not make clear exactly how these two elements are related to the production of excess blood at puberty. The role of food is suggested by *Mul.* i. 1 (viii. 14. 6–7) where the author says that one of the reasons women produce menstrual blood is that they do not work hard enough to use up all the nourishment in their bodies. Presumably the author of *Virg.* believes that prior to puberty girls do use all or most of their nourishment in growing, and that the little they do not use does not present a health hazard even if it remains in their bodies. Once growing slows down or ceases girls do not use up all their food, resulting in an over-abundance of blood that cannot be accommodated in the body and begins to flow into the womb for evacuation. It might therefore seem surprising that the second reason the author of *Virg.* gives in addition to food for the commencement of menstruation is growth rather than the cessation of growth. However, *Genit.* 2 (vii. 472. 16–474. 4) explains the significance of the increase in body size. In children, it is claimed, the vessels of the body are narrow so the humours (body fluids) cannot become agitated. As the children grow the vessels of the body grow with them so there is more room for the humours to be set in motion. Women contain more fluid than men, and once growth provides

[19] ἅμα τε καθοδῷ τῶν ἐπιμηνίων, 'the descent of the menses', cannot mean actual menarche or any other menstrual period because what causes the *parthenoi*'s problems is that the blood cannot leave their bodies (cf. King 1983, 113 and n. 10). Similarly, at *Mul.* i. 141 (viii. 98. 10–11), although the menarchal blood that is causing the problem is called 'the first appearance' (τὰ ἐπιφαινόμενα πρῶτα) of the menses, it causes the problems before it appears outside the body.

room the fluid is more easily set in motion by the variations in temperature from month to month, producing menses.[20] It is to this aspect of growth that the author of *Virg.* is referring when he cites it as a cause of menstruation beginning at puberty.

But the author of *Virg.* would need to cite only one of these causes to explain menarche. The utilizing of all nourishment in growth prior to puberty is sufficient in itself to explain why young girls do not menstruate, and the author of *Mul.* makes no reference to an expansion of the vessels of the body helping to cause menstruation. In fact, as we shall see, he frequently draws attention to the narrowness of the passages in a woman's body until she has given birth. Conversely, the author of *Genit.* and *Nat. Puer.* implies that girls are considerably moister than boys at any age: 'Now a woman's body has more fluid than that of a man.... This is simply a fact of woman's original constitution' (*Nat. Puer.* 15 (vii. 494. 13–15)),[21] so he has to cite a reason other than the lack of excess fluid to explain why young girls do not menstruate before puberty. *Genit.* and *Nat. Puer.* are concerned to explain parallel developments in the male and the female, so they develop an explanation of puberty which accounts for both the production of menses in a girl and the production of semen in a boy. *Mul.* is concerned with the mature woman and does not try to correlate the menstrual process with any normative physiological function in men. Even in *Genit.* and *Nat. Puer.* the parallelism between male semen and menses breaks down if it is pushed too far. Semen is produced when the male is aroused sexually—as is 'female seed'; this is not true of menses. The author seems to be aware of the difficulty in *Nat. Puer.* 20 (vii. 508. 6–7) where he says that the way is opened in young girls for the passage of both menses and seed at the same time, two secretions where the male has only one.[22] In general, throughout the work, the author treats semen and female seed as more alike than semen and menses, and he gives no indication of a process whereby female seed might be derived from menstrual fluid. Elsewhere in the Hippocratic Corpus, semen is thought to correspond to female seed, not menses. The author of *Genit.* and *Nat. Puer.* makes the additional equation of

[20] *Nat. Puer.* 15 (vii. 494. 11–15)
[21] τὸ σῶμα ὑγρότερον γάρ ἐστιν ἢ τὸ τοῦ ἀνδρός ... καί πως τοῦτο ἐν τῇ ἀρχῇ τῇ φύσει ὑπῆρξεν.
[22] The lack of interest in explaining this doubling, which has no therapeutical repercussions for the Hippocratics, shows how pragmatic even their theoretical treatises were.

semen and menses because they first appear at roughly the same time in young men and women while there is not necessarily any outward sign of female seed in pubescent girls. The menarchal theory of *Genit./Nat. Puer.* can be combined with the menstrual theory of *Mul.* as it is in *Virg.*, but together they produce an over-determination of the phenomenon of menarche and menstruation which suggests that the author of *Virg.* was attempting to take account of two separate theories.[23]

Puberty, then, was a socially determined age (probably around fourteen) at which young girls were thought to have an accumulation of blood in their bodies. This blood drained into the womb and from there issued as menstrual blood if the girl was 'opened up'. However, if it could not flow out of the womb, the author of *Virg.* explains, it could move off to the area around the heart where it caused a deadening sensation leading to symptoms similar to those of epilepsy and often ending in attempted suicide. To prevent this, says *Virg.*, the girl should be married and deflowered as soon as she reaches puberty (i.e. the socially determined age of puberty).[24] This indicates that intercourse was thought to remove some impediment to menstruation. Sissa claims that it achieves this not by rupturing the hymen (which she believes is a Christian idea), but by dilating the body's network of veins and the mouth of the cervix (stoma).[25] Hanson disagrees, citing the evidence of *Virg.*, and argues that the images of defloration in Greek literature liken the first penetration of the vagina to the breaking of a seal on a wine jug or the breaching of a city's walls.[26] She cites Soranus' arguments against the existence of a hymen at *Gyn.* i. 16–17 as showing that some authorities in the ancient world did believe that the hymen was imperforate before defloration.[27] Sissa points out that the theories Soranus is arguing

[23] In an earlier published version of this material (Dean-Jones 1991, 117) I suggested that the theory of menstruation put forward in *Genit.* was an alternative to the dominant theory put forward in *Mul.*, and this might be taken to imply different authors. I now think that the differences can be explained in terms of the purpose of each treatise, and that the same author may have put forward both theories on different occasions without being concerned to make them cohere.

[24] Rousselle 1988, 27, argues that prepubertal marriage was a Roman rather than a Greek practice. King 1983, 112, also assumes menarche preceded defloration in Classical Greece.

[25] Sissa 1984, 1133–4.   [26] Hanson 1990, 325.

[27] Soranus argues that the blood and pain a woman suffers on first intercourse come from a 'spreading of the furrows' in the vagina, and that there cannot be a membrane across the vagina because menses can flow out unobstructed and a doctor can insert a probe without meeting any resistance in most virgins.

against are anonymous and cannot be attributed to any medical school before the Christian period.[28] She argues that as the Hippocratics thought of a sealing membrane across the vagina as a pathological rather than a natural state,[29] *Virg.* can be more coherently explained by assuming that the blood was thought to be trapped inside the body by the narrowness of a young girl's veins. *Superf.* 34 (viii. 504. 20–506. 7) supports this interpretation. The passage describes symptoms which *parthenoi* suffer if their menses do not appear when they are supposed to in terms very similar to those of *Virg.* However, the *Superf.* passage recommends fumigations and warm applications to relieve these symptoms rather than intercourse, showing that what was being treated was the constricted nature of the body rather than an imperforate membrane in the vagina. Moreover, *Virg.* does not describe the trapped blood as descending from the womb into the upper part of the vagina, which is where it would have to be imagined as halted on its downward path if the upward thrust of the penis through a membrane was thought to release it. The blood is trapped in the womb by a constricted stoma which the moist, warming friction of intercourse will open up. In the absence of intercourse, closure is the normal state of the stoma, which is why all women in their reproductive years should remain sexually active.[30]

Hanson argues that as the womb was constantly opening and closing throughout a woman's life, the first opening of the stoma could not signal the irrevocable change of a young girl's body to that of a woman. She claims that the stoma closes during periods of extended sexual inactivity, pregnancy, and most of the month, when the woman is not actually menstruating, to trap the blood in the womb. This in itself would suggest that we should expect the stoma of *parthenoi* to be closed over initially, and insisting on a sealing membrane in addition seems unnecessary. It is the production of blood internally which irrevocably changes the body of a young girl to that of a woman. Moreover, the Hippocratics did not believe that once a woman had been deflowered complete closure of the womb was a common occurrence outside cases of sexual abstinence,

---

[28] Sissa 1984, 1131.

[29] *Mul.* 1. 20 (viii. 58. 15–60. 3); *Nat. Mul.* 67 (vii. 402. 6–12).

[30] *Mul.* 1. 2 (viii. 16. 1–2): 'At any rate this is the cause of the womb closing up in the case of a woman who does not have coitus' (τοῦτ᾽ οὖν αἴτιον γίνεται ὥστε αὐτὰς ξυμμύειν, οἷα μὴ λαγνευομένης τῆς γυναικός).

pregnancy, or disease.[31] Hanson notes that on several occasions in antiquity authors claim that a girl's throat expands when she has been deflowered. Her suggestion that this claim illustrates a belief in the sympathy between a woman's upper and lower 'throats' is surely correct, but the imagery seems to fit better with a widening of the stoma than with the rupturing of a membrane.

Equating defloration with loosening the stoma rather than with rupturing a sealing membrane allows the blood which often appears on first intercourse to be identified with the blood supposedly collecting in a young girl's womb and to act as confirmation that the girl was ready to take on her adult role. Hymenal blood could be explained as the first drops of menstrual blood.[32] If full menstruation did not begin immediately after defloration, its absence could be explained by claiming that a large amount of blood had not yet accumulated or that the blood had moved off to another part of the body and needed some time to return to the womb.[33]

There is further evidence for the confusion of hymenal and menarchal blood in the Hippocratics. At *Epid.* 3. 12 (iii. 136. 9–10) it is said that a young girl's period appeared for the first time because she was a *parthenos*.[34] This term usually signifies a young unmarried girl, so the doctor could be attributing the girl's not having menstruated previously to either her age or to her virgin

---

[31] See p. 62 below.

[32] Menarche *per se* does not seem to have been ritually marked in Classical Greece. Linders 1972, 58–9, convincingly refutes the claim that there is evidence for the dedication of first menstrual rags to Artemis. If hymenal and menstrual blood were thought to be identical, the clothes a girl wore either just before or just after defloration/marriage (such as we know were dedicated to Artemis) would be more significant than her subsequent first menstrual rag. In some societies hymenal and menarchal blood are thought to be identical, but the confusion operates in the opposite way; menarche is taken to be loss of virginity to an unseen demon and premenstrual girls are sent to the local holy man to be deflowered in safety, sometimes artificially, see Delaney–Lupton–Toth 1976, 27. In later antiquity Pliny explicitly equates menarchal blood with hymenal when he says that many women lose their virginity through age alone (*NH* 28. 79), and even Soranus says virginity should be preserved until menarche has come on 'by itself' (*Gyn.* 1. 33), though this is probably a way of saying that intercourse stimulated menstruation.

[33] *Steril.* 246 (viii. 458. 24–460. 2) describes a condition in which a woman feels pain and bleeds during intercourse. The nature of the blood she sheds is characterized as 'fresh' or 'recent' (νεαρόν), probably to differentiate it from menstrual blood that had been building up in the body over the course of a month. Any non-menstrual blood which accompanied intercourse (from ruptured membranes, furrows, or lesions in the vagina, or any other reason) was considered pathological.

[34] Cf. *Epid.* 2. 2. 8, 3. 1 (v. 88. 7–8, 104. 1).

state.[35] But the very fact that the physician felt it necessary to append an explanation as to why it was the girl's first period suggests that it was her unmarried state which seemed significant to him. If menarche occurred simply because the girl had reached the age to menstruate there would have been less reason to account for why she had not menstruated previously. An explanation is only needed if she was old enough to have menstruated previously but had not done so.[36] This shows that the Hippocratics accepted that it was possible for women's wombs to 'open up' of their own accord without intercourse, but that the 'opening up' would be delayed beyond the optimum age in an unmarried girl. Another equation of the blood of puberty and that of first sexual intercourse is given at *Epid.* 6. 3. 14 (v. 300. 1–2) where it is said that young men can bleed either on their first sexual encounter or when their voice breaks. Bleeding is not naturally associated with either of these events, and the statement would seem to be another attempt at correlating male and female puberty.

Aristotle believes that the developments of boys and girls at puberty are parallel, and explains both as the redirection of nourishment previously used in growth to the production of reproductive fluids: semen and menses. It is easier for him to maintain this parallelism than it is for the author of *Genit.* and *Nat. Puer.* because he does not believe that a woman produces 'female seed' as well as menses. He argues that no animal can produce two seminal residues, and since menses obviously parallel male semen, they have to be a woman's seminal residue.[37] While Aristotle sets puberty at 14 for both boys and girls, thereby concurring with what seems to be the socially accepted norm, he believes that a boy's semen remains infertile till he reaches 21, and that although young women conceive readily, they have difficult pregnancies and therefore should wait till 21 to reproduce also.[38] In fact, modern research has shown that most men are fertile from their first ejaculation while young girls do

[35] Sissa 1984, 1119–20, cites examples of *parthenoi* who had had sexual adventures and were still called *parthenoi*, but the circumstances of their stories show that their status was exceptional.

[36] A remark at *Nat. Mul.* 3 (vii. 314. 16–17), that the movement of the womb towards the liver is more likely to happen especially to 'aged *parthenoi*' (παρθένοισι ... παλαιῇσιν), suggests that the term's virgin connotations were more important for the Hippocratics than its normal age connotations. It is true that the term 'aged' leaves the actual age of the *parthenoi* unspecified, but the adjective *palaios* has connotations of extreme age rather than simply 'older than average'.

[37] *GA* 727ᵃ26–30.   [38] *HA* 582ᵃ16–29.

not ovulate with every menstrual cycle for the first two years at least, so it would be more correct to postulate a gap between puberty and the capacity to reproduce for girls rather than boys.[39] Aristotle may have been led to his conclusion from the fact that he had seen some very young mothers in his society, while men were not encouraged to marry before 30, so young men who were acknowledged as fathers would have been comparatively rare.[40] Nevertheless, because he believed the female body was more like the male than did the Hippocratics, Aristotle argued that puberty for a woman extended over a period of time as it did for a man; the fact that a young girl could conceive did not mean that she should conceive. For Aristotle, menarche was the beginning, not the end, of a girl becoming a woman.

Aristotle believed that any sealing of the womb was a pathological condition. At *GA* 773^{a}15–29 he describes the growing together of the stoma as a pathological condition which has to be corrected by surgery. His coalescing of the vagina and the urethra (see pp. 81–3 below) would prevent him from positing an imperforate membrane across the passage itself. It is not clear how he accounted for hymenal blood because he does not deal with defloration *per se* in his biological works, so he presumably felt that initial intercourse was significant in a social rather than a biological context. He could not have believed in the constricted stoma which would be opened by intercourse since he argues against early marriage and sexual experience for both boys and girls, and therefore must have thought that there was no general impediment to virgins' menstruation. He did believe that intercourse widened the passages (*poroi*) in the male and female bodies,[41] and his claim that premature attempts at ejaculation through masturbation caused pain as well as pleasure in young boys may have been an inappropriate assimilation of a boy's first sexual experience to those of a girl, as at *Epid.* 6. 3. 3. 14 (v. 300. 1–2).

The Hippocratic confusion of hymenal and menarchal blood shows the importance of menstrual blood in the Classical definition

[39] See Mackay *et al.* 1983, 62.

[40] For age of marriage of men and women in the Classical period, see Pomeroy 1975, 64. Sally Humphreys has collected epigraphical and prosopographical evidence that men did marry at the age recommended in the literary texts, i.e. 30 (personal communication). The speaker of Dem. 40. 12–13, 56 feels he has to explain why he married so young that people can mistake his daughter for his sister.

[41] *HA* 581^{b}19.

of a woman's body. If a body is to be that of a woman and not a child it has to contain menstrual blood, even if there is no evidence of it outside the body. The Hippocratic texts upheld the socially accepted age for female puberty by arguing that menstrual blood was present in the bodies of those supposedly pubertal and post-pubertal girls who were not menstruating, identifying the blood which often appears at defloration (particularly in very young girls) with blood that could only be produced by a mature woman's body. This justified, scientifically, requiring young girls to assume their adult responsibilities at about 14. Aristotle also believes that girls start to become women around 14 and that the significant event marking this is the presence of blood inside their bodies. However, just as the male body takes several years to reach its full generative capacities once it has begun to produce semen, Aristotle argues, so the presence of blood in a female body does not automatically mean that a girl is ready to assume the role of a woman.

THE HIPPOCRATIC ACCOUNT OF THE ACCUMULATION
OF MENSTRUAL BLOOD

Mul. i. i (viii. 12. 6–21) attributes menstruation to the nature of a woman's very flesh, which is loose and spongy, causing her body to soak up excess blood from her stomach (where it has been converted from the food she has consumed). The author uses an analogy to explain the difference between female and male flesh. If wool and cloth of equal weight are stretched over water and left for two days and nights, at the end of this period the wool will have become much heavier than the cloth. It soaks up more moisture because it is more porous (ἀραιά).[42] So it is with men and women. A woman's spongy, porous flesh is like wool (εἴριον)[43] and soaks up more moisture from her belly than a man's from his. *Nat. Puer.* 21 (vii. 512. 2–3) remarks that women can have dense- or loose-textured flesh (πυκνοσάρκοισι ἤ ἀραιοσάρκοισι), so it was recognized that women's bodies were not all exactly alike, but the differences between them were

[42] Hanson 1990, 317 and n. 42, has detailed how fleeces were used in this way to locate underground water sources in Mother Earth.
[43] Faraone 1989, 298–9, cites an erotic spell in which a pair of idols representing a man and a woman are used. The female figure is made from wool. Hesych., s.v. στέφανον ἐκφέρειν, says that Attic Greeks hung wreaths of wool over door lintels to announce the birth of a girl. I am grateful to Charles Ramos for this reference.

those of degree. *Mul.* 1. 1 (viii. 12. 2) identifies women who have
never given birth as having more solid and denser bodies (στερεώ-
τερου καὶ πυκνοτέρου), but their bodies are still loose-textured
enough to soak up menses; they simply do not evacuate the blood as
well.
If a man should have any excess moisture in his body after exercise, it is absorbed by his glands which are especially constructed for
this purpose. The author of *Gland.* 1 (viii. 556. 1–7) describes their
nature as spongy, porous, and plump (σπογγώδης, ἀραιαὶ καὶ
πίονες), says that if they are cut they haemorrhage violently (εἰ δὲ
διατάμοις αἱμορραγίη λάβρος), and likens the texture of glands to
wool (ἐπαφομένῳ δὲ οἷον εἴρια). The author emphasizes how
much they differ from the rest of the body in this: 'and there is no
flesh like it in the rest of the body, nor anything like it at all in the
body.'[44] In chapter 16 (viii. 572. 2–3), however, he says: 'The nature
of glands in women is porous, just like the rest of the body',[45] and
indeed, his description of glands in his first chapter would fit the
female flesh of the Hippocratic gynaecology admirably. The body
of a mature woman was one big gland and therefore similar to that
flesh in a male body which functioned only after a man had evacuated or used up most of his excess fluid through vigorous activity.
The implication is that a truly feminine woman would be incapable
of developing the sort of flesh that would enable her to perform the
same tasks as a man, despite the fact that many female slaves worked
very strenuously and must have developed leaner and more muscular bodies than some men.
    Moreover, the greater porosity of female flesh may have been
advanced as an explanation for certain supposedly feminine dis-
positions. *Vict.* 1. 36 (vi. 522. 17–524. 10) says that while some
personality traits can be altered by a regimen which redresses the
balance between the fire and water in the soul, there are other
characteristics which are caused by the nature of the *poroi* (passages)
in the flesh and which cannot be altered by regimen. The author lists
these as being irascible, frivolous, deceitful, straightforward, hos-

[44] καὶ ἔστιν οὔτε σαρκία ἴκελα τῷ ἄλλῳ σώματι, οὔτε ἄλλο τι ὅμοιον τῷ
σώματι (viii. 556. 2–3).
[45] τῇσι μὲν γυναιξὶν ἀραιή τε ἡ φύσις κατὰ τῶν ἀδένων, ὥσπερ τὸ ἄλλο
σῶμα. Littré suppresses the καί that appears in the manuscripts before κατά, but Joly
adopts Zwinger's emendation to κάρτα. This could be interpreted as an even stronger
statement: women's glands were very porous, even more porous than a man's glands,
just as the rest of her body was more porous than a man's body.

tile, and kindly (ὀξύθυμος, ῥάθυμος, δόλιος, ἁπλοῦς, δυσ-μενής, εὔνους). At *HA* 608ᵃ11–609ᵃ18, Aristotle lists traits that are typical of male and female. The male is depicted consistently as more spirited and savage (which would correspond to 'irascible' and 'hostile') and the female as softer and more easily tamed (which would correspond to 'frivolous' and 'kindly'). He also describes the female as 'more deceptive' (ψευδέστερον) and the male as 'more simple' (ἁπλούστερον). The correlation between *Vict.*'s list of personality traits attributable to *poroi* and Aristotle's list of male and female traits suggests that the nature of female flesh was used to support the affective as well as the physical stereotyping of women.

The breasts are regarded as glands and the difference in the size of male and female breasts is used as another indication of the extent to which a woman's body is looser than a man's. In both sexes they swell at puberty, but *Gland.* 16 (viii. 572. 1) says that breasts become prominent (διαίρονται) only in those who make milk,⁴⁶ because man's firm flesh prevents the spongy parts of his body from swelling too far. Even where the bodies of both sexes are constructed to soak up moisture, women soak up more. *Epid.* 2. 6. 19 (v. 136. 11–12) states, 'there is a thick vein in each breast; these hold the greatest part of consciousness.'⁴⁷ From this the author draws the conclusion that if a person is about to become mad, blood collects in the breasts. Women would always be more susceptible to having more blood in their breasts than men, so this would give a scientific basis to the belief that women were always closer to the irrational than men.⁴⁸

Here we see how the empirical observation of menstruation and breasts was used to create a biological construct which upheld the

---

⁴⁶ It is perhaps surprising that in *Prorrh.* 2. 24 (ix. 54. 11), when listing factors which predict good childbearing capacity, the Hippocratic author gives a positive endorsement to large breasts, since, as Henderson 1975, 148–9, remarks, 'firmness and thus youthfulness is the usual attribute' desired of breasts in a *parthenos*. The Hippocratics, on this issue, did not ratify the culture's ideal female body type, perhaps because the culture's erotic ideal for a woman's body was too boyish and hence too masculine to allow her to fulfil her female role as wife and mother easily. It may be relevant that the gradual movement away from assimilation of the proportions of female statues to male, documented by Guralnick 1981 (and cf. Delcourt 1961, 56–7), began in Ionia, the geographical birthplace of Hippocratic medicine. However, even the more feminine shapes of the Hellenistic period retained small breasts, and Soranus at *Gyn.* 2. 84 advises swaddling an infant girl tightly around the chest, but letting the bandages loose around the buttocks, for this is a more becoming shape. On breasts in Greek literature, see Gerber 1978.
⁴⁷ φλὲψ ἔχει παχείη ἐν ἑκατέρῳ τιτθῷ· ταῦτα μέγιστον ἔχει μόριον συνέσιος.
⁴⁸ Cf. Padel 1983.

cultural characterization of a woman as inherently weaker, softer, and less stable than a man. Underlying the Hippocratic characterization of male and female flesh is a value judgement: firm and compact = good; loose and spongy = bad. This is clear from the fact that a contributory reason to a man's flesh remaining compact was his more excellent mode of life. He was thought to work much harder than a woman and thereby to use up all his nourishment in building a stronger body. A woman soaks up moisture through inactivity (διὰ τὴν ἀργίην), a man does not because labour strengthens his body (ὁ πόνος κρατύνει αὐτοῦ τὸ σῶμα).[49] *Vict.* 1. 34 (vi. 512. 14, 17–18) says that women are colder and moister than men in part because they use a more frivolous regimen (ῥᾳθυμοτέρῃσι τῇσι διαίτῃσι χρέονται). *Morb.* 4. 45 (vii. 568. 14–16) states that if a person remains at rest and does no work (which, to the Greek male mind, would be to follow a more typically feminine way of life) then there is illness (κακόν) in their body, even if they are not immediately aware of it because they are otherwise so healthy. Less work, therefore, does not simply result in a different type of body; characterizing the result of idleness as illness shows that the change was looked upon as a deterioration. This might seem to indicate that a woman could change her body type and cease to menstruate if she led a strenuous enough life. But although women of a masculine appearance menstruate less, to the point of being infertile, they do not cease altogether (*Mul.* 1. 6 (viii. 30. 20)), and while there are various means for reducing the menstruation of women who menstruate too abundantly,[50] no Hippocratic author recommends that an over-menstruating woman should work harder or increase her exercise, and nowhere in the Hippocratic Corpus is there a suggestion that a woman could overcome her inherently inferior *physis* to the extent that she could cease to menstruate altogether.

By the second century AD, when, partly as a result of dissection,

---

[49] *Mul.* 1. 1 (viii. 14. 5–7); *Gland.* 16 (viii. 572. 13). Hes. *Th.* 592–9, and Semon. 2–6, 24, 46–7, 58–62, also characterize the typical female lifestyle as slothful. Xen. concurs in this judgement but attributes it to nature rather than choice (*Oec.* 7. 23). Eur. *El.* 527–9 suggests that the extra activity men undertook in the gymnasium was thought capable of changing even the nature of their hair.

[50] e.g. *Mul.* 1. 5 (viii. 28. 12, 15) implies excessive menstruation could be lessened by curtailing food intake, and *Aph.* 5. 50 (iv. 550. 5–6) recommends bleeding at the breasts. *Steril.* 213 (viii. 412. 1–3) says that if the condition exists by nature it is incurable. However, an excess of other humours in a woman's body could be controlled by exercise. *Mul.* 1. 11 (viii. 44. 20) advises a woman who is too moist because of phlegm to exercise (γυμνάζεσθαι) frequently.

partly under the influence of Aristotelian theories, male and female
bodies were treated as members of the same species partaking in
basically the same *physis*, Soranus expressed the opinion that excessively active women did cease to menstruate.[51] It is recognized today
that female athletes, gymnasts, dancers, etc. can cease to menstruate
if the ratio of body fat to total body weight drops below a certain
level,[52] and perhaps Soranus had seen this syndrome. On the other
hand, as the exercises he cites explicitly are singing-competitions
and travelling towards the sea, perhaps he had not; he was more
probably simply following his theory through to its logical conclusion: men and women have the same *physis*; if women lived more
like men their bodies would become more like men's. Because the
Hippocratics believed that the difference between men and women
was to be explained primarily by biology rather than by their
socially allotted way of life, they did not believe the female could
ever assimilate to the male in this way and so could never expect to
live more like a man. On the other hand, the description of Scythian
men in *Aër.* 20–2 (ii. 72. 22–82. 5) shows that if a man pursues a
sedentary life-style, his body becomes loose, flabby, and moist
(though he does not begin to menstruate), and therefore more like a
woman's. The Scythians who develop this condition are able to
follow a female life-style (apart from bearing children) because this
always lay within the capabilities of every man, though it was
usually avoided.

Because the majority of Hippocratic gynaecological treatises deal
with pathology, and most pathological conditions were thought to
originate after menstrual blood had passed into the womb, it is not
possible to say with certainty that all the gynaecological authors
believed that menstrual blood was originally nourishment soaked
from the stomach into the flesh of a woman, but no alternative theory
is put forward apart from that of *Genit.* and *Nat. Puer.* In this theory,
menstrual blood is a secretion, or 'foam' (ἀφρός), of the humours
coursing through the vessels of a woman's body in great abundance
because she is so moist by nature. The secretion is produced by the
agitation of the body fluids due to the monthly fluctuations in
temperature. Because a man's body is drier it takes the violent
agitation of sexual intercourse to produce the foam from his body
fluids which is emitted as semen. As mentioned above, pp. 49–50, the
correlation between menses and semen is made in a rather *ad hoc*

[51] *Gyn.* i. 22–3. [52] Mackay *et al.* 1983, 75; Jones–Wentz–Burnett 1988, 351.

manner, and the author is not entirely successful in maintaining it for the length of *Genit.* and *Nat. Puer.* No other Hippocratic treatise adopts the correlation of menses and semen, so in view of the close links which generally hold between the gynaecological treatises, we can assume that most of them subscribed to the view of *Mul.* I. I. Among the general works of the Hippocratic Corpus, *Gland.* appears to accept *Mul.*'s theory. Once again, the focus on pathology and therapy means that the subject is not touched on in most treatises, but no statement made about women is inconsonant with this theory.

ARISTOTLE'S ACCOUNT OF THE ACCUMULATION OF MENSTRUAL BLOOD

Aristotle's theory of menstruation includes elements present in both *Mul.*'s theory that women could not convert nourishment as men could and *Genit.*'s theory that parallel physical developments in male and female produced semen in the former and menses in the latter.[53] He considered the stomach to be like the earth from which an animal took nourishment after the food had been converted by concoction (a form of heating) into blood.[54] This is drawn from the stomach to the diaphragm where it is infused with *pneuma* (vitalized breath) from the heart making it more suitable to nourish a living body.[55] The residue of blood which is not used up in nourishment (of which residue the male has less than the female because he uses more material in maintaining his larger body, producing hair, etc.[56]) is further concocted by the natural heat of the male into semen.[57] The female is unable to perform this final concoction both because

[53] For a more detailed discussion of Arist.'s theories of male and female in the context of his whole philosophy, see pp. 176–83 below. Briefly, Arist. believed that the two sexes existed in the higher animals for the sake of separating the two necessary elements of reproduction (he believed that specialization of parts increased corresponding to an animal's higher place on the *scala naturae*). The two elements are form (the male contribution) and matter (the female). Form is superior to matter in so far as it makes a thing the sort of thing it is. The female is a 'stunted' male because while she possesses the form herself, she is unable to pass it on to her offspring, *GA* 731^{b}18–732^{a}12.

[54] *PA* 650^{a}3–32.   [55] Peck 1953, III–21.   [56] *GA* 727^{a}16–19.

[57] Ibid. 725^{a}11–22. As evidence of its origin as blood, Arist. remarks that the loss of semen is just as exhausting as the loss of healthy blood, ibid. 726^{b}3–13.

she has a greater amount of blood left over (Nature does not allow her to use all her nourishment on her own body as it is needed to form and nourish the foetus should she become pregnant[58]) and because of her colder nature. Her seminal residue, therefore, remains bloodlike.[59]

Both semen and menses are presumed to come from the same source, as in *Genit.*, and, from the same reasoning, they appear in adolescent males and females at the same time,[60] but this source is the immediate residue of nourishment, as in *Mul.*, not the agitated humours. Males are unable to concoct semen before puberty because they lack sufficient heat, and in this a boy's physique is thought to be like a woman's and a woman's like a sterile man's, all because of the same inability.[61]

For Aristotle, the manifestation at puberty of the male's greater heat was a result not of a superior flesh or life-style, but of the development of his genitals.[62] At *GA* 718ᵃ11–15 Aristotle mentions that a small initial part of the vas deferens contains blood; it is thus the seminal ducts around the testes which perform the last stage of the concoction. He adduces further evidence for this from the feminine appearance of men who have been castrated.[63] After puberty, when the penis is rubbed, *pneuma* rushes down to the seminal ducts directly from the heart and enables them to perform the final concoction of the seminal residue into generative material.[64] It is possible that Aristotle thought the *pneuma* was at work in the womb too; the blood that is stored there is suitable for procreation, unlike the rest of the blood in either the male or the female body, and he likens the womb to an oven (*GA* 764ᵃ12–20).

Aristotle believed the same *pneuma* caused the swelling in both male and female breasts.[65] Room was made for this swelling by the descent of the seminal residue for generative purposes at puberty; the thoracic region became emptier in women in proportion to their greater amount of residue, and was therefore more easily inflated.[66]

---

[58] Ibid. 730ᵇ2–4.   [59] Ibid. 726ᵇ31–727ᵃ1.   [60] Ibid. 727ᵃ5–7.
[61] Ibid. 728ᵃ17.   [62] Ibid. 728ᵇ28–31.   [63] Ibid. 716ᵇ5–12.
[64] *HA* 510ᵃ13–29; *GA* 717ᵇ23–718ᵃ15.   [65] Ibid. 728ᵇ27–31.
[66] Ibid. 776ᵇ19–22.

THE EVACUATION OF MENSTRUAL BLOOD

Nat. Puer. 15 (vii. 492. 21–494. 2) says that the descent of menstrual blood from a woman's flesh to her womb happens all at once (βύζην) when the woman is not pregnant.[67] Though stated nowhere else explicitly, this view of a month's menses as a discrete quantity of blood which entered the womb only at the end of the month is reflected in such remarks as the claim that one month's menses could make an opening for previous months' menses which had been trapped in the womb (e.g. *Mul.* 1. 2 (viii. 16. 3–4)). Since the menses were stored in the flesh during the month there would be no need for the womb to close to contain the blood in a non-pregnant woman. The Hippocratics believed that the most favourable time for conception was just after menstruation when the passages of a woman's body (along which her seed travelled) as well as her womb were empty, but they were aware that conception could take place at any time of the month,[68] so they would have had to imagine the womb as being open throughout the month to receive the male seed. *Mul.* 1. 24 (viii. 64. 3–5) states that: 'In the time before [menstruation], the stoma of the womb is rather/more closed and the vessels [φλέβες] being full of blood do not draw in the seed as well [as just after menstruation].'[69] Even just before menstruation the womb was not completely closed and the blood was stored in the veins rather than the womb. Menstrual blood filled the womb up at the end of the month because it flowed in faster than it flowed out. In a healthy, sexually active, non-pregnant woman the stoma of the womb was not expected to open and close every month.[70]

From the flesh, the blood passed into the passages or small veins (φλέβια) which formed a network through the body; from there it flowed into larger veins (φλέβες) and eventually drained into the womb.[71] The passing of the blood into the womb was easiest in those women who had given birth:

[67] The same term (βύζην) is used at *Mul.* 1. 5 (viii. 28. 13) of the menstrual flow of a woman who has a pathologically heavy period. The morbid element in her condition is not the fact that the blood is descending all at once but that there is so much of it.

[68] e.g. *Mul.* 1. 17, 24 (viii. 56. 17–22, 62. 20–1); *Nat. Puer.* 15 (vii. 494. 18–20).

[69] ἐν δὲ τῷ πρὶν χρόνῳ τό τε στόμα τῶν μητρέων μέμυκε μᾶλλον, καὶ αἱ φλέβες πλέαι αἵματος ἐοῦσαι οὐχ ὁμοίως σπῶσι τὴν γονήν.

[70] If it closed over so often, closure of the womb would not have been considered so significant a sign of pregnancy or ill health.

[71] On the passages in a woman's body, see Hanson 1991, 85–7.

I say that a woman who has never given birth suffers more intensely and more readily from menstruation than a woman who has given birth to a child. For whenever a woman does give birth, her small vessels become more easy-flowing for menstruation. The lochia and the breaking down of the body make them easy-flowing. The small vessels—especially those near the belly and the breasts—are broken down; the rest of the body is also broken down. ... When the body is broken down the vessels necessarily are more open and become more easy-flowing for menstruation.[72]

From this it would appear that the lochial flow made the body more 'easy-flowing' in two ways. It not only widened the passages it passed through, but also broke down the flesh surrounding these passages so that they could expand. This it did presumably as it was passing into the vessels.

The Hippocratics believed that those parts of the body which were spongy and porous readily soaked up moisture but did not easily discharge it. It would seem that they assumed some mechanism which impelled a woman's flesh to surrender its blood so that it was ready to soak up the next month's excess instead of retaining the blood it had first soaked up and hardening so that it could absorb no more, as the spleen was wont to do.[73] *Nat. Puer.* 15 (vii. 494. 10–15) attributes the movement of the blood to the fluctuations of temperature from month to month, but this treatise does not claim that the menstrual blood has been soaked into the flesh, and as we shall see, most Hippocratics assume that the time of the menstrual flow is peculiar to individual women and is not controlled by environmental factors. The author of *VM* 22 (i. 628. 3–5) asserts that the womb actively draws blood to itself, and it is possible that the Hippocratic gynaecological writers also believed that the impulse of the flesh to release the blood at the appropriate time originated in the womb. They do not describe the womb explicitly as drawing the blood to itself; the most commonly used verb of the blood's movement to the womb is 'flow' (χωρέω). However, the author of *Nat. Puer.* 15 (vii. 494. 4) says that in a pregnant woman the blood flows (χωρέει) into her womb on a daily basis because the seed in the

[72] φημὶ γυναῖκα ἄτοκον ἐοῦσαν ἢ τετοκυῖαν χαλεπώτερον καὶ θᾶσσον ἀπὸ τῶν καταμηνίων νοσέειν· ὁκόταν γὰρ τέκῃ, εὐρωότερά οἱ τά φλέβιά ἐστιν ἐς τὰ καταμήνια· εὔροα δέ σφιν ποιέει γίνεσθαι ἡ λοχίη κάθαρσις καὶ ἡ καταρραγὴ τοῦ σώματος. τά πλησιάζοντα δὲ μάλιστα τῆς τε κοιλίης καὶ τῶν μαζῶν καταρρήγνυται· καταρρήγνυται δὲ καὶ τὸ ἄλλο σῶμα. ... καταρραγέντος δὲ τοῦ σώματος, ἀνάγκη τὰς φλέβας μᾶλλον στομοῦσθαι καὶ εὐρωτέρας γίνεσθαι ἐς τὰ καταμήνια, *Mul.* ι. ι (viii. 10. 1–9).
[73] *Aff.* 20 (vi. 228. 20–230. 22); *Int.* 30–4 (vii. 244. 6–252. 16).

womb draws (ἕλκει) the blood from the body. The frequent use of the verb to flow, therefore, does not necessarily preclude the idea of the womb exerting a drawing force at regular intervals on the menstrual blood in the flesh.

Aristotle, on the other hand, believed that the womb existed in the body as the proper receptacle for the female seminal residue when it had been finally concocted and that the menses flowed into the womb naturally throughout the month without any force. At *GA* 737[b]28–34 he explicitly contradicts the theory that the womb exerts any force on the menses:

> Each of the residues is carried to its proper place without the exertion of any force from the *pneuma* and without compulsion by any other cause of that sort, although some people assert this, alleging that the sexual parts draw the residue like cupping-glasses and that we exert force by means of the *pneuma*, as though it were possible for the seminal residue or for the residue of the liquid or of the solid nourishment to take any other course unless such force were exerted.[74]

Menstrual blood remained in the womb until it was used in conception and reproduction or had reached such a volume that it had to be evacuated to prevent the menses swamping the semen. At this point the womb would open and remain open until it had emptied itself.

The role of menstruation in the context of a woman's general health and pregnancy[75] in the Hippocratic and Aristotelian theories is reflected in the functions they attribute to the womb. The Hippocratics thought that menstruating made it possible for a woman to maintain her health and that menstrual blood was only utilized in pregnancy after the foetus had been conceived, which occurred more readily if the womb was empty. Therefore, while remaining empty for most of the month in preparation for conception, the womb also played an active prophylactic role in Hippocratic conceptions of female physiology. Aristotle, on the other hand, believed that a woman's heavy menstrual flow caused her paleness and deficiency of

---

[74] φέρεται γὰρ ἕκαστον εἰς τὸν οἰκεῖον τόπον οὐθὲν ἀποβιαζομένου τοῦ πνεύματος, οὐδ' ἄλλης αἰτίας τοιαύτης ἀναγκαζούσης, ὥσπερ τινές φασιν, ἕλκειν τὰ αἰδοῖα φάσκοντες ὥσπερ τὰς σικύας, τῷ τε πνεύματι βιαζομένων, ὥσπερ ἐνδεχόμενον ἄλλοθί που πορευθῆναι μὴ βιασαμένων ἢ ταύτην τὴν περίττωσιν ἢ τὴν τῆς ὑγρᾶς ἢ ξηρᾶς τροφῆς. The reference to cupping-glasses (σικύας) shows that the passage in *VM* 22 was one of the 'people' Arist. had in mind here (see pp. 65–7 below). However, the inclusion of *pneuma* as an agent suggests that he was also thinking of some Sicilian source.

[75] For theories of conception and pregnancy, see pp. 148–224 below.

physique.[76] The sole purpose of menstrual blood in his theory was to provide material for the conception and growth of a foetus, so if it was not present in the womb when a man ejaculated semen into a woman the production of it by the woman's body would have been wasted. In Aristotle's theory a woman possesses a womb solely for the purpose of reproduction.

ANATOMY OF THE WOMB

The Hippocratics refer to the womb as a 'vessel' (ἄγγος, *Epid.* 6. 5. ii (v. 318. 14–15)), and Hanson has suggested that it was conceived of as a jug.[77] However, *Nat. Puer.* 30 (vii. 532. 6) describes the womb as 'soft' (ἀπαλάς), and a hydropsical or distended womb is likened to a swollen wineskin (ἀσκός) at *Mul.* 1. 61, 2. 170 (viii. 124. 15–21, 350. 16–17). The *askos* seems intuitively more likely to have been the general image of the womb, as the Hippocratics have to imagine it having the capacity to expand to contain the foetus in pregnancy.[78] Moreover, at *Mul.* 1. 2 (viii. 14. 10) the author uses the term ἰδνωθῇ to describe a configuration of the cervix. The word is used by Homer to describe the doubling up of pliant bodies.[79] It would therefore seem to imply a drooping motion, one more applicable to a wineskin than a jar.[80]

VM 22 (i. 626. 17–18) further describes the shape of the womb by saying that the hollow organs best suited to attract moisture from the rest of the body are 'those which are wide in part and narrow down' (ἐς στενὸν συνηγμένα ἐκ κοίλου τε καὶ εὐρέος). The author continues:

---

[76] *GA* 727ᵃ22–5.

[77] See Hanson 1990, 317. This view is accepted by King 1989, 23, though she calls the womb a 'jar'.

[78] It is true that *Genit.* 9 (vii. 482. 9–22) implies that the womb can restrict the growth of the foetus, but this would be because it did not expand enough, not because it did not expand at all. *Nat. Puer.* 30 (vii. 532. 16–18) explicitly says that the womb can become inflated and swell.

[79] For example, at *Il.* 2. 266 and 13. 618 it is used of the doubling over of a human body in pain or death, at *Il.* 12. 205 of a snake bending back on itself to bite an eagle who was carrying him in his beak, and at *Od.* 8. 375 of a ball thrown up into the air and coming back down again.

[80] This is not to say that there were no occasions on which the Hippocratics used the analogy of a jug or a jar for the womb. Analogies can be altered to suit the exigencies of an argument, see Lonie 1981, 77–86. I believe, however, that generally speaking the wineskin analogy was uppermost in the minds of the Hippocratics.

Such things have to be deduced from a consideration of what clearly happens outside the body. For instance, if you gape with your mouth wide open you cannot suck up any fluid, but if you pout and compress the lips and insert a tube you can easily suck up as much as you like. Again, cuppingglasses are made concave for the purpose of drawing and pulling the flesh up within them, and there are other examples of this kind of thing. Among the inner organs of the body, the bladder, the skull and the womb have such a shape.[81]

'Such a shape' in the last sentence refers generally to an organ which is 'wide in part and narrow[s] down', i.e. not specifically to the shape of a cupping-glass, though Aristotle seems to have read the passage in this way (see p. 64 above). The shape of a cupping-glass may be appropriate to describe the skull, but the simile is not apt for the bladder or womb. The Greeks used bladders (among other things) as wallets, to administer clysters, and to contain hot water as a poultice,[82] and knew that they were shaped more like a pouch than a bowl. Similarly, when too much blood accumulates in the womb, it does not simply overflow its vessel into the surrounding organs, as it would be imagined as doing if the womb were conceived of as a cupping-vessel, but moves off through the passages of the body to other locations. The openings of the bladder and womb into urethra and vagina respectively approximate to the first example of this shape given in the passage, that of pursed lips, but they are pointing in the wrong direction to draw fluids into themselves from the body. We need to imagine similar openings on the other side of the bladder and the womb directed towards the interior of the body. *Nat. Puer.* 17 (vii. 498. 14–15) says that during pregnancy a passage forms in the foetus to the bladder from the belly and intestines. This may be the narrow opening to which the author of *VM* refers through which the bladder draws fluids to itself from the body. There is no description of such a tube for the womb, but *Superf.* 1 (viii. 476. 3) describes the womb as having two 'horns' (κέρατα). This term was later used by Herophilus and Galen to designate the Fallopian tubes, but the

---

[81] καταμανθάνειν δὲ δεῖ αὐτὰ ἔξωθεν ἐκ τῶν φανερῶν. τοῦτο μὲν γὰρ τῷ στόματι κεχηνὼς ὑγρὸν οὐδὲν ἂν ἀνασπάσαις· προμυλλήνας δὲ καὶ συστείλας, πιέσας τε τὰ χείλεα, ἔτι τε αὐλὸν προσθέμενος, ῥηιδίως ἀνασπάσαις ἂν ὅ τι θέλοις. τοῦτο δὲ αἱ σικύαι προσβαλλόμεναι ἐξ εὐρέος ἐς στενώτερον ἐστενωμέναι πρὸς τοῦτο τετεχνέαται, πρὸς τὸ ἕλκειν ἀπὸ τῆς σαρκὸς καὶ ἐπισπᾶσθαι, ἄλλα τε καὶ πολλὰ τοιουτότροπα. τῶν δ' ἔσω τοῦ ἀνθρώπου φύσις καὶ σχῆμα τοιοῦτον· κύστις τε καὶ κεφαλὴ καὶ ὑστέρα γυναιξί *VM* 22 (i. 626. 18–628. 4).

[82] Ar. *Fr.* 504; *Steril.* 220 (viii. 430. 8–9); *Acut.* 7 (ii. 268. 9–11).

Hippocratics show no knowledge of these.[83] The 'horns' of *Superf.* seem to be thought of as pockets inside the womb. However, 'horn' implies a tapering structure, and there is no obvious reason why the Hippocratics should imagine the interior of the womb as having this shape unless they were aware of the general shape of the exterior of the womb and thought the interior conformed to these contours. It would be the projections or stumps of the Fallopian tubes which the author of *VM* identified as the narrow openings through which the womb drew blood into itself. *Mul.* 2. 146, 162 (viii. 322. 3, 338. 14) refers to plural mouths (*stomata*) of the womb. One interpretation could be that the author was thinking of the mouths facing the interior of the body through which the woman's seed and blood entered the womb, as well as the external mouth from which the blood and foetus exited.[84]

Nat. Puer. 31 (vii. 540. 1–16) says that the womb can contain many pockets and that those animals which produce a great many offspring at one birth do so because the semen is divided between several pockets and a separate foetus develops in each. This is the explanation of the birth of twins from women; semen falls into each of the womb's two pockets. The author does not explain what causes this to happen on some occasions and not on others, nor does he account for multiple births of triplets or more. Obviously, these would be much rarer than twins, so he may have thought that women who had more than two pockets to their womb were unusual, if not abnormal. The human uterus, in fact, has no separate compartments at all, but the misapprehension could have arisen from observation of other mammalian uteri, particularly of the pig, which are divided. The belief that the womb consisted of two or more pockets may explain why the Hippocratics generally refer to the human womb in the plural.

Aristotle says that all wombs 'are in two parts' (εἰσὶ διμερεῖς), but his reasoning is that the testicles of the male are always two in number.[85] It has been suggested that in describing the womb as bipartite Aristotle is referring to the external duality of the ovaries.[86] However, at *HA* 632ª22–30 Aristotle remarks that swineherds remove the *kapria* from sows in order to quench their

---

[83] See von Staden 1989, 232–3, 239–40.

[84] Galen, *Ut. Diss.* 10, imagines a plethora of veins carrying blood into the womb and roughening its interior surface when open.

[85] GA 716ᵇ32–3.   [86] Thomas Laqueur, personal communication.

sexual appetite and fatten them up. The *kapria* is said to be located in the lower abdomen in the same area where boars have testicles and to adhere to the womb. It is generally believed that *kapria* refers to the ovaries (even though it is a singular noun), so since Aristotle differentiates the ovaries from the womb here, he cannot mean the two parts of the womb to be identical with the ovaries, though again, it seems likely that his belief that the womb is in two parts would be confirmed by what he had seen of the configuration of the Fallopian tubes leading to the ovaries. Although he accepts in this passage that the ovaries are in some way analogous to testicles, Aristotle does not describe the role they play in reproduction. As he knew that the removal of the *kapria* resulted in sterility, it might seem that Aristotle would have to expend some energy in denying that its presence showed that women could contribute seed to the foetus as well as menstrual blood. But in fact nobody during the Classical period seems to have advanced this argument, and since to Aristotle's mind it is not simply physically unlikely, but logically impossible that women should contribute seed as well as menstrual blood (see p. 53 above), it is not surprising that he did not see the possible significance of the *kapria* himself. Aristotle would have to posit that its function was to concoct the female seminal residue before it passed on to the womb, but he makes no mention of this in his discussions of menstruation. He believes the menstrual fluid passes from the diaphragm directly to the womb. Unlike Aristotle, the Hippocratics did not consciously apply knowledge gained from other female animal bodies to women, so although they did believe that women contributed seed to the conception of a foetus they too failed to recognize the significance of the *kapria* in sows. Nor did they feel it necessary to discover a female analogy to the testicles. In both sexes they believed that the seed was drawn either from all over the body at the time of copulation or from a reservoir in the head. Although both sexes supplied seed it was accepted without question that they differed in reproductive anatomy. Moreover, the Hippocratics were not compiling an anatomy for its own sake and their models of disease and procreation in women worked well for them without having to invoke two small organs which had only been seen in quadrupeds and whose function was not immediately apparent.

Both the Hippocratics and Aristotle therefore believed that a woman's reproductive apparatus was limited to the womb. The use of a plural noun to refer to the womb is to be ascribed to the belief that the human womb contained two or more pockets, as had been observed in the wombs of other mammals. *Superf.*'s description of these pockets as 'horns' suggests that the ancients had some vague knowledge of the shape of a human uterus and assumed that the interior pockets conformed to the contours produced from the initial projections of the Fallopian tubes. Aristotle's description of *kapria* supports the likelihood that the Greeks were aware of the basic shape of the mammalian uterus. It is through openings in the projections of the Fallopian tubes that the womb was thought to fill with blood from the body. This 'horned' shape would make the womb resemble an *askos* even more.

THE 'WANDERING WOMB'

Once the blood had flowed into the womb, it was discharged through the stoma into the vagina. As we have seen, the Hippocratics believed that outside pregnancy a closed stoma was a pathological condition, especially common among virgins and women who had ceased to be sexually active. In the case of a closed stoma, the blood could either remain and fester in the womb or drain off to some other part of the body and form an abscess.[87] When we remember that the Hippocratic model of a woman's body postulated a network of channels leading to the womb from all over the body, we can understand how they could conceive of menstrual blood flowing back along these channels and gathering at another point in the body. As modern medicine recognizes that the angling of the cervix towards the anterior or posterior wall of the vagina can signal anteversion or retroversion of the womb,[88] we can also understand why the Hippocratics believed that the womb could tip in one direction or another and, again, either trap its blood in itself or spill it back out along the channels. However, it is hard to comprehend how the Hippocratics could have imagined the womb as having the ability to relocate anywhere else in the body, yet the gynaecological authors cite in-

[87] For a discussion of the pathological repercussions of suppressed menstrual blood, see pp. 125–36 below.
[88] Mackay *et al.* 1983, 13.

stances of the womb attaching itself to the heart, the liver, the brain, the bladder, and the rectum.[89] The concept of a mobile womb is not restricted to the Hippocratics. In *Ti*. 91 B–D Plato characterizes the womb as an irrational animal wandering round the body of a woman seeking satisfaction in sexual intercourse and pregnancy. The Hippocratics never describe the womb explicitly as an individual animal wandering at will within the body of a woman, in fact the gynaecologists never use the verb 'to wander' (πλάνω) to describe the womb's movements.[90] The womb is said to 'turn' (στρέφω) if it is simply displaced to one side or another;[91] if it turns and moves away from its normal position completely the verb for 'turn' is τρέπω.[92] Sometimes the motion begins with some form of στρέφω followed by a verb such as ἐπιβάλλω or ἐμβάλλω ('to leap upon') or προσπίπτω ('to fall towards').[93] Some verbs describing womb movements imply a very swift motion, e.g. θέω ('to rush'), σεύομαι ('to be set in swift motion'), or παροτρῦναι ('to urge on').[94] The womb usually has a destination, and the vocabulary used shows that the Hippocratics envisaged it as actually reaching these destinations. The womb 'becomes contiguous' (ὁμοῦ γίνονται) with the liver; it can be 'set against' (προσιστάμεναι) the heart; it can become inflamed 'alongside' (παρά) the lungs; it can 'touch' (ψαύωσι) and 'cling to' (προσκέωνται) the hips.[95] The movements of the womb in the Hippocratic gynaecological treatises are therefore conceived of as very violent and directed, and there is no doubt but that it was thought to relocate physically.

The Hippocratics account for the womb's movements throughout

[89] e.g. *Mul.* 2. 123, 124, 127, 137 (viii. 266. 11, 20, 272. 9, 310. 6–7). In recent scholarship this syndrome has often been referred to as 'hysteria', a term which derives from the Greek word for womb (*hystera*), which has in turn been translated as 'wombiness' by Lefkowitz 1981, 13. However, King 1985, 101–6, points out that this term is not used by the Hippocratics themselves, and that a displaced womb can give rise to many different 'syndromes', see Micale 1989, 230–3; King 1990.

[90] Though this verb is used of the womb in *Art.* 57 (iv. 246. 9). For more details of uterine displacement, see Hanson 1991.

[91] e.g. *Mul.* 1. 2 (viii. 14. 16, 18, 19). 'To be displaced' (μεθίσταμαι) also has this connotation and is used for displacement of the bladder to one side or the other, as well as of the uterus, e.g. ibid. 2 (viii. 18. 19).

[92] e.g. ibid. 2. 127, 150 (viii. 272. 9, 326. 8).

[93] e.g. ibid. 1. 7 (viii. 32. 7–8, 34. 1–2).

[94] e.g. ibid. 1. 7, 2. 138, 201 (viii. 32. 8, 310. 23–4, 384. 1).

[95] e.g. ibid. 1. 7 (viii. 32. 7–8); 2. 124 (viii. 266. 20); 2. 128 (viii. 274. 10); 2. 134 (viii. 302. 13).

a woman's body by explaining that if it is not anchored in place by pregnancy or kept moist by intercourse, it becomes dry and is attracted to the moister organs. Older women, women who are not having regular sexual intercourse, and young widows who have had children are prone to these displacements.[96] The wombs of older women are lighter not only because they have their wombs moistened less by sexual intercourse and pregnancy, but also because after a certain point they cease to produce menstrual fluid.[97] A womb which was full of menstrual blood or a foetus was not quite as peripatetic as an empty womb.

The womb could prolapse completely and issue from the vulva as a result of intercourse too soon after childbirth or a difficult birth.[98] A prolapsed womb is recognized as a medical condition today, and it has been suggested that it was this which gave rise to the belief that the womb could wander in other directions.[99] However, the prolapse of the womb is simply a falling-down of the organ through the vagina. It can, and does, occur in spite of the tendons that usually hold it in place; it does not in and of itself suggest that the female body is possessed of an ambulatory womb. More significant is Hanson's remark that since men's bodies held no uterus, the human body had no special place for it to reside.[100] Once again, although the Hippocratics were presumably aware that the wombs of female animals were generally found held in place by tendons in the lower abdomen, they did not apply this knowledge to their construction of a woman's body, and their belief that women were considerably different from men meant that knowledge gained about the nature of organs in the human body from war wounds, sporting accidents, etc., could be disregarded if it proved difficult to incorporate into their construct of the female.

One aspect in which a woman's body had to be imagined as

[96] Ibid. 1. 7 (viii. 32. 2); *Nat. Mul.* 3 (vii. 314. 16–18).
[97] *Mul.* 2. 137 (viii. 310. 10–11).
[98] *Nat. Mul.* 4–5 (vii. 316. 9–318. 23); *Mul.* 2. 143, 144, 145, 153 (viii. 316. 1–3, 13, 318. 21, 328. 3–5). *Mul.* 2. 144 and *Nat. Mul.* 5 suggest as treatment for this condition that a woman be strapped upside down on a ladder, bounced up and down a few times, and left overnight. Succussion on a ladder was also practised on male patients in *Art.* 42–4 (iv. 182. 13–188. 16), but this does not seem so bizarre nowadays when people buy special boots to hang upside-down to cure backache. Indeed, the effects of gravity probably brought about some short-term relief for a prolapse, and many women may have sanctioned the treatment. It is also possible that many women claimed to be cured to avoid any similar solicitous intervention in their welfare.
[99] King 1985, n. 158.   [100] Hanson 1991, 82.

differing from that of a man was in possessing thoroughfares along which the womb could pass. Although a woman's body was considered to be more loose-textured than a man's, the Hippocratics do not seem to have thought of the abdomen as an empty body cavity. A large part of female menstrual dysfunction was attributed to the vessels and flesh being too tightly packed to accommodate the excess blood in a woman whose body had not been broken down by the lochial flow after giving birth. That a woman's flesh was thought to soak up blood from her stomach, and the vessels around the stomach were among the first to be broken down by the lochia, suggests that the Hippocratics imagined the abdominal organs to be surrounded by flesh. 'A wide space' (εὐρυχωρίη) in the abdomen could sometimes be provided by the stomach being emptier than usual, but this seems to afford space for the preliminary turning of the womb, not its relocation to distant parts of the body.[101] The womb, however, was connected to all parts of the body by *phlebia* and *phlebes*, and after the breaking down of the body these too could develop into 'a wide space' so that they did not become overfull or strained with the menses.[102] A pliable womb could be thought to travel along these widened pathways with some ease, and those women thought to be most susceptible to displacements of the womb were women whose passages would have been widened either by the lochia (widows who had had children and some, at least, of women who had once been sexually active but had ceased) or by the length of time menstruation had been occurring in their bodies (older virgins). Even in young virgins or women who had not given birth, the preferred destinations of the womb (heart, liver, brain) would be connected to the womb by the larger *phlebes* since they were among the moistest organs in the body and so would be served by a vessel capable of carrying a large quantity of blood. It is quite possible that these *phlebes* were tributary to a 'tube' which both Manuli and King hypothesize was thought to pass through the diaphragm and to connect the nostrils and vagina of a woman, giving the womb free passage from the top to the bottom of the body.[103] Evi-

[101] *Mul.* 1. 2, 7 (viii. 14. 17–16. 1, 32. 4–7).

[102] Ibid. 1. 1. (viii. 10. 16–19). Blood was always thought to be contained in vessels in the body (see Harris 1973, *passim* and figs. 1–5), so the text cannot mean that the blood was easier for a woman to bear because it was in the wide spaces of her body cavity.

[103] Manuli 1983, 157; King 1989, 22–3. Hanson 1991, 86 argues that 'there is no evidence, so far as I am aware, that Hippocratics thought that the uterus actually arrived at and made contact with the wet places and the moist organs above the diaphragm', but at *Mul.* 2. 124 (viii. 266. 20) the womb is said to be 'set against' the

dence for this conception is furnished by a favourite Hippocratic method for deciding whether a woman can conceive or not. The doctor sits her over something strong smelling (garlic is a standard ingredient for these recipes) and tests whether it can be smelled through her mouth. If it can all is well; if not, her tube is blocked and steps must be taken to unblock it before she can conceive.[104] The model of a tube connecting the head to the vagina perhaps explains why the gynaecology includes a specific cure for bad breath in women. This involves taking the head of a hare and three mice or rats (two of them having had all their innards removed apart from their brains and liver), mixing these up with various other ingredients and smearing them on a woman's gums for a period of days. One would imagine that however rancid a woman's breath was naturally it would smell sweet in comparison to the cure![105]

The relocation of the womb to different areas of the body, therefore, can be accounted for by scientific principles in the Hippocratic construction of the female body. However, these principles are not apparent in the method the Hippocratics suggest for drawing the womb back to its proper position. The general procedure is to administer foul-smelling substances to the nostrils at the same time as the woman is sitting on a bowl filled with sweet perfumes, simultaneously repelling the womb from one end of the body and attracting it to the other (sweet and foul smells are

heart (προσιστάμεναι), and although *Mul.* 2. 123 (viii. 266. 11) describes the womb's movement only as 'turning towards the head' (ἐς τὴν κεφαλὴν τραπῶσιν), the remarks that 'the stifling settles there and weighs down the head' (τῇδε λήγῃ ὁ πνιγμός, κεφαλὴν βαρύνει) suggest that the womb does reach its destination.

[104] *Mul.* 2. 146 (viii. 322. 8–14); *Nat. Mul.* 96 (vii. 412. 19–414. 3); *Aph.* 5. 59 (iv. 554. 3–6). The rationale for this procedure would be that blocked tubes prevented the semen from being drawn to the womb from the rest of the body, and particularly from the brain, not that the passage into the womb for the male semen was blocked. *Steril.* 219 (viii. 424. 1–13) says the odour shows on the hair, not the breath, and that the test is no use if the woman has not already been pregnant (presumably because the passages throughout her body would not be open enough to carry the smell). Moreover, in a woman who conceives easily the smell will permeate even when there has been no purgation (presumably she is so fertile because her passages are wide enough to carry the smell—and therefore seed—even when they are also carrying menstrual fluid).

[105] *Mul.* 2. 185 (viii. 366. 6–20). There is no specific cure for halitosis in a male in the Hippocratic Corpus, but the *Philogelos* (a collection of jokes put together in the second century AD, though containing some jokes dating from much earlier) has a section of twelve jokes on 'smelly-mouths' (ὀζόστομοι), in one of which (235) the patient complains to his doctor that his uvula (σταφυλή) has 'gone down' (κατέβη). The doctor recoils from his examination and says, 'No, your anus has come up' (ἀλλ' ὁ κῶλός σου ἀνέβη). This suggests a connection between mouth and anus in men paralleling that between mouth and vagina in women.

reversed if the womb has travelled down the body).[106] The belief in the efficacy of this therapy depended upon the womb being assumed to have the sense of smell in some way,[107] and derives from some pre-rational theory of womb movements. It would seem that there was a common traditional source from which the Hippocratics and Plato derived their accounts of the mobile womb.

Now, although the Hippocratics did accept and rationalize many folk beliefs in their medicine, they did not usually give credence to any belief that smacked purely of irrational superstition (e.g. *Morb. Sacr.* poured ridicule on traditional explanations of the causes of epilepsy), so it lay within the purview of the gynaecological writers to dissent from the common opinion that the womb reacted to smells. Indeed, although Hippocratic female physiology can accommodate a mobile womb, there is nothing in the physical theory of the Hippocratics which demands it (the illnesses attributed to the relocation of the womb could all be explained more easily as the abscession of menstrual blood), and accounting for the efficacy of the odour-therapies could cause them some embarrassment. That rational medicine did not reject the concept of a mobile womb out of hand suggests that it fulfilled an important cultural role in characterizing the female sex.[108]

In recent years several theories have been advanced for the origin and function of the concept of the 'Wandering Womb' in Greek thought.[109] Simon argues that 'a hysterical symptom, for a Greek woman, permitted a safe expression of certain unmet needs, and the

[106] e.g. *Nat. Mul.* 3, 14 (vii. 314. 21, 332. 6–7); *Mul.* 1. 13, 2. 126, 142 (viii. 50. 19–52. 8, 270. 20–272. 1, 314. 22–4).

[107] Soranus, *Gyn.* 3. 29, denies that this treatment has any efficacy, but he indicates that some of his contemporaries were still using it on the theory that 'the uterus fleeing the first-mentioned [evil] odours, but pursuing the last-mentioned [fragrant] might move from the upper to the lower parts'. For more information on other measures used in concert with odour-therapies, see Hanson 1991, 81–7; Lefkowitz 1981, 16.

[108] The importance of a mobile womb in the cultural construction of the female is shown by the tenacity of the concept in Greek scientific literature. After the dissection of human bodies at Alexandria in the 3rd and 2nd c. BC, Greek physicians had a much clearer idea of female reproductive organs and knew that they were held in place by tendons and connected to other organs in the abdomen. Even so, in the 2nd c. AD Soranus, *Gyn.* 1. 8, Galen, *Ut. Diss.* 4, and Aretaeus, *CD* 2. 11, describe the uterus as being very loosely moored and capable of causing severe discomfort by displacement in all directions. Hanson 1991, 103 n. 52, describes odour-therapies that were still used in the later period.

[109] e.g. Simon 1978, 238–68; Lefkowitz 1981; Gold 1988; Manuli 1983, 149–204. King 1985, 113–16, asserts that the idea of the womb as an independent animal is not present in the Hippocratic texts and would not suggest itself if we were not reading

relationship with the doctor allowed a form of gratification that would otherwise be forbidden.'[110] Lefkowitz believes that the symptoms of a displaced womb or of Dionysiac possession developed as women's expression of their feelings of oppression; in this she is followed by Gold. Manuli believes the concept of a mobile womb was an entirely male construct, the threat of which was designed to deprive women of control over their own sexuality and to justify their subordination to their husbands. She has demonstrated that, within their rationalization, the Hippocratics take account of the model of the womb which Plato was to use in the *Timaeus*, that of the womb as a separate animal within the woman which, without the intervention of a man (husband or doctor), is in danger of subjugating the woman's own life-force ($\psi\upsilon\chi\acute{\eta}$) if it does not have its own wants satisfied. Its preferred destinations (heart, liver, brain) were all thought to be possible seats of the *psyche*.[111] She points out that employing perfumes in attracting the womb parallels the use of incense in invoking a god, an entity which it was not easy for even a man to control.

All these theories assume that women of the Classical period were and felt sexually repressed. It is not, of course, to be denied that men had much greater sexual freedom in the ancient world than women did, but it is anachronistic to attribute to the women of the ancient world a concern with their sexuality *per se*. The construct of the male body in the Hippocratic Corpus ratified the culture's definition of acceptable male sexual conduct, and the concept of a womb which was prone to relocation if it was not weighed down by semen or a foetus did condone the belief that a woman should submit to her husband's sexual appetite for her own good, whether she desired it or not. However, given the array of socially acceptable sexual outlets available to Greek men (concubines and hetairai, male lovers, male

back from the *Timaeus*. In citing the principles of attraction of the dry to the moist, she says, the Hippocratics give a completely mechanical explanation of the movement of the womb, which does not necessitate attributing to it any desires of its own. She does not address the problem of the presumed efficacy of the odour-therapies (but see now King (forthcoming)). Rousselle 1988, 24–6, has argued that the concept of a mobile womb was developed entirely by women to account for bodily ailments, particularly stifling, though she does not suggest why this sensation should be so widespread among women or why they should want to attribute it to the relocation of their reproductive organ.

[110] Simon 1978, 242.

[111] *Mul.* I. 38 (viii. 94. 9–10) says that the womb is in sympathy with many things and specifically lists the bregma, throat, and intelligence ($\beta\rho\acute{\varepsilon}\gamma\mu\alpha$, $\sigma\tau\acute{o}\mu\alpha\chi\sigma\varsigma$, $\gamma\nu\acute{\omega}\mu\eta$).

and female slaves and prostitutes),[112] it would seem that Greek wives would have been in danger of suffering from the neglect of their husbands rather than over-attentiveness. Despite Simon's claim, actually manifesting the symptoms of *pnix* would not have obtained sexual satisfaction for a woman,[113] but the threat of such symptoms developing would have allowed her to insist on the sexual attention she wanted from her husband without threatening his dominant position. The concept of a mobile womb, then, could function in Classical Greek culture to the benefit of both men and women, ratifying the social expectations of male and female sexual conduct while allowing a forum in which women could justifiably demand that their sexual desires be fulfilled without usurping the male social role of erotic initiative.[114]

As Aristotle denied that the womb was active in even so minor a role as drawing the blood to itself, he was hardly likely to allow it the capacity to perceive smells. Moreover, as he did not regard the human female as quite so anomalous in comparison with the female gender of other species or the other gender of the human species, he asserts that the womb is held in place by tendons, just like the wombs of other animals and like the seminal passages in the male.[115] Nevertheless, even he thinks that when the womb is empty it can be pushed upwards and cause a stifling sensation.[116] Surprisingly, at *HA* 582[b]22–6 Aristotle explains a prolapsed womb as a result of lack of sexual intercourse. The womb descends and will not return to its proper position until it has conceived.[117] No rationale is offered for this, and it is hard to imagine a rational explanation that could justify weighing down a uterus that was already protruding beyond the vulva with a foetus. A prolapsed

[112] Of course, not all Greek men would be able to afford all of these, or would necessarily want to frequent any of them; but all except the poorest could avail themselves of one of them instead of forcing unwelcome advances on their wives if, as Ar. *Lys.* 163–6 suggests, most men did not enjoy intercourse with an unwilling partner.

[113] See King 1985, 110; (forthcoming). Manuli, who argues that 'hysteria' is a male construct, is the only scholar who assumes that the significance of 'hysteria' lies more in the threat than in the actual manifestation of symptoms. She says it functioned as 'hygienic blackmail', 1980, 402; 1983, 160.

[114] For further development of these views, cf. Dean-Jones (1992).

[115] *GA* 720[a]12–14.

[116] Ibid. 719[a]21–2.

[117] This echoes the description of the 'Wandering Womb' in the *Timaeus*. This may indicate that this section was part of Arist.'s earliest biological work when he was still heavily influenced by Plato.

womb is one of the rare female conditions for which the Hippocratics recommend abstinence from intercourse.[118] Aristotle may
have been more rigorously scientific in observing anatomical and
physiological phenomena, but to some extent (perhaps because he
never had to translate his theories into therapy) he was sometimes
less critical of folk beliefs than the Hippocratic doctors.

Aristotle mentions using pessaries to test if a woman can conceive.[119] He accepts that if the pessaries cannot be smelled through
the mouth it shows that the passages in the body have closed over.
However, the connection he posits between the genital area and the
breath is not quite so simplistic as the Hippocratic tube. He believes
the seminal secretion originates in the area of the diaphragm, and
just as this passes down to the genitalia, any movement set up in the
lower area passes back to the chest and it is from here that the scent
becomes perceptible on the breath. The seminal discharge can also
pass from the chest to the eyes (the most 'seminal' part of the head),
so another way of checking whether all the passages in the body are
open as they should be is to rub pigments on the eyes and see if they
colour the saliva.[120] The appearance of the coloured fluid from the
eyes in the mouth could only come about if it was flowing or being
drawn down the body, demonstrating that the passages to and from
the genitals were clear.

EXTERNAL GENITALIA

Because they are compiling a pathology rather than a physiology,
the Hippocratics do not describe in detail every part of the female
anatomy of which they are aware. They generally refer to the genitalia by the commonplace plural form 'privy parts' (τὰ αἰδοῖα) and
use the singular (τὸ αἰδοῖον), to refer to the vagina when describing

[118] e.g. *Mul.* 2. 149 (viii. 326. 1), see Hanson 1991, 84 n. 63.
[119] *GA* 747[a]7–23. He does not identify the passage in which they should be
inserted, merely that the smell should penetrate 'from below upward' (κάτωθεν
ἄνω). Note that Arist. is concerned with the movement of seminal fluids around the
body, not with the movement of organs.
[120] *Nat. Mul.* 99 (vii. 416. 1–3) advocates rubbing a woman's eyes with a red stone to
find out whether or not she is pregnant. If the substance penetrates she is pregnant.
This seems to belong to the same tradition as Arist.'s test for the possibility of conception, but it is unclear how it was thought to work when conception had taken place.

treatment for the womb. The labia are only differentiated when they are part of a pathological condition, e.g. at *Mul.* 1. 40 (viii. 96. 10) the 'lips' (τὰ χείλεα) are described as sticking together across 'the mouth of the vagina' (τὸ στόμα τοῦ αἰδοίου), i.e. the external opening of the vagina, not the stoma of the cervix. *Loc. Hom.* 47 (vi. 344. 7) calls the labia 'overhanging banks' (οἱ κρημνοί) when describing a condition in which the mouth of the womb adhered to them.

All these parts are named when they are involved in describing a pathological condition in which the physician has to deal with the individual parts in therapy. The Hippocratics make no mention of the clitoris, the existence of which was known to their contemporaries.[121] Hanson says that this is due to a 'sense of propriety and proper conduct', but the detail with which the Hippocratics describe the most intimate recesses of a woman's body shows that they could cross the bounds of everyday decorum in the cause of maintaining a woman's health. The clitoris is omitted from their vocabulary of female genitalia because it played no role in health and disease. Because the Hippocratics believed a woman's seed was necessary for conception, and because they assumed, on the basis of the male model, that the seed was produced by ejaculation, we might expect that among the many recipes to promote conception one or two would be found to refer to the clitoris in descriptions of how to produce orgasm in a woman—but no such recipes exist. The author of *Genit.* attributes the pleasure leading to the ejaculation of seed by a woman during intercourse to the friction of the penis in the vagina. The woman ejaculates seed directly into her womb, and in the normal course of events the seed remains there, so the author does not necessarily expect a woman's pleasure to be marked by the lubrication of her vagina:

In the case of women it is my contention that when during intercourse the vagina is rubbed and the womb is disturbed, an irritation is set up in the womb which produces pleasure and heat in the rest of the body. A woman also releases something from her body, sometimes into the womb, which

---

[121] Hanson 1987, 31, notes that Xanthos of Lydia remarks that the Lydian king had clitoridectomies performed to create female eunuchs for his harem; Hipponax and Aristophanes both refer to it under the name of 'myrtle-berry' (τὸ μύρτον), and it seems likely that Sappho used the word νύμφη as a pun referring to a bride and the clitoris, see Winkler 1981, 78–81.

then becomes moist, and sometimes externally as well, if the womb is open wider than normal.[122]

This does not mean that the Hippocratics were oblivious to the clitoris and its effects; but despite their belief in female seed, they were aware that a woman's subjective feelings of pleasure—or lack of them—were irrelevant to whether or not she conceived. So one author, in giving advice on how to promote conception in circumstances where the cause of infertility is assumed to be the woman's failure to produce seed, does not suggest that a husband modify his love-making in any way. He simply advises him to continue to have sex with his wife, 'for the habit causes desire in them [i.e. women] and opens up the passages. And if the semen given off from the man immediately flows together with that from the woman she will conceive.'[123] That is, if a man has intercourse with a woman often enough she will eventually become pregnant, which proves she has come to enjoy the experience.

Aristotle may show his awareness of the clitoris at *GA* 728ᵃ32–4: 'An indication that the female emits no semen is actually afforded by the fact that in intercourse the pleasure is produced in the same place as in the male by contact, yet this is not the place from which the liquid is emitted.'[124] Aristotle is here arguing that neither menstrual fluid nor the vaginal lubricant (cf. *GA* 727ᵇ33–728ᵃ2, 739ᵃ32–7) can be equated with semen because they are not emitted from the place where a woman feels pleasure during intercourse. Menses and the fluid sometimes produced by a woman during intercourse are emitted from the stoma of the cervix. The place where a woman feels pleasure is identified as 'the same place as in the male by contact'. This cannot be meant to signify the spot where the penis is in contact with the vagina as this would be too close to the stoma of the cervix to be so categorically differentiated from it. It would therefore seem to indicate a spot on a woman's body that corresponded to the place

[122] τῇσι δὲ γυναιξί φημι ἐν τῇ μίξει τριβομένου τοῦ αἰδοίου καὶ τῶν μητρέων κινευμένων, ὥσπερ κνησμὸν ἐμπίπτειν ἐς αὐτὰς καὶ τῷ ἄλλῳ σώματι ἡδονὴν καὶ θέρμην παρέχειν. μεθίει δὲ καὶ ἡ γυνὴ ἀπὸ τοῦ σώματος, ὁτὲ μὲν ἐς τὰς μήτρας, αἱ δὲ μῆτραι ἰκμαλέαι γίνονται, ὁτὲ δὲ καὶ ἔξω, ἢν χάσκωσιν αἱ μῆτραι μᾶλλον τοῦ καιροῦ, *Genit.* 4 (vii. 474. 14–18).

[123] προθυμίην γὰρ σφίσι ποιέει ἡ μελέτη, καὶ ἀναχαλᾶται τὰ φλέβια, καὶ ἢν τὸ ἀπὸ τοῦ ἀνδρὸς ἀπιόντα ὁμορροθῇ κατ' ἴξιν τῷ ἀπὸ τῆς γυναικὸς κυήσει, *Mul.* 1. 17 (viii. 56. 20–2).

[124] σημεῖον δὲ τοῦ τὸ θῆλυ μὴ προΐεσθαι σπέρμα καὶ τὸ γίνεσθαι ἐν τῇ ὁμιλίᾳ τὴν ἡδονὴν τῇ ἀφῇ κατὰ τὸν αὐτὸν τόπον τοῖς ἄρρεσιν· καίτοι οὐ προΐενται τὴν ἰκμάδα ταύτην ἐντεῦθεν.

80   *Female Anatomy and Physiology*

on a man's body which produced pleasure when it was touched, i.e.
the penis. This would suggest a spot just below the pubes on a
woman's body, i.e. the clitoris. Aristotle is led to refer to the clitoris
because he wishes to disassociate women's experience of pleasure
from the process of conception.[125] Unlike the Hippocratics, however, he does find a use for a woman's subjective feeling of pleasure;
the fluid a woman produces when she feels pleasure assures that the
womb is open and allows the semen of the man easier passage into
the womb.[126] The Hippocratic gynaecologists recognized that the vagina, and
the urethra were separate. They frequently advise inserting pessaries
into the vagina, to be left there for several days, without any directions for steps to avoid obstructing the flow of urine.[127] A passage
from *Aër.* may suggest that physicians without gynaecological experience did not recognize the separation of the two passages, but
problems with the text make it possible that the passage originally
said exactly the opposite. In explaining that stone in the bladder
causes great pain by blocking the passage of urine, the author comments, 'As a result, children suffering from stone rub or pull at their
private parts because they think that in them lies the cause why they
cannot make water.'[128] Later in the chapter he continues, 'Female
children are less liable to stone because the urethra is short and wide
and the urine is passed easily. Neither do they masturbate as the
males do, nor touch the urethra. †For their urethras open through a
passage into their private parts. (In men the urethra does not
immediately join the private parts, and accordingly their urethras
are not wide)†.'[129] The manuscript tradition of this passage is
extremely confused, and the obelized sentence is generally excised
as an interpolation. However, if we omit the phrases for which evidence that they were in situ in antiquity is weak (the letter-spaced

[125] *GA* 727ᵇ7–11.
[126] Ibid. 739ᵃ32–7. For the significance of Arist.'s recognition of the clitoris in his
theory of female sexuality, cf. Dean-Jones (1992, 83–7).
[127] e.g. a pessary left in for three days and then replaced by another for a further
three days, *Mul.* 1. 19 (viii. 58. 11, 13); a pessary left in for a day and a night, ibid. 1.
37 (viii. 90. 9–10); a pessary left in for two to three days, ibid. 1. 59 (viii. 118. 10).
[128] ὥστε τὰ αἰδοῖα τρίβουσι καὶ ἕλκουσι τὰ παιδία τὰ λιθιῶντα· δοκέει γὰρ
αὐτέοισι τὸ αἴτιον ἐνταῦθα εἶναι τῆς οὐρήσιος, *Aër.* 9 (ii. 38. 23–5).
[129] τοῖσι δὲ θήλεσι λίθοι οὐ γίγνονται ὁμοίως· ὁ γὰρ οὐρητὴρ βραχύς ἐστιν
ὁ τῆς κύστιος καὶ εὐρύς, ὥστε βιάζεσθαι τὸ οὖρον ῥηιδίως. οὔτε γὰρ τῇ χειρὶ
τρίβει τὸ αἰδοῖον ὥσπερ τὸ ἄρσεν, οὔτε ἅπτεται τοῦ οὐρητῆρος. †ἐς γὰρ τὰ
αἰδοῖα ξυντέτρηται. (οἱ δὲ ἄνδρες οὐκ εὐθὺ τέτρηνται, καὶ διότι οἱ
οὐρητῆρές εἰσιν οὐκ εὐρέες)†, *Aër.* 9 (ii. 40. 7–42. 5), trans. L.D.-J.

Greek in n. 129), and retain the negative before 'open through' (ξυν-
τέτρηνται) as in MS 2146, we arrive at the sense we might expect, 'for
their [i.e. women's] urethras do not open through a passage into their
privy parts and accordingly their urethras are wide.'[130] This not only
corresponds more closely to female anatomy but also is more
coherent with the author's explanations as to why girls do not suffer
stone as much as boys—their urethras and privy parts are distinct.
If the confusion in the manuscripts is due to a later interpolation,
it could be attributed to the influence of Aristotle, because he failed
to recognize the separation of the urethra and the vagina. This is a
direct result of one of the founding principles of Aristotle's biology:
that the female is a less perfect representative of the human form
than the male. The same principle led him to make other erroneous
claims. He states that a man has more sutures in his skull because he
has a bigger brain and a bigger brain needs more ventilation.[131] Men
and women have the same number of sutures in their skulls, so it
may seem as if here Aristotle is citing completely non-existent evidence as proof of the male's superiority over the female. However, at
HA 491ᵇ3–5 he enumerates the sutures as three in a man and one
circular one in a woman. Ogle records, 'it is by no means uncommon
for the sutures on the vertex to become more or less effaced in
pregnant women; so common is it, that the name "puerperal
osteophyte" has been given to the condition by Rokitansky.'[132] In
this condition the sagittal suture disappears and the lamboid, lat-
eral, and coronal sutures form a circle. Aristotle may have seen or
heard of such a skull and, as it was different from a normal skull
(perhaps seen most commonly on battlefields and therefore easily
identified as male), explained its unusual features by saying it was
female, even if he did not know for a fact that it was a woman's
skull. At another point, based on the principle that men are naturally superior to women, he claims that men have more teeth,[133]
which he associates with a longer life-span (perhaps because it
allows men to masticate more and therefore digest their food better).[134] Again, men and women have exactly the same number of
teeth, at least to start with, but we should not assume that Aristotle
could have corrected his error 'by the simple device of asking Mrs.

---

[130] I am grateful to Ann Hanson for bringing this possibility to my attention.
[131] *PA* 653ᵃ27–9, 653ᵇ1–3.   [132] Ogle 1882, 168.   [133] *HA* 501ᵇ20–4.
[134] At *PA* 661ᵇ34–6 Arist. says that the female has the parts needed for feeding 'in
a lesser degree' (ἧττον) than the male.

Aristotle to keep her mouth open while he counted.'[135] Aristotle's statement that female sheep, goats, and pigs also have fewer teeth than their male counterparts but that other animals had not yet been examined (ἐπὶ δὲ ἄλλων οὐ τεθεώρηταί πω) suggests he had conducted some sort of survey, and it is conceivable that, by sheer coincidence, in all the mouths he examined the male had lost fewer teeth than the female.[136] In this case Aristotle's presupposition of female inferiority would have led him to the wrong inference from correctly observed empirical phenomena.

Now, Aristotle claims that in most blooded animals and in all Vivipara there are two passages for evacuating fluid and solid residues from the body.[137] The existence of two passages is a sign of the superiority of the Vivipara over the Ovipara and lower animals, since the higher up the *scala naturae* an animal is, the more it is specialized in its parts.[138] That passage through which the fluid residue is voided lies higher up and in front of that for the evacuation of solids. However, the existence of the forward passage is for the sake of generation, a channel for the reproductive fluids of semen and menses. Urine uses this passage as it is a fluid residue and it is reasonable that things that are alike should share the same part, though when possible the superior should be separated from the inferior, so ideally the useful seminal residue should also be separated from useless urine. It is easy to understand why Aristotle would think that men had only two passages for voiding residues from the body, but the urethra and the vagina in women are distinct. That Aristotle did not distinguish the two is shown clearly at *PA* 689ᵃ 6–9: 'Nature employs one and the same part for the discharge of the fluid residue and for copulation in all blooded animals (with a few exceptions), male and female alike, and in all Vivipara without exception.'[139]

At *HA* 493ᵇ4–6 Peck translates, 'there is an "urethra" outside the

[135] Russell 1950, 135.

[136] It may not have been so much a coincidence if men had a consistently superior diet and women had lost more teeth owing to calcium deficiency in pregnancy. This would also account for Arist.'s observation that women were more knock-kneed than men (*HA* 538ᵇ10). Alternatively, Arist. may have been comparing the dentition of young wives (pre-wisdom teeth) with their older husbands.

[137] *GA* 719ᵇ29–34, 720ᵃ7–10; *PA* 689ᵃ4–17; *HA* 493ᵇ24–ᵇ 6, 497ᵃ24–35.

[138] *PA* 656ᵃ2–7. On the biological continuum, see Clark 1975, 28–47, esp. 44–5.

[139] καταχρῆται δ' ἡ φύσις τῷ αὐτῷ μορίῳ ἐπί τε τὴν τῆς ὑγρᾶς ἔξοδον περιττώσεως καὶ περὶ τὴν ὀχείαν, ὁμοίως ἔν τε τοῖς θήλεσι καὶ τοῖς ἄρρεσιν, ἔξω τινῶν ὀλίγων πᾶσι τοῖς ἐναίμοις, ἐν δὲ τοῖς ζῳοτόκοις πᾶσιν.

womb; it serves as a passage for the semen of the male. In both sexes
the urethra serves as an outlet for the liquid residue.'[140] He encloses
the word 'urethra' in inverted commas presumably to indicate that
Aristotle does not mean to use the word in its proper sense here. The
only evidence for this interpretation is our own knowledge that the
urethra does not lie directly outside the womb. In fact, the urethra
and vagina in other female mammals do share the same external
orifice, but had Aristotle made an even cursory examination of a
human female he would have discovered that this was not the case in
all Vivipara 'without exception'. It may be that such intimate examination, even of his own wife, was taboo for a non-medical investi-
gator, but Aristotle could have asked his wife to make the
examination herself. His usually astute readings in contemporary
medical literature should also have suggested this anatomical fact
to him. Aristotle did not assimilate this knowledge because what
would here seem to be a legitimate difference between man and
woman, unlike the spurious differences he lists elsewhere, would
make a woman superior in some respect by the further specialization
of her body to separate her two fluid residues. This is one difference
Aristotle simply failed to register because he did not expect it or
think of looking for it: it went against one of his most basic tenets.
Had he noticed it, of course, it would not have caused him to re-
evaluate his opinion of the inferiority of the female. His theory
would have developed to accommodate this apparent anomaly.

HAIR GROWTH

The seemingly most superficial of physical differences between men
and women, that men are on the whole hairier, is credited to a man's
greater volume and agitation of semen by the author of *Nat. Puer.* 20
(vii. 506. 23–510. 17). Hair, he claims, needs moisture (primarily
semen) to grow, and the reason humans have so much on their heads
is because that is where the semen is stored and the epidermis is most
porous. Secondary body hair first makes its appearance at puberty
around the genital area as a direct result of the agitation of semen in
the body and the flesh in this area becoming more porous. According
to this author, women have some semen, but not as much as males,

---

[140] οὐρήθρα ἔξω τῶν ὑστερῶν, δίοδος τῷ σπέρματι τῷ τοῦ ἄρρενος, τοῦ δ'
ὑγροῦ περιττώματος ἀμφοῖν ἔξοδος.

nor does it become agitated throughout the whole body, so the genital area is the only place where secondary body hair grows. On the other hand, during intercourse the agitated semen of a man has to pass from his brain through the length of his body. Hair grows on his chin and chest because he is normally facing downwards and these project beyond the straight course of the semen and so act as reservoirs which have to be filled up before the semen can continue on its journey.[141] The same theory is used to explain why men become bald and women do not. The semen in the brain, in becoming agitated, heats up the phlegm which burns through the roots of the hair on the head. The theory is consistent within itself and with the observed physical differences between men and women. It is predicated upon the assumption that men derive greater pleasure from intercourse (a view not held universally in the ancient world) and that they will normally face downwards during the act of intercourse, though the theory can obviously accommodate men with hairy backs too.

Aristotle thought hair grew when moisture was able to seep through the skin and evaporate, leaving an earthy precipitate behind. Humans divert a greater amount of their nourishment to producing a greater volume of seminal residue in accordance with their size than do other animals, so there is not as much nourishment left over to be diverted into hair, nor is their flesh as loose-textured.[142] We have most hair on our heads because the brain is the moistest part of the body and the sutures in the skull allow the fluid to seep through.[143] Pubic hair grows when the seminal fluids begin to be produced because the flesh is less firm in the genital area.[144] At *GA* 782^{b}18, Aristotle states that it is because the brain is fluid and cold that it causes most hair growth.[145] From these considerations the adult man would seem to be the most fluid, cold, and loose-textured member of the human race. However, Aristotle attributes the hairier appearance of the adult male in comparison with other humans to the fact that women, children, and eunuchs are unable to concoct semen, which men can do because of their heat. He does not explain further, but it would seem that he imagines the semen in a man's body coming near the surface at times and being encouraged to evaporate by the man's heat, while a woman's unused fluid residue

---

[141] Cf. pseud.-Arist. *Prob.* 893^{b}10–17. 　　　　　[142] *GA* 728^{b}19–23.
[143] *PA* 658^{b}2–6. 　　　　　　　　　　　　　　　[144] *GA* 728^{b}26–7.
[145] And at *GA* 783^{a}23–7 Arist. says sea-urchins produce long spines because they are too cold to concoct nourishment and have to use up the residue.

remains as blood in the interior of her cold body.[146] Men go bald at the front of their heads because this is where semen is stored. Hair begins to drop out after sexual activity begins because the emission of semen results in a deficiency of hot fluid.[147] Again, one could ask why women, children, and eunuchs do not begin to go bald much more readily than men as they are always deficient in hot fluid. Aristotle has difficulty in attaining consistency in his theory of hair growth because while adult men produce more they also lose more, and he wants both to be indications of male superiority.

SUMMARY

To summarize: the sexual differentiae of menstruation and breasts are accounted for in Hippocratic theory by the nature of female flesh, and function together with the womb as a prophylactic system in a woman's body. They are utilized in procreation, but they are the result of a difference between men and women which does not have sexual generation as its sole purpose. For this purpose men possess a penis and both women and men produce seed; as a man produces more and it becomes more agitated he produces more hair. In Hippocratic theory, therefore, there are two fundamental causes for the observable differences in male and female physiology and it is the difference between male and female flesh rather than that between reproductive fluids which dictates a woman's incapacity to perform in a man's world. Aristotle's theory is more economical in that it ties all differences to a man's naturally greater heat which allows him to concoct nourishment to a greater degree for the purposes of sexual reproduction.

Because this is one small difference, Aristotle considers women to be less 'Other' and more like men than the Hippocratics, but he can maintain this theory only while adhering to the principle of male superiority in every feature at the loss of some consistency (as in hair growth) and the neglect of some observable anatomical realities (as in the distinction of the urethra and the vagina). Because they thought woman was a completely different creature and not simply a substandard man, the Hippocratics did not have to look for a correspondence between all male and female body parts. They felt woman was inferior of course, but her 'Otherness' allowed her body

[146] Cf. *HA* 521^{a}24–5.   [147] *GA* 783^{b}9–784^{a}12.

to be defined more by its own parameters. However, because they thought a woman was so different, these parameters sometimes spread a little too widely (as in the case of spongy flesh and the 'Wandering Womb').

Hippocratic and Aristotelian models of a woman's interior space were inferred from observable phenomena such as menses and breasts, and analogy with such things as sponges and wineskins. In so far as the Classical Greeks did not dissect human bodies, they had no evidence to gainsay the societal assumption of female physiology and the extent to which it differed from the male. Comparisons with dismembered animals could give some testimony to what lay inside humans, but as there was no reason to think that humans bore any but a superficial resemblance to quadrupeds, the Greeks would naturally select those observations which confirmed their ideas about the human body and reject those that contradicted firmly established beliefs, e.g. the compartmentalized wombs of other mammals were taken as confirmation that the human womb had at least two compartments while the sedentary nature of most animal reproductive organs was never brought forward to challenge the belief in the 'Wandering Womb' in women. Such egregious errors in ancient theories about female anatomy were the result of wrong inferences stemming from presuppositions which the individual never thought to challenge, rather than a wilful neglect of the facts before his eyes.

However, menstrual blood itself does not remain part of a woman's internal environment: it becomes external and accessible to direct observation. As this information was available to the Hippocratics and Aristotle, they had more opportunity to rectify erroneous notions about when and in what quantity a normal woman bled; yet their statements on menstrual flow are frequently as mistaken as their pronouncements on more unverifiable matters. That women menstruate was the primary evidence upon which they based their theories of the unseen innards of a woman, but in turn these theories, themselves influenced by societal assumptions of the female, controlled their empirical observations of the amount, frequency and consistency of menstrual blood.

Both the Hippocratics and Aristotle posited what we would consider exceptionally heavy blood loss in normal, healthy women.
The Hippocratic gynaecological theories constructed a creature
whose entire flesh had the same quality as the glands in a man's
body, and one of these qualities was to release a lot of blood when
forced to give it up—'if you were to cut into one [i.e. a gland] it
would haemorrhage violently'.[148] As we have seen (see pp. 55–6
above), a woman's body was one big gland, with even spongier flesh
in those parts of her body corresponding to glandular parts in a
man—hence her more prominent breasts. As a woman did less work
than a man, she also had more unused nourishment to be soaked up
which had to be discharged from her body in the form of menses.
Because even the firm body of an active man produced some excess
moisture[149] (which was soaked up by the glands causing a slight
swelling of the breasts even in a male), the Hippocratics would be
looking for a woman to shed a large amount of blood. They thought
that women who regularly bled in small amounts were not bleeding
'as necessary' (ὡς χρεών, *Aër.* 21 (ii. 76. 4–5)).

Like the Hippocratics, Aristotle believed that woman used up less
of her nourishment than a man did of his in building her smaller
body and fuelling her less active life-style. Moreover, concoction
refined and reduced the volume of any residue, so the volume of a
woman's seminal material, being initially more abundant and then
less concocted, vastly exceeded that of a man. The degree of discrepancy is revealed at puberty by the descent of the seminal residues,
hitherto lodged around the heart; the chest region became emptier in
woman in proportion to her greater amount of residue and was
therefore more inflated by the *pneuma* emanating from the heart.
Aristotle would expect the amount of blood lost in menstruation to
exceed the amount of semen lost over the month by a quantity
reflecting the difference in the size of male and female breasts.

The quantity of a woman's blood loss had to be calculated from
the duration and intensity of her menstrual flow. *Mul.* 1. 6 (viii. 30.
6–11) is the fullest description we have of the menstrual bleeding of
a healthy woman:

[148] εἰ δὲ διατάμοις, αἱμορραγίη λάβρος, *Gland.* 1 (viii. 556. 4).
[149] *Gland.* 3 (viii. 556. 18–558. 7). *Morb.* 4. 45 (vii. 568. 13–16) says a man who is
inactive becomes ill because of excess moisture in his body, and *Salubr.* 5 (vi. 78. 3–80.
17) advises even healthy men to purge themselves regularly to avoid a build-up of
excess fluids.

88   *Female Anatomy and Physiology*

Menses flow most thickly and most abundantly during those days in the middle, but at the beginning and end of the menstrual period they are less in quantity and thinner in consistency. An average amount of menses for any healthy woman is about two Attic kotyls—or a little more or a little less—and this appears, moreover, for two or three days; a time longer or shorter than this is unhealthy and suggests barrenness.[150]

The passage goes on to say that a doctor should ascertain from each female patient the duration of her own normal flow; but the parameters for variance appear very narrow. If a healthy woman bleeds for more or less than two to three days disease and barrenness follow. To lose two kotyls (about one pint) of menstrual blood over the course of two to three days implies heavy bleeding indeed, and if two to three days is meant to represent the entire period, it is difficult to give much significance to the phrase 'those days in the middle'. *Septim./Oct.* 13 (vii. 458. 16–17) says that three days is the minimum length of a healthy period; *Mul.* 1. 37 (viii. 92. 2–3) refers to 'the first three days of menstruation' (τὰς μὲν ἐν ἀρχῇ ἡμέρας τρεῖς), as though more were to follow and *Nat. Mul.* 53 (vii. 394. 13) advises inserting a pessary on the third or fourth day of a woman's period without any indication that the bleeding should have ceased by then.[151] Aristotle too says that two to three days was a short time for a menstrual period.[152] These figures for the shortest duration of healthy menstruation are a day or so higher than modern research would put it,[153] but as his contemporaries do seem to view it as a lower limit, the author of *Mul.* 1. 6 may have intended his remark on two to three days to refer solely to the heavy part of the flow—'the middle days'—the length of the entire period to be calculated by adding the lighter days on each side.

The accepted upper limit for the duration of a menstrual period in antiquity is not clear, though references to periods lasting longer than normal indicate that there was one. Occasionally 'longer than normal' might refer to a patient's aberrant flow in comparison to her own healthy period, as at *Nat. Mul.* 13 (vii. 330. 12–13) or *Aph.* 5. 57 (iv. 552. 11) but the statement at *Steril.* 213 (viii. 412. 24–414. 3) that

[150] χωρέει δὲ τὰ καταμήνια παχύτατα καὶ πλεῖστα τῶν ἡμερέων τῇσιν ἐν μέσῳ, ἀρχόμενα δὲ καὶ τελευτῶντα ἐλάσσονα καὶ λεπτότερα. μέτρια δ' ἐστὶ πάσῃ γυναικὶ χωρέειν, ἢν ὑγιαίνῃ, τὰ ἐπιμήνια ἐλθόντα ὅσον κοτύλαι δύο ἀττικαὶ ἢ ὀλίγῳ πλέονα ἢ ἐλάσσονα, ταῦτα δὲ ἐφ' ἡμέρας δύο ἢ τρεις· ὁ δὲ πλείων χρόνος ἢ ἐλάσσων ἐπίνοσος καὶ ἄφορός ἐστι.

[151] Cf. *Mul.* 1. 19 (viii. 58. 10).   [152] *HA* 582^b5–6.

[153] Mackay *et al.* 1983, 65.

some women menstruate longer than normal by nature and not as the result of an illness shows that the number of days which constituted a normal period was an arbitrary figure set up for all women regardless of those who regularly went beyond it when they were not ill. The situation is similar in our own society. Modern research has set the upper limit for a regular, healthy menstrual period at about eight days, but as the average and the mean is much nearer five days,[154] a woman who regularly menstruates for over a week might be said in layman's terms to have an abnormally long period. The ancient evidence reflects the same attitude; there was an average length for a period around which most women clustered and which the Hippocratics and Aristotle continued to class as normal, though they knew that women could lie beyond the boundaries in each direction without being pathological. The number of days continued to be the most flexible of ancient criteria in determining whether a woman's period was healthy or not. Soranus at *Gyn.* I. 21 says a woman has menstruated in the right measure if she feels healthy afterwards, and this can cover anything from one to seven days. As his gynaecological theories allowed for a woman using up much, and in some cases all, of her menstrual material in exercise, and therefore did not necessarily predict heavy blood loss, he could accommodate a shorter menstrual period in a healthy woman.

More important than the number of days a woman menstruated was that she should lose the right amount of blood during that time. The figure that *Mul.* I. 6 gives as the normal amount of blood lost during menstruation is two kotyls. This is about one pint and therefore seven to eight times what is considered the normal amount today, but commensurable with the Hippocratic expectation of heavy blood loss. Even Soranus mentions this inordinate quantity, though he does add that it is the absolute maximum amount of the flux.[155] King remarks that this is 'an excessively large amount by modern standards and most unlikely'.[156] Liddell, Scott, and Jones thought it so unlikely that they suggest that κοτύλη could be used to refer not only to the usual half-pint measure, but in this case alone to an eighth of a pint, though a quarter pint would still give an excessive reading. Hanson recognized that this was an unsatisfactory

[154] Asso 1983, 18. A World Health Organization report, 'Women's bleeding patterns: ability to recall and predict menstrual events', *Studies in Family Planning*, 12 (1981), 17–27, has suggested that cultural factors may affect the length of bleeding.
[155] *Gyn.* I. 20. [156] King 1985, 135.

explanation and commented 'the discrepancy may be due to inaccurate methods of measuring or estimating the quantity of menses or any number of other factors.'[157] But an inaccurate method of collecting and measuring menses would be more likely to result in a failure to record all the two to three ounces rather than a magnification of them by such a large margin. It is true that people tend to exaggerate their own blood loss,[158] and women may have described their menstrual blood flow as being heavier than it actually was. Moreover, it takes only a small amount of liquid to produce a large stain, so estimation of blood loss based on menstrual cloths would also tend to the high side. However, the quantification at two kotyls is not an arbitrary figure used by the Hippocratics simply to represent 'a lot'.

The Hippocratics did not (and could not) know that menstrual blood was only the discarded lining of the womb. Their theories assume that in order to provide the best drainage of a woman's over-moist flesh the womb was filled to capacity with blood at each menstrual period. At *Mul.* 1. 1 (viii. 12. 2–4) the author remarks that women whose bodies have not been broken down by the lochia feel more pain when they are menstruating because the stoma is less open than in other women. Since the blood flowed into the womb faster than it flowed out even in women who had given birth, a womb that was not open very wide would become engorged to the point of pain. The Hippocratic doctors, therefore, estimated the amount of blood a healthy woman should lose by the amount of fluid they thought the average non-pregnant womb could hold. Now, one of the therapies recommended for various gynaecological complaints was to irrigate the womb with a clyster administered through the cervix (not, it should be noted, a vaginal douche). They regularly warn against administering a clyster to the womb of over two kotyls. 'Administer a clyster of two kotyls at most: do not use more when administering any clyster.'[159] 'A clyster of more than two kotyls

---

[157] Hanson 1975, n. 12.

[158] 'There is ... no correlation between measured menstrual blood loss and subjective assessments of blood loss', Jones–Wentz–Burnett 1988, 379.

[159] κλύσαι δὲ δύο κοτύλῃσι τὸ πλεῖστον· πάντα δὲ τὰ κλύσματα μὴ πλέονι κλύζειν, *Mul.* 1. 78 (viii. 190. 3–4). At 194. 13–15 in the same chapter a clyster recipe calls for four kotyls of wine or boiled milk to be mixed with wild cucumbers, but the mixture is to be strained before injection into the womb, and *Mul.* 1. 80 (viii. 200. 18–21) repeats the same recipe with the instruction to mix narcissus oil with what had been strained off before injection.

should be used on practically no one.'[160] A clyster of more than two
kotyls is used in the case of phlegmatic women, but then the author
indicates that this exceeds the normal amount. 'Irrigate the womb, if
necessary, with a clyster of more than two kotyls.'[161] The average
volume of a non-pregnant womb is two to three ounces, though it
obviously can expand enormously.[162] It would be possible to infuse
a pint of fluid into a non-pregnant womb, although the woman
would have to be practically upside down to prevent the fluid
coming back out through the dilated cervix, and a good part of the
fluid would pass through the Fallopian tubes into the body cavity.[163]
The procedure would cause extreme discomfort long before the pint
mark was reached, but this in and of itself would not deter the
Hippocratics from using the full two kotyls because of the amount
of material they knew a womb could hold when pregnant. Alternatively, the Hippocratics may never have intended the two kotyls
from the clyster to remain in the womb all at once. *Steril.* 222 (vii.
430. 15–16) says that when using a clyster of milk to wash out pus
from the womb, a doctor can tell the treatment has been successful
when the pus no longer comes out along with the milk. The amount
of two kotyls would still be significant in matching the amount of a
therapeutical clyster with the amount of pathological fluid (or re
tained menses) a womb was generally thought capable of holding.

Aristotle does not state what he considers to be the normal
volume of blood of one month's menstruation, but he thought it
heavy enough to cause a woman's paleness and deficiency of physique (*GA* 727^{a}22–5). At *GA* 728^{b}15 he says that woman produces
the largest amount of any animal, and at *HA* 573^{a}7 he estimates the
amount of menses a cow produces before copulation at half a kotyl.
In the same passage he states explicitly that he believes that besides
women all female quadrupeds who bend their hind legs inwards
menstruate. In this he is obviously confusing the menstrual cycle of
humans with the oestrus cycle or 'heat' of other mammals. Oestrus
serves a completely different purpose and does indeed involve much

[160] πλέον δὲ κλύσμα δύο κοτύλαι μηδενὶ ὡς ἔπος εἰπεῖν, *Mul.* 2. 209 (viii. 404.
21–406. 1).
[161] κλύζε δὲ, ἢν δέῃ, κλυσμῷ πλέον ἢ δυσὶ κοτύλαις, *Nat. Mul.* 33 (vii. 370.
11–12).
[162] Gohari–Berkowitz–Hobbins 1977, 257, gives a normal volume towards the end
of pregnancy as 4,500 ml, approximately 1,521 fl. oz.
[163] Personal communication from Austin Women's Medical Centre and Dr John
Maxwell. As this procedure is no longer practised it proved very difficult to get
information on it.

less blood loss than menstruation (and a great deal less than half a kotyl or quarter of a pint), so if Aristotle directly compared a woman's menses to other animals' oestrus it is not surprising that he commented upon the abundance of the flux, especially as he expected there to be a large amount from the size of a woman's breasts. It would have been possible for both the Hippocratics and Aristotle to make a more accurate estimate of menstrual blood loss from observation, if not collection, and from this to revise theories on how little of the nourishment she ingested a woman actually utilized compared to a man. Instead, they took society's evaluation of woman and her lifestyle as the facts that accounted for a heavy blood loss which they never thought to dispute.

The amount of blood a woman was thought to lose during her menstrual flow appears to have been constant no matter how long or short that period was. *Steril.* 213 (viii. 408. 15–16, 412. 1) remarks that while a sparse flow can last many days an abundant menstrual flow lasts a short period. Aristotle says that the blood in a woman's womb can flow away from her copiously or little by little.[164] The speed of the blood loss depends on whether the stoma is more open or closed, but the amount of blood that the womb can hold and draw to itself for discharge each month is finite. All orifices of a woman's body were thought to be connected in some way to her womb, and if she discharged blood through any of them, because of the limited amount of blood to be lost, her menses were either depleted or completely suppressed: 'Speaking generally, unless the menstrual discharge is suspended, women are not troubled by haemorrhoids or bleeding from the nose or any other such discharge, and if it happens that they are, then the evacuations fall off in quantity, which suggests that the substance secreted is being drawn off to the other discharges.'[165]

King, however, has drawn attention to a couple of remarks which seem to suggest that the amount of blood which could be lost was not always so finite:[166] 'If, contrary to nature, the womb gapes open, the menses flow more heavily, are sticky [congealed?] and frequent.

[164] *HA* 582ᵇ7–8.
[165] ὡς γὰρ ἐπὶ τὸ πολὺ οὔθ' αἱμορροΐδες γίνονται ταῖς γυναιξὶν οὔτ' ἐκ τῶν ῥινῶν ῥύσις αἵματος οὔτε τι ἄλλο μὴ τῶν καταμηνίων ἱσταμένων· ἐάν τε συμβῇ τι τούτων, χείρους γίγνονται αἱ καθάρσεις ὡς μεθισταμένης εἰς ταῦτα τῆς ἀποκρίσεως, *GA* 727ᵃ12–16. Cf. *Mul.* I. 2 (viii. 20. 25–22. 1); *Aph.* 5. 32, 33, 50 (iv. 542. 14, 544. 1–2, 550. 5–6); *Morb.* I. 7 (vi. 152. 20–2).
[166] King 1985, 135–6, 142.

... If the mouth of the womb gapes wide more than is natural during menstruation, the menses are heavier, worse in every way, more liquid and flow for a longer period.'[167] The menstrual flow resulting from the stoma of the womb opening more than usual can be either 'more' and 'occurring frequently' (πλέονα and θαμινά), or 'more' and 'extending over a longer period' (πλείω and διὰ πλείονος χρόνου). It is easy to explain why a stoma that was open too much should cause a heavier period than usual (the blood would gush out all at once instead of seeping out more gradually as at *Steril.* 213); but for a blood loss heavier than normal to occur frequently or to continue for a longer time than usual requires that there be a larger amount of blood to be discharged.

The characterization of the blood in abundant menses that flow for a longer period of time as 'more liquid' (ὑγρότερα), and in those that occur more frequently as 'sticky' or 'congealed' (γλίσχρα) provide a partial answer to the problem. In the first case the volume of fluid is increased by the blood being more dilute than usual, so the womb would have to expand more than it usually does in a non-pregnant woman to hold the extra fluid. In this case the excessive opening of the womb is said to take place only once a month, during menstruation. In such a situation, even if the womb shed a large amount of blood every day through the stoma opening more widely than usual, it would still take longer for it to shed all its fluid. In the second case, if the blood was more than normally compacted, the womb would be holding more actual blood, even if it only drew the same volume of fluid to itself when the body became full. Since, in this instance, the womb's gaping contrary to nature is not confined solely to the time of the menstrual period, the abundant blood could flow out heavily at any point during the month when the womb was drawing the blood to itself from the body—hence explaining the larger amount of blood flowing at a greater frequency. However, it is difficult to account for an open womb in and of itself causing the body to produce an increased quantity of blood which is either more liquid or more congealed than usual. The author seems to have been describing the sort of menstrual flow that resulted from a stoma opened more widely than usual when it

[167] ἢν παρὰ φύσιν αἱ μῆτραι χάνωσι, τὰ ἐπιμήνια χωρέει πλέονα καὶ γλί-σχρα καὶ θαμινά. ... ἢν τὸ στόμα τῶν μητρέων ἀναχάνη μᾶλλον ἢ ὡς πέφυκεν ἐν τοῖς ἐπιμηνίοις, τὰ ἐπιμήνια γίνονται πλείω καὶ κακίω πάντα καὶ ὑγρότερα καὶ διὰ πλείονος χρόνου, *Mul.* 2. 166, 167 (viii. 344. 12–13, 22–4).

coincided with the production of blood of an abnormal type, and there is no evidence that he disagreed with Aristotle and the author of *Steril.* that normal blood in conjunction with an open stoma would lead to a short but heavy period.

FREQUENCY OF MENSTRUATION

The theory that menstruation could take place more often than usual presupposes an accepted standard frequency for menstruation. Modern research has indicated that a normal menstrual cycle can take anywhere from twenty-one to thirty-five days to complete,[168] and although nowadays the average cycle lasts about twenty-nine and a half days, this is a phenomenon of improved nutrition in post-industrial society; in earlier periods of history the average cycle was probably much longer.[169] However, there must always have been many (which is not to say most)[170] women who did menstruate at fairly regular monthly intervals. It is only after a culture has identified menstruation as a monthly occurrence that it can then go on to connect it with the phases of the moon, as so many societies do.[171] Words for menstrual blood in Greek and Latin (καταμήνια and *menses*) show that ancient Mediterranean society did expect it to flow monthly. Soranus at *Gyn.* i. 19 claims that menses were given the name ἐπιμήνια because this was the word for a sailor's monthly rations and the menses acted as monthly rations for the growing foetus.

Both the Hippocratics and Aristotle thought women who menstruated more often than once a month were ill in some way.[172] If it is

[168] Mackay *et al.* 1983, 65. 1–2% of women can have regular cycles outside these limits.

[169] Asso 1983, 17, 90, 148.

[170] Rousselle 1988, 37, implies that women in ancient Greece would not have had many menstrual periods at all because they would have spent most of their reproductive life in a state of pregnancy and breast-feeding. The concern of the Hippocratic gynaecological treatises with women who had not conceived does not support this interpretation. Even in contemporary Western society, the infertility rate among healthy couples is about 15% (1 in 7), see Jones–Wentz–Burnett 1988, 263.

[171] Préaux 1970, 89, argues that the ancient Greek connection between menses and the moon was originally one of sympathy (both were cycles of repletion and diminution) rather than observed periodic coincidence. However, to say women had a cycle like the moon's need not lead to saying that their cycle was synchronized with the moon's, as some Classical Greeks appear to have believed. Moreover, the Greek term for menstruation suggests the regular periodic measure rather than the waxing and waning nature of the moon's cycle, cf. Préaux 1970, 66.

[172] *Nat. Mul.* 16 (vii. 336. 1–5); *Mul.* i. 57 (viii. 114. 8–13); *HA* 582^{b}25.

true that improved nutrition has shortened the average menstrual cycle, few women in antiquity were likely to have had regular cycles which repeated in under a month, and medical and scientific opinion that bleeding twice in one month was an indication of disease was probably based on more than the culture's beliefs, though it is possible that they attempted to cure perfectly healthy women whose cycle was naturally shorter than four weeks.[173]

The same ancient medical opinion, with perhaps less basis in the ancient world than it had for insisting that women should not menstruate *more* than once a month, firmly endorsed the cultural belief that women should menstruate regularly once a month. 'But females use a regimen that is moister and less strenuous besides purging the heat out of their bodies every month.'[174] Concerning a pregnant woman: 'if the womb gapes open more than it should, it releases the blood each month, just as it has been accustomed to do in the past.'[175] However, because amenorrhoea can be one of the earliest signs of pregnancy, which the Hippocratics did all in their power to promote, it is unlikely that an extended menstrual cycle by itself would call down upon a woman who was sexually active the battery of Hippocratic measures for dealing with suppressed menses—since they would not wish inadvertently to cause an abortion.[176] There would have to be a significant time lapse without any menstrual blood and without any other sign of pregnancy or with some signs of an illness before a woman was thought to require the services of a doctor. If there was no reason to believe a woman could be pregnant, these services might be called into play much sooner, simply to deal with a cycle that was longer than the canonical month.

There are indications in the texts that ancient theorists intended the menstrual period to take place at exactly rather than roughly monthly intervals. The author of *Septim./Oct.* 9 (vii. 448. 5–7) states:

[173] There may have been a few women, as now, who bled fairly heavily at ovulation. Some women bleed so heavily at ovulation that they describe themselves as menstruating twice a month, see Jones–Wentz–Burnett 1988, 260. If this is a regular phenomenon it need not be pathological.

[174] τὰ δὲ θήλεα ὑγροτέρῃσι καὶ ῥᾳθυμοτέρῃσι τῇσι διαίτῃσι χρέονται, καὶ κάθαρσιν τοῦ θερμοῦ ἐκ τοῦ σώματος ἑκάστου μηνὸς ποιέονται, *Vict.* i. 34 (vi. 512. 17–19).

[175] ἢν δὲ χάνωσιν αἱ μῆτραι μᾶλλον τοῦ καιροῦ, παραμεθίασι τοῦ αἵματος κατὰ μῆνα, ὥσπερ εἴωθε χωρέειν, *Mul.* i. 25 (viii. 66. 1–3). Cf. *Mul.* i. 1 (viii. 14. 2–3); *GA* 767ᵃ2–6.

[176] See pp. 172–5 below, for the Hippocratic recognition of amenorrhoea as an early sign of pregnancy, and the claim that women could tell the instant they conceived because the seed did not fall out.

'In healthy women the menses appear every month, because the month has a particular power over the body.'[177] The Hippocratic authors do not direct their treatises at any one *polis* (state), so we must assume that when they use the term 'month' they are referring to a lunar month (lunation) as this would be the only month universally recognized among the ancient Greek *poleis* (who all had their own calendars). *Prorrh.* 2. 24 (ix. 54. 14–15) says a woman should be so regular that she menstruates on the same days each month.[178] If she menstruated at irregular intervals, she might not only be unsure whether or not she was pregnant[179] but also have difficulty in conceiving. It would seem that because a woman's regimen (unlike a man's) did not vary enormously from month to month, her body was thought to produce and store menstrual blood at the same rate throughout the year,[180] and therefore to reach the point where it needed to be emptied on the same day each month. Aristotle expected a woman to menstruate at regular monthly intervals because he believed that Nature aimed at measuring all things by 'periods': day, night, month, year, and times measured by these.[181] Again, as Aristotle refers to Nature's periods he must mean the lunar rather than any calendar month.

[177] τὰ καταμήνια τῇσι γυναιξὶ τῇσιν ὑγιαινούσῃσι φαίνεται καθ' ἕκαστον τῶν μηνῶν, ὡς ἔχοντος τοῦ μηνὸς ἰδίην δύναμιν ἐν τοῖσι σώμασιν.

[178] Cf. *Mul.* 1. 4, 2. 128, 133 (viii. 26. 5, 11, 274. 17, 298. 3–4); *Nat. Mul.* 59 (vii. 398. 7).

[179] See *Epid.* 4. 21 (v. 160. 15–162. 1).

[180] Though both Hes. *Op.* 582–9, and Arist. *HA* 542ª32, say that women desire intercourse more during the summer, so the heat was thought to have some effect on women's moistness and/or coldness, cf. pseudo-Arist., *Prob.* 879ª26–35, 880ª11–22.

[181] *GA* 777ᵇ17–30. An early passage in Arist.'s biology, *HA* 582ᵇ3–4, disputes the idea that all women menstruate regularly every month: 'And while in a few cases the menses come regularly every month, in the majority of cases they come every third month' (καὶ ταῖς μὲν συνεχῶς καθ' ἕκαστον ὀλιγάκις τὰ καταμήνια φοιτᾷ, παρὰ δὲ μῆνα τρίτον ταῖς πλείσταις). In his commentary on this passage, Louis explains this statement as a result of correct observation and inclusive reckoning. Arist. noticed that women usually menstruated at intervals longer than 29 days. If a menstrual period was counted as marking the end of one month and the 29 days that followed without a menstrual period as the second month, the next period would be said to take place in the third month. But *Mul.* 1. 2 (viii. 16. 3) uses the phrase 'in the third month' (ἐν δὲ τοῖσι τρίτοισιν) to signify menstruation which occurs after one period has been missed, not regular monthly menstruation. Moreover, while it is true that the Greeks did count inclusively, the use of the preposition παρά seems to indicate a particular way of enumerating time periods. Arrian used καθ' ἡμέραν, παρ' ἡμέραν, παρὰ δύο, παρὰ τρεῖς to mean, 'every day, every second, every third, and every fourth day' (*Epict.* 2. 18. 13), and παρὰ τρία in *IG* V (2), 422 probably means every fourth year. If a Greek said women menstruated παρὰ δὲ μῆνα τρίτον he would mean that they menstruated every fourth month, i.e. three times a year. Arist. may have been aware of many women who did menstruate infrequently and, at an

Many statements suggest that in antiquity it was widely believed
not only that the lunar and menstrual cycles were the same length,
but that the one controlled the other. The statement in *Septim./Oct.*
9 on the month's 'particular power' (*ἰδίην δύναμιν*) over the body
would seem to suggest the correspondence of a woman's menstrual
period to a particular phase of the moon—though it could also (less
probably) mean simply that the period of twenty-nine and a half
days was significant for the body. At *Gyn.* 1. 21 Soranus reports
Diocles and Empedocles as saying that all women menstruated with
the waning moon, though Soranus himself does not subscribe to this
belief.[182] Now, the ideal for a respectable Athenian man of the
Classical period was to be wealthy enough to have no need for his
women to leave the home, and there is some modern evidence that
women who live in close quarters with each other, especially if they
are confined and their day is controlled largely by artificial light,
can become synchronized in their menstrual cycles.[183] It is therefore
conceivable that the wife, concubine, daughters, and female slaves
of many families did menstruate at about the same time, and as it is
unlikely that the average Greek man inquired into the menstrual
cycle of households other than his own this may have given support
to the belief that all women menstruated at the same time. But even
if we allow that women within a household became synchronized in
their menstruation, this is not sufficient to explain the further notion
that menstruation tended to coincide with the waning moon. Even
Aristotle accepts this as the norm: 'Also the fact that the menstrual
discharge in the natural course tends to take place when the moon is
waning is due to the same cause. That time of month is colder and
more fluid on account of the waning and failure of the moon.'[184] He
rationalized this belief by saying that the moon's waxing and waning
caused temperatures on the earth to rise and fall respectively and
that women released their blood at the coldest time of the month.

earlier period of his thought, have tried to explain menstrual periodicity by tying it to the
cycle of the seasons (i.e. spring, summer, and winter). Whatever the reason for his calcu-
lation, it may be connected with Pliny's assertion at *NH* 7. 66, that although women
menstruate once a month, their flow is heavier at three-month intervals, *et hoc tale tan-
tumque omnibus tricenis diebus malum in muliere exsistit et trimenstri spatio largius.*

[182] The belief, however, was still current in later antiquity. Galen reports it as a
fact at *Dieb. Dec.* 3. 2.

[183] Asso 1983, 7.

[184] *καὶ τὸ γίνεσθαι δὲ τὰ καταμήνια κατὰ φύσιν φθινόντων τῶν μηνῶν μᾶλλον
διὰ τὴν αὐτὴν αἰτίαν συμβαίνει. ψυχρότερος γὰρ ὁ χρόνος οὗτος τοῦ μηνὸς καὶ
ὑγρότερος διὰ τὴν φθίσιν καὶ τὴν ἀπόλειψιν τῆς σελήνης, GA* 767[a]2–6.

He does admit that some women do not conform to this pattern, but rather than using them to challenge his culture's assumption, he classes them as exceptions to the rule.[185] The Hippocratics never explicitly refute the belief that all women menstruate at the same time, but they are less willing to commit themselves to supporting it. This could be a direct result of their having intimate knowledge of more than one household. It should have become obvious to them very rapidly that whether or not one woman was menstruating could not be used to predict whether another woman would be. Whenever their therapies have to be administered just before or at the onset of menstruation, they advise action with regard to the regular time or the actual appearance of the menses without any reference to the moon to indicate when this time should be.[186] As they do not appear to have believed in synchronicity between all women, it would seem even less likely that they would posit synchronicity between women and the moon. The author of *Nat. Puer.* 15 (vii. 494. 10–13), however, explains that a woman's menstruation is controlled by the environment beyond herself: 'In the first place, the blood in the body is set in agitation each month by the following cause. There is a great difference in temperature between month and month. Now, a woman's body has more fluid than that of a man and is therefore sensitive to this change.'[187] This not only suggests that all women menstruated at the same time, but that the time was controlled by the temperature change from month to month. It would therefore seem legitimate to assume that the author was referring to the same tradition as Aristotle, and believed that a woman lost her blood during the coldest part of the month, i.e. during the waning moon.

Septim./Oct. 13 (vii. 458. 11–460. 9) is another Hippocratic passage which implies synchronicity of menstruation without stating it in so many words. The author argues that most women conceive after their menstrual period (which takes at least three days, usually a lot longer) and that the process of conception takes the same amount of time.[188] Beginning his calculations from the new moon (*neomēniē*),

[185] Ibid. 738ᵃ17–21.
[186] e.g. *Mul.* 1. 74 (viii. 154. 12–13); cf. *Nat. Mul.* 59 (vii. 398. 7).
[187] πρῶτα μὲν ταράσσεται τὸ αἷμα ἐν τῷ σώματι κατὰ μῆνα ἕκαστον, ὑπὸ ἀνάγκης τοιῆσδε· ὅτι μὴν μηνὸς διαφέρει πουλὺ καὶ κατὰ ψύξιν καὶ κατὰ θερμασίην, καὶ τούτου αἰσθάνεται τῆς γυναικὸς τὸ σῶμα, ὑγρότερον γάρ ἐστιν ἢ τὸ τοῦ ἀνδρός.
[188] On the process of conception see pp. 172–6 below.

he concludes that most women conceive around the 'half-month' (*dichomēniē*), i.e. the full moon. If *neomēniē* and *dichomēniē* are used in their usual sense, it would seem that this author thinks women begin menstruating on the new moon. And even if the terms are here being used in the technical sense (found nowhere else) of 'the beginning of the menstrual cycle' and 'the middle of the menstrual cycle' and have no bearing on the actual phase of the lunar cycle, the two cycles must have been thought to coincide at one time for the medical sense of the terms to develop.[189] The author counts the first day of menstrual bleeding as the first day of the menstrual cycle; and if the author thought this coincided with the first day of the lunar month he would expect women to menstruate with the waxing moon. His aim in including this chapter is to contradict popular opinion and demonstrate that most women conceive in the second part of the month. This implies that popular opinion held that most women became pregnant at the beginning of the month, i.e. that they had finished menstruating at the end of the previous month.[190] This would indicate that the common belief was that menstruation took place during the waning moon, and would identify *neomēniē* (the first day of the menstrual cycle if the term had a specialized sense in common parlance) as the first day after the menstrual bleeding. This seems instinctively more likely as the Greeks looked on menstruation as the end result of a process rather than itself causing the next stage of the cycle. It would also seem more likely that the Greeks would use the terminology of the new moon (an auspicious day[191]) to refer to the more auspicious segment of the menstrual cycle. It therefore seems likely that any popular synchronization of *neomēniē* and *dichomēniē* with the menstrual cycle reflects the same theory as Diocles, Empedocles, Aristotle, and the Hippocratic *Nat. Puer.*—that women menstruate with the waning moon.

[189] The author makes a point of commenting that the *neomēniē* lasts one day, which suggests that the term held primarily astronomical connotations. It would be tautologous to remark that the first day of a woman's period lasted one day, but the period of the new moon could be defined as anything from when the actual conjunction of the moon and sun took place to the first observed appearance of the new crescent. This was usually one or two days, but in exceptional cases could be three, see van der Waerden 1960, 169.

[190] The belief that the best time for conception, or at least 'fertilization', was right at the end of the menstrual period seems to have been widespread, e.g. *Mul.* 1. 17 (viii. 56. 16–17); *Nat. Puer.* 15 (vii. 494. 18–20); *GA* 727^{b}10–14, 23–5; *HA* 582^{b}11–12. The new moon was considered the best time for marriages at Athens, see Préaux 1970, 99.

[191] See Préaux 1970, 86–7.

The theory that women's bodies were influenced by the external environment explained why all women should be expected to menstruate at the same time; but the fact remains that although the women in a Greek household could all have menstruated around the same time, it would only be by coincidence that this synchronization would coincide with the waning moon. Nor does the admission that not all women conform to this norm have the same force as similar disclaimers. Preconceived notions of the 'normal' duration of a menstrual period or length of a menstrual cycle could have been confirmed by observation of the majority of women, which would mean that those falling outside the mean or average could legitimately be classed as exceptions. There is, however, nothing inherent to the menstrual cycle which would confirm the expectation that the majority of women bled during the waning moon. That Aristotle, and perhaps some Hippocratics, adhered to this ideology in spite of what they saw, raises the possibility that the belief had been absorbed into Greek culture at a very fundamental level and still played an important role in the structure of that society.

The moon had always been associated with women in popular mythology; *HA* 582^{a}34 says that some would argue that the moon itself was female from the fact that menses always occur during its waning phase. The waning of the moon was considered to be the most inauspicious time of the month for living things in general.[192] The presumed coldness of this phase of the month probably influenced this belief, as warmth was considered necessary for generation. Generally, the least fertile period for a woman was thought to be when her passages were full of blood and her womb more closed than usual, just before and during the first part of her menstrual period,[193] and husbands who wished either to promote or inhibit the production of heirs would presumably try to ascertain when this actually took place in the case of their particular wives. The fact that despite this, they assented to the belief that menstruation generally took place during the waning moon would seem to be the result of strong cultural conditioning. The Hippocratics and Aristotle were, on occasion, willing to reject what they considered mistaken superstitious beliefs. Those that they never thought to

---

[192] The author of the *Geoponica* remarks at 1. 6 and 5. 10 that many people believe that nothing should be planted during a waning moon, though he himself disagrees with them.

[193] *Mul.* 1. 24 (viii. 64. 3–5).

challenge but rather attempted to accommodate and explain must
have been more deeply rooted. It may be that the efficacy of many
female rituals (which were often of extreme importance to the state
in promoting fertility) depended upon the women being physically
in harmony with each other and the moon. Several scholars of
Greek religion have seen connections between the woman's annual
festival of the Thesmophoria and rites of menstrual seclusion in
other cultures.[194] Burkert comments, 'Naturally, this striking connection does not imply the biological miracle of a collective menstruation in some primitive age.' True: but it may indicate the desire to
believe in such a 'miracle' even in the Classical period. For whatever
the reason, the cultural need for this belief was so strong that it
influenced the theories of the Hippocratics and Aristotle, though
their incidental remarks show that they had observed that synchronicity was not universal.

QUALITY OF MENSTRUAL BLOOD

Ritual considerations may also have influenced the scientific observation of the consistency of menstrual blood once it had left a
woman's body. *Mul.* 1. 6 (viii. 30. 16–17) states: 'If a woman is
healthy, her blood flows like that from a sacrificial animal (*hiereion*)
and it speedily coagulates.'[195] *Mul.* 1. 72 (viii. 152. 7) and *Nat. Puer.*
18 (vii. 502. 6–7) make the same observation, almost verbatim, on
lochial blood. Menstrual and lochial blood is provided with an
anticoagulant and therefore quick clotting should give rise to
concern rather than optimism. However, it is the failure of menstrual blood to clot which is taken as a sign of illness in Hippocratic
gynaecology.[196] King 1987 demonstrated that in the Hippocratic
Corpus only the blood of a woman in her menses and lochia was
likened to that of a *hiereion* because the presentation of the first
woman to men coincided with the institution of sacrifice, and on her
first appearance Pandora was decked out like a beast about to be
slaughtered. Both sacrifice and woman serve to distance men from
the gods, but also offer the only means by which men can communicate with the gods and achieve immortality. In both sacrifice and

[194] Kerényi 1972, 126–7; Detienne 1979, 213; Burkert 1985, 245.
[195] χωρέει δὲ αἷμα οἷον ἀπὸ ἱερείου, καὶ ταχὺ πήγνυται, ἢν ὑγιαίνῃ ἡ γυνή.
[196] e.g. *Mul.* 1. 30, 61 (viii. 74. 11, 124. 7).

defloration it is men who shed blood and the beast or the woman
who bleeds. Woman was therefore felt to be like a sacrificial beast
in her origin and nature.

King's analysis is undoubtedly correct; however, it would be possible to compare the blood of a menstruating woman to that of a
sacrificial beast without appending the mistaken observation that
menstrual blood clotted quickly. *Mul.* 2. 113 (viii. 242. 9–10) likens a
morbid flow of blood, a 'reddish flux' (ῥόος ἐρυθρός), to the blood
of a sacrificial beast, using the term *neosphakton* for the victim, and
says that the blood sometimes contains 'shining clots' (θρομβία δια-
λάμποντα) and sometimes is simply a flux. This could be interpreted
as describing a flow that failed to coagulate, and since, in sacrificial
vocabulary, *neosphakton* refers explicitly to a beast that has just had
its throat slit,[197] the use of the analogy to characterize non-
coagulating blood would appear to be accurate.[198] Aristotle uses the
same image of the blood of a *neosphakton* to describe menstrual
blood at *HA* 581ᵇ1–2, presumably referring to its non-coagulating
quality. *Hiereion*, the term for a sacrificial victim which the Hippocratics use in their analogies characterizing normal menstrual blood,
was a general term which could be used of a sacrificial animal at any
type of sacrifice, or at any point during a sacrifice—even up to the
animal being served as meat. Unlike a *sphagion*, a *hiereion* was
usually destined to be consumed. The role of blood was not essential
in the concept of a *hiereion* as it was in that of a *sphagion*.[199] The blood
of a *hiereion* (unlike that of most sacrifices, which would be cleared
away as soon as possible[200]) would have time to congeal while the
animal was being dressed for consumption, and it is to this blood that
the Hippocratics compare the menstrual and lochial blood of a
healthy woman.

If the blood of a sacrificial victim clotted quickly it would
signify that the animal had been healthy and would be an
auspicious sign for the well-being of the city.[201] The blood of a
healthy man who was injured would presumably also clot quickly,

[197] Casabona 1966, 194 and n. 56.
[198] Aretaeus, *SA* 2. 11, indicates that the blood of a *sphagion* was not thought to
clot when he likens sudden death due to a fatal haemorrhage to the slaughter
(*sphagē*) of an animal.
[199] Casabona 1966, 30–4.   [200] See Girard 1978, 36–7.
[201] Most specialists believe that signs taken from the blood were essential in the
sacrifices before battle, but we know no details of the signs the Greeks looked for.
Colour and flow are mentioned as criteria in the scholion to *Lys.* 203–5, see Pritchett

but this would not be a predictable, regular event and would be good news primarily for the man himself, so the clotting of male blood is never likened to that of a propitious animal sacrifice. A woman's healthy blood had wider, civic significance; it affirmed that she could replenish the citizen body as well as her own. Loraux has shown how closely in ancient Greece marriage and sacrifice interact in what she calls 'the deadly equation of nuptials and throat-cutting'.[202] She deals primarily with the tragic sacrifices of *parthenoi*, and states that, 'the virgins cannot fight alongside the men, but, in times of peril, their blood flows so that the community of *andres* [men] may live.'[203] In times of peace, a *parthenos* shed her blood at defloration/marriage, but this was simply the first of many occasions when a woman would bleed and show herself ready to replenish the community of *andres*. Loraux's comment, 'Once one immerses one-self in the medical thought of the Greeks ... one can find no way of rejoining the tragic universe',[204] is contradicted here. The events in women's lives in the gynaecology may be less dramatic than those of tragic heroines, but the Hippocratics endowed their blood with the same sacrificial significance.

It is in areas such as the amount, frequency, and quality of men-strual blood, where an author takes for granted 'facts' which are open to direct contradiction, that we can see most clearly the contours of the cultural construct of the female within which the scientific texts were being produced. Women in the fifth and fourth centuries BC did not bleed more heavily, more often, or more thickly than contem-porary Western women; the theories that were developed to explain why they menstruated at all predicted a heavy, frequent, and quickly coagulating blood loss, and wherever possible scientists interpreted their observations to support their theories and classed contrary evidence as deviations from the norm.

THE MORE RAPID AGEING OF WOMEN

Another 'fact' which the Hippocratics and Aristotle state with confi-dence is that women reached puberty, maturity, and old age more

1979, 85–7. Pritchett remarks (87), 'Omens were taken from the colour of the blood and the manner of coagulation.' I am grateful to Professor M. H. Jameson for this reference.

[202] Loraux 1987, 38.   [203] Ibid. 34.   [204] Ibid. 61.

quickly than men.[205] This is in contrast to the development of male and female foetuses in the womb where the female is said to be much slower than the male in reaching critical stages (articulation, quickening, parturition). The beliefs about foetal development could not have been verified by empirical observation and are obviously simply a reflection of the cultural values of the inferior 'lazy' female. Saïd 1983, 108–9 (followed by King 1985, 133), attributes the belief in earlier female ageing also simply to cultural values. In the womb the foetuses are developing towards a positive outcome—birth—so the male achieves it first. In the world, male and female are advancing to a negative outcome—death—so the female achieves it first; an inferior entity deteriorates more quickly.[206] But if the Greeks were concerned simply to symbolize the inferiority of women in the ageing process, they could have done so by retaining the image of the lazy female and claiming that although women had an inferior body, they aged at the same rate as men because they did not work as hard. Aristotle, who associates old age with coldness and dryness, does claim that hard work dries out living beings, but he pre-empts objections that men should therefore age more quickly than women by adding that the greater heat of men keeps them young longer.[207] He believes women age more quickly despite their more leisurely lifestyle because they are colder than men. But if the male lifestyle could be offset by his hot *physis*, it is not clear why the female moist *physis* could not counterbalance her lifestyle with the result that both sexes age at the same rate.[208] *Septim./ Oct.* 9 (vii. 450. 10) claims that one reason women age more speedily than men is their weakness of body (ἀσθενείη), but he does not elaborate on this weakness. Old age is normally associated with wetness

[205] *Septim.* 9 (vii. 450. 9); *GA* 775[a]14; *HA* 582[a]21–4, 583[b]23–8.
[206] *GA* 775[a]20–2.
[207] *Long.* 466[b]14–16.
[208] At *GA* 727[a]9–10 Arist. says that the power to generate in men and menstruation in women ceases at the same time of life, without identifying the age. *HA* 545[b] 26–31, which puts the cessation of the power to generate at 45 to 50 for women and 65 to 70 for men, more closely reflects Arist.'s claims that women age faster than men and also conforms to observations on fertility in our own society. The comments in *GA* 727[a]9–10 are made as part of an argument to prove that menses are a woman's contribution to conception, and Arist. is therefore assimilating them as closely as possible to male semen. The argument is *ad hoc* and should not be taken as challenging Arist.'s general views on the matter.

among the Hippocratics,[209] but in the gynaecology older women are
said to be drier than younger,[210] which would seem to give them an
advantage in staving off the effects of age in the context of the rest of
the Corpus. If the Hippocratics were concerned simply to maintain
an ideological programme in claiming that women aged faster, we
should expect them to put forward some arguments as to why
speedier ageing should be associated with increased dryness in the
case of women.

It therefore seems probable that the scientific claims on female
ageing reflect a perceived fact about the ageing of the sexes in Classical
Greece, which neither the Hippocratics nor Aristotle felt they had to
argue for,[211] especially since osteoarchaeological studies have shown
that adult women died considerably younger than adult men at all
periods of antiquity.[212] The average age of death for women could be
lowered by many women having died in childbirth at a young age, but
early pregnancy and bad nutrition would leave their mark at a comparatively early age on the bodies of those women who survived.[213]
Aristotle recognized that pregnancy could wear out a woman's
body.[214] Therefore, while the claim that women aged more quickly
than men may have had an ideological component (especially for
Aristotle), it was a claim ancient authors could support by the
observed facts of the ageing of the sexes in their society.

MENOPAUSE

One of the reasons for arguing that women reached old age sooner
than men would be that their reproductive lives were shorter.
Aristotle advises that men should marry women about twenty years
younger than themselves, so that a man's own reproductive
capacities should cease at the same time as his wife's,[215] but in

---

[209] *Salubr.* 2 (vi. 74. 21–76. 1); *Vict.* 1. 33 (vi. 512. 11–12). Both passages also say
that old age is cold. *Nat. Hom.* 12 (vi. 64. 3–10) associates old age with cold but not
specifically with moistness. If, as seems likely (see pp. 45–6 above), the Hippocratic
gynaecologists thought women were hot because of the quality and/or quantity of
their blood, having less of it as they became drier would also make them colder.

[210] *Nat. Mul.* 1 (vii. 312. 6–7); *Mul.* 2. 111 (viii. 238. 22–240. 1).

[211] Cf. Byl 1980, 139–41.

[212] Grmek 1989, 104.

[213] See Rousselle 1988, 34. I do not believe that the average Greek woman was
pregnant as frequently as Rousselle argues that she was.

[214] *HA* 583ᵇ23–8.   [215] *Pol.* 1335ᵃ28–32.

general very little attention is paid to menopause. Although Classical Greeks were very concerned with the advent of menstruation and its regular recurrence throughout a woman's reproductive life, they showed no great interest over the cessation of menstruation. They were not concerned to explain in detail how or why a woman's body stops producing blood, nor do they seem to have been aware of the problems which many women in our society experience around menopause.[216] Angel's osteoarchaeological investigations have put the average age at death of a Greek adult female of the Classical period at 36 to 37 years.[217] The evidence of skeletal remains puts the average age at death for adult men at 44 to 45 years, but while there is a scarcity of skeletons of older men, we know from literary evidence that many men continued to be active well into their sixties, and some could live to be centenarians.[218] Therefore, although the average female life-span in the Classical period was considerably shorter than in our own society,[219] many women would have lived to menopause and beyond. That the Hippocratics numbered older women among their clientele is shown by their references to 'elderly' female patients (γεραίτεραι, πρεσβυτέρη, and ἀφηλικεστέρη).[220] *Nat. Mul.* 1 (vii. 312. 6–7) and *Mul.* 2. III (viii. 238. 22–240. 1) both say that older women are dry and have less blood than younger women (αἱ δὲ πρεσβύτιδες ξηρότεραι καὶ ὀλίγαιμοι πρεσβύτεραι), probably because older women ceased to menstruate. The author of *Mul.* 2. 137 (viii. 310. 10–11) specifically refers to post-menopausal women when he says that displacement of the womb occurs more often in older women around the cessation of menses (πρὸς τὰς ἀπολείψιας τῶν ἐπιμηνίων), and *Mul.* 1. 7 (viii. 32. 1–7) says older women suffer from *pnix* more often because their wombs are empty and light. At *HA* 545^b 26–31 Aristotle puts the age at which a woman's power to generate ceases (i.e. menopause) at 45 to 50.[221] The lack of interest in meno-

---

[216] A great many climacteric and post-climacteric syndromes in our society may be caused by cultural and environmental pressures, see Flint 1982.

[217] Grmek 1989, 103.   [218] Ibid. 107–9.

[219] The overall average age was probably even younger than 36, but it is impossible to calculate it on the available evidence, ibid. 101.

[220] *Mul.* 2. 119, 121 (viii. 260. 21, 264. 19). The first 'elderly women' cannot bear the flux (perhaps because their bodies are too dry) and the second group are older than those who can have children. Cf. *Epid.* 6. 3. 1, 7. 8, 101 (v. 334. 13, 378. 19, 454. 4).

[221] This is the generally agreed average age of menopause in our own society, see Asso 1983, 5, 100–1. Just as the maximum age of life in any culture rarely exceeds 100 no matter how good the medical knowledge and nutrition, so the upper age of menopause seems to remain constant across cultures.

pause in the scientific texts, therefore, cannot be attributed to ignorance of the phenomenon.

That the Hippocratics describe older women as drier shows that they thought that the bodies of post-menopausal women had ceased to produce blood rather than that the blood was irrevocably trapped somewhere in their bodies. They give no indication as to whether this came about because older women ate less, because their stomachs were unable to convert their nourishment into blood, or because their flesh had ceased to absorb blood from their stomachs. The claim that the bodies of older women grew drier might seem to be particularly in need of support and explanation since the general theory on ageing in other Hippocratic works associates old age with increased wetness, but the Hippocratics do not seem to view the claim as contentious. It would seem that they took the empirical fact of menopause as proof enough that old women were dry.

But that the claim should be uncontested is not sufficient reason for menopause to generate so little interest. Menarche could be taken as sufficient proof that women's bodies became more moist at puberty, but the Hippocratics and Aristotle do not omit to explain in detail why and how this should be so, and, in the case of the Hippocratics, to describe the dangers associated with the transition. Other than claiming that post-menopausal women were among the high risk categories for a displaced womb, the Hippocratics did not consider menopause as dangerous a transition as menarche. Whereas menarche differentiated women from men, menopause signalled the reassimilation of the female body to the male (and hence more tractable) body. Whatever the change was that brought about menopause, therefore, did not require specialized knowledge. Cessation of menstruation with no dire effects was empirical evidence that a woman's body had become physiologically more like a man's and, in a gynaecology, there was no reason to explain how this sort of body worked.

Aristotle likewise does not explain the phenomenon of menopause *per se*, but it can be easily extrapolated from his theory of ageing. In the process of living an animal uses up its innate heat, thereby becoming colder, and the production of various fluid residues eventually dries out its body.[222] Aristotle believes that life is dependent upon heat and moisture, so a body which is cold and dry is nearer to death and exhibits characteristics of old age. Meno-

[222] *Long.* 466^{a}17–21, 466^{b}9–10; *Resp.* 479^{a}15–21.

pause is perfectly consistent with this theory, but Aristotle does not discuss the cessation of the production of seminal residues with the same detail as he does their initial production. The relative problematization of menarche and menopause in Classical Greece is significant when compared to the reverse emphasis in our own society. In modern Western culture we hear very little of biological threats besetting pubertal girls, but a host of disorders (hot flushes, migraines, palpitations, osteoporosis, insomnia, depression, to name only a few[223]) afflict the menopausal woman. Modern research suggests that these difficulties attend menopause in the West because menopausal women are devalued in Western society. In those cultures where women gain in stature with age there are few reports of menopausal difficulties.[224] In Classical Greece, while a woman was most valuable to society during her reproductive years, the anomalies of her body compared to a man's meant it was a dangerous period in many ways. The medical and biological attention bestowed on a woman in her reproductive years reflects the concern Greek society had in defining and containing her behaviour within the *oikos*. An older woman had greater authority and freedom because her behaviour posed less of a threat to the integrity of the *oikos*,[225] and her body also posed fewer problems as it was less anomalous when compared to the male's. Since the reproductive years were culturally defined as more problematic for women than the years before and after, women were expected to (and perhaps did) experience biological disorders during the transition into these years rather than the transition out.[226]

CONCLUSION

In constructing their theories of female physiology, both the Hippocratics and Aristotle took menstruation as their main explanandum and developed models which predicted and required heavy and regular bleeding in most women. The relative status of men and women in Greek society meant that although the female body was

[223] Asso 1983, iii–26.   [224] Flint 1982, 368–71.
[225] Henderson 1987, 108. This does not mean, of course, that women wanted to look old, see *Mul.* 2. 188 (viii. 368. 19–22) for a recipe to remove wrinkles.
[226] In Roman society older women were valued less highly than those in their reproductive years (see Richlin 1984, 68–72) and menopause was perceived as a medical problem (Soranus *Gyn.* 1. 26, 3. 26).

acknowledged to be necessary, and its differences from the male valuable for society as a whole (a woman was most precious to society in her reproductive years when her body was thought to diverge most widely from the male's), science used menstruation to construct a female body inherently weak and in need of supervision, thereby buttressing woman's subordinate and restricted position in society. For the Hippocratics, the weakness of a woman's body (her porous flesh) caused menstruation; the release of excess matter in menstrual blood once a month prevented a woman's body from becoming diseased. Even if menstrual fluid had no role to play in childbearing, a woman would have had to produce it, as it was only thus that she could approach the male ideal of health. For Aristotle, on the other hand, the production of menstrual blood for the sake of generation caused woman's physical weakness. Moreover, he comments on the abundance of menstrual fluid in women in comparison not only with men's seminal fluid but also with the 'menstruation' of other female animals. Consequently, while Aristotle considers the male of almost every species as physically superior to the female, the ascendancy in humans is more marked.

2

Female Pathology

THE DOMAIN OF GYNAECOLOGY IN ANTIQUITY

At the beginning of Book 3 of his *Gynaecology*, Soranus records a debate among physicians of antiquity as to whether or not women have conditions peculiarly their own. Soranus agrees with the view that, apart from the areas of the female reproductive system, pregnancy, parturition, and the care of the new-born child, women do not need a specialized branch of medicine; they otherwise suffer the same diseases as men and should be treated the same.[1] This point of view appears unremarkable because it coincides with what we would consider the legitimate domain of gynaecology. There are indeed functions and diseases peculiar to women to which men are not subject because they do not possess the female reproductive organs; in other aspects of the body, however, we assume that men and women are alike and are subject to the same range of diseases. But we should not assume that this has always been the dominant view. The range of opinions recorded by Soranus shows that the issue was hotly debated in antiquity.

Many of the Hippocratic treatises reflect the point of view that Soranus was arguing against, that is that a woman did need a specialized branch of medicine and that any illness she suffered should be treated as a specifically female complaint. Like Soranus, supporters of this view regarded gynaecology primarily as the medicine of the female reproductive system, but they believed that a woman's reproductive system was of central importance whenever she fell ill. There was for some of the Hippocratics, on the one hand, a gynaecology for women and, on the other hand, a general medicine, or 'andrology', for men. This disjunction would be consistent

---

[1] *Gyn.* 3. 1–5. In fact, Soranus believes that only natural conditions in the areas mentioned are peculiar to women. He says that conditions contrary to nature in women are due to the same causes as those responsible for conditions contrary to nature in men.

with the ancient Greek tendency to organize the world by dichotomy and gender and would conform to the traditional ideas the Greek doctors inherited concerning death and disease.

GENDER CATEGORIES OF DISEASE IN EARLY GREEK POETRY

In the *Iliad*, outside the battlefield, male death and disease are said to emanate from the arrows of Apollo, which not only cause the plague that afflicts the Greek army as a whole, but are also a source of death to individual men. Hecuba, addressing Hector's body, says: 'You lie, like to one whom Apollo of the Silver Bow has slain, visiting him with his gentle darts.'[2] Female death, on the other hand, is the province of Apollo's sister Artemis. Addressing Artemis, Hera says: 'Zeus placed you as a lion towards women, and granted that you kill whomever you wish.'[3] The brother and sister preserve their respective roles in this diptych when taking revenge upon Niobe for insulting their mother; Apollo kills her sons and Artemis her daughters (*Il.* 24. 605–6). Even when it is on his own behalf that Apollo wishes to exact retribution from an individual woman, he sends his sister to bring about her death. In Pindar's *Pythian* 3. 32–4, it is Artemis who assails Coronis for her unfaithfulness to Apollo. This symmetry in the representation of a divine source of death—a male for a man, a female for a woman—is an index of the extent to which the culture believed the female body differed from that of the male. The dichotomy shows that not only were women thought to be susceptible to certain forms of suffering and death to which men were not, but that there was also believed to exist a range of diseases which afflicted men to which women were immune. A concept of

---

[2] κεῖσαι, τῷ ἴκελος ὄν τ᾽ ἀργυρότοξος ᾽Απόλλων | οἷς ἀγανοῖσι βέλεσσιν ἐποιχόμενος κατέπεφνεν, *Il.* 24. 758–9. It is true that gods other than Apollo could cause sickness among men. Hes. (*Op.* 102–4) says that Zeus sent diseases upon mortals, and the plague in Soph.'s *OT* is sent by Ares (*OT* 190–202). However, this only emphasizes the fact that whereas disease and death among the general population can be said to have any one of several origins, an individual woman's death was always attributed to Artemis, cf. *Il.* 6. 428, 19. 59; *Od.* 11. 324, 15. 478, 18. 202, 20. 61.

[3] ἐπεί σε λέοντα γυναιξὶ | Ζεὺς θῆκεν, καὶ ἔδωκε κατακτάμεν ἥν κ᾽ ἐθέλῃσθα, *Il.* 21. 483–4. On a Graeco-Roman amulet of the second century BC the womb is addressed and requested to cease 'roaring like a lion', see Bonner 1950, 90 n. 52; Barb 1953, 193–238. I am grateful to Christopher A. Faraone for this reference.

gender categories for death and disease is suggested in the earliest Greek poetry.

'ANDROLOGY' IN THE HIPPOCRATIC CORPUS

We cannot know to what extent these gender categories were recognized in the earliest scientific accounts of disease. Accounts of Presocratic views on the matter may have been preserved in Aristotle's *On Medicine* 1-2, but this exists only as a title in the lists of his works compiled by Diogenes Laertius, Hesychius, and Ptolemy. It follows that we have also lost a large part of Aristotle's own opinions on the subject. Remarks on human and female pathology are scattered through his biological works, but we have no systematic treatises as we do for his opinions on physiology and reproduction. However, in the case of the Hippocratics, we can see that just as mythology followed the contours of social ideology in recounting tales of death and disease, so also much medical doctrine, which attempted to base its theories on empirical observation and rational theorizing, reflected the same cultural beliefs.

The author of *Mul.* 1. 62 (viii. 126. 14–19) writes:

At the same time the doctors also make mistakes by not learning the apparent cause through accurate questioning, but they proceed to heal as though they were dealing with men's diseases (τὰ ἀνδρικὰ νοσήματα). I have already seen many women die from just this kind of suffering. But at the outset one must ask accurate questions about the cause. For the healing of the diseases of women differs greatly from the healing of men's diseases.[4]

Here women's diseases are not set apart from a general medicine dealing with both sexes, but are opposed to a medicine which deals exclusively with the male sex. Manuli says that while there is a specialized field of gynaecology in ancient medicine there is no analogous field for the study and treatment of the male genital apparatus,[5] and Hanson says that the author wields 'the term "diseases of men" as a club with which to batter opponents, since, as he

---

[4] ἅμα δὲ καὶ οἱ ἰητροὶ ἁμαρτάνουσιν, οὐκ ἀτρεκέως πυνθανόμενοι τὴν πρόφασιν τῆς νούσου, ἀλλ' ὡς τὰ ἀνδρικὰ νοσήματα ἰώμενοι· καὶ πολλὰς εἶδον διεφθαρμένας ἤδη ὑπὸ τοιούτων παθημάτων. ἀλλὰ χρὴ ἀνερωτᾶν αὐτίκα ἀτρεκέως τὸ αἴτιον· διαφέρει γὰρ ἡ ἴησις πολλῷ τῶν γυναικηίων νοσημάτων καὶ τῶν ἀνδρώων.
[5] Manuli 1983, 186.

knows, there are no diseases of men—only diseases of women and
human diseases.'[6] It is quite possible that the author did coin the
term *ta andrika* to make his argument appear more dramatic, but in
so doing he did not mean to denote a fictional branch of medicine
dealing with the male reproductive organs which other doctors confused with the female; *ta andrika* simply denotes all medicine which
is not *ta gynaikeia* and which is normally referred to simply as
'medicine'. Manuli claims that the author acknowledges that
women could be afflicted by non-gynaecological diseases in the
phrase 'women have a share in diseases' (*αἱ γυναῖκες μετέχουσι
τῶν νούσων, Mul.* I. 62 (viii. 126. 7)), which she understands (following Littré) to mean that women share diseases in common with
men. However, as the phrase occurs in a sentence explaining why
women's diseases are so hard to deal with, it seems to be more
appropriate to interpret the Greek as saying that women have diseases in common with each other (as Hanson does: 'These diseases
... are difficult to understand because of the fact that women are the
ones who share these sicknesses'). In either case we would normally
expect a dative after the genitive to show with whom women shared
the diseases. It is more easily supplied if the phrase is taken to be
reflexive. To treat a woman without regard to her sex is a mistake,
claims this author. The passage makes it clear, though, that a range
of opinions are possible on this matter; some doctors are castigated
because they do treat men and women the same, so we should not
expect to see so firm a disjunction represented in all the Hippocratic
treatises.[7] However, many of them do share the view articulated in
this passage to a greater or lesser extent.

The most obvious failure to take female physiology into account
in the general medicine is the scarcity of reference to menses. These
are of crucial importance in the gynaecological works. Thus, in
Mul. I. 6 (viii. 30. 11–13) doctors are advised to question a woman
closely about her current and previous menstruation to determine
whether her menstrual flow is morbid or not before proceeding to
treat her. In a more general context, the condition of a woman's
menstrual discharge could be just as informative about the internal

[6] Hanson 1987*a*, 38

[7] e.g. *Nat. Hom.* 9 (vi. 52. 14–54. 1) says that while male and female lifestyles
might result in men and women generally being susceptible to a different range of
diseases, they can catch the same disease from the air. However, *Aër.* 3–4 (ii. 14.
20–22. 14) suggests that even in these cases men and women would manifest different
symptoms, see pp. 118–19 below.

environment of her body as any other secretion. *Hum.* 5 (v. 482. 14)
and *Alim.* 17 (ix. 104. 5) list discharges from the womb along with
other discharges as one of the things a doctor should look at when
treating an illness, and doctors in the *Epid.*, when dealing with
individual female cases, do take them into consideration.

One doc-
tor states as a general rule: 'And [observe] the menses if they appear,
especially for those women in whom they appear for the first time,
but also for young girls and women in whom they occur at intervals,
and for those in whom they do not appear at the usual time, nor as
they ought to appear and then are very pale.'[8] Yet even though
menses, like any discharge, could be a valuable sign of the type of
disruption occurring unseen in a woman's body, other non-
gynaecological treatises ignore them completely. Throughout *Prog.*
and *Acut.*, while the authors pay great attention to sputum, urine,
and stools in generalizing about how to forecast the course of an
illness, they make no mention of the use of menses. Moreover,
Morb. 4. 41 (vii. 562. 8–10) states that there are four ways a person
can be purged of harmful substances: mouth, nostrils, rectum, and
urethra. No mention is made of the vagina although this is
supremely important in purging a woman.

It may be countered that the omission of references to specifically
female anatomy and physiology suggests rather that the authors
believed that if a woman was affected in her reproductive mechanism
in any way, she was suffering a specifically gynaecological complaint, and that the general medicine includes only material relevant to both sexes. The first part of this contention is, in a sense,
correct, but its significance can be understood fully only if we appre-
ciate how frequently the Hippocratics believed a woman's reproductive organs were involved in her illness—even when she was
suffering from the same pathological agents as a man. The second
part of the contention is refuted by the frequency of statements which
are relevant only to the male sex.

Unless an author in the Hippocratic Corpus is writing a specifically gynaecological treatise, when he indicates the expected sex of a
patient, the sex is male.[9] Given the restricted sphere of activity of
women this is understandable for several areas of medicine, such as

---

[8] καὶ γυναικεῖα ἦν ἐπιφαίνηται, μάλιστα δὲ ᾗσι πρῶτον, ἀτὰρ καὶ παρθένοισι καὶ γυναιξὶν ᾗσι διὰ χρόνου, ἀτὰρ καὶ ᾗσι μὴ ἐν ᾧ εἴθισται χρόνῳ, ἢ
ὡς δεῖ, ἐπιφαίνονται, ἔπειτα ἔξωχροι γίνονται, *Epid.* 2. 3. 1 (v. 102. 20–104. 3).
[9] See Lloyd 1983, 63–5.

those dealing with fractures or head wounds, and for other areas it may be argued that the Hippocratics used the male body as a shorthand for both sexes of the human species, indicating that the Hippocratics saw no difference between male and female bodies of the same age and constitution in the same environment. However, many remarks and recommendations made in the 'general' treatises would be totally inappropriate for female patients, and in these contexts the Hippocratics do not append instructions modifying their remarks to make them relevant to women. In the 'general' medicine, where gender differences would be germane, women are often overlooked.

Vict. 1–3 emphasize the need for a person to engage in regular exercise over and above normal daily exertion to remain healthy. *Vict.* 1. 2 (vi. 470. 6–10) says exercise should be proportioned to the bulk of food that is consumed, the *physis* and age of the individual, and the season, winds, and situation of the environment, but it makes no mention of considerations of sex. The amount a man should exercise is to be determined as he undresses and exercises in the gymnasium,[10] and different specifications of the amount and kind of exercise are given for different types of men. Throughout *Vict.* the exercise envisaged seems to be running on the track, wrestling, and the like.[11] *Vict.* 2. 60 (vi. 574. 4) says that an easy-going (ῥᾳθυμίη) regimen moistens and weakens the body, so it would be a regimen that women, who were already moist and weak, should avoid; yet it is just the regimen *Vict.* 1. 34 (vi. 512. 17–18) says women follow. To counteract their moistness women should follow a drying regimen, but advice to those who need to follow a dry regimen includes instructions to wrestle in the dust.[12] This would obviously be considered out of the question for most Greek women,[13] but there is no corresponding activity in which they are advised to participate. Walking is mentioned frequently, but in the 'general' treatises always as preparatory or subsequent to more vigorous exercise, e.g.

[10] *Vict.* 1. 2 (vi. 470. 19–20).

[11] e.g. *Vict.* 3. 68 (vi. 594. 3–604. 19) gives advice for the majority of men. The lightest exercise, undertaken during the summer months, still includes wrestling and running on the track (vi. 602. 15–20).

[12] *Vict.* 2. 64 (vi. 580. 9–16).

[13] So too the advice to a person who has exercised too much 'to get drunk once or twice' (μεθυσθῆναι δὲ ἅπαξ ἢ δίς, *Vict.* 3. 85 (vi. 636. 11–12)). Athletics were not open to women until the Hellenistic period, see Pomeroy 1975, 137. Spartan women seem always to have taken part in some physical exercise, but in this they were exceptional among Classical Greeks.

Vict. 4. 90 (vi. 654. 10–11). *Vict.* does not describe alternative
exercise a woman might undertake to maintain her health, nor how
it should be regulated in accordance with her particular
constitution, or vary with the time of year. What is advanced as a
general concept of health is in fact directed primarily at men.

This is not to say that Greek women took absolutely no exercise.
Mul. 1. 11 (viii. 44. 20) advises a phlegmatic woman to exercise
frequently (γυμνάζεσθαι συχνά), but it does not indicate what type
of exercise is to be undertaken, and this regimen is only to be
followed before attempts at conception. Afterwards she is to move
as little as possible, and if she wishes to walk she should take care to
do so on level ground (viii. 46. 22–4). *Mul.* 1. 12 (viii. 50. 9) tells a
woman whose womb is weak from an affection or too many fumigations to take much light exercise (πόνοισι πρηέσι πλέοσι), but
again it does not specify the type of exercise. The exercise envisaged is
probably little more than walking. The general impression in the
gynaecological treatises is that violent movement of any sort is bad
for a woman. *Nat. Mul.* 44 (vii. 388. 6–8) says that simply standing
up or bending over can cause womb displacement. A woman is safest
when reclining—but even then not completely protected against
womb movement. Such complete immobility would obviously be
impractical for most women, especially slaves and lower-class
women. *Mul.* 2. 138, 153 (viii. 312. 1–2, 328. 1–3) describe various
strenuous activities they would undertake such as dancing, win-
nowing grain, chopping wood, and running up and down hills. Once
again, however, this exercise is dangerous to women as it can cause
uterine displacement. It cannot be used as the prophylactic which
the 'general' medicine advocates with such enthusiasm.

Symptoms that manifest themselves in male genitals are
mentioned without any restricting adjective or noun to show that
they are solely masculine symptoms, e.g. 'The drawing up of the
testicles and privy parts signals strong pains and the risk of death',[14]
whereas if a non-male anatomical part is mentioned attention is
drawn to the fact that it is female, e.g. in describing parts of the body
that draw fluids to themselves: 'Among the inner organs of the body,
the bladder, the skull, and the womb [in women] have such a

---

[14] ὄρχιες δὲ καὶ αἰδοῖα ἀνεσπασμένα πόνους ἰσχυροὺς σημαίνει καὶ κίν-
δυνον θανατώδεα, *Prog.* 9 (ii. 134. 3–4). Cf. *Hebd.* 51 (viii. 669. 16). Inflammation of
the bladder is shown on the prepuce (ἀκροποσθίη) in *Morb.* 4. 55 (vii. 604. 6). The
spleen passes water into the scrotum at *Morb.* 4. 57 (vii. 610. 3).

shape.'[15] Even if an observation applies manifestly only to women, as in references to the womb, the text is at pains to exclude men— another token of the degree to which the male body was the dominant model in the minds of the authors and the intended audience of the general medical works. References to the male body do not deliberately except the female because women's physiology does not fall within the archetype.

On occasions, authors feel impelled to make it plain that a specific prognosis is not restricted to males. In *Epid.* 1. 9 (ii. 656. 2–6) it is stated that of those who succumbed (τῶν καμνόντων) to a particular disease, the ones most likely to die were the young, those in their prime, the smooth, fair-skinned, straight-haired, black-haired, black-eyed, those living recklessly and carelessly, the thin-voiced, rough-voiced, lispers, and the passionate. These are all designated by masculine adjectives, the gender a Greek would use when describing a group containing both male and female, so women would not *de facto* be excluded; but the list is immediately followed by the phrase, 'And very many women of this type died' (καὶ γυναῖκες πλεῖσται ἐκ τουτέου τοῦ εἴδεος ἀπέθνησκον). Similarly, in *Epid.* 3. 14 (iii. 96. 4–98. 1) the physical characteristics of consumptives (τῶν φθινωδέων) are listed: smooth skin (white, lentil, or reddish coloured), bright (blue/grey?) eyes, a leucophlegmatic condition, and projecting shoulder-blades. The author then laconically remarks, 'And women likewise' (καὶ γυναῖκες οὕτω). Grammatically, τῶν καμνόντων and τῶν φθινωδέων could both encompass women. The explicit statement that women suffered these diseases as well shows that normal grammatical idiom was not strong enough here; steps had to be taken to ensure that the reader did not assume that women who exhibited the physical features characteristic of men who fell ill were somehow naturally protected from the disease in question.[16]

The usual word for 'patients' in the Hippocratic Corpus is 'humans' or *anthrōpoi*, notionally embracing both men and women,

[15] τῶν δ' ἔσω τοῦ ἀνθρώπου φύσις καὶ σχῆμα τοιοῦτον· κύστις τε καὶ κεφαλὴ καὶ ὑστέρα γυναιξί, *VM* 22 (i. 628. 3–4). Jones and Chadwick–Mann omit 'in women' (γυναιξί) as superfluous in their English translations.

[16] The weaker reading of this passage, that the author intended simply to deny that there were different characteristics for women who fell ill, still points to the same general conclusion; although there is nothing about the characteristics of men who fell ill which definitely excludes women, the author and his readers would not necessarily assume that they were applicable to both sexes unless specific reference was made to women.

and one might well imagine that this word was preferred to 'men', *andres*, for the reason that the authors in some sense aim at a general medicine and not at a specifically male medicine. However, the term is used with the female article in the gynaecological treatises simply to signify 'the patient' where there can be no question of an attempt to include both sexes. Furthermore, when symptoms in younger people are said to differ from those in older patients, the older group of *anthrōpoi* is identified as 'men and women', *andres kai gynaikes*.[17] This very qualification indicates that the author could not be sure that his readers would understand that he wished particularly to include both sexes in the older group unless he made an explicit statement to that effect. Children were not differentiated by sex before puberty and so could be referred to as a homogeneous group. If older patients were thought to exhibit this same homogeneity there would be no need to specify that both sexes were included; *anthrōpoi* would suffice. It could not be used without qualification in cases where women were to be included because the generic *anthrōpos* of the general medical works was all too readily identified as an *anēr*.[18]

When women are mentioned in the general treatises as being affected by the same diseases as men they do not suffer the same sort of symptoms. *Aër.* 3–6 gives a classification of the different types of environment and the diseases that follow upon each. When listing the symptoms of those diseases associated with a city exposed to hot winds (*Aër.* 3 (ii. 14. 19–18. 17)), the writer describes the men as suffering from dysentery, diarrhoea, ague, fever, eczema, and haemorrhoids. The women suffer barrenness and abortions. In a city exposed to cold winds (*Aër.* 4 (ii. 18. 18–22. 14)) the men suffer pleurisies, internal lacerations, inflamed eyes, and nosebleeds. The women are barren, childbirth is rare, abortions frequent, and their menses are scanty and bad. It might be argued that the Hippocratic doctor intended the women's reproductive illnesses to be understood as symptoms in addition to those suffered by the men, but the use of the antithesis 'men on the one hand ... women on the other

---

[17] *Prog.* 12, 24 (ii. 142. 1–3, 184. 8–12).
[18] Loraux 1981, 92–4, remarking on Hes.'s use of 'the female race' (θῆλυ γένος) and 'the race of women' (γένος γυναικῶν), notes that nowhere does Hes. mention a corresponding 'race of men' or 'male race', but instead contrasts 'the female race' to 'the human race' (γένος ἀνθρώπων).

hand' (μὲν ... δέ (ii. 18. 2–5, 22. 1–3)), shows that the author was seeking to set up an opposition rather than a progression of symptoms. A particularly illuminating example of the dichotomy is given in *Aër*. 10 (ii. 46. 3–4) when, after giving a list of ailments during childbirth following a mild winter and cold spring, the author says, 'These things happened to women. But to the rest dysentery and dry eyes' (ταῦτα μὲν τῇσι γυναιξίν. τοῖσι δὲ λοιποῖσι δυσεντερίας καὶ ὀφθαλμίας ξηράς). In one passage, while stating that, in one instance at least, women could suffer the same disease as men and manifest the same symptoms, the author still relegates discussion of the treatment of the disease in women to the gynaecology. *Morb.* 4. 57 deals with a man suffering from dropsy. At the end of the chapter the author adds: 'Women also suffer from dropsy—on the uterus, on the stomach, and on the legs: the symptoms, too, are all the same. I have described the disease in *Diseases of Women*.'[19]

Thus it appears that even when exposed to the same pathological agents as men, a woman is thought to be affected first and foremost in her reproductive function. It is this medical principle that is the root of the strong disjunction, at times almost a polarization, of the general ('andrological') and the gynaecological works. The major source of female suffering was alien to men. Jaap Mansfeld has conducted an independent study on the female case histories of the *Epid.* and noted that they are virtually all gynaecological in nature.[20] As there were only half as many female as male case histories, Mansfeld arrived at the conclusion that the Hippocratics were only interested in recording the case histories of female patients when they were suffering from a gynaecological illness. I believe the findings (which replicate my own) are more satisfactorily explained by arguing that the Hippocratics did not have as many women as men as patients, and when they did have a female patient they tended to concern themselves automatically with her reproductive mechanism.

---

[19] γίνεται δὲ καὶ τῇσι γυναιξὶν ὁ ὕδρωψ ἐν τῇσι μήτρῃσι καὶ τὰ ἐν τῇσι κοιλίῃσι, καὶ τὰ ἐν τοῖσι σκέλεσι καὶ τἆλλα σημήια ταὐτὰ ἴσχει· ἀποπέφανται δέ μοι ἐν τοῖσι γυναικείοισι νουσήμασι περὶ αὐτοῦ (vii. 612. 19–21). This may be a reference to the chapters discussing dropsy in *Mul.* 1–2.

[20] Personal communication.

CLASSIFICATION OF CONSTITUTIONS IN 'GENERAL' MEDICINE

Despite the dichotomy which many Hippocratics would see in the treatment of men and women, the principles of health and disease were the same for both. In general, throughout the Hippocratic Corpus an individual is considered to be in good health when the various constituents of their body are combined in the correct amounts. These can be the classic four humours (blood, phlegm, yellow bile, and black bile) as in *Nat. Hom.* 4 (vi. 38. 19–40. 1) or in *Morb.* 4. 32 (vii. 542. 9) which substitutes *hydrops* (a watery humour) for black bile, or a vast number of properties such as the sweet, the acrid, the salty, etc., as in *VM* 14 (i. 602. 9–11). A superabundance of any one of these constituents causes a person to be unhealthy and susceptible to certain specific illnesses, and has to be rectified. Most often in the treatises men are characterized as tending towards a bilious, phlegmatic, dry, or humid constitution, (as at *Aër.* 4 (ii. 18. 23), *Acut.* 34 (ii. 296. 1–6), *Morb. Sacr.* 5 (vi. 368. 10–11)), but can maintain the various substances in their body in a harmonious balance by modifying their lifestyle according to body type and time of year, (as at *Salubr.* 2 (vi. 74. 14–76. 5), *Vict.* 1. 35, 3.68 (vi. 512. 20–522. 16, 594. 3–604. 19).

As human beings women contain as many components as men,[21] yet unlike men they are not classified under varying types of constitution in the general medicine. Time and again throughout the Hippocratic treatises they are assimilated generally into the humid category. *Salubr.* 2 prescribes different regimens for men of different physical builds, saying that those of a fleshy, soft, and red physique should adopt a dry regimen for the greater part of the year, 'for the *physis* of these types of people is moist' (ὑγρὴ γὰρ ἡ φύσις τῶν εἰδέων τουτέων (vi. 74. 14–16)). Women are treated *en masse* as being of this same physical type: 'Women do best on a drier diet as

---

[21] It is specifically stated at *Morb.* 4. 32 (vii. 542. 6–7) that men and women both contain four humours. *Nat. Hom.* 5 (vi. 42. 20–44. 2) says that the four humours must be congenital in humans, 'because they were procreated by a human being who had them all and mothered in a human being similarly endowed with all the elements which I have indicated and demonstrated' (γέγονεν ἐξ ἀνθρώπου ταῦτα πάντα ἔχοντος, τέθραπταί τε ἐν ἀνθρώπῳ ταῦτα πάντα ἔχοντι, ὁκόσα ἐγώ γε νῦν φημί τε καὶ ἀποδείκνυμι).

dry foods are most suited to the softness of their flesh, and the less diluted drinks are better for the womb and for pregnancy.'[22]

What is said to be good for the humid constitution is said to be beneficial for women as well, e.g. no rainfall during the Dog Star or Arcturus.[23] In several passages throughout the Corpus a disease is said to affect those of a humid disposition and women, e.g. *Aph.* 3. 11 (iv. 490. 4–5): 'There were dysenteries, especially among women and men with a humid *physis*' (δυσεντερίας γίνεσθαι, μάλιστα τῆσι γυναιξὶ καὶ ἀνδρῶν τοῖσιν ὑγροῖσι τὰς φύσιας). *Morb.* 4. 57 (vii. 612. 19–21) is the only chapter in a work dealing with the types of illnesses arising from different humours to draw specific attention to women—and it is in the context of diseases arising from an excess of *hydrops*. When women suffer an illness caused by another humour in men they are still said to suffer because of their humidity, e.g. *Aër.* 10 says that phlegmatics are liable to dysentery—as are women because the phlegm is attracted down from their brains by the humidity of their constitutions; they are not classed as phlegmatics themselves (ii 46. 5–7).

DIFFERENCES BETWEEN WOMEN IN THE
GYNAECOLOGICAL TREATISES

In a chapter dealing with barrenness due to abnormalities in the cervix, the author of *Steril.* remarks:

Try to be an enquirer into nature (φυσικὸς εἶναι),[24] attending to the patient's physical appearance (ἕξις) and strength, for there is no standard (σταθμός) of these things, but try to gather evidence from these things, using purgations and evacuations of the whole body and the head, and fumigations and pessaries of the uterus. These are your elements, and treatment of these ⟨conditions⟩ lies in the part of each of them, and whichever of these you do not use, always employ fumigations for this is the softening remedy and leads out the humours (τοὺς ἰχῶρας). And when you have finished the

---

[22] τὰς δὲ γυναῖκας χρὴ διαιτᾶσθαι τῷ ξηροτέρῳ τῶν τρόπων· καὶ γὰρ τὰ σιτία τὰ ξηρὰ ἐπιτηδειότερα πρὸς τὴν μαλθακότητα τῶν γυναικείων σαρκῶν, καὶ τὰ ἀκρητέστερα πόματα ἀμείνω πρὸς τὰς ὑστέρας καὶ τὰς κυοτροφίας, *Salubr.* 6 (vi. 82. 2–6).

[23] *Aër.* 10 (ii. 50. 6–9), cf. *Aph.* 3. 14 (iv. 492. 3–4).

[24] This could simply be exhorting the doctor to follow the method detailed in the passage, but it may also be meant to indicate that the doctor is to determine the woman's *physis* before proceeding to treat her.

treatment and the natural discharge has ceased (ληγόντων τῶν κατὰ φύσιν), you must draw some blood from the arm.[25]

This passage explains that it is difficult to identify a woman's underlying constitution because there is no *stathmos* by which to measure it. Instead a doctor has to rely on a group of signs—and particularly on discharges from the womb via fumigations because these lead down the humours.[26] Littré takes the phrase *lēgontōn tōn kata physin* to mean 'after the menses have finished'. It is true that *ta kata physin* is sometimes used to mean menses,[27] but the author of this passage has already used the more common word for menses, *katamēnia*, earlier in the chapter (viii. 438. 15), so here it is more likely that he is using the term 'natural discharge' to signify that the fumigations bring down not just menstrual blood but whatever other humour is naturally in excess in a woman's body. Immediately after this passage, the author says he has described the regimens to be used with these treatments elsewhere (viii. 444. 10–11). He may be referring to *Mul.* 1. 8–12 (viii. 34. 6–50. 12) where the identification and treatment of bilious, phlegmatic, and humid women, and whether treatment should focus on the womb, the head and womb, or the womb and the entire body are discussed. Diagnosis is made from the state of the menstrual discharge. Bilious menses are black, gleaming, scanty, and slow to coagulate. Phlegmatic menses are membranous and whitish. In each case it is the whole body which is in a bad state (viii. 34. 6, 38. 6), but the pathological agent can be identified only in the menses.[28]

Hippocratic gynaecological authors do say it is important to take a female patient's *physis* into account, e.g. *Nat. Mul.* 1 (vii. 312. 3, 9–10), *Mul.* 2. 111 (viii. 238. 16–17), but despite the above references to bile and phlegm affecting the whole body and discussions of

[25] *Steril.* 230 (viii. 442. 27–444. 9). πειρῶ δὲ φυσικὸς εἶναι, πρὸς τῆς ἀνθρώπου τὴν ἕξιν καὶ τὴν ἰσχὺν ὁρέων τούτων γὰρ οὐδεὶς σταθμός ἐστιν, ἀλλ᾽ ἐξ αὐτέων τουτέων τεκμαιρόμενος πειρῶ, ὅλου τοῦ σώματος, κεφαλῆς καθάρσεσι, φαρμακείῃσι, καὶ πυρίῃσι τῆς ὑστέρης καὶ προσθέτοισι χρῆσθαι· στοιχεῖα δέ σοι ταῦτά ἐστιν· ἡ δὲ θεραπείη τουτέων ἐστὶν ἐν μέρει ἑκάστου, καὶ ὅ τι ἂν μὴ ποιῇς τουτέων, αἰεὶ ἐπὶ τῆς πυρίης διατριβέτω· αὕτη γάρ ἐστιν ἡ μαλθάσσουσα καὶ ἄγουσα τοὺς ἰχῶρας. ὅταν δὲ καταπαύσῃ τῆς θεραπείης, ληγόντων τῶν κατὰ φύσιν, χρὴ αἷμα ἀφαιρέειν ἀπὸ τῆς χειρός.
[26] *Ichōr* signifies the serous part of the blood and seems here to mean any fluids carried in the blood.
[27] See King 1989, 15.
[28] *Mul.* 2. 182 (viii. 364. 15) has a reference to black bile, rare in the gynaecological works, which causes the woman to be fearful and gloomy. The humour is specifically located in her womb.

illness caused by phlegm in the womb,[29] the differences between
female constitutions as evidenced by their colouring, stature, and
age tend to be more degrees of humidity. Fair and young women are
more humid and more subject to fluxes;[30] dark and older women are
firmer and stiffer; ruddy-complexioned women and those between
the extremes of age have a constitution between the two extremes.[31]
However, while the gynaecology may consider some women dry in
comparison to others, the author of *Nat. Mul.* i, when he says he will
begin discussing the treatment of women from 'the moist according
to nature' (ἀπὸ τοῦ ὑγροῦ κατὰ φύσιν (vii. 312. 12–13)), proceeds
immediately to talking about the disease of dropsy rather than any
illness caused by excess phlegm or bile. Even dark women will be
considered to have a humid constitution in comparison to men, so
the author of *Mul.* i. 11 (viii. 44. 3) can claim, 'On the whole, most
treatment is the same for all women' (σχεδὸν δὲ πάσῃσιν ἡ
πολλὴ θεραπείη ἡ αὐτή ἐστι).

MAINTENANCE OF HEALTH IN WOMEN AND HUMID MEN

As was shown in the previous chapter, the humidity of the female
constitution resulted from a combination of women's inherently
loose flesh and their supposedly more indolent lifestyle, which
meant they were unable to utilize all the food they ingested. A man
who had a naturally humid constitution could keep himself healthy
by following the correct regimen of diet and exercise. *Vict.* i. 35 (vi.
512. 20–522. 16) discusses the regimen of different types of men.
Those who tend to humidity are benefited by following a regimen
inclined towards fire, i.e. no surfeit of food or drink and regular use
of emetics. Those who tend only a little to water should take sharp
runs for exercise. Individuals tending more to water should eat less
and drier food and should resort to more vigorous exercise and more
frequent vomiting. Those whose fire is completely mastered by
water need vapour baths and purgings with hellebore (remedies
which are frequently used in the gynaecology). While these
measures may have been considered sufficient to keep a humid man

[29] e.g. *Mul.* i. 53–4, 57, 58 (viii. 112. 6–20, 114. 8–116. 19).
[30] Arist. echoes this in *HA* 583ᵃ12 when he says that in intercourse fair women
secrete more moisture than dark.
[31] Groupings of women in the context of susceptibilities to disease are often made
on the basis of age rather than constitutions, e.g. *Mul.* 2. 145 (viii. 320. 11–12). In the
case of young and old women, humidity is related to the possession or lack of blood
in excess, see *Nat. Mul.* i (vii. 312. 1–8); *Mul.* 2. 111 (viii. 238. 16–240. 4).

healthy, neither diet, exercise, nor artificial purgings could relieve a woman of her congenital proclivity to humidity. To ensure that her body did not become overburdened by excess substances she had to rely on her monthly evacuation. Aristotle says of menses and 'whites' (a vaginal discharge which was thought to be particularly common in young girls): 'These two secretions of residue, if moderate in amount, keep the body in a sound condition, because they constitute an evacuation of the residues which cause disease. If they fail to occur, or occur too plenteously, they are injurious, producing either disease or a lowering of the body.'[32]

The ultimate source of any illness—food, environment, lack of exercise, etc.—and the proximate source—an imbalance of bodily constituents—might be the same for male and female, but the threat of imbalance had to be countered in fundamentally different ways for each of the sexes. In a man, the Hippocratics placed the emphasis on preventing an accumulation of any excess. Different measures had to be taken to maintain the balance of the humours in the body depending on an individual's constitution, and for humid men particularly emetics and enemas could be used as adjuncts in a health maintenance regimen,[33] but they were not as important as correct diet and exercise. Some men had to be more careful than others, as they were weaker and more prone to suffer from any miscalculation in their regimen,[34] but in general the male health which resulted from following the correct regimen would be of a higher order than any female health because a man had less disposition to build up excess substances and more control over ridding himself of them. No amount of care over the food she consumed or the life she led could ever relieve a woman from the innate weakness of her body.[35] No matter what regimen she followed, her body accumulated an excess of blood and she had to have her monthly courses to maintain a healthy balance of her bodily components. The gynaecological

---

[32] *GA* 738ᵃ26–33 μετριάζουσαι μὲν οὖν ἀμφότεραι αὗται αἱ ἀποκρίσεις τῶν περιττωμάτων τὰ σώματα σώζουσιν, ἅτε γιγνομένης καθάρσεως τῶν περιττωμάτων ἃ τοῦ νοσεῖν αἴτια τοῖς σώμασιν· μὴ γινομένων δὲ ἢ πλειόνων γιγνομένων βλάπτει· ποιεῖ γὰρ ἢ νόσους ἢ τῶν σωμάτων καθαίρεσιν.

[33] *Salubr.* 5 (vi. 78. 3–80. 17) details the use of emetics and clysters in a health maintenance regimen. It advises those who are accustomed to induce vomiting twice a month to do so on consecutive days rather than once a fortnight (πεντεκαίδεκα). It is significant that this would more closely resemble the frequency of menstruation.

[34] *VM* 12 (i. 596. 1–5).

[35] *Septim.* 9 (vii. 450. 10) shows that a woman's weakness (ἀσθενείη) of body was not simply a product of her regimen.

works are not devoid of dietetic recommendations,[36] but these are not the main area of concern in maintaining a woman's health. Hippocratic advice to women aimed at keeping the mechanism for evacuating the inevitable excess in working order, ideally by becoming pregnant, which would utilize the excess and also, after parturition, leave the mechanism in a more efficient state than before. Since the best way to achieve this for most women was simply regular intercourse, the Hippocratics would have less need to devise regimens for individual women.

MENSTRUATION AS AN ILLNESS

Often when a woman fell ill, the Hippocratics looked no further for a cause than the retention of menstrual blood, e.g. 'If the menses do not flow, women's bodies become prone to sickness.'[37] As was mentioned above (pp. 94–6), many women probably did not menstruate with the regularity that the Hippocratics expected, so even if a patient's normal menstrual cycle had not been disrupted by her illness, if more than a month had passed since her last period a doctor could insist that her problems were caused by the retention of menstrual blood beyond its due time.[38] Those illnesses severe enough really to interfere with the menstrual cycle would only provide further ammunition for the diagnosis.

The most common and least pathological affliction caused by menstrual blood in the body is that suffered just before normal menstruation. At *HA* 582^{b}7–9 Aristotle describes menstruation as a painful illness in itself, and the Hippocratics say it is heralded by coldness, tiredness, headaches, and sore throats, and that a mist in front of the eyes appears if the flow is going to be heavy.[39] This

[36] *Mul.* 2. 162 (viii. 340. 3) recommends evacuating a woman 'upwards if that is her habit' (εἰ ἠθάδες εἶεν ἄνω), perhaps showing that women could also employ a regimen involving emetics, though it could also be referring to women who regularly bled through the nose at menstruation.

[37] τῶν δὲ καταμηνίων μὴ χωρεόντων τὰ σώματα τῶν γυναικῶν ἐπίνοσα γίνεται, *Genit.* 4 (vii. 476. 14–15), cf. *Mul.* 1. 2, 62 (viii. 14. 8–9, 126. 8) where the author states that the diseases women suffer come from their menses.

[38] It may be as an argument against this view that the author of *HA* 10 states that menstruating at irregular intervals does not signify disease, 634^{a}35–40.

[39] *Coac.* 537, 541 (v. 706. 15–16, 708. 2–3); cf. *Prorrh.* 1. 142–3 (v. 562. 6–10). It is noteworthy that the Hippocratics make no mention of tenderness in the breasts, one of the most commonly reported symptoms of PMS today, and it is interesting to speculate whether this contrast should be attributed to their society's lack of interest in the breasts or our society's preoccupation with them. The mood swings associated with the pre-menstrual phase today are also absent from the Hippocratic list, perhaps

suffering is attributed to the sudden accumulation of blood inside the woman, straining to get out through the womb. *Nat. Puer.* 15 (vii. 492. 21–494. 5) says that in a woman who was not pregnant the blood was pictured as crowding into the uterus all at once each month rather than flowing in little by little throughout the month as it did in pregnancy. A woman who had never given birth is said to suffer 'more seriously and more quickly' (χαλεπώτερον καὶ θᾶσσον, *Mul.* 1. 1 (viii. 10. 1–2)), than a woman who has, not simply because the passage of her uterus is narrower and the uterus itself, never having been stretched by pregnancy, cannot accommodate a large amount of blood with the same degree of comfort, but because her body has not experienced the abundant lochial flow which follows upon giving birth and breaks down the whole body, enabling the blood to flow through the veins all over the body into the womb more easily.[40] Menstrual blood drains from the whole physical being of the woman, not just one part. Although the use of the comparative adverbs (χαλεπώτερον, θᾶσσον) to describe the suffering of a childless woman shows that giving birth did not guarantee absolutely pain-free menstruation, motherhood was generally viewed as the ultimate solution to women's problems,[41] and easing normal menstruation was no exception. During pregnancy menses did not crowd into the womb all at once, and after parturition a woman's body could accommodate the crush more easily.

RETENTION OF MENSES IN VIRGINS AND SEXUALLY INACTIVE WOMEN

Giving birth facilitated the passage of menstrual blood from the body into the womb, but it did not guarantee that the blood would pass out of the womb with no problem. The Hippocratics believed that to ensure this a woman should have frequent sexual inter-

because a woman's emotional life did not impinge on the male sphere so much, or perhaps because they were not perceived to occur in Classical Greek culture. Soranus, who believed that even normal menstruation was unhealthy as it sapped a woman's strength, lists the effects as listlessness, tension, flushing, nausea, and lack of appetite (*Gyn.* 1. 24).

[40] *Mul.* 1. 1 (viii. 10. 11–12. 5).

[41] Cf. *Nat. Mul.* 2, 3, 8, 35, etc. (vii. 314. 13, 316. 5, 324. 9, 378. 18–20); *Mul.* 2. 121, 128, 133, 169, etc. (viii. 264. 18–19, 276. 8, 302. 11, 350. 9–10); *Epid.* 5. 12 (v. 212. 9–10). However, it is not always clear that the standard formula of 'if she conceives, health, (ἐν γαστρὶ ἴσχῃ, ὑγιής) is meant to signify that if the woman becomes pregnant she will be cured rather than that becoming pregnant is a sign that she has been cured. Arist. thinks pregnancy generally undermines a woman's health, *HA* 584[a]3–[b]19.

course.[42] This moistened the womb thereby preventing it from being
displaced,[43] heated the blood thus making the passage of blood
easier,[44] and kept the mouth of the womb open so that none of the
blood was retained.[45] The idea that intercourse was needed to ensure
normal menstruation may reflect the desire of Greek men to play
some active part in causing menstruation, as they did in defloration
and bringing about pregnancy and childbirth. Making the comfort
of such a common female experience contingent upon sexual intercourse could also be a subtle reinforcement of the assumption that a
woman should submit regularly to her husband's advances whether
she was sexually aroused or not; it implied that she should do so for
her own good.

CONTINUED MENSTRUATION IN SEXUALLY INACTIVE
AND SUPPRESSED MENSES IN SEXUALLY ACTIVE
WOMEN

Of course, it must have been apparent that not all sexually inactive
or nulliparous women did cease to menstruate and fall ill, and that
not all sexually active or parous women menstruated regularly and
remained healthy, so the Hippocratics developed categories to
explain why some women would be more susceptible to retaining
menstrual blood than others. *Mul.* 1. 2 (viii. 14. 9–10) says that the

---

[42] *Mul.* 1. 2 (viii. 14. 8–24. 19) opens by stating that it will discuss the problems
caused by suppressed menstruation in women who have not been pregnant. By implication *Mul.* 1. 3 (viii. 23. 5) must deal with problems caused by suppressed
menses in women who have been pregnant. In fact, the problems of the first group are
blamed more on the fact that the women do not have coitus, rather than on their not
becoming pregnant: 'This then is the reason that the womb closes over, because the
woman does not have intercourse' (τοῦτ᾽ οὖν αἴτιον γίνεται ὥστε αὐτὰς ξυμμύειν,
οἷα μὴ λαγνευομένης τῆς γυναικός (viii. 16. 1–2)). If a woman had not been pregnant it was often assumed that she was sexually inactive. In contrast, one of the
possible symptoms of the second group is that intercourse with their husband causes
pain (μισγομένη ἀνδρὶ ἀλγέει (viii. 22. 13)).
[43] *Mul.* 1. 2 (viii. 14. 16–17); *Genit.* 4 (vii. 476. 8–12).
[44] *Genit.* 4. (vii. 476. 12–14).
[45] *Mul.* 1. 2 (viii. 16. 1–2). Soranus (*Gyn.* 1. 31) says that many widows who menstruated with difficulty were fine after remarrying. He, for his part, believed that intercourse aided menstruation by relaxing the whole body. Some modern researchers
also subscribe to this belief, blaming the refusal of some men to have intercourse at
this period of the month for contributing to pre-menstrual tension since menstruation
is accompanied by erotic impulses in many women. It is also thought that the vaginal
contractions of orgasm may help to alleviate cramps, Asso 1983, 56.

blood can be trapped in the womb by the cervix closing or bending (*ἰδνωθῇ*),[46] or by part of the vagina twisting, and goes on to say (viii. 14. 12–14) that this is especially likely to happen in those women who have a narrow stoma or a cervix lying far into the vagina.[47] The chapter continues:

> For if either (*θάτερον*) of these conditions exists, and if the woman in question does not have intercourse, and if her belly is more emptied than usual from some suffering, the womb is displaced. The womb is not damp of its own accord (as, for example, in the case of a woman who does not have coitus) and there is empty space for the womb (as, for example, when the belly is more empty than usual), so that the womb is displaced when the woman is drier and more empty than usual.[48]

This passage seems to explain not why the womb closes over, but why it becomes displaced. This is because displacement is needed to explain why a far-projecting cervix should make a woman susceptible to retaining menstrual blood. Any woman who does not have intercourse will develop a dry womb which is prone to displacement, but this will be more likely to cause closure of the womb if the body has room in which the womb can move[49] and the cervix is so long as to be brought up against the wall of the vagina when the womb tips. Those with shorter cervices will continue to menstruate even in the absence of coitus. The genital configuration of a narrow stoma could be used to explain why some women who were sexually active suffered from retained menses. Their stomata were so narrow

[46] Cf. *Mul.* 1. 10 (viii. 42. 1) where it is stated that a cervix which is bent (*ἰδνοῦνται*) fails to grasp the seed, and ibid. 1. 36 (viii. 84. 23) which attributes the closing of the womb after childbirth in one patient to the bending (*περιιδνοῦνται*) of the cervix.

[47] It is difficult to know what significance to give to the term *πρόσω τοῦ αἰδοίου*, which I have translated 'far into the vagina'. I have taken it to mean a cervix which projects into the vagina so that it lies close to the vulva. However, this is better represented by the phrase 'close to the privy part' (*πλησίον τοῦ αἰδοίου*), and *Mul.* 1. 5 (viii. 28. 11) says a cervix of this configuration would be liable to excessive flows of blood rather than the retention of menses. *πρόσω τοῦ αἰδοίου*, therefore, could signify a short cervix that lies far back in the vagina away from the vulva. However, a short cervix would seem less prone to doubling up. I have therefore taken *πρόσω τοῦ αἰδοίου* and *πλησίον τοῦ αἰδοίου* to signify the same configuration which is liable both to bending and to excessive flows of blood when straight.

[48] *ἢν γὰρ τουτέων θάτερον ᾖ, καὶ μὴ μίσγηται ἡ γυνὴ τῷ ἀνδρί, καὶ κενωθῇ ἡ κοιλίη μᾶλλον τοῦ καιροῦ ὑπό τευ παθήματος, στρέφονται αἱ μῆτραι· οὔτε γὰρ ἰκμαλέαι εἰσὶ κατὰ σφέας, οἷα μὴ λαγνευομένης, εὐρυχωρίη τε σφίσιν ἐστίν, ἅτε τῆς κοιλίης κενοτέρης ἐούσης, ὥστε στρέφεσθαι ἅτε ξηροτέρης καὶ κουφοτέρης ἐούσης τοῦ καιροῦ, Mul.* 1. 2 (viii. 14. 14–19).

[49] The *εὐρυχωρίη* in the body which is advantageous in accommodating menstrual blood can be a liability if the womb becomes too dry.

as to impede the entrance of semen into the womb, so their wombs remained dry even after intercourse. The beginning of the passage, then, would perhaps be better rendered as: 'For if *one* of these conditions [i.e. the narrow stoma] exists *or* if the woman in question does not have intercourse . . . the womb is displaced.' Most manuscripts (DGHIJK) give the reading 'or' (*ἤ*), rather than 'and' (*καί*), and since the sentence is explaining the causes of womb displacement, the first arm of the disjunction would refer to only one of the two genital configurations under discussion. A far-projecting cervix would not cause the displacement of the womb; it is only significant in trapping menstrual blood after the womb has been displaced. The displacement can result in any woman from a failure to have intercourse, or in sexually active women from a narrowness of the stoma. This chapter, then, while still maintaining that sexual intercourse was a valuable measure for health maintenance, accounts for the fact that some virgins remain healthy and some sexually active women fall ill.

PROGRESSION FROM DISCOMFORT TO DISEASE

To begin with, suppressed menses simply cause a woman pain or discomfort, e.g. *Mul.* I. 1 (viii. 12. 19–21), and once again a parous woman finds it easier to deal with the situation than a nullipara: 'If some additional suffering (*pathēma*) should befall a woman who has already given birth so that her menses cannot be got rid of, she will endure the pain more easily than a woman who has not borne a child.'[50] In this case, a *pathēma* over and above parturition causes menstrual suppression. In the case of nulliparous women, 'more conditions [*pathēmata*] befall them so that their menses are shut in their body' (*τὰ παθήματα προσπίπτει πλείονα ὥστε τὰ καταμήνια ἀποφράσσεσθαι*). It should be noted that in these situations what a woman suffers is called a *pathēma*, 'condition', not a *nosos*, 'disease', and that the retained menstrual blood is still called *katamēnia*, 'menses', rather than a *rhoos*, 'flux', which at *HA* 521ᵃ27 Aristotle says is the term used to signify a diseased menstrual flow.

---

[50] *εἰ δὲ καί τι πάθημα τῇ γυναικὶ γένοιτο τῇ ἤδη τετοκυίῃ, ὥστε τὰ καταμήνια μὴ δύνασθαι καθαρθῆναι, ῥηιτέρως τὸν πόνον οἴσει ἢ εἰ ἄτοκος ἦν, Mul.* I. 1 (viii. 10. 13–15).

Ordinary menses, even when suppressed, are not a morbid discharge. [51] If the menses are not evacuated, however, they lead to disease either by moving to a different part of a woman's body, by turning purulent, or by taking on an admixture of a pathological agent. In these cases, a woman's suffering is termed a *nosos* and the discharge of blood a *rhoos*, cf. *Mul.* 1. 3 (viii. 22. 12). [52] *GA* 773ª16–20 says that in a woman whose stoma has closed over, there are no problems until the time comes for discharge of the menses. Then the constriction either bursts open naturally or is forcibly opened by a doctor. In the latter case, and in cases where the opening was not made at all, some women died. Aristotle is not himself a doctor, but he here records the belief that suppressed menses could cause serious illness as a result of a condition that is not itself life-threatening.

Although one cure for retained menses in virgins is to have them married and deflowered as soon as possible, for women who have fallen victim to retained menses despite being sexually active, intercourse can be painful, [53] and the Hippocratics prescribe treatment such as purges and pessaries (which draw the womb back to its proper place or open the vagina) before advising a woman to return to her husband. The appearance of the menses brings relief and indicates that the treatment is successful. In these cases, however, the Hippocratics do not concern themselves primarily with the pre-existent pathological state. Their treatment is aimed at curing the symptom of retained menses rather than attacking the root of the problem directly, and although to do this the condition which caused the retention must be circumvented in some way, the specific ailment that is causing any particular woman to retain her mens-

---

[51] Arist. likens menses to diarrhoea and other morbid discharges at *GA* 728ª21–5, but he still insists that they are a natural discharge.

[52] Bilious and phlegmatic menses are termed a *rhoos* at *Mul.* 1. 8, 9 (viii. 36. 10, 40. 1); pathological menses are termed a *rhoos eruthros* at *Mul.* 2. 110, 113 (viii. 234. 3–5, 242. 9–10), and *Mul.* 1. 24 (viii. 64. 9–11) says that a pathological discharge of seed from a too relaxed womb should be treated as a *rhoos*. *Mul.* 2. 114 (viii. 246. 6–9) says that sometimes a woman will bleed from her joints after childbirth or illness and some doctors take this to be a *rhoos*, but it is something else—'a viscous discharge like blood' (κολλῶδες ὁμοῦ τῷ αἵματι). A true *rhoos* comes from the womb or hollow veins and is pure blood.

[53] 'If the flux does not come, it happens that they seem to be pregnant, and intercourse with a man is painful' (ἢν δέ οἱ ῥόος μὴ γίνεται, ἔσται ὥστε δοκέειν ἐγκύμονα εἶναι, καὶ μισγομένη ἀνδρὶ ἀλγέει, *Mul.* 1. 3 (viii. 22. 12–13)).

trual fluid is rarely mentioned in actual cases—the important thing for an ailing woman is to begin menstruating again.[54]

TYPES OF ILLNESS ASSOCIATED WITH RETAINED MENSES[55]

Among the hardships caused by the suppression of menses were headaches,[56] gout,[57] fever,[58] haemorrhoids,[59] pains in the hips and flanks,[60] consumption of the lungs,[61] suffocation,[62] and loss of reason, particularly in young virgins.[63] In other cases the accumulated menses could fester and turn to pus, causing intense pain in the stomach. When the periods eventually came the pus would flow out with them for seven to nine days. Following this the woman might be left with ulcers, which if they were considerable caused her to be sterile. If the mixture of blood and pus could not come out via the genitals it could eat its way out and erupt as a malodorous stream in the flank above the groin. This showed that the mouth of the womb had been diverted to this place, and henceforth the menses issued from here and the woman was sterile, if she survived at all. If the menses accumulated but did not fester they could not eat their way out through the flank but collected there in the flesh causing a tumour. Doctors who cut this put their patients in danger. Sometimes the condition could right itself by the womb's reverting to its

---

[54] Soranus seems to be referring to this attitude in *Gyn.* 1. 28 when he comments on the lack of efficacy in bringing on impeded menstruation if the impediment itself is not dealt with directly.

[55] This section does not deal with those illnesses said to have been caused by a displaced womb (see pp. 69–71 above). This was another important source of diseases among women, but often the suppression of menses that resulted from the displacement would be the major cause of concern anyway. The Hippocratics would be looking for the appearance of menstruation as a sign that the womb had returned to its normal place. The close association of the two conditions is shown in *Nat. Mul.* 18 (vii. 338. 3–22) which advises the use of odour-therapies (usually employed on a displaced womb) on a woman said to be suffering simply from suppressed menses.

[56] *Nat. Mul.* 18 (vii. 338. 7).   [57] *Aph.* 6. 29 (iv. 570. 6).

[58] *Mul.* 1. 3 (viii. 26. 10–12).

[59] *Epid.* 4. 24 (v. 164. 9–10).

[60] Ibid. 4. 38, 5. 91 (v. 180. 5–14, 254. 7–10). Rousselle 1980, 1090, notes that pains in the neck, forearms and loins have been connected with amenorrhea in this century owing to blockage of extra-uterine tubes.

[61] *Mul.* 1. 2 (viii. 18. 16–18).   [62] *Nat. Mul.* 18 (vii. 338. 5–6).

[63] *Virg.* (viii. 468. 8–17). The author states that if the young girls do not kill themselves because of the suppression of menses they will die of another disease.

natural position, but otherwise the same dangers held in this case as in the previous.[64] Diseases in the general medicine could have any one of several different origins and each disease was treated in the light of this assumed origin. For headaches *Morb.* 2. 12 (vii. 20. 11–15) advises shaving the patient's head and strapping to it a leather hide filled with water as hot as the patient can stand, refilling the hide with hot water whenever it grows cold. *Loc. Hom.* 40 (vi. 330. 16–19) advises venesection and cauterization. *Prorrh.* 2. 8 (ix. 28. 2–6) says that gout in a young man can be cured if he 'takes care to follow the correct way of life, loves exercise, has a good digestion, understands what is suitable, and follows the advice of a knowledgeable doctor'.[65] Haemorrhoids are ascribed to bile or phlegm lodging in the veins in the rectum, and the treatise *Haem.* (vi. 436. 9–442. 25) gives seven chapters of alternative remedies for them.[66] Pains in the loins could be treated by administering hellebore to make the patient vomit up large amounts of foamy matter (ἀφρώδεα συχνά).[67] *Int.* 10–13 (vii. 188. 26–200. 23) lists three different types of consumption arising from phlegm, blood, bile, exertion, and especially from intercourse (μάλιστα καὶ ἀπὸ λαγνείης, *Int.* 13 (vii. 200. 3)), all of which are to be treated by specified emetics, enemas, fumigations, and exercise. A person suffering from sanguineous pleurisy should abstain from intercourse, *Morb.* 3. 16 (vii. 148. 17–21).

The solution to all these problems for women was to bring on the menses by vapour baths,[68] pessaries,[69] fomentations,[70] diet, and emmenagogues of various ingredients. A typical emmenagogic prescription calls for taking five dung beetles without wings, heads, or

[64] *Mul.* 1. 2 (viii. 18. 21–20. 25).

[65] τὸν τρόπον ἐστὶν ἐπιμελής τε καὶ φιλόπονος καὶ κοιλίας ἀγαθὰς ἔχων ὑπακούειν πρὸς τὰ ἐπιτηδεύματα, οὗτος δὴ ἰητροῦ γνώμην ἔχοντος ἐπιτυχὼν ὑγιὴς ἂν γένοιτο.

[66] A short final chapter, *Haem.* 9 (vi. 444. 1–5), gives the treatment for haemorrhoids in women, and while this is admittedly not directed at securing the descent of the menses, it illustrates once again that the general medicine was not necessarily considered applicable to women. Failure to recognize this causes Littré to claim (ad loc.) that in this chapter ἕδρην (which normally is translated as 'rump', and hence in this context seems most likely to signify the anus) signifies the vulva, and Joly to argue (ad loc.) that the author includes this chapter because women were thought to be especially prone to haemorrhoids, not because there was a specific treatment for them.

[67] *Coac.* 2. 304 (v. 650. 15–17).   [68] *Aph.* 5. 28 (iv. 542. 5–6).
[69] *Mul.* 1. 3 (viii. 22. 9–10).
[70] *Nat. Mul.* 18 (vii. 338. 8–9).

Female Pathology 133

feet and grinding them up with a water chestnut from the seashore complete with shell and root, mixing this with an equal amount of yellow camomile and celery seed, and fifteen cuttlefish eggs and finally giving it to the woman to drink in a draught of sweet wine.[71] This chapter continues for ten pages in Littré's edition, cataloguing similar recipes, and *Mul.* 1 and 2 end with similar extensive lists, perhaps showing the extent to which folk remedies influenced the Hippocratics in their treatment of women as opposed to men.

These potions and the advice on diet were perhaps guided by the aim of rendering the menses as fluid as possible so that they would pass out more easily. Vapour baths and fomentations would no doubt have a relaxing, if not a debilitating, effect which would be thought to loosen any general constrictions in the body, while pessaries would address any constriction specifically in the vagina or cervix.

Individuals of both sexes could be subject to bouts of delirium, those that turned violent being due to black bile, *Prorrh.* 1. 123 (v. 552. 5–554. 1).[72] Women were at extra risk because in their case menses could turn the fits positively savage (θηριώδεα). The author mentions the case of a tanner's daughter who had suffered from loss of voice, lethargy, and spasms, 'which began with the appearance of the menses' (ἤρξατο γυναικείων παρεόντων). Littré's note demonstrates that the text is corrupt here, and remarks that Galen commented that the wild fever which attacked the tanner's daughter was due to the suppression of menses.

According to the Hippocratics, menstrual suppression can lead to great suffering and eventually death if the material lies in the womb. At the end of three months' accumulation of menstrual fluid (which can be heard gurgling in the womb), the woman suffers intermittent suffocation, fever, coldness, and backache. By the end of the fourth month she also has thick urine, a hard stomach, she grinds her teeth, loses her appetite, and cannot sleep. In the fifth month all these symptoms increase, and in the sixth she throws herself round, swoons, coughs up phlegm and yellow bile, has a raging thirst and backache, cannot pass faeces or urine, slurs her speech, and her legs and lower body swell up.[73] After this, death is inevitable.

---

[71] Ibid. 32 (vii. 346. 14–18).
[72] At *Mul.* 2. 182 (viii. 364. 14–15) a woman suffering from anxiety, depression, and despair is said to have black bile lodged in her womb.
[73] *Mul.* 1. 2 (viii. 16. 2–18. 14).

A woman's body could use up the extra material of suppressed menses in the production of extra flesh or masculine traits, particularly if the suppression was due to lack of intercourse. Two cases are recorded of women whose husbands had left them and whose menses stopped.[74] Both began to grow hairier and their voices grew deeper. The only hope of reversing the process was to bring back the menses, but the doctor failed in both cases. Aristotle says that in fat women the menstrual fluid is used up to maintain the body and that if a woman has no menses from puberty she tends to look masculine.[75] He also remarks that after menopause some women grow hair on the chin.[76] It seems as if the actual symptoms of masculinity were thought to be caused directly by the suppression of the menses and the using up of the material in the production of hair, extra fat, etc.

Occasionally a woman could be thought to be menstruating too abundantly, which caused its own problems.[77] *Mul.* 1. 6 (viii. 30. 17–19) says women who menstruate for more than four days are 'delicate' (λεπταί). The illnesses included such things as loss of colour, lethargy, fever, anorexia, anxiety, loss of weight, and general weakness. The woman would suffer pains in the hips and would finally become sterile. The original problem could be due to the fact that her body was naturally disposed to flux or that the mouth of the uterus was placed close to the vulva.[78] In either case the condition was exacerbated by frequent intercourse or large meals. Indulging in intercourse too often is attributed to the woman's own desires (viii. 28. 16), not to her simply acceding to her husband's desires as a dutiful wife should—behaviour against which the Hippocratics pronounce no health sanctions. This is one of the rare places in the Corpus where women are described as having a conscious appetite for intercourse, and it is part of a pathological condition. Aristotle's cure for a sexually incontinent woman was for

---

[74] *Epid.* 6. 32 (v. 356. 4–15).   [75] *GA* 746^{b}27–9, 747^{a}1–3.

[76] *HA* 518^{a}33–5. The belief that hair could grow on the chin as a result of suppressed menses, which were best freed by intercourse, may explain the Argive law that a woman with a beard must occupy the same bed as her husband, Plut. *Mor.* 245F. *Acta Sanctorum Oct.* III, 162, records that Galla, a daughter of Symmachus, was unwilling to marry again after she had been widowed. She was warned that this would result in an excess of heat which would cause the growth of a beard, and this did happen. She died of cancer of the breast, see Delcourt 1961, 91–2.

[77] *Aph.* 5. 57 (iv. 552. 11).   [78] *Mul.* 1. 5 (viii. 28. 10–11).

her to give birth several times, thus using up the excess material which caused her desire for sex.[79]

FEMALE REPRODUCTIVE MECHANISM AS THE CAUSE OF DISEASES IN WOMEN

However, the cases of a woman menstruating too abundantly are rare in comparison with the number of occasions on which the Hippocratics find cause to suspect suppression of menses. The expectation of frequent and heavy blood loss, which probably few women achieved, may have led to treatment for suppression of menses when the woman was in fact perfectly healthy and merely had a longer cycle than the mean, once again requiring men to intervene in controlling female sexuality. More importantly though, the focus on the suppression of menses as the cause of a disease, even when this was a complaint completely unrelated to a woman's reproductive organs, and one which a man could suffer equally, emphasizes the Greek male negative estimation of the female body. Not only did it fall short of the male ideal in a manner that required a monthly readjustment to keep it healthy, but the mechanism that performed this readjustment was itself in constant danger of malfunction and therefore posed a threat to the health of a woman. The development of many illnesses in a woman was traced to a malfunction in her reproductive system because this was her first line of defence against disease. The aetiology of men's diseases was more varied, in part at least, precisely because men did not have a common cycle in which they regularly emitted a specific humour, nor an anatomical analogue of the womb which could act as a collecting point for all this humour and hence a focus for disease. This explains why the author of *Morb.* 4. 57 (vii. 612. 19–21) says that even though women get dropsy as men do and show the same symptoms, he will deal with female dropsy in his *Diseases of Women*.[80]

Loc. Hom. 47 (vi. 344. 3–4) says, 'The diseases called "gynaecological": the womb is the cause of all these diseases (τὰ γυναικεῖα νοσεύματα καλεύμενα· αἱ ὑστέραι πάντων τῶν νοση-

---

[79] *GA* 774ᵃ5–6. Given the discomfort, pain, and risks inherent in childbirth at this period, it is quite understandable that this course of action would make a woman somewhat wary of intercourse.

[80] This may be a reference to *Mul.* 1. 59–61 (viii. 116. 20–126. 3).

μάτων αἰτίαί εἰσιν). For many Hippocratic physicians, any disease a woman suffered was gynaecological and the cause of all these diseases was the womb. However, in many cases the symptoms of the diseases were thought to be caused by the resulting suppressed menses rather than the womb itself.[81] Menstruation kept a normal woman healthy; if a woman became sick the blame was put on the breakdown of this mechanism.

Obviously, I do not want to argue that none of the female patients in the Hippocratic Corpus was suffering from specifically gynaecological complaints,[82] and as I stated (above, p. 113) not all Hippocratic physicians would centre their therapy of a female patient exclusively on her reproductive system. What I wish to emphasize is the frequency with which illnesses attributed to a variety of causes in men are traced to a breakdown in the reproductive mechanism in women.

MENSTRUATION AS A CURE

Being female, therefore, was viewed as a biological hazard which led to most women living on the brink of ill health. In view of this, it is surprising that on several occasions in the *Epid.*, when discussing diseases which afflicted the population as a whole, the authors claim that more men than women suffered and died from the illnesses under discussion. To some extent this could reflect the fact that since women tended to seek therapy from more traditional sources, the doctors' patients had been mostly men; there are twice as many male as female case histories recorded in the *Epid.* However, women would not have had to keep their visits to wise-women and other healers secret, so the Hippocratics would have known that women were falling ill even if they were not giving the Hippocratics their custom. Failing a survey to establish how many women were seeking alternative treatment, a survey which it is unlikely the Hippocratics conducted, the estimate of how many women fell ill would be based

---

[81] Arist. was of the opinion that women were the only female animals to suffer from affections of the womb (*GA* 776ª9–15), and he attributed this to the volume of a woman's menstrual flow compared to what he thought other animals produced.
[82] e.g. breast cancer, *Mul.* 2. 133 (viii. 282. 10–284. 1); vaginal warts, ibid. 2. 212 (viii. 406. 16); uterine prolapses, ibid. 2. 144 (viii. 316. 13); uterine ulcers, ibid. 1. 38 (viii. 94. 5–10); uterine 'moles', ibid. viii. 1. 71 (viii. 148. 24–150. 22).

on assumption, an assumption supported not by statistical evidence but by cultural expectations.

One doctor remarks that women's restricted sphere protected them from contracting diseases; men had to go out of the house more and were therefore more often exposed to the influence of the environment. Only two free women contracted κυνάγχαι (an inflammation of the throat) and that in a mild dose, though it affected slave women (who lived a less restricted life than free women) more frequently and very violently, and they died extremely quickly.[83] It seems possible that not frequenting public places would afford women some measure of protection from disease, but in widespread epidemics this must have amounted to little more than a delay in contracting the illness rather than complete protection from it. Not knowing the mechanism of contagion, a woman would not quarantine her husband, at least not before the symptoms manifested themselves, and it is often prior to the manifestation of symptoms that a disease is most contagious. If a man was likely to catch a disease from being exposed to large gatherings of people, his wife would be likely to catch it from being exposed to him in an intimate manner, and when epidemics attack a general population there is no medical reason that they should generally manifest themselves in a less virulent form among women than among men. In fact, since women seem to have been less well nourished, and the home was perhaps an equally fertile ground for breeding disease as the more open public spaces,[84] we might expect women to be more rather than less susceptible to disease. It therefore seems unlikely that the cultural perception that women suffered less frequently and less severely from disease was based on empirical evidence. Furthermore, the theory that women were protected because they were exposed less to the environment does not have much support among the Hippocratic treatises. More significant in Hippocratic explanations of women's comparative immunity to fatal diseases is the fact, once again, that they menstruate.

Even the author who argues that women are protected by their remaining in the home does not make it his primary reason for their

[83] *Epid.* 6. 7. 1 (v. 334. 14–18).
[84] Pomeroy 1975, 79, describes the residential quarters of the average Greek family in Classical times as 'dark, squalid and unsanitary', but cf. Wycherley 1969, 187. Patterson 1985, 121, argues that the enclosed spaces, undernourishment, and nursing duties of women in Classical Greece would have made them more susceptible to diseases than men.

immunity; he says, 'I think *this* is responsible, and the fact that they do not go out like men, and that they do not otherwise fall ill like men' (*ἠτιώμην τοῦτο, καὶ τὸ μὴ ἐξιέναι ὁμοίως ἀνδράσι, καὶ ὅτι οὐδ' ἄλλως ὁμοίως ἀνδράσιν ἁλίσκονται, Epid.* 6. 7. 1 (v. 334. 14–15)). Littré says that *τοῦτο* signifies menstruation, and that the author wishes to argue that the menstrual purgation was one of the reasons that women did not fall ill as often as men. The previous sentence contains no discussion of menstruation to provide such a reference for the pronoun *τοῦτο*, but it contains the remark that those women who did succumb to the disease were older, and *τοῦτο* seems to be referring to this aspect of age in some way. The major physiological distinction setting older women apart from other members of her sex in Hippocratic eyes was that she had passed menopause, so Littré's inference would seem to be correct. In any case, it is difficult to see to what else *τοῦτο* could refer. Even in cases where women were afflicted with a disease which had the same origins as the disease which was attacking men simultaneously, menstruation brought relief.[85]

An epidemic was sometimes the stimulus which caused young girls to menstruate for the first time; they, too, invariably recuperated, e.g. *Epid.* 1. 8 (ii. 646. 9–648. 5):

Though many women fell ill, they were fewer than the men and less frequently died.... Now, menstruation appeared during the fevers in most cases, and with many maidens it occurred then for the first time. Some bled from the nose. Sometimes both epistaxis [bleeding from the nose] and menstruation appeared together; for example, the maiden daughter of Daitharses had her first menstruation during fever and also a violent discharge from the nose. I know of no woman who died if any of these symptoms showed themselves properly.[86]

The individual cases recorded in the *Epid.* corroborate this generalization. For instance, the cases of three *parthenoi* are recorded, all of whom were suffering from fever. The first never

[85] *Epid.* 6. 5. 1 (v. 314. 5–13) says that Nature effects cures by the various evacuations from the body, including what takes place in females (*τοῖσι θήλεσι, ἃ τούτοισι*). Pliny also thought menstruation could cure many diseases, see *NH* 28. 44.

[86] *γυναῖκες δὲ ἐνόσησαν μὲν πουλλαί, ἐλάσσους δὲ ἢ ἄνδρες, καὶ ἔθνησκον ἥσσους· ... τῇσι μὲν οὖν πλείστῃσιν ἐν τοῖσι πυρετοῖσι γυναικεῖα ἐπεφαίνετο, καὶ παρθένοισι πολλῇσι τότε πρῶτον ἐγένετο· ἔστι δ' ὅτε καὶ ἐκ ῥινῶν καὶ τὰ γυναικεῖα τῇσιν αὐτῇσιν ἐπεφαίνετο, οἷον τῇ Δαιθαρσέως θυγατρὶ παρθένῳ ἐπεφάνη τότε πρῶτον καὶ ἐκ ῥινῶν λαῦρον ἐρρύη, καὶ οὐδεμίην οἶδα ἀποθανοῦσαν, ᾗσι τουτέων τι καλῶς γένοιτο. Cf. Epid.* 1. 9 (ii. 658. 6–10).

menstruated and died; the other two began to menstruate during their illness and survived.[87] Menstruation could also bring relief in cases of mental distress. *Epid.* 3. 17, case xi (iii. 134. 1–14), records how a woman of gloomy temperament, after a grief, wandered in her speech in a slightly feverish state uttering obscenities until the crisis of her disease, when copious menstruation occurred. Later in the same book another woman is recorded, case xv (iii. 142. 6–146. 6), who was seized with grief and was often speechless. No menstruation is recorded for her and she died.

There are several cases where recovery is specifically ascribed to menstruation, e.g. *Coac.* 520 (v. 704. 9–10) says, 'In a spasm, menses appearing at the beginning, fever not developing, release' (σπασμῷ, γυναικείων ἐν ἀρχῇσι φανέντων, πυρετοῦ μὴ ἐπιγενομένου, λύσις), and *Epid.* 4. 25 (v. 168. 15–17) gives four cases where the appearance of menstruation relieved a tension in the hypochondria: 'Tension in the hypochondrium, menses appearing on the seventeenth day, the patient came to a complete crisis. A woman whose menses were not suppressed in this way came to a crisis on the third day; another on the fifth; another came to a crisis on the sixth.'[88] Only one of these cases attributes the woman's illness to suppressed menses, but menstruation is effective as a cure in all four cases. *Epid.* 5. 12 (v. 212. 5–10) attributes the easing of a headache directly to menstruation.

Epistaxis was also looked upon as a very favourable occurrence during the course of a woman's illness. This resulted from the belief that if the menses could not flow from the uterus they could flow from the nose or the anus—the latter being more common in young girls:[89] 'For a woman, if when the menses are lacking, blood flows from the nose, good' (γυναικὶ τῶν καταμηνίων ἐκλειπόντων, αἷμα ἐκ τῶν ῥινῶν ῥυῆναι, ἀγαθόν).[90] Aristotle thought that a woman could not have haemorrhoids, a nosebleed, or any other similar discharge if she was menstruating; if she did, her menses were

---

[87] *Epid.* 3. 1, case vi; 17, cases vii and xii (iii. 50. 1–52. 9, 122. 1–17, 136. 1–12).

[88] ὑποχονδρίου ἔντασις, γυναικεῖα ἐπεφάνη δεκάτῃ καὶ ἑβδόμῃ, ἐκρίθη διατελέως. ἥ γε μὴ οὕτως ἐνέμεινεν, ἐκρίθη τρίτῃ· ἄλλη, πέμπτῃ· ἄλλη ἑβδόμῃ ἐκρίθη.

[89] *Mul.* 1. 2 (viii. 22. 3–4).

[90] *Aph.* 5. 33 (iv. 544. 1–2). Sometimes it would seem as if an emission from any other part of the body was considered to be the menses in another form, e.g. vomiting, *Mul.* 1. 2 (viii. 20. 25–22. 1); *Aph.* 5. 32 says menstruation cures a woman of vomiting blood (iv. 542. 14), a sentiment echoed at *Morb.* 1. 7 (vi. 152. 20–1). Conversely, if a woman is 'badly affected by flux' (ὑπὸ ῥόου δὲ πιεζομένη), she is benefited by the flux going to the mouth or nose (vi. 152. 21–2).

depleted.[91] In fact this syndrome (vicarious menstruation) does occur, though it is rare.[92] Oestrogen has a powerful effect on mucous membranes and occasionally the membranes of the nose can become gorged with blood then release it at the same time as the uterus; but this seldom, if ever, completely supersedes normal menstruation. The Hippocratics believed that this epistaxis could cure a disease in the same way as menstruation. In fact, if a woman died after epistaxis it was thought to require some explanation: 'For the daughter of Philo, who died, though she had violent epistaxis, dined rather unseasonably on the seventh day.'[93] Another young girl is reported to have died even though she bled from the nose: 'In the daughter of Leonides, the *physis* having made a start, turned aside; after it had turned aside, she bled at the nose. When she had bled at the nose a change occurred. The doctor did not understand, and the young girl died.'[94] Helen King has argued that the reason this girl died is that she was too young to benefit from an epistaxis. As a *pais* ('child') rather than a *parthenos* her vessels were too narrow to permit the menses to flow upwards, and it was this that the doctor did not understand.[95] However, the comment, 'the doctor did not understand', is made after the case history states that a change occurred upon epistaxis and before it notes that the girl died, imputing responsibility to the doctor for her death. The change could well have been for the good, and the doctor's failure to understand this and his continuation of treatment the direct cause of her death. Because the Hippocratics believed that menstruation led to recovery and that a nosebleed was the menses in another form, they would have to blame this death on external circumstances.

Menstruation was thought to cure so many diseases because it was

[91] *GA* 727ᵃ12–16. Soranus also believed the substance of the menses could be evacuated through a nose bleed (*Gyn.* 3. 7).
[92] Jones–Wentz–Burnett 1988, 259.
[93] Φίλωνος γὰρ τῇ θυγατρί, ἐκ ῥινῶν λαῦρον ἐρρύη, ἑβδομαίη δὲ ἐοῦσα ἐδείπνησεν ἀκαιροτέρως· ἀπέθανεν, *Epid.* 1. 9 (ii. 658. 10–12).
[94] τῇ Λεωνίδεω θυγατρὶ ἡ φύσις ὁρμήσασα ἀπεστράφη, ἀποστραφεῖσα, ἐμυκτήρισεν· μυκτηρίσασα διηλλάγη· ὁ ἰητρὸς οὐ ξυνεῖδεν· ἡ παῖς ἀπέθανεν, *Epid.* 7. 123 (v. 468. 4–6).
[95] King 1989, 28. She details a great deal of evidence which shows that the 'way up' was considered to be constricted in young girls, but because of the position of the remark concerning the doctor's lack of understanding here, I am not sure that it is applicable to this case. Believing that epistaxis was generally inhibited in young girls does not entail that it would not perform the same service for them as it did for older women if it did take place.

a natural purging process of the whole body; when it was functioning properly, it drew off the excess humours and with them all the morbid substances building up inside a woman who had become diseased. *Aph.* 5. 36 (iv. 544. 7–8) implies that it is only if the menses are not doing their job that purging is called for: 'If the menses of a woman are pale, and do not always appear at the same interval, it is a sign that the woman is in need of purging.'[96] The Hippocratic prescriptions for purging bile or phlegm with emetics or enemas were probably directed primarily at men; in women the harmful substances were drained through the reproductive system rather than the digestive tract. When the author of *Mul.* I. II claims that therapy is the same for almost all women he adds the rider, 'except for drawing down the menses' (πλὴν τοῦ κατασπάσαι τὰ ἐμμήνια), and then account needs to be taken of whatever is bad in the menses.[97]

Female bodies as a whole can be treated the same because any morbid residues that would differentiate them from one another drain from the rest of the body into the womb with the menses and it is only in this one particular spot that differences become material. A woman suffering from an accumulation of bile or phlegm is relieved by bilious or phlegmatic menses.[98] Initially these are said to bring only temporary relief, but after complete suppression of the menses a *rhoos* from the womb is the best hope of a cure. However, if the *rhooi* continue too long they can ulcerate the womb and make the woman more ill than she was before. In this case the *rhoos* is said to be flowing from the womb itself and no longer from the whole body.[99] *Mul.* I. II (viii. 44. 22–4), after prescribing emetics, diet, and vapour baths to rid women of excess bile, phlegm, etc., says, 'If the womb does not respond to this treatment, it is necessary to purge it with pessaries from non-irritant remedies' (τὰς δὲ ὑστέρας χρή, ἢν μὴ πρὸς ταύτην τὴν δίαιτην ἐνακούωσι, καθαίρειν φαρμάκοισιν ἀδήκτοισι προσθέτοισιν), showing that even when a

[96] γυναικὶ τὰ καταμήνια ἄχροα, καὶ μὴ κατὰ τὰ αὐτὰ αἰεὶ γινόμενα, καθάρσιος δεῖσθαι σημαίνει.

[97] *Mul.* I. II (viii. 44. 3–8).

[98] *Mul.* I. 8 (viii. 36. 9–10, 14–15) says that although bilious vomit, stools, or flux can relieve a woman of excess bile, the most common remedy is the *rhoos*, and *Mul.* I. 9 (viii. 38. 10–12), says that the phlegm from a phlegmatic woman's body leaves by the menses rather than the nose, anus, or urethra.

[99] Ibid. I. 8 (viii. 38. 1–2). A phlegmatic woman has a similar experience, ibid. I. 9 (viii. 40. 5–6).

doctor employs remedies which are not specifically emmenagogues, he is still targeting the womb in his treatment.

The Hippocratics do not advise bleeding women often—unless it was to check menstruation or as a substitute for it.[100] There are fourteen recorded instances of bleeding in the case histories, twelve of them male, of whom nine survived. Of the two women who were bled, one died.[101] In *Nat. Hom.* ii (vi. 58. 13), when describing the vascular system so that a doctor might know where to bleed for various complaints, the author mentions the testicles but no female genitalia. *HA* 512^{b}1–5 describes Diogenes of Apollonia's theory of blood vessels, which is very similar to that in *Nat. Hom.*, but mentions the uterus as well as the testicles. Bleeding is recommended at the end of a course of treatment at *Steril.* 230 (viii. 444. 8–10), but when it is mentioned in the gynaecology it is usually as a last desperate resort. *Mul.* 1. 77 (viii. 172. 6–7) recommends bleeding at the ankle for women during difficult childbirth, and *Mul.* 1. 38 (viii. 94. 17) advises bleeding if the lochia do not come out after all other remedies have been tried, but the author makes it clear that it is much better to obtain relief using clysters or vomiting if possible. Bleeding is also the last resort in treating a mole, a very dangerous undertaking which Hippocratics are advised to refuse attempting at all, *Mul.* 1. 71 (viii. 150. 19–22). *Mul.* 2. 110 (viii. 236. 20–238. 1) advises applying cupping-glasses to breasts in case of a *rhoos eruthros*, but warns against actually drawing any blood. *Steril.* 232 (viii. 446. 2) remarks that this treatment failed to cure a *rhoos eruthros* anyway. Venesection was a remedy for the male body.

One explanation for the preference of menstruation as a purge can be found in *Epid.* 2. 5. 6 (v. 130. 3): 'For this flux comes from the Great Vein' (ὅδε γὰρ ὁ ῥόος, ἐκ τῆς μεγάλης φλεβός). The previous statement discusses women who did not have menses,[102] so we are

---

[100] *Aph.* 5. 50 (iv. 550. 5–6). At *Epid.* 2. 5. 5 (v. 130. 2) Littré's text reads, 'For flatulence, venesection' (ἀνεμίην, φλεβοτομίη). Manuscript H reads, 'For lack of blood, venesection' (ἀναιμίην, φλεβοτομίη). Bleeding a person who was suffering from anaemia would be paradoxical to say the least, and this may explain Littré's adoption of ἀνεμίην from D's reading of ἠνεμίην. However, if the lack of blood referred to a lack of menstrual blood, bleeding would be acting as a substitute for menstruation here. If this were the case, it would be easier to understand the following statement in the Greek text which gives advice on staunching a *rhoos*. As it stands, and as Littré himself recognizes, it is hard to give any significance to the *rhoos* which is discussed there (see pp. 142–3 below).

[101] *Epid.* 5. 63 (v. 242. 8). For the survivor see p. 214 below.

[102] If we follow H's reading ἀναιμίην over D's and Littré's ἀνεμίην/ἠνεμίην.

justified here in taking ῥόος to signify the menstrual flux, particularly as the following statement deals with women who are unable to conceive, thereby firmly placing the remark in a gynaecological context. The menstrual fluid is thus said to come from the Great Vein itself, which would surely have effected the most efficient purging as the blood was drawn from all over the body, not from one particular area. It would be extremely dangerous to attempt venesection on the Great Vein, so artificially stimulated blood loss could not evacuate blood from every corner of the body as could menstruation.

In addition, because menstrual blood is a natural and not a forced discharge, it is more likely to bring away waste products than is blood drawn arbitrarily. A natural purging is more likely to bring away appropriate material in the appropriate quantity through the appropriate passage than purging a patient by artificial means, where it is possible for a doctor to make a mistake in each of these areas.[103] Menstruation effected a natural cleansing of harmful substances from the body which no artificial purgations could equal as a cure. Therefore, any childhood disease which persisted after menarche was thought to be incurable and likely to become chronic.[104] If the onset of menstruation could not cure a woman, nothing could.

This is indicative of why copious nose bleeds, paralleling vicarious menstruation, were looked on so favourably during a man's illness, e. g.: 'As to the peculiarities of the ardent fevers, the most likely patients to survive were those who had a proper and copious bleeding from the nose, in fact I do not know of a single case in this constitution that proved fatal when a proper bleeding occurred.'[105] And again in *Prog.* 7 (ii. 126. 13–128. 1), 'A heavy flow of blood from the nose is advantageous' (αἵματος ῥῆξις ἐκ τῶν ῥινῶν καὶ κάρτα ὠφελέει).[106] If epistaxis could take the place of normal menstruation in a woman, this blood could be thought of as flushing waste products from all over the body in a man also. Like menses, epistaxis was an evacuation that appeared at puberty, *Aph.* 3. 27

[103] See *Aph.* 1. 21–5 (iv. 468. 11–470. 7).
[104] Ibid. 3. 28 (iv. 500. 4–8); *Epid.* 6. 1. 4 (v. 268. 1–2).
[105] ἢν δὲ τὰ παθήματα τῶν καύσων, οἷσι μὲν καλῶς καὶ δαψιλέως ἐκ ῥινῶν αἱμορραγῆσαι, διά τουτέου μάλιστα σώζεσθαι, καὶ οὐδένα οἶδα, εἰ καλῶς αἱμορραγήσειεν, ἐν τῇ καταστάσει ταύτῃ ἀποθανόντα, *Epid.* 1. 8 (ii. 642. 4–8).
[106] This is said to happen most often in patients under 35 years of age (ii. 128. 3–4); *Prog.* 21 (ii. 172. 12–14); cf. under 30, *Aër.* 4 (ii. 20. 13–14).

(iv. 500. 1–3). It was discharged naturally, and was therefore more likely to effect a cure than emetics or even venesection. *Morb.* 4. 38 (vii. 556. 3–6) says that an excess of blood causes pain: 'If the amount which accrues is small, the body does not feel it and it is eventually passed on to the stomach or the nostrils: these parts expel it and it is rendered harmless.'[107] *Aph.* 6. 21 (iv. 568. 7–8) says that varicose veins and haemorrhoids, which could also be viewed as natural purgings of blood in a man, can cure madness, and in treating cases of severe haemorrhoids doctors are advised to leave one pile so that the patient does not develop dropsy or consumption,[108] diseases which can be caused by the retention of menses in a woman.

SURVIVAL RATES FOR MENSTRUATION

Of the 129 individual female case histories in the seven books of the *Epid.*, 38 women were at some stage of pregnancy and so could not menstruate. Of the 91 who could menstruate, 22 are recorded as having done so and survived;[109] of the remaining 69, 32 died. That is to say, that in a woman who was not pregnant, aborting, giving birth, or nursing, the survival rate of those for whom no menstruation is recorded is 53.6% while for those who did menstruate it is 100%. (The overall survival rate is 65.9%). The statistics are even more striking in some of the individual books when taken separately. In *Epid.* 1. and 3. there are 17 female case histories, 9 of whom had illnesses related to pregnancy or childbirth and were unable to menstruate. Only two survived. The other eight had illnesses ranging from pains in head and neck to inflammation of the bowels.[110] Four of them were specifically said to have menstruated and survived. No mention is made of the other four menstruating and they all died, although they suffered some of the same types of illnesses. The correlation of the individual male case histories with the generalizations made throughout the Corpus is not as complete

---

[107] ἢν δὲ ὀλίγον προσγένηται, οὐκ ἐσάσσειεν ἂν ἐς τὸ σῶμα, χρόνῳ δὲ διαδίδοται.

[108] *Aph.* 6. 12 (iv. 566. 7–8).

[109] If a day of death is not recorded I have presumed the woman survived.

[110] *Epid.* 1. 13, case xiv (ii. 716. 5–14), 3. 1, case ix (iii. 58. 1–7); the former menstruated and survived, the latter did not and died. *Epid.* 3. 1, case vii (iii. 52. 11–54. 7) records a case of a woman with angina. No menstruation occurred and the woman died.

as in the female cases, but it is still strong enough to be significant. The overall death rate of men in the *Epid.* is 33.6%. Of the 19 men who suffered nosebleeds 15 survived, giving a death rate of 21.2%. Of the 25 male case histories in *Epid.* 1. and 3. eleven survived, five of whom had epistaxis and one of whom underwent venesection.[111] Of the fourteen who died only two had any epistaxis recorded,[112] both times described as 'scanty', (σμικρόν). Of the other two cases in the *Epid.* when a man dies after bleeding from the nose, one is a doubtful case of epistaxis anyway, since the word which appears in the manuscripts to describe the symptom is ἀπόσταξις,[113] a word which appears nowhere else in the *Epid.* (and only six times in the whole Corpus).[114] To bring it into conformity with the rest of the *Epid.* it would probably be better here either to follow the manuscript reading of ἀπὸ στήθεος (referring generally to a haemorrhage 'from the chest') or to emend to ἀπόστασις, which would then refer to an abscess. The other fatality was that of a man who died after a particularly heavy fall in the gymnasium in which his wrestling-partner had fallen on top of him,[115] so he cannot strictly be said to have died from an excess of morbid humours which would be cured by purging. If these factors are taken into account, epistaxis as a cure for male diseases (the nearest they could get to a woman's monthly purging) approaches the hundred-per-cent success rate of menstruation in women.

None of the artificial purgings which Hippocratic doctors practised on their patients was credited with this success rate. The natural excretions of vomit, urine, or faeces were also considered to be less effective because it was patently obvious that a patient could die shortly after evacuating himself by any one of these three methods. As the menstrual cycle is longer than the digestive process, there would not be so many occasions on which a woman died just after her monthly period, so the evacuation would not necessarily be thought of as taking place but failing to purge the patient. More-

[111] Ibid. 3. 17, case viii (iii. 124. 7).
[112] Ibid. 1. 13, case i (ii. 682. 14–15); ibid. 3. 17, case i (iii. 104. 5).
[113] Ibid. 5. 80 (v. 250. 8).
[114] *Acut. App.* 9, 10 (ii. 442. 2, 450. 4); *Prorrh.* 1. 132, 141 (v. 558. 1, 562. 5); *Coac.* 406, 513 (v. 676. 9, 702. 18–19). The two occurrences in *Acut. App.* are emendations not present in the manuscripts.
[115] *Epid.* 5. 14 (v. 212. 20–214. 6). It is true that purging after blows and wounds was standard practice, but the loss of blood caused by a blow would not be looked on as necessarily advantageous as it might be perfectly healthy blood dislodged by violence.

over, those women who were seriously ill over a long period of time could very well cease to menstruate before death, whereas those suffering from minor complaints, which were not in danger of becoming fatal anyway, would continue to bleed each month. Most of those who survived even a serious illness would presumably menstruate at some point thereafter. In these cases the appearance of menstruation can be viewed as a sign of the relative mildness of the disease and an improvement in the state of the patient. But just as the Hippocratics viewed the absence of menstruation not as a symptom but as a cause of ill health, so they viewed its appearance as a cure rather than as a mere indication of recovery. We should not be surprised to find that those women who were ailing for a long time without menstruating eventually died, and that the Hippocratic doctors are able to make an explicit note of the occurrence of menstruation for many women who survived an illness. What is surprising, however, is the hundred-per-cent correlation between menstruation and survival. There is not a single case of a woman recorded as having menstruated during her illness where the illness proved fatal. In a smaller sampling, menstruation could perhaps indicate a less virulent form of disease. However, the number of case histories in the *Epid.* precludes this possibility. It seems that the Hippocratics were so sure that menstruation would bring recovery that if a woman menstruated before her death they either failed to record it at all, as not being true menstruation and therefore irrelevant, or they recorded it as a *rhoos*, contaminated menses that may not have brought away all the pathological agent.

WOMEN'S BODIES AS A PARADIGM FOR 'GENERAL' MEDICINE

By sins of omission and commission, various Hippocratic authors show that women do not hold a guaranteed place in the general medicine. Many of the illnesses there attributed to a variety of causes are ascribed to a woman's reproductive system in the gynaecological works. The varied aetiology of the general medicine calls for a variety of therapies, but a woman's reproductive system acts as her own natural purging process. Paradoxically, therefore, the source of a woman's physical infirmity which led to her having a generally lower standard of health than a man, also led to her succumbing less often to, and recuperating more quickly from, serious disease.[116]

This perception of the causes of female health and illness may have been partially responsible for the concerns in the 'general' medicine, perhaps even the exemplar on which the theory of the need for purging, by venesection particularly, was based. Because men had no single organ which naturally gathered and flushed excess humours from their bodies, the medicine which dealt with them had to be more diverse.[117] The 'general' medicine is focused on men because women do not need this diversity. Given that the Hippocratics had no opportunity to look inside a woman's body, the wide range of their gynaecology is rational, explicable, and no less effective than the medicine they practised on men.

---

[116] Arist. similarly attributes a womans lower susceptibility to headaches to an otherwise inferior physical state. He says that they have more lice than men due to their moister body, *HA* 557^{a}8–10.

[117] *Nat. Hom.* 12 (vi. 60. 20–64. 14) says that patients over 35 who expectorate a lot (without showing fever), pass a large quantity of sediment in their urine, or suffer continually from bloody stools, as in cases of dysentery, are ill due to a single cause. As young men such individuals were very active, and on stopping exercise they run to seed very quickly. If a person like this contracts a disease he escapes for the time being, but after the illness his body wastes. These individuals generally recover of their own accord within forty-five days. This describes men who on passing out of first youth, develop a body of soft flesh which evacuates large quantities of material at regular intervals. Their bodies become like those of women, prone to diseases from one cause but also able to survive them more easily without the intervention of the medical art. Conversely, although older women do not suffer any specific menopausal symptoms, they are more susceptible to diseases in general, e.g. *Mul.* 2. 120, 121, 137 (viii. 262. 10, 264. 19–20, 310. 10–12); *Epid.* 6. 7. 1 (v. 334. 13), reflecting the assimilation of their bodies to the male model.

3

The Female's Role in Reproduction

EARLY THEORIES ON A WOMAN'S CONTRIBUTION TO CONCEPTION

Early years of childhood, for boys as well as girls, would have been spent at home with the mother, and there is no reason to doubt that, generally speaking, a strong bond existed between a mother and her children.[1] But while Athenians recognized the affective power of the maternal bond, a mother played only a small role in determining a child's public or private identity. So, while Aristotle claims that mothers love their children more than fathers, he still asserts that the child is part of its father until it reaches a certain age.[2] In the case of widowhood or divorce, children of a marriage usually remained in their father's house while their mother returned to her father's house.[3] If a man had had a daughter but no sons, the sons of his daughter (who in this situation was called an *epiklēros)* would inherit his property, but they were only considered to be the true continuance of their maternal grandfather's line if one of his close male relatives (e.g. his brother or first cousin) were the father.[4] A woman was not thought capable of perpetuating her father's line without an infusion of the family's male principle in her offspring. In such a culture, theories of reproduction were bound to emphasize the importance of the male component over the female.

In the realm of mythology this emphasis took the form of stories

---

[1] See Lacey 1968, 111; Golden 1990, 97–100.   [2] *EN* 1161^{b}27, 1134^{b}10.
[3] See Harrison 1968, i. 44–5. Evidence about the disposition of children in cases of divorce is speculative. Harrison suggests (38–9) that if a woman had borne her dead husband sons she had the choice of remaining in his house under the guardianship of the sons' *kurios*, but that this option would not be available to a woman who had borne only daughters.
[4] For a fuller discussion of the epiklerate, see Harrison 1968, i. 9–12, 108–115, 132–8; MacDowell 1978, 95–108; Sealey 1990, *passim*.

in which parturition was within the powers of the supreme male deity. Zeus was said to have given birth to Athena from his head and to Dionysus from his thigh.[5] At *Eum.* 658–66 Aeschylus makes Apollo argue that Orestes is vindicated in killing his mother because the mother is not a true parent of the child, only its nurse; the god cites Athena's nativity as proof of this view, and in casting her ballot for Orestes, Athena says she is taking the male side because she has no mother (736–8). Obviously, no human father could claim to have given birth himself, but some 'scientific' theories did support Apollo's contention that only the father contributed seed to the child, while the mother simply provided the place and the nourishment for its growth. Assertions that women did not contribute seed to the embryo were made, for example, by Diogenes and Hippon (according to Censorinus), Anaxagoras (according to Aristotle), and some Pythagoreans (according to Aetius).[6]

However, from the earliest period there was also an opposite point of view that women did contribute seed to the embryo. Among the upholders of this theory were Anaxagoras, Alcmaeon and Empedocles (according to Censorinus), Parmenides (according to Caelius Aurelianus), and Democritus (according to Aetius). Indeed, given that this point of view informs most of the Hippocratic gynaecology, it would seem to have been the predominant theory in the Archaic and Classical periods.[7] Modern readers may think this is only to be expected because theorizing that women provide seed explains why children should take after their mother as often as their father, a difficulty raised by the theory that the male and female contribution to generation was qualitatively different.[8] However, if women did provide seed as well as place and nourishment for the foetus, it became difficult to explain why a male was

[5] This was also the part of the body which was used for the gestation of the foetus in the moonmen of Lucian's *True Histories* 1. 22. Skinner 1970, 173, notes of the obscure etymology of femur that the origin may be '*feo* (the root of foetus), meaning "to be fruitful", due to some relationship between the thighs and sex or the bearing of children'.

[6] See Lloyd 1983, 86–8.   [7] Ibid. 107 n. 182.

[8] Though it should be noted that among the Trobriand Islanders, who do not believe a male contributes anything to the conception of a child, it is generally accepted that a child will grow to look like its father through a process of 'moulding', Malinowski 1929, 176–7. Resemblance to both parents, therefore, is not necessarily seen as an objection to a 'one-seed' theory by proponents of it.

needed at all, why women did not reproduce parthenogenetically as the Greeks believed locusts and some fish did.[9]

Diodorus Siculus reports that the Egyptians also thought the father was the true parent of the child and that the mother supplied only nourishment and place. In consequence (presumably because they did not understand the mechanism of pollination), the Egyptians called those trees which bore fruit male and those which did not female—the opposite of Greek custom.[10] This is a telling detail because it shows that, however important the Greeks thought the role of the male in begetting a child, where there was no observable difference between the 'sexes' other than the fact that one bore fruit and the other did not, the Greeks, in contrast to the Egyptians, followed a convention of calling the one which visibly reproduced the female. As there was no observable contribution from the non-productive tree this automatically implied that the male principle in generation was more dispensable than the female. The insistent claim that in animals, at least, the father provided the most important element to the generation of the child functions as the Greek male response to the underlying fear that a mother could be a sufficient, not merely a necessary, condition for procreation.

However, the theory that in the vast majority of animals the female could not provide seed herself did have explanatory value where the alternative theory was lacking (why a father should be necessary at all), and while acknowledging that the 'male seed only' theories did undermine a mother's claim to her children, we should not assume that their appeal was based solely on a desire to perpetuate the subordinate social and political status of women. Many scholars have maintained that it was.[11] Horowitz in particular, in castigating Aristotle for allotting reproductive roles as he did, refers to societies which believe women to be solely responsible for repro-

[9] *GA* 741ᵃ5-9, 32-7; *HA* 539ᵃ30-ᵇ5; *HA* 10. 637ᵇ17-20. See Detienne 1977. A scholion to *Il.* 18. 483 (Erbse 1969, iv. 528) and Antiochenus fr. 13. 5 (Müller 1868, iv. 547) may suggest that there was a time when Greeks believed that women did reproduce parthenogenetically. The scholion says that it was on account of Cecrops that 'men first recognized that they were begotten from two', and Antiochenus reports that before Cecrops women were totally responsible for reproduction and could give their offspring to whomever they chose, see Tyrrell 1984, 30.

[10] τῶν δένδρων ἄρρενα μὲν καλοῦσι τὰ καρποφόρα, θήλεα δὲ τὰ μὴ φέροντα τοὺς καρπούς, ἐναντίως τοῖς Ἕλλησι, Diod. 1. 80. 4. However, cf. *Nat. Puer.* 26 (vii. 526. 19–528. 2) where the author says that trees that bear fruit have passages wide enough to draw a fatty substance (πῖαρ) from the ground without classing such trees as either male or female.

[11] e.g. Horowitz 1976; Saïd 1983; Clark 1982; Rousselle 1988, 24–46.

duction, and seems to accuse Aristotle and others who attributed any importance to the male contribution of doing so in the teeth of the evidence.[12] But it is hardly fair to fault the Greeks for observing that human reproduction is sexual and in the light of this attempting to identify the unique element that a father brought to reproduction. Bettelheim has noted:

> The less men understand of the masculine contribution to pregnancy and childbirth ... the more eager may they be to assert that they, too, play an important part in procreation. ... In tribes where the male role is somewhat better understood, the envy of women and the tendency to overstress the male contribution may lead to belief that the semen is all important and the female contribution to childbirth negligible.[13]

Those who argued against the existence of female seed believed that a woman's contribution to reproduction was menstrual fluid. Those who believed that both men and women provided seed saw menses as a further female contribution to reproduction without which the conceptus of the two seeds could not be nourished and grow. No Greek theorist ever argued that the male could provide this element to reproduction.[14] If we look at the myths of Dionysus' and Athena's nativities more closely, we find that even in the case of the supremo male deity the Greeks acknowledged that a female was needed for the original forming and nurturing of the embryo. Zeus swallowed Metis after she had conceived Athena, and he appeared to Semele as a thunderbolt when she was pregnant with Dionysus, carefully removing the embryo and secreting it in his thigh when the corpse was about to be burned. In contrast, Hera, piqued at Zeus' procreative coup with Athena, gave birth to Hephaistos and Typhon without any male contribution whatsoever.[15] Zeus could produce his own seed and, in an emergency, could find a place in his body to lodge the foetus. Hera was even more self-sufficient, since she could provide

---

[12] She cites Malinowski's work on the Trobriand Islands in 1903 (185–6), but Malinowski himself later wrote, 'The so-called ignorance of paternity is nothing else but a very imperfect knowledge that intercourse is a necessary though not sufficient condition of the women being "opened-up" as my Trobriand friends put it', quoted in Ashley-Montagu 1937, 3. Leach 1966 addressed the problem and Spiro 1968 responded. The articles generated a prolific correspondence. My own opinion is that of Malinowski's reappraisal.

[13] Bettelheim 1954, 110–11.

[14] Lucian's moonmen had their anuses blocked so that their excrement could be diverted to provide nourishment for the foetuses in their thighs.

[15] Hes. *Th.* 927–8, *h. Ap.* 307–52.

evidence? for herself that for which Zeus had to turn to the opposite sex, i.e. the material to form a child—menses.

The cultural significance of menstrual blood in conception and gestation, whatever theories were held about female seed, is reflected in the frequency with which menses were recommended as an ingredient in traditional fertility or contraceptive recipes.[16] Though the Hippocratics profess to believe in female seed, when explaining why a woman has not conceived and attempting to promote conception they direct their therapies towards the menstruation rather than the sexual arousal of a woman, and some of their advice shows signs of folkloric origins. *Mul.* I. II (viii. 42. 9–18) advises letting a woman's menses fall on to cloths (two for day and two for night) over cinders and observing them to see if they were too bilious or phlegmatic. The daytime cloths should be washed the next day and the night-time ones after lying in the cinders for a day and a night. *Nat. Mul.* 22 (vii. 340. 15–20) advises mixing the menses with sand and allowing the mixture to dry in the sun. If the blood turned yellow it was too bilious, and if mucous too phlegmatic.

All the attention lavished on menses in promoting or preventing conception, regardless of what theories were held about male and female seed, shows how important they were considered to be. In the ancient world, where the production of heirs was one of the major considerations in contracting a marriage,[17] the fertility of a young girl being married for the first time could only be gauged from her family history and her own state of health. Regular menstruation was an indication not only that the girl herself was healthy, but also that she was likely to be able to bear children. Soranus advised a prospective husband to inquire after his intended wife's menstrual flow to make sure that it was regular, neither too much nor too little and more bloody than ichorous.[18] Whatever theory was held on female seed, there was a general consensus among the Greeks that menstrual blood was indispensable in procreation.[19] In some man-

[16] e.g. *PMag* xxxvi. 320–32 calls for a frog to be stuffed with a mixture of vetch and menstrual blood. Pennyroyal was a traditional contraceptive which achieved its effect by stimulating menstruation, see Scarborough 1989, 22.

[17] Xen. *Mem.* 2. 2. 4.

[18] *Gyn.* I. 34. There are indications that in Greece as well as Rome, marriage and defloration often took place before menarche (see pp. 50–3 above). In both societies, however, despite the concern that a first-time bride should be a virgin, *divorcées* or widows with a proven childbearing capability do not seem to have been disadvantaged in the marriage stakes, see W. E. Thompson 1972, 222–3.

[19] Galen was an exception in this, Lloyd 1983, 109 n. 196.

ner it formed the fabric of the child's body and also its staple diet when it first came into being. So, despite the patrilineal structure of Greek society in which children were part of the family of their father and not their mother, Athenian law allowed the marriage of half-siblings from the same father but not those from the same mother: originating from the same womb made such a relationship incestuous where springing from the same seed did not.[20]

Rel to Law ?

STIMULATION OF FEMALE SEED ACCORDING TO THE HIPPOCRATICS

Despite the emphasis the therapeutical texts place on the menstruation of a woman who is attempting to conceive, the Hippocratics did not believe that menstrual blood was used in the actual conception of a foetus. The one treatise in the Hippocratic Corpus which takes a totally theoretical approach to the subject (*Genit.*) attests a belief in female seed, as does *Vict.* I. in advising the mode of life that both a man and a woman should adopt in order to determine the sex of the child that is to be conceived. The lack of attention paid to female seed elsewhere in the Corpus should not be taken to indicate an alternative theory. Those works that deal primarily with therapies to promote conception focus on the menses partly because they indicate the state of a woman's own health, partly because they show the environment into which the seeds will fall and in which the foetus will be nurtured,[21] and partly because the doctors are employing traditional procedures. Yet even in *Mul.* I, which concerns itself almost exclusively with menstrual fluid in diagnosing sterility and promoting fertility, the author remarks in chapter 8 that if the menses are bilious 'the seed of both the male and the female is

[20] See Pomeroy 1975, 66. It is possible that the law was promulgated expressly to prevent an *epikleros* marrying a half-brother by her mother as her nearest male relative and taking the property away from her agnate kin. Even so, it remains surprising that the Athenians sanctioned the marriage of half-siblings related through their father. Themistocles' daughter, Mnesiptolema, by his second wife married his son, Archeptolis, by Archippe (Plut. *Them.* 32. 1–2), and the speaker of Dem. 57. 20 says, 'My father married his sister by a different mother.' As the husband in these marriages would be the son, the father's property would already be assured of remaining in his family and the daughter would not have the status of an *epikleros*, so there would be no need for her to marry inside her father's family at all.

[21] *Vict.* I. 26 (vi. 498. 13–14) says, 'whatever enters a woman grows if it meets with the things that suit it' (ὅ τι δὲ ἐς τὴν γυναῖκα, αὔξεται, ἢν τύχῃ τῶν προσηκόντων).

154   The Female's Role in Reproduction

destroyed' (καὶ ὁ γόνος ἀμαλδύνεται ἀμφοῖν, τοῦ τε ἄρσενος καὶ τοῦ θήλεος (viii. 34. 9–10)), and at *Mul.* I. 24 (viii. 62. 20–21) he says that female seed is strongest if women have intercourse when they ought, just after menstruation.[22] Moreover, despite the emphasis placed on menstrual blood in the gynaecological works, there is nowhere any statement that this was a woman's only contribution to generation. Although the Hippocratics do not generally communicate their theory of reproduction explicitly, as in the case of normative physiology their assumptions can be detected underlying their therapeutical advice and comments on pathological states. Moreover, in the case of reproduction we have extensive arguments from Aristotle against elaborate scientific theories which posited a role for female seed in conception. These arguments seem to be directed against a well-established and widely held view.[23] The view would not be exclusive to the Hippocratics, but we might expect an author who disagreed with the prevalent opinion to say so explicitly. We have no such statement in the Hippocratic Corpus. Therefore, while the Corpus exhibits varying opinions on such points as the mechanism of resemblance, sex differentiation, and embryonic development, it is reasonable to assume that the majority of the authors adhered to some theory of female seed,[24] and that Aristotle's rebuttals can give us an idea of the finer points of the theories where they are lacking in the Hippocratic treatises themselves.

Genit. begins by describing the origin of semen in a human male. It is said first to appear in boys at puberty, and to result from an agitation of the body which causes the most potent part of the humours to separate out into a foam. The agitation is caused by friction on the penis, which is connected to passages containing the humours all over the body, and so the friction instigates a movement

---

[22] Though at *Mul.* I. 16 (viii. 54. 1) the author describes the seed that is expelled from a woman's womb after six or seven days as 'the stuff from the man' (τὰ ἀπὸ τοῦ ἀνδρός), cf. ibid. II (viii. 46. 20–21). For a possible explanation of this phraseology, see pp. 173–4 below.

[23] See Lonie 1981, 65.

[24] *Steril.* 241 (viii. 454. 8–10), for example, implies that a woman contributes something to conception over and above menstrual fluid, but the author seems to differentiate it from the seed contributed by the man. He says that sometimes the womb is open too far and the menses are too abundant and watery, 'so that the thing that comes from the woman is not received for conception, and the seed emitted from the man is destroyed' (ὥστε τὸ ἀπὸ γυναικὸς μὴ ξυλλαμβάνεσθαι πρὸς τὴν τέκνωσιν, τήν τε τοῦ ἀνδρὸς γονὴν ἐπιοῦσαν διαφθείρεσθαι).

through the whole man. This is not possible in a child as the passages are too narrow to allow the humours to become agitated and produce a foam. For the same reason a girl does not menstruate until puberty. The author was obviously led to make this equivalence by the similar age of puberty in young men and women; night emissions and menarche start around the same time. However, the emission of menses is not tied to the occasion of intercourse as the ejaculation of semen is. Accordingly, the author appears to think that while in young girls menses parallel semen, they are not the full female analogue of the male secretion. This does not appear until the woman becomes sexually active. So, while *Genit.* 3 ends, 'I have now dealt with the subject of sperm: its origin, how and why it originates, and in the case of those who do not have sperm, why this is so; and I have dealt with menstruation in girls',[25] *Genit.* 4 (vii. 474. 14) opens with the words, 'In the case of women' (τῆσι δὲ γυναιξί), and proceeds to deal with the secretion emitted by a woman during intercourse. In *Nat. Puer.* 20 (vii. 508. 6–7) the author remarks that the passages are opened for menses and seed in a young girl at the same time, but unlike a man a woman could not become agitated enough to separate out completely the most potent part of the humours into seed until she had actual sexual contact.

It is important to note that the female seed was not necessarily a visible secretion as a man's was; it was postulated because of its explanatory value in a hypothesis, not because it had been empirically observed. The vaginal lubricant sometimes produced by a woman during intercourse could be used as evidence that women did produce seed, but then so could pathological leucorrhoea. At least, this seems the most likely explanation for the secretion described in the comment, 'If the seed flows away continuously and does not cease, she will not welcome intercourse with her husband.'[26] *Genit.* 4 says: 'A woman also releases something from her body, sometimes into the womb, which then becomes moist, and sometimes externally as well, if the womb is open wider than normal.'[27]

---

[25] καὶ ταῦτα μὲν εἰρέαται μοὶ περὶ γονῆς, ὁπόθεν γίνεται καὶ ὅπως καὶ διότι, καὶ οἷσιν οὐ γίνεται ἡ γονὴ καὶ διότι οὐ γίνεται, καὶ περὶ καταμηνίων παρθένων (vii. 474. 11–13).

[26] ἢν δὲ ὁ γόνος ἀπορρέῃ διπετής, καὶ μὴ λήγῃ, οὐ μίσγεται ἀσπασίως τῷ ἀνδρί, *Mul.* 1. 24 (viii. 64. 5–6).

[27] μεθίει δὲ καὶ ἡ γυνὴ ἀπὸ τοῦ σώματος ὁτὲ μὲν ἐς τὰς μήτρας, αἱ δὲ μήτραι ἰκμαλέαι γίνονται, ὁτὲ δὲ καὶ ἔξω, ἢν χάσκωσιν αἱ μήτραι μᾶλλον τοῦ καιροῦ (vii. 474. 16–18).

A woman's remaining dry through intercourse did not prove that she had failed to emit seed; it could have been retained in her womb, waiting for the man's seed which was emitted at the mouth of the womb and had to be drawn in so they could mingle and produce a foetus. This pre-empts Aristotle's criticism that the moisture secreted by a woman during intercourse could not be female seed as it was emitted outside the womb and would have to be drawn back in again if conception was to take place. His objection is that this would be a superfluous action and Nature does nothing superfluous (ἡ δὲ φύσις οὐδὲν ποιεῖ περίεργον).[28] The author of *Genit.* says that female seed is by nature emitted into the womb. It only appears outside the womb if the womb is open contrary to nature. The author of *HA* 10 disagrees with the author of *Genit.*, saying that the female seed is emitted at the *os uteri* and not directly into the womb, but he also answers Aristotle's objection by claiming that this serves a purpose. It means that a woman can conceive in any position because the seed of both sexes is emitted in the same place and can mingle, which could not happen if a woman emitted her seed directly into her womb: 'That is why women may conceive while copulating in any of the positions; for in every case the semen is emitted, both by them and by men, into the region in front of the womb, whereas if it were emitted into the womb, they would not conceive after every form of copulation'.[29]

After the seeds have been emitted at the *os uteri*, the womb draws them in 'like a nose'. It could presumably draw in the male seed without its being mixed with the female, so it might seem as if there was nothing to prevent conception in every position even if the woman did ejaculate directly into her womb. But the author of *HA* 10 thinks that in this case the two seeds would remain separate in the womb because they had not initially been emitted in the same place. *HA* 10. 636ᵇ12–24 also says that male and female semen must be ejaculated at the same time. If the partners do not 'keep pace' with one another conception will be hindered. Male and female seed have to make contact the instant they are ejaculated if they are to transfer their powers to a new being. However, the author of *HA* 10 seems to contradict himself on this point in a slightly earlier pas-

[28] *GA* 739ᵇ17–20.
[29] διὸ καὶ παντὶ σχήματι συνοῦσι κυΐσκονται, ὅτι εἰς τὸ πρόσθεν παντελῶς ἐχούσης γίνεται καὶ αὐταῖς καὶ τοῖς ἀνδράσιν ἡ πρόεσις τοῦ σπέρματος· εἰ δ᾽ εἰς αὐτήν, οὐκ ἂν πάντως συγγινόμεναι συνελάμβανον, *HA* 10. 634ᵇ36–9.

sage. At 635ᵇ19 he describes the female secretion during intercourse as 'a sort of local sweating—just as we often emit saliva at the mouth on the approach of food'.[30] The passage then goes on to say that this prevents the womb from inhaling male seed in a pure state: 'But in some there is so much moisture that they cannot draw up the man's emission in a pure form because it is mixed with the moisture from the woman.'[31] Since this statement is diametrically opposed to the earlier argument that it is necessary for female seed to mingle with the male before it is drawn into the womb, the passage is either an interpolation trying to bring the book into conformity with the rest of the *HA* and Aristotle's biology, or an earlier or later opinion of the same author.[32]

The belief that both male and female seed were needed to generate a child is Rousselle's prime evidence that the Hippocratics derived their reproductive theories from a female oral tradition which wished both to have it acknowledged that women played an equal role in procreation and to ensure that their desires were taken into consideration during intercourse.[33] The description of a woman's pleasure in *Genit.* 4 (vii. 474. 14–476. 8), however, hardly shows an intimate knowledge of feminine experience. A woman's pleasure is said to be produced by the friction of the penis in her vagina, just as a man's is produced by friction on his penis, and to last from the moment intercourse begins for as long as the penis remains in her vagina until the man ejaculates, when her desire flames up to greet his semen and is then completely doused, like a candle flame that has had wine thrown on it. Occasionally a woman could reach orgasm before a man and her pleasure was then somewhat less during the remainder of the intercourse, but no matter to what extent she was or was not aroused during the act, her pleasure always terminated along with the man's.

[30] *οἷον ἵδρωμα τοῦ τόπου ὥσπερ καὶ τῷ στόματι σιάλου, πολλαχοῦ μὲν καὶ πρὸς τὴν φορὰν τῶν σιτίων.*

[31] *ἀλλ' ἐνίαις τοσαύτη ὑγρασία γίνεται, ὥστε μὴ δύνασθαι καθαρὸν τὸ τοῦ ἀνδρὸς ἀνασπάσαι διὰ τὴν σύμμιξιν τῆς γιγνομένης ἀπὸ τῆς γυναικὸς ὑγρότητος,* HA 10. 635ᵇ29–31.

[32] If later, it would be compatible with the claim in Balme 1985 that the book is an early work of Arist. and that he had originally believed in female seed.

[33] Rousselle 1988, 27. This would only be advantageous as long as every act of intercourse was directed towards pregnancy. It could obviously backfire if, once he had engendered as many children as his *oikos* could support, a man directed his sexual favours elsewhere or even deliberately attempted to suppress his wife's enjoyment as a means of contraception.

Excepting Aristotle, only *HA* 10 shows any knowledge of the role of the clitoris.[34] The passage states that as a man has a penis which is a channel through which he deposits his semen in front of a woman's womb, so a woman has a similar tube (καυλός) through which semen passes inside her body. This tube has two openings, a wider one in front of the womb through which the seed is deposited to mingle with the man's and a small duct (μικρὸς πόρος) which opens to the outside air just above the place where women urinate and through which the kaulos respires. The disposition of the tubes seems to be as shown in Fig. 1. When a woman desires intercourse the area (τόπος) is not in the same condition as before the desire arose (οὐκ ἔχει ὁμοίως καὶ πρὶν ὀργᾶν). Although the *kaulos* does not exist, this description of female sexual excitement reflects women's subjective experience more closely than the description in *Genit.* 4.

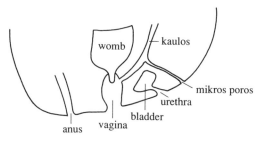

Fɪɢ. 1

In all the therapies for sterile women in *Steril.* there is no account of how to stimulate a woman's seed, and *Mul.* 1. 17 (viii. 56. 19–21) directs a man whose wife does not conceive straightaway simply to continue having intercourse with her as the activity itself will excite her desire, i.e. she will eventually become pregnant. A woman's enjoyment of intercourse is not proof that she will become pregnant; becoming pregnant is evidence that she enjoyed some previous act of intercourse.[35] This smacks a great deal more of wishful thinking on

---

[34] *HA* 10. 637ᵃ23–8.

[35] This is not to say that every Greek man was completely insensitive to his wife's desires, simply that a belief in female seed would not ensure he would be attentive to her.

the part of the male than does Aristotle's acceptance of the proposition that many women conceive without ever having felt any pleasure in intercourse.[36] Since only the woman concerned can say whether or not she enjoyed a specific act of intercourse, in this statement Aristotle is giving the subjective testimony of women more credence than did the Hippocratics, who used the success or failure of conception as objective evidence about her enjoyment. Even the author of *HA* 10 (who believed a woman's seed was emitted outside the womb and knew the importance of the clitoris) believes that women can emit seed without its being obvious and without knowing it themselves because it is immediately all drawn into the womb: 'And it is then especially that women conceive without realising it; for they do not think that they have conceived if they are not aware of their emission, and they understand that the emissions must occur in both partners, the man and the woman, at the same time.'[37]

Rousselle's theory that the belief in female seed stemmed from a female oral tradition aimed at ensuring that men paid attention to women's sexual needs, and that the denial of female seed was a male 'sexist' tradition which caused to disappear 'the traditional basis of reciprocal pleasure in heterosexual love-making',[30] results in her placing Soranus in the 'sexist' tradition of Aristotle. At *Gyn.* 1. 37 Soranus remarks that 'if some women who were forced to have intercourse have conceived, one may say with reference to them that in any event the emotion of sexual appetite existed in them too, but was obscured by mental resolve.' This, says Rousselle, goes one further than Aristotle by ruling out conscious desire as well as pleasure as necessary for conception.[39] But this passage, as well as others, shows that Soranus is following the opposite tradition to Aristotle on this point, insisting that female pleasure *is* necessary for conception. He is aware that women conceive best at one particular time of the month (when the womb and passages have been emptied

[36] *GA* 727b8, 739a29.

[37] καὶ λανθάνουσι τότε μάλιστα κυισκόμεναι. οὐ γὰρ οἴονται συνειληφέναι, ἐὰν μὴ αἴσθωνται. προιέμεναι δὲ τυγχάνουσιν ὑπολαμβάνουσαι ὡς δεῖ ἀπ' ἀμφοῖν συμπεσεῖν ἅμα, καὶ ἀπὸ τῆς γυναικὸς καὶ ἀπὸ τοῦ ἀνδρός, *HA* 10. 636b35-40. I have translated τυγχάνουσιν ὑπολαμβάνουσαι as 'understand' rather than accepting Barnes's 'actually suppose', as I think this is a belief in which the author of *HA* 10 concurs, cf. 636b12-24.

[38] Rousselle 1988, 29.   [39] Ibid. 39-40.

by menstruation) but comments that the woman must also be desirous of sexual intercourse for conception to take place. He seems to be upholding a woman's right to enjoy sex in spite of the (correct) observation that the time of the month has more to do with conception. His claim that if a woman conceived after being raped she must have enjoyed it in some way but have suppressed this emotion through mental resolve, is the most lenient expression possible of the logical consequence of believing a woman's enjoyment was indispensable to conception. It is the position the Hippocratics would be constrained to support and that Aristotle would be forced to deny. Taking into consideration the description of what stimulated a woman during intercourse in *Genit.* and the belief that pregnancy was considered testimony that she had enjoyed it, the theory of female seed is not sufficient or indeed convincing evidence that Hippocratic reproductive theory could only have derived directly from the female oral tradition.

This is not to say that women's testimony did not contribute to Hippocratic theories. It very obviously did. But such testimony often reflects traditional folk belief rather than women's desire to reassert their rights to sexual pleasure. In fact, over and over again the Hippocratics record that women say they can tell they have conceived when they are dry after intercourse, not when there is evidence they have been stimulated.[40] This results, they say, because the womb has drawn in the seed (whether male alone or male mingled with female) and it has not fallen back out. *HA* 10. 637^{a}1–4 says some women assume they have not conceived if they are moist after intercourse but that they can be mistaken as the womb sometimes requires only a small portion, not all, of the semen that was ejaculated for conception.

MALE CONTRIBUTION TO CONCEPTION IN HIPPOCRATIC THEORIES

Female seed was championed by the Hippocratics because it was the most obvious explanation of a child's resemblance to its maternal family. As has been remarked, however, it does raise the question of

---

[40] e.g. *Mul.* 1. 10 (viii. 40. 13–14); 2. 162, 168 (viii. 338. 15–16, 346. 19–20); *Steril.* 220, 222 (viii. 424. 16–21, 428. 15–18); cf. *HA* 583^{a}15.

why a father was necessary at all. *Vict.* I. 27 (vi. 500. 10–22) explains that seed is needed from both parents in order to master the ἐπι-ρρέον (probably the menses).[41] In and of itself the seed of each parent has too much moisture and too little fire to solidify the menses; even both seeds together can only achieve this on one day in each month before the menses become too overwhelming.[42] This explains most of the phenomena known at the time: (*a*) women only conceive at a certain point in a (roughly) monthly cycle marked by the appearance of menstrual blood, so the presence or absence of menses must play some role in conception; (*b*) children can take after either parent equally, so male and female contributions to generation must be similar; (*c*) a woman cannot conceive without a man, so the father's contribution is needed to bring the seed up to a full complement, even when the child does not resemble him at all. This last point bears a resemblance to the modern theory of double chromosomes and dominant and recessive genes.

Most Hippocratic theories, while accounting for the first two points, have difficulty in explaining why, if a woman can produce her own seed, she cannot produce parthenogenetically. *HA* 10 says that the females of some species (e.g. locusts, 637^b16–18) do, but that in other animals if seed from only one parent vitalized the material in the female uterus it would produce a mole or *mylē* (an undifferentiated fleshy lump) rather than a foetus, analogous to a wind-egg produced by a bird who had not been impregnated by a male:

For it is when women are in this state [i.e. their wombs are hot and dry] and there is no mixture from both partners but, like a wind-egg, matter is released from one only, that the so-called moles occur; and they are neither animals (for they do not come forth from both partners) nor yet inanimate (for what was received was animate) as in the case of wind-eggs.[43]

[41] It should be noted that the author gives this explanation as a reason why a woman has to emit seed as well as a man, but in framing it in this way he has a ready-made explanation as to why she cannot reproduce from her seed alone.

[42] See pp. 169–70 below.

[43] ἐὰν μὴ μεμιγμένον ἐστὶ τὸ ἀπ' ἀμφοῖν, ἀλλ' ὥσπερ τὸ ὑπηνέμιον ἐνδέξαιτο ἀπὸ θατέρου, τότε γίνεται ἡ καλουμένη μύλη, οὔτε ζῷον, διὰ τὸ μὴ παρ' ἀμφοῖν, οὔτε ἄψυχον, διὰ τὸ ἔμψυχον ληφθὲν εἶναι, ὥσπερ τὰ ὑπηνέμια, *HA* 10. 638^a22–5. *Mul.* I. 71 (viii. 148. 24–150. 1) says moles are caused by a large amount of menses mingling with a little seed that is diseased, but it does not indicate whether the seed is male, female, or a mixture of both.

This has obviously been influenced by Aristotle's theory of the different faculties of soul which are needed to bring about complete conception,[44] but because this author believes in a similarity between male and female seed, and that male seed uncombined with female seed would also produce a mole rather than a foetus,[45] it is not clear what, if any, was the unique contribution of each sex or whether, as in *Vict.*, the author believed that semen from one sex would simply not be sufficient in quantity to produce a foetus. However, this possibility is unlikely since *HA* 637ª3–15 makes it clear that a very small portion of the semen emitted by both sexes is needed for successful conception to take place. Unfortunately, immediately after the passage where the author poses the question, 'Why don't women reproduce parthenogenetically?', there is a lacuna (637ᵇ10), so he may have had a specific answer that we cannot reconstruct *ex silentio*. *Genit.* 8 (vii. 480. 13–14) remarks that it is impossible that a child should resemble one parent in all respects and the other in none, but again offers no explanation as to why two sets of seed were always needed in generating a child.

THEORIES OF RESEMBLANCE AMONG THE HIPPOCRATICS

The Hippocratics explained the resemblance of children to their parents by the theory of pangenesis, that is to say that the seed emitted during intercourse was drawn from all over the body.[46] Some asserted that it was drawn directly from the body to the reproductive organs during intercourse, citing the pleasure felt throughout the body as evidence.[47] Aristotle rebutted this with the comment that the sensation only occurred at the culmination of intercourse, not gradually throughout it, as one would expect if the semen had to be drawn from the extremities.[48] Others believed that it was stored in the brain and conveyed to the reproductive organs during inter-

---

[44] Cf. *GA* 741ª15–32

[45] See *HA* 10. 637ᵇ22–4: διὸ οὐδὲ τὰ ἀπὸ τοῦ ἄρρενος ἅπαντα γόνιμα φαίνεται, ἀλλ' ἔνια ἄγονα, ὅταν μὴ ἐξ ἀμφοῖν ὡς δεῖ συναρμοσθῇ.

[46] *Aër.* 14 (ii. 60. 1–2); *Morb. Sacr.* 2 (vi. 364. 19–20). *Vict.* 1. 7 (vi. 480. 11), in a very confused and confusing section, states, 'it is necessary that whatever enters has all the parts' (ἀνάγκη δὲ τὰ μέρεα ἔχειν πάντα τὰ ἐσιόντα). This seems most likely to refer to seed at conception, but it may be meant to refer to the consumption of food by living humans.

[47] *Genit.* 1 (vii. 470. 1–21).   [48] *GA* 723ᵇ33–724ª4.

course via the spinal marrow—the theory favoured in *Aër.* 22 (ii. 78. 10–11). *Aër., Morb. Sacr., Genit.,* and *Vict.* 1. are the only treatises to mention pangenesis specifically. *Genit.* tries to combine both of these theories, indicating that the image of the brain as a reservoir was only an extra stage in the semen's progress towards emission and did not imply the brain was the sole and ultimate origin of seed.[49] Once the seed from both parents had been emitted and mingled together, the characteristics of their child were determined by which parent had supplied the most seed from each part.[50] If the mother had drawn more seed from her eyes than the father had from his the child would have its mother's eyes, though it could still take after its father in the nose if its father had provided more seed from this physiognomic feature.

Inherent in the theory of pangenesis is some degree of preformationism. The most radical of these ideas is that which Aristotle attributes (perhaps unfairly) to Empedocles.[51] This states that the parts of the body actually exist in miniature in the semen. Aristotle demolishes it by saying, 'Further, if the parts of the future animal are separated in the semen, how do they live? and if they are connected they would form a small animal '[52] If the parts of the body existed in a dismembered state in the seed of both parents, they would have to have some sort of soul or life of their own, and if this were the case each part would be a separate animal and they could not join together to form a single animal.[53] If, on the other hand, the parts of the body were joined together in the semen, the seeds of the parents could not combine with each other but would produce two animals, and a woman could produce a homunculus by herself without any need for a man. The more sophisticated theory of pangenesis claimed that semen provided the material from each part in an

[49] Lonie 1981, 101.

[50] *Mul.* 1. 24 (viii. 64. 1) says that whichever seed (mother's or father's) gains mastery determines the resemblance of the child, but it does not indicate where the seed is thought to be drawn from.

[51] *GA* 722[b]7–30. 'Perhaps unfairly' because he quotes Empedocles as saying merely that 'the nature of limbs is separate' (διέσπασται μελέων φύσις), which could indicate simply that the material of the seed from one parent was not sufficient by itself to form any part of an animal, similar to the theory expounded in *Vict.* 1. Arist. however, connects this pronouncement with another cosmogonical one, which speaks of neckless heads existing at an earlier time in world history, to show that Empedocles imagined the actual parts of the body to exist in a dismembered state.

[52] ἔτι εἰ μὲν διεσπασμένα τὰ μέρη ἐν τῷ σπέρματι, πῶς ζῇ; εἰ δὲ συνεχῆ, ζῷον ἂν εἴη μικρόν, *GA* 722[b]4–5.

[53] Ibid. 722[b]22–4.

unshaped state, not each part ready-formed in miniature. It was thus a question of which parent provided the most material from their nose, not which nose nudged its way on to the face. This material was undifferentiated when the foetus was first conceived, though it had to be in the position corresponding to the part of the body whence it originated,[54] and only assumed its shape as the foetus developed. Aristotle retorted that we do not say a child resembles its parents in the materials of its body, its flesh and blood (the uniform parts, *ta homoiomerē*) but in the arrangement of the flesh and blood, its face, hands, etc. (the non-uniform parts, *ta anomoiomerē*). If the flesh and blood does not come prearranged, there has to be some factor over and above it to do the arranging and it is this that causes the resemblance. If resemblance to a parent in non-uniform parts is the result of this factor of organization on uniform parts, why should resemblance in uniform parts in turn not be the result of the organization of even less differentiated material? Animals grow by converting elements in food into flesh and blood (Aristotle remarks that the supporters of pangenesis are not followers of Anaxagoras), so why should the seed have to carry actual flesh, blood, and bone?[55]

Moreover, if resemblance in any particular feature required receiving material in any form at all from it, how could a child inherit such non-material traits as a good singing voice or a particular gait? And how could such traits as a beard or grey hair be inherited— traits not necessarily apparent in the father or mother at the time of conception?[56] This last objection could be accommodated by invoking the extra heat of a young body which could do more with the same materials than an older. The pangeneticists, however, did find themselves in difficulties when called upon to explain how it was that parents did not pass on to their children acquired characteristics such as the loss of a hand or a shrivelling caused by a burn. *Aër.* 14 (ii. 60. 2) solved the difficulty by saying that they did; deformed parents produced deformed children. Aristotle objected that a parent who had been mutilated in some part of their body often produced a child who resembled the parent before mutilation.[57] The

---

[54] *Nat. Puer.* 17 (vii. 496. 19–20). The material was separated off to its appropriate place by respiration (vii. 498. 15–25).
[55] *GA* 722ᵃ16–ᵇ4, 723ᵃ2–23.   [56] Ibid. 722ᵃ3–8.
[57] Ibid. 724ᵃ4–8. Arist. does not deny the possibility of the inheritance of acquired characteristics outright. He accepts the case of a man in Chalcedon whose children were born carrying on their arms the same mark as he had been branded with, *GA* 721ᵇ30–4.

author of *Genit.* also realized that this was the case, and in trying to explain how this should happen, in chapter II (vii. 484. 15–16) made the first few stumbling steps towards the realization that seed carried information on how to structure the material rather than the material itself: 'Although an animal may be deformed it still has exactly the same *components* as what is sound' (ἔχει γὰρ τὸν ἀριθμὸν πάντα τὸ πεπηρωμένον τῷ ὑγιεῖ). 'Components' here probably refers to the four humours, so this is still a form of preformationism, but the author realizes that the material does not have to originate from a particular part of the body to transfer the structure of that part. Therefore a parent who had lost, say, a hand could still pass on the components causing a child's hand to resemble the parent's before it had been lost. Logically this should have led him to reject the theory of pangenesis altogether in favour of an organizational principle in the seed, but unfortunately his thinking on the issue was still confused by his belief that inheritance of acquired characteristics did occur sometimes and that in these cases the seed was 'not complete, but deficient in the deformed part'.[58]

Aristotle believed that once it was admitted that resemblance could not be explained by pangenesis, there was no call to hypothesize that the mother produced seed.[59] However, an argument for the seed's material not having been drawn from all over the body will not suffice to dismiss it altogether as the factor that causes resemblance. *HA* 10 brings a strong argument of its own against pangenesis, but still insists that 'it is clear that every female contributes something to the semen'.[60] He argues that as only a small part of the semen is used up in conception, this small fraction cannot itself have received seed from all over the body. Even if it could, in cases of multiple birth this small part would have to be divided up so that a correct proportion of each part of the semen predestined to develop into specific limbs and organs should go to each foetus: 'It is clear that the semen does not proceed from the whole body but that it divides up according to each form. For it is possible for some to be separated off from the whole and for the whole to be divided

[58] οὐχ ὅλην, ἀσθενέστερον δὲ τὸ κατὰ τὸ πεπηρωμένον (vii. 484. 18–19). In his favour, it should be added that even Darwin, who maintained that acquired characteristics were never inherited, held a pangenetic rather than an organizational theory to explain resemblance.

[59] *GA* 721ᵇ11. Conversely, at 724ᵃ10 he says that if the female does not emit semen, it is reasonable to suppose it does not come from the whole body of male.

[60] δῆλον ὅτι συμβάλλεται εἰς τὸ σπέρμα πᾶν τὸ θῆλυ, *HA* 10. 637ᵇ18–19.

into many parts; but it is impossible for it to act as a whole on different parts at the same time.'[61] As multiple births were usually explained in the Hippocratic theories by the mechanical process of the seed falling into separate compartments in the womb,[62] it is difficult to see how the requisite selection of some amount from every different part of the semen could have taken place without some organizational principle in the seed above and beyond pangenesis. Once this organizational principle is admitted, the necessity for pangenesis evaporates.

SEX DIFFERENTIATION IN HIPPOCRATIC THEORIES

Many Hippocratics recognized the need for some sort of organizational theory in explaining sex differentiation at least, though this led them to the inconsistency of saying that sex organs themselves did not provide seed like the rest of the body. Democritus earned Aristotle's commendation for trying to extend his theory of pangenesis to account for the sex of a child by the relative amounts of seed it received from each of its parents' sex organs, but these parts were even less amenable to such a theory than the rest of the body. Assuming that a child could draw seed from its mother's eyes and father's nose to make up its face, why should it not receive seed from its mother's uterus and also from its father's penis to make up its reproductive system? Despite the invariable correspondence of internal reproductive organs and external genitalia, the uterus, vagina, labia, etc., seemed to be no less separable than the parts of the face. If the correspondence was attributed simply to the proximity of the parts involved, Aristotle asked, why did receiving seed from any other part of one parent's body not entail the seed from all the surrounding areas, and ultimately from the whole body?[63]

In attempting to explain the almost invariable coincidence of certain details that go along with being one sex or the other, the Hippocratics followed one of two tactics: the seed was either male or female by its overall quality, or became male or female accord-

[61] δῆλον ὅτι οὐκ ἀπὸ παντὸς ἔρχεται τὸ σπέρμα τοῦ σώματος, ἀλλ' ἐφ' ἑκάστου εἴδους ἐμερίζετο. ἀπὸ παντὸς μὲν γὰρ ἐνδέχεται ἀποχωρισθῆναι, καὶ τὸ πᾶν εἰς πολλά. ὡς δὲ πᾶν ἅμα καὶ κατὰ μέρος ἀδύνατον, *HA* 10. 637[a] 11–15. For a full discussion of different accounts of multiple birth, see Lonie 1981, 252–5.

[62] e.g. *Vict.* 1. 30 (vi. 504. 14–22).   [63] *GA* 764[b]20–8.

ing to its environment. Often in both of these models the final sex of
the seed was established by the male or female element overcoming
the other either through sheer quantity or through the quality of the
surroundings in which conception took place. A common belief was
that the sex of a child was determined by which side of the womb the
seed fell into, or by which testicle it had come from.[64] Aristotle cites
those who copulate with the right or left testicle tied up in a bid to
produce specifically male or female offspring,[65] and *Epid*. 6. 4. 21 (v.
312. 10–11) says that if the right testicle drops first the man will
procreate boys. Boys were always associated with the right and girls
with the left, since the right side of the body was, in and of itself,
regarded as more auspicious than the left. A concomitant to this was
that the right side of the body was thought to be hotter than the left,
so Aristotle admitted there was some rationality behind associating
males with the right testicle as hotter semen had more chance of
'mastering' the female matter, but he argued that it was ultimately
the ratio of semen to menses which determined the sex of the child. It
thus seems a little unreasonable of him to ridicule Empedocles for
saying that girls were produced in a cold womb (an effect of the
amount of menses present), as this was far closer to his own theory
than that of Democritus which he had praised. However, because he
represents Empedocles as saying that the parts of the body were
already formed in the seed before they entered the womb, he could
claim that this implied that a body which already had a penis could
fall into a cold womb and have to be counted a female (*GA*
764ª12–20).

It is not obvious that this was Empedocles' meaning at all. It was
not the meaning of those Hippocratics who accepted that the temperature of the womb determined the sex of the child; in their
opinion the seed was sex-neutral until it was differentiated by its
environment at conception.[66] Here again it was the negatively
valued categories of cold and moist which produced a girl. *Superf*.
31 (viii. 500. 5–10) says that if a man wishes to have a son he should

---

[64] Parmenides, DK 28 B 17; Anaxagoras, *GA* 763ᵇ33; *Epid*. 6. 2. 25 (v. 290. 7–12);
Aph. 5. 38 (iv. 544. 11–13) says that in a woman carrying twins, if the right breast
becomes thin she will miscarry a boy, if the left a girl, see Hanson 1992, 44–6.

[65] *GA* 765ª23–5.

[66] *Vict*. 1. 34 (vi. 512. 13–19) implies the same belief when it says that 'originally
each sex was born *in* such things' (ἀπ' ἀρχῆς ἐν τοιούτοισιν ἑκάτερα ἐγένετο),
rather than '*from* such things'. Elsewhere in *Vict*. 1, however, the author assumes
mother's and father's seed could be male or female.

have intercourse when the menses are stopping or have finished altogether, and he should push as hard as he can till he ejaculates. For a girl he should have intercourse while menses are as heavy as possible. The passage also suggests tying up the right testicle to engender a girl and the left for a boy. *Genit.* chooses to explain a child's sex by claiming that seed itself is either male or female and that both mother and father can produce either type. As evidence of this the author refers to couples who have produced a child of one sex together and children of the other sex with other partners.[67] The author's description of the two types of seed is not 'male' and 'female' but 'strong' and 'weak'. If both parents supply strong seed, a boy results, and if both provide weak, a girl. If there is a mixture of strong and weak seed, whichever predominates determines the sex. The fact that girls can resemble their fathers is used as evidence that men have female (weak) seed, and that boys can resemble their mothers that women can have male (strong) seed. However, following the theory of pangenesis the author says that weak seed is drawn from weak parts and strong from strong.[68] Since the father has no female parts in his body and the mother has no male parts in hers,[69] it is hard to see how they could provide weak and strong seed respectively. Fraternal twins of different sexes could both look very like their father. The son would have received seed from the same parts of his father's body as the daughter; how could one lot of seed be said to have been drawn from 'strong' parts and the other from 'weak'? A possible answer is that the 'parts' from which the seed is drawn are the humours which have different potencies. When mixed in a ratio that affords strength the humours can engender a male, and a female when the weak elements predominate. In this case, the sex of the child would be determined solely by the quality of the seed and not by its place of origin

[67] Chapter 7 (vii. 478. 16–24). This is of course fallacious reasoning, as it could result purely from the relative amounts of the female seed emitted by the woman and the male seed emitted by the man, as Democritus believed, or (as we believe) by only one parent determining the sex and the other being neutral.

[68] ἀπὸ τῶν ἀσθενέων ἀσθενὴς καὶ ἀπὸ τῶν ἰσχυρῶν ἰσχυρή, *Genit.* 8 (vii. 480. 8–9).

[69] Though *Vict.* 1. 28 (vi. 502. 13–14) says that in men who received male seed from their father and female seed from their mother, 'the female body decreases into another part' (τὸ δὲ θῆλυ μειοῦται καὶ διακρίνεται ἐς ἄλλην μοίρην). This would mean that the most masculine men who had received male semen from both parents could not beget daughters and the most feminine women could not beget sons. But both *Vict.* and *Genit.* imply that all men and women have both male and female seed.

in the body or the nature of the womb in which it is conceived. The fact that the same seed in the same act of intercourse could engender twins of opposite sexes is explained in *Nat. Puer.* 31 (vii. 540. 16–542. 2) as resulting from the emission of semen in a series of spasms, each spasm yielding a different quality of seed. *Vict.* 1⁷⁰ is the only other treatise which describes both men and women as possessing male and female seed. The author describes seed as consisting of a fiery and a moist element; when the fiery element predominates the seed is male and when the moist, female. The amount of each can be controlled by following a dry regimen to produce a boy and a wet to produce a girl. This is not so sweeping a value judgement as it would be in other treatises, since the author believes that mental and physical health lies in a balance between the two elements, and an overabundance of the fiery element can cause disease.⁷¹ Nevertheless, it is better where possible to have more fire than moisture for 'if in any case fire receives a power inferior to that of water, such a soul is of necessity slower, and persons of this type are called silly'.⁷² If both seeds are male the best type of man is born. The next best type is that in which although the mother produces female seed, the father's male seed is sufficient to overwhelm it. The most effeminate type of men, hermaphrodites, are those in whom the sex was established by their mothers' male seed, even though their fathers contributed female seed. The hierarchy is the same for women: the best are those resulting from two sets of female seed, then those in whom the female seed came from their mothers, and finally those 'mannish' (ἀνδρεῖαι) women who received male seed from their mothers but more dominant female seed from their fathers.

This elaborate typology would seem to leave no room for the influence of the womb, yet in an earlier chapter, *Vict.* 1. 27 (vi. 500. 14–19), the author states that if the fires in the seeds join together and fall into a dry place the fire masters the moist part of the seed and solidifies the menstrual fluid, while if it falls into a moist part of the womb it is quenched and 'dissolves into the lesser rank' (διαλύεται ἐς τὴν μείω τάξιν). Littré translates this as 'passant au rang de décroissance' and Jones asks, 'Does it refer to "lifeless" matter, i.e.

⁷⁰ *Vict.* 1. 26–8 (vi. 498. 13–502. 23).
⁷¹ And it should be noted, incidentally, that the author is of the opinion that some men will want to produce daughters.
⁷² εἰ δέ τινι ἐνδεεστέρην τὴν δύναμιν τὸ πῦρ λάβοι τοῦ ὕδατος, βραδυτέρην ἀνάγκη ταύτην εἶναι, καὶ καλέονται οἱ τοιοῦτοι ἠλίθιοι, *Vict.* 1. 35 (vi. 516. 7–9).

matter that cannot form a living embryo?' Given that the first alternative (the fire mastering the moist part of the seed) would result in the conception of a boy, it seems more likely that the failure of the fire in the seed completely to master the moist part, and its subsequent reduction to a lower rank, describes the conception of a girl as opposed to a boy being effected by the environment of the womb. The difficulty of interpretation is caused by the author's attempt to assimilate two theories of sex differentiation.[73] In the one, a female is generated by the same type of process as a male—and is not necessarily any more likely to occur. (Of course, a son might still be hoped for over a daughter, but she is not the result of a less than perfect conception). In the second theory, the true aim of conception is a male child and a female results when this process is hindered.

THE PROCESS OF CONCEPTION IN HIPPOCRATIC THEORIES

Vict. 1. 27 (vi. 500. 19–20) states that the seed can solidify and master the 'things that advance' (τῶν ἐπιόντων) on only one day in each month. This implies that there was only a very short time in the month, before menstrual fluid started to flood the womb, when a boy could be conceived. Once menstrual blood had started to moisten the womb, the fire in the seed would have to contend with so much moisture that it could not assert itself and a girl would be conceived.[74] As it is unlikely that the author thought that the conception of girls vastly outnumbered that of boys, he must have believed that the period of time in which the menses did not completely overwhelm moist seed also was very circumscribed, to one or two days beyond the period in which male seed was viable. Other treatises do not appear to share the opinion that the period in which a woman could become pregnant was so circumscribed, but in general they do agree on the most favourable time for conception. This was just after

---

[73] This may also be evident in *Vict.* 1. 34, see p. 167 n. 66 above.

[74] Because female sperm can survive in higher acidity, males tend to be conceived slightly less often, and later (rather than earlier as the ancients thought) in the menstrual cycle, Harlap 1979. The higher female birth-rate could not have been proven statistically in antiquity, but the ancients may have felt that fewer boys were being conceived if the birth of a daughter was generally less desirable than that of a son. The theory that menstrual blood flowed into the womb throughout most of the month is contrary to the theory in the gynaecological works, see p. 62 above.

menstruation when the womb would be empty and the seed would not be flushed out by the flow of blood: 'It is necessary for her to go to her husband whenever the treatment has been successful and the menses are either tapering off or just beginning, but it is better when they have ceased. She should try especially on those days if she is able to become pregnant, for these are the most decisive.'[75]

The less favoured alternative, that a woman should go to her husband just as her menses were beginning to flow, while it may have been considered favourable because the flow of blood was still not too heavy, would still be advocating intercourse while the womb was full of blood and could be a vestige of the confusion between human menstruation and mammalian oestrus. It may also reflect the belief that during most of the month menses were stored in the woman's flesh and that it was only after the fluid had drained into her womb that the passages in her body were free to carry seed[76] —hence the supposed efficacy of odour tests to discover whether a woman could conceive. Another possibility is that intercourse as menses were finishing was believed to produce boys and during menstruation girls.[77] *Mul.* 1. 17 goes on to say that if a woman does not become pregnant straightaway she is to continue to have sex with her husband as this excites desire and causes her seed to flow. If both seeds flow together there will be conception. This shows that the Hippocratics knew what many practitioners of the rhythm method have discovered for themselves: a woman may be able to conceive at any time of the month, though certain periods are more likely. Because they believed that conception was the combination of male and female seed, the Hippocratics thought the most likely period was that in which there was nothing in the womb to impede the mingling, or nothing in the veins to hinder the flow, of seed; many therapies aimed at promoting conception were therefore purgatives.[78] At the beginning of this century the medical profession was

---

[75] ἰέναι δὲ χρὴ παρὰ τὸν ἄνδρα, ὅταν τὰ ὑπὸ τῆς θεραπείης καλῶς ἔχῃ, ληγόντων ἢ ἀρχομένων τῶν ἐπιμηνίων· ἄριστον δὲ καὶ ἐπὴν παύσηται· μάλιστα δὲ ἐν ταύτῃσι τῇσιν ἡμέρῃσι πειρηθῆναι, ἢν δύνηται κυΐσκεσθαι· αὗται γὰρ κυριώταται, *Mul.* 1. 17 (viii. 56. 15–19); cf. *Nat. Puer.* 15 (vii. 494. 18–20), 'The most favourable time for conception is just after menstruation' (μετὰ γὰρ τῶν καταμηνίων τὴν κάθαρσιν αἱ γυναῖκες μάλιστα λαμβάνουσιν ἐν γαστρί). Cf. also *HA* 582b11–19. *Mul.* 1. 24 (viii. 62. 20–1) says that it is at this period that a woman's seed is strongest.

[76] Cf. *Mul.* 1. 24 (viii. 64. 4–5).

[77] Cf. *Superf.* 31 (viii. 500. 5–10), pp. 167–8 above.

[78] e.g. *Epid.* 2. 5. 6, 5. 42 (v. 130. 2–5, 232. 9–16).

of the opinion that menstruation scoured the mucous lining of the
womb, leaving it more sanitary for the reception of the fertilized
ovum; conception was most likely when the womb was cleanest,
directly after menstruation.[79] At present the most favourable time for conception is believed to
be around mid-cycle, two weeks after the onset of menstruation.
This has been hard to document as it is possible for sperm to live for
two to three days in the Fallopian tubes and also for ovulation to
occur at any point in the cycle (even during menstruation itself,
though this is very rare). *Septim./Oct.* 13 (vii. 458. 11–460. 9) begins
by saying that the best time for conception is directly after menstruation. This lasts for at least three days (usually longer): 'And it is
not possible for either the discharge of menses or the conception of
embryos to take place in shorter periods of time. Therefore, as a
result of all these things it is necessary for most women to conceive
around the middle of the menstrual cycle.'[80] This apparent conson-
ance with modern medical knowledge is vitiated by the fact that the
author seems to think that the process of conception takes at least
three days, and that it results from intercourse directly after menstruation rather than *at* mid-cycle, full conception being viewed as
an end point of an extended process. The alternative is that he
believed menstruation itself could last for the first half of the
month.

There are several statements indicating that the Hippocratics did
not believe conception occurred the instant male and female seed
came into contact with each other,[81] but that a period of mingling
and solidifying had to take place before an embryo could be said to
have been conceived. The claim that a woman can tell she has
conceived if she is dry after intercourse because her womb has drawn
in the seed deposited at the *os uteri* is simply an indication that the
process of conception is under way. *Genit.* 5 (vii. 476. 17–19) says that
in these circumstances, if a woman does not want to conceive, 'it is
her practice to expel the sperm produced by both partners whenever
she wishes to do so' (πρὸς τῷ ἔθει χωρέει ἔξω ἡ γονὴ ἀπ'
ἀμφοτέρων, ὁκόταν ἡ γυνὴ ἐθελήσῃ), i.e. this practice is seen as

[79] Crawfurd 1915, 1331.

[80] καὶ οὐχ οἷόν τε ἐν τοῖσιν ἐλάσσοσί γε μορίοις γίνεσθαι οὔτε τὴν λύσιν
τῶν καταμηνίων οὔτε τὴν ξύλληψιν τῶν ἐμβρύων. ἐκ τουτέων οὖν ἁπάντων
ἀναγκαῖόν ἐστι τῇσι πλείστῃσι τῶν γυναικῶν περὶ διχομηνίην ἐν γαστρὶ λαβεῖν.

[81] For purposes of exposition I shall term this event 'fertilization'.

a contraceptive rather than an abortifacient.[82] Even if a woman does not deliberately expel the semen emitted by both partners during intercourse, there is no guarantee that the two will mingle sufficiently if the woman does not take the correct precautions—though there is disagreement over what these are. *Nat. Puer.* 12 (vii. 486. 2) says that the seeds mingle as long as the woman does not stay still, and *Mul.* 2. 162 (viii. 338. 15–16) says that when a woman moves her legs after coition it causes the seed to fall out if her womb is closed, indicating that in normal circumstances moving the legs aided conception. On the other hand, *Mul.* 1. 11 (viii. 46. 14) says to ensure conception a woman should remain still and cross her legs after intercourse, and *Steril.* 220 (viii. 424. 16–21) says a woman should remain quiet (ἡσυχαζέτω) after coming from her husband. It may be the necessity of this correct mingling which makes the first day after intercourse particularly significant for embryos.[83]

The second most significant day, according to the same passage, is the seventh, because it is in the first seven days after fertilization that most pregnancies terminate spontaneously, and in that case 'such events are called effluxions rather than miscarriages/abortions' (ὀνομάζεται δὲ τὰ τηλικαῦτα ἐκρύσιες, ἀλλ' οὐ τρωσμοί).[84] This seems to be a cultural belief, for it is echoed by Aristotle at *HA* 583ᵃ25 where he says, 'If the seed remains within for seven days then it is certain that conception has taken place; for it is during that period that what is known as effluxion takes place',[85] and *Mul.* 1. 10 (viii. 40. 12–42. 8), in discussing various reasons why a woman can-

---

[82] There are few references to contraceptives in the Hippocratic Corpus. *Mul.* 1. 76 (viii. 170. 7–8) and *Nat. Mul.* 98 (vii. 414. 20–1) both give the same recipe: 'Dissolve about a bean-sized piece of *misy* [either copper ore or truffle] in water, give it to the woman to drink, and she will not become pregnant for a year' (μίσυος ὅσον κύαμον διεὶς ὕδατι, δίδου πίνειν, καὶ ἐνιαυτὸν οὐ κυΐσκεται).

[83] *Septim./Oct.* 9 (vii. 446. 19–448. 1).

[84] Ibid. 9 (vii. 448. 2). The passage goes on to say (vii. 448. 19–21) that a period of seven days is significant in human development because it is formed from a triad and a tetrad. Grensemann 1968, 100, athetizes the passage because it does not fit into the scheme of days, months, forty-day periods, and years which the author is drawing up to show the periods of time which have recognized significance in the development of the embryo as well as in human health and disease. If the seven-day 'effluxion' was a traditional belief, however, the author may have included his complex argument on triads and tetrads precisely so that he could introduce the hebdomad as a significant period. Empedocles stated that 'In seven times seven days [the unborn child is formed]', DK 31 B 153a.

[85] ἐὰν δὲ ἐπτὰ ἐμμείνῃ ἡμέρας, φανερὸν ὅτι εἴληπται· αἱ γὰρ καλούμεναι ἐκρύσεις ἐν ταύταις γίνονται ταῖς ἡμέραις.

not conceive, takes as examples of failed conceptions seed that is expelled up to the seventh day. In such a case, the author says, the seed has putrefied and the whole body should be treated. *Mul.* 1. 11 (viii. 46. 19–24) says that a woman should maintain a drying regimen for seven days after intercourse with her husband, and if she has conceived after this period she should sit on something soft. In these passages seed that is expelled from a woman's womb is referred to simply as 'the stuff from the man' (τὰ τοῦ ἀνδρός), as if no mingling of seeds had taken place.[86]

In this context it is significant that abortions in which Hippocratic doctors admit to having played a part are all said to be of embryos of seven days or less. In *Nat. Puer.* 13 the author repeats three times that the entity he describes is a six-day seed,[87] and the author of *Carn.* 19 (viii. 608. 22–610. 10) claims to have seen many seven-day foetuses. The aborted foetuses described by these authors are manifestly further advanced than seven days,[88] but in classifying them as effluxions rather than abortions the authors may be attempting to operate within the terms of *Jusj* which states 'I will not give a woman an abortive pessary'.[89] Women's claims that they could tell when their wombs had imbibed the seed immediately after intercourse may have developed as a 'safety-valve' for themselves and for doc-

---

[86] Cf. *Mul.* 1. 16 (viii. 54. 1). *Mul.* 1. 12 (viii. 48. 19) says seed must remain in the uterus for ten to twelve days for conception to take place.

[87] ἐξ ἡμέρας μείνασαν ἐν τῇ γαστρὶ γονήν (vii. 488. 22); τὴν γονὴν ἑκταίην (vii. 490. 2–3); ἑκταίην οὖσαν τὴν γονήν (vii. 492. 2).

[88] Lonie 1981, 161, says that if what the author of *Nat. Puer.* saw was indeed a foetus, it could not have been aborted earlier than one month into pregnancy. The *Carn.* passage claims that by seven days the foetus is fully formed in miniature, a stage which other Hippocratic treatises place at thirty to forty days at the earliest, e.g. *Vict.* 1. 26 (vi. 498. 17–21). Hanson 1987b, 596, argues that the author claims that the fully-formed foetuses he has seen are seven days old as proof of his contention that human life and development is governed by the number seven. This may well be the primary motive for the author's statements; however, the point could have been made by stating that all the seven-day foetuses the author had seen were already fully formed. The author's assertion that all the foetuses he had seen were seven-day foetuses suggests he had some reason for assuming or insisting that the abortions he had seen occurred on the seventh day and no later. Lonie 1981, 53–4, believes that the author of *Carn.* bases his account on that of *Nat. Puer.*, but the foetuses are said to be of different ages (six and seven days) and at different stages of development. Apart from the fact that both authors cite their observations as support for their theory of significant days during embryological development, there do not seem to be many points of contact.

[89] οὐδὲ γυναικὶ πεσσὸν φθόριον δώσω (iv. 630. 9–10).

tors in situations where abortion was frowned on, allowing them to
terminate their pregnancies actually several weeks after conception
(when they began to recognize typical symptoms of pregnancy in
themselves) under the title 'contraception' because all they were
expelling was supposedly an effluxion (since they could claim that
their knowledge of their pregnancy stemmed from recognizing the
moment of conception within the last few days). It seems to be in
situations where a pregnancy would be unwelcome that claims are
laid to immediate recognition of fertilization.[90] In other circumstances the Hippocratics and Aristotle record the delayed signs by
which a woman knows she is pregnant; for example, *Nat. Puer.* 30
(vii. 532. 17–19) says a woman might think she is pregnant because
her belly swells and her menses stop. *Steril.* 215 (viii. 416.
8–11) says, 'If you cannot tell whether a woman is pregnant by any other
means' (κύουσαν γυναῖκα ἢν μὴ ἐν ἄλλῳ γινώσκῃς), you can
tell from her drawn and sunken eyes of which the whites will be dis-
coloured, by the rash on her face, her loss of appetite for wine and
food, heartburn, and profuse salivation. The non-appearance of the
menses is considered particularly significant,[91] and the controversy
over the length of human gestation in the ancient world[92] suggests
that in most cases women calculated backwards from the first
missed period to arrive at the date of conception.

The reasons advanced in the treatises for treating terminations of
pregnancy within the first seven days as effluxions rather than abortions or miscarriages is that it takes seven days for the seed to set or

[90] The foetuses of *Nat. Puer.* and *Carn.* are all said to have derived from prostitutes. It may have been more difficult for a married woman to make such a claim if her
husband had not had intercourse with her within the previous seven days. Helen King
has suggested to me (private communication) that the belief that women could tell
when they had conceived might also have enabled women to procure an abortion
from a Hippocratic who might have been unwilling to perform one even at the earliest
stages of pregnancy, i.e. they could claim, 'I'm not menstruating, and no, I am
definitely not pregnant.' Hdt. 1. 5 says that the Phoenicians disputed the Persians'
account that Io had been abducted by a Phoenician captain. Rather, they said, when
Io realized she was pregnant she insisted on running away with the captain. If
maritime trade was to be profitable, the captain could not be expected to have
remained in any one port over-long, so the Phoenician account assumes that most
people would assent to the possibility that Io could realize she was pregnant almost
as soon as she conceived.
[91] e.g. *Epid.* 2. 3. 17, 4. 21 (v. 118. 2–3, 160. 13–162. 3); *Mul.* 1. 10, 2. 133 (viii. 40.
12, 280. 7–282; *Aph.* 5. 61 (iv. 554. 9–11); *Nat. Puer.* 30 (vii. 532. 18–534. 10).
[92] e.g. *Septim./Oct.* 4, 13 (vii. 440. 13–442. 1, 458. 11–460. 1); *Nat. Puer.* 30 (vii. 532.
14–15).

solidify.⁹³ *GA* 758ᵇ2–6 says: 'With animals internally viviparous the embryo becomes egg-like in a certain sense after its original formation, for the liquid is contained in a fine membrane, just as if we should take away the shell of the egg, and that is why they call the abortion of an embryo at that stage an "efflux".'⁹⁴ The author of *Nat. Puer.* 13 (vii. 490. 13–14) says of the six-day embryo he saw: 'It was as though someone had removed the shell from a raw egg, so that the fluid inside showed through the inner membrane.'⁹⁵ The membrane contained white fibres and thick red serum and possessed a small projection through which the author believed the seed and later the embryo respired. Between fertilization and full conception it appears that all the seed takes in is air and it is this which produces the swelling and the membrane. It is only after this is in place that the seed begins to draw in menstrual fluid which coagulates and causes the embryo to grow.⁹⁶ *Epid.* 2. 3. 17 (v. 118. 2–3) asks if the nine months of pregnancy should be counted 'from the menses ... or from conception' (ἀπὸ τῶν γυναικείων ... ἢ ἀπὸ τῆς συλλήψιος). That is to say that although the author concedes that a 'conceptus' might exist before the menses began to be utilized, the being within a woman's womb would not be considered a foetus proper until it began to gestate.⁹⁷ In Hippocratic theories, therefore, menstrual blood is not brought into play until conception is complete.

SEXUAL HIERARCHY IN ARISTOTLE'S THEORY OF CONCEPTION

Aristotle, as we have seen, brought several cogent objections against the theory of female seed as expressed by the Hippocratics. His

---

⁹³ *Carn.* is an exception in this.

⁹⁴ τὰ δ' ἐν αὐτοῖς ζῳοτοκοῦντα τρόπον τινὰ μετὰ τὸ σύστημα τὸ ἐξ ἀρχῆς ᾠοειδὲς γίνεται· περιέχεται γὰρ τὸ ὑγρὸν ὑμένι λεπτῷ, καθάπερ ἂν εἴ τις ἀφέλοι τὸ τῶν ᾠῶν ὄστρακον· διὸ καὶ καλοῦσι τὰς τότε γιγνομένας τῶν κυημάτων φθορὰς ἐκρύσεις.

⁹⁵ οἷον εἴ τις ᾠοῦ ὠμοῦ τὸ ἔξω λεπύριον περιέλοι, ἐν δὲ τῷ ἔνδον ὑμένι τὸ ἔνδον ὑγρὸν διαφαίνοιτο; see also pp. 202–3 and n. 193 below.

⁹⁶ *Nat. Puer.* 14 (vii. 492. 7–15). Antiphon the Sophist had commented, 'That in which the embryo grows is called a membrane', DK 87 B 36. *Steril.* 213 (viii. 412. 5–6) says it is the blood of the menses which causes the seed to coagulate, and if it does not because it is diseased, the seed will flow away from the woman.

⁹⁷ The author's terminology shows that he considers both events (fertilization and the missed menstrual period) to be identifiable. He is addressing the question 'What counts as pregnancy?', rather than 'How can one tell that a woman has conceived?'

alternative theory of the female contribution to reproduction did
away with the notion of female seed altogether and asserted that a
woman's only contribution to the conception of a foetus was her
menstrual fluid. The appearance of semen in young men and menses
in young women at puberty led him, like the author of *Genit.*, to
assert that the two secretions were analogous,[98] but unlike the
author of *Genit.* he believed it was therefore impossible that a
woman should later produce a second seminal secretion:

Now, it is impossible that any creature should produce two seminal
secretions at once, and as the secretion in females which answers to semen in
males is the menstrual fluid, it obviously follows that the female does not
contribute any semen to generation; for if there were semen, there would be
no menstrual fluid; but as menstrual fluid is in fact formed, therefore there is
no semen.[99]

Aristotle also claims, 'Similarly, in the decline of life, the power to
generate ceases in males and the menstrual discharge ceases in
females.'[100] This gives the impression that just as menses and semen
appear at the same age in men and women (14), they stop at the same
age, giving Aristotle more support for his contention that the two
secretions are parallel. It obscures the fact that in another context
Aristotle places 'the decline of life' some twenty years earlier for
women than for men.[101]

Aristotle was aware that just like men women could produce a
liquid when they were aroused during intercourse, but he argued
that the site of its emission, which differed from the part of the
genitals where women felt pleasure, disqualified it from counting as
a parallel to semen.[102] He also disputed that a woman's contribution to generation had anything whatsoever to do with her state of
arousal during intercourse because many women conceived without
ever having ejaculated or experiencing any pleasure, while often
those who did enjoy intercourse did not become pregnant. Whether

---

[98] *GA* 727ᵃ5–9.
[99] ἐπεὶ δὲ τοῦτ' ἐστὶν ὃ γίγνεται τοῖς θήλεσιν ὡς ἡ γονὴ τοῖς ἄρρεσιν, δύο
δ' οὐκ ἐνδέχεται σπερματικὰς ἅμα γίνεσθαι ἀποκρίσεις, φανερὸν ὅτι τὸ θῆλυ
οὐ συμβάλλεται σπέρμα εἰς τὴν γένεσιν. εἰ μὲν γὰρ σπέρμα ἦν, καταμήνια οὐκ
ἂν ἦν· νῦν δὲ διὰ τὸ ταῦτα γίγνεσθαι ἐκεῖνο οὐκ ἔστιν, *GA* 727ᵃ26–30.
[100] καὶ παύεται τῆς ληγούσης τοῖς μὲν τὸ δύνασθαι γεννᾶν, ταῖς δὲ τὰ
καταμήνια, *GA* 727ᵃ9–10.
[101] *HA* 545ᵇ26–31. In this passage Arist. is explaining that the inferiority of a
woman's body causes her to age more quickly.
[102] *GA* 728ᵃ31–4.

or not a woman conceived depended on what was in her womb at the time of intercourse, not any emotions she might or might not feel during the act:

Here is an indication that the female does not discharge semen of the same kind as the male, and that the offspring is not formed from a mixture of two semens, as some allege. Very often the female conceives although she has derived no pleasure from the act of coitus; and, on the contrary side, when the female derives as much pleasure as the male, and they both keep the same pace, the female does not bear—unless there is a proper amount of menstrual liquid (as it is called) present.[103]

Aristotle's objection that no secretion emitted by the female during intercourse could be seed because its appearance had no correlation to conception is sound, and as he cannot be blamed for failing to discover the mammalian ovum he cannot be faulted for coming to the conclusion that menstrual fluid was a woman's only contribution to conception. What does need some further explanation is his insistence that it was a less perfect form of seed than the male's.

It is not sufficient to cite Aristotle's sexism here.[104] The Hippocratic doctors were equally convinced of female inferiority. Their theory of female seed did not in any way amount to saying that women were equal to men (note their description of female seed as weak seed); it was merely the most obvious way of explaining the undeniable resemblance many children bore to their mothers. The possibility of resemblance to the mother was just as obvious to Aristotle, but he appreciated the difficulties inherent in the unsophisticated theory of equivalent male and female seed. His solution to these difficulties demonstrates an appreciation of the logical and biological complexities of embryonic development which were not fully addressed until the beginning of the twentieth century;[105]

---

[103] σημεῖον δ' ὅτι οὐ τοιοῦτο σπέρμα προίεται τὸ θῆλυ οἷον τὸ ἄρρεν, οὐδὲ μιγνυμένων ἀμφοῖν γίνεται, ὥσπερ τινές φασιν, ὅτι πολλάκις τὸ θῆλυ συλλαμβάνει οὐ γενομένης αὐτῇ τῆς ἐν τῇ ὁμιλίᾳ ἡδονῆς· καὶ γιγνομένης πάλιν οὐδὲν ἧττον, καὶ ἰσοδρομησάντων τοῦ ἄρρενος καὶ τοῦ θήλεος, οὐ γεννᾷ, ἐὰν μὴ ἡ τῶν καλουμένων καταμηνίων ἰκμὰς ὑπάρχῃ σύμμετρος, *GA* 727ᵇ7–12. The vocabulary Arist. uses at *HA* 489ᵃ9–12, when distinguishing between male and female, is not meant to imply that the female could inject semen into her womb as a male did, simply that her generative fluid was released to do its work inside her body: 'of those animals which generate, one will emit semen into itself, one into another individual. The former is known as "female", the latter as "male"' (τούτων ἐν οἷς μὲν ὑπάρχει γένεσις ζῴων τὸ μὲν εἰς αὐτὸ ἀφιέν, τὸ δ' εἰς ἕτερον. καλεῖται δὲ τὸ μὲν εἰς αὐτὸ ἀφιὲν θῆλυ, τὸ δ' εἰς τοῦτο ἄρρεν).

[104] See Morsink 1979, 83–112; 1982, 43–59.   [105] Kullmann 1979, 4.

however, his assertion that the male and female contribution to
conception was totally dissimilar made it impossible to give a convincing explanation of why a child had an equal chance of resem-
bling either parent. In fact, his theory lent itself more readily to
explaining resemblance to the mother, and Aristotle had to make
some very contentious claims to preserve resemblance to the father
as the normal outcome of reproduction. The fact that he held
staunchly to his theory, when the problem could have been more
readily resolved by allowing the male to fulfil some of the functions
of the female as well as his own, shows that he was not motivated by
a simple desire to elevate the male contribution over the female.

One question never fully addressed by the Hippocratics was
answered by Aristotle's theory—Why did a woman require a man to
produce children? That he needed her capability of nurturing a
foetus until it was ready to be born was obvious, but why did she
need him? Arriving at the conclusion that she did is, of course, a
matter of empirical observation; but if women were able to produce
their own seed, what could they lack which only a man could provide?[106] As neither sex could reproduce without the other, Aristotle
made the reasonable assumption that they played different and
complementary roles in causing a new individual. Aristotle found it
easy to identify the causal roles of male and female with two of the
four causes he thought necessary for the existence of any substance;
he argued that the male provided the 'formal' cause and the female
the 'material'.[107]

To be intelligible, Aristotle's theory of reproduction has to be set
in the context of other aspects of his philosophy which are themselves highly complex and controversial. However, constraints of
space necessitate a somewhat cavalier approach to Aristotle's on-
tology, epistemology, and psychology. For a general discussion on
the issues which follow the reader is directed to Ross 1949, Allan
1952, and Guthrie 1981.

For Aristotle, all things that exist can be allotted to one of
several categories: substance, quantity, quality, relation, place,
date, action, passivity, and perhaps posture and possession. All the
other categories are dependent upon the category of substance.

---

[106] *GA* 741^{a}6–33.

[107] I do not mean to say that Arist. inferred the relationship of male to female from
that of form to matter, or vice versa. The distinctions fed off and nourished one
another without one necessarily being the origin of the other.

Apart from this no category can exist independently. The really existent things are substances, material objects with some unity (a heap or part of a body, for instance, is not a substance) which can have other qualities predicated of them. A substance is compounded of matter (the stuff a thing is made from) and form (the type of thing the stuff is in that particular incarnation). Neither matter nor form can exist in the sublunary world except in conjunction with each other; there is no such thing as pure matter without form, or pure form without matter. For a new substance to come into being in the world, matter, that existed previously in some other form, must be brought into conjunction with a form, that existed previously in some other matter. The lump of rock before it is made into a column drum has the form 'stone', and the form of the column drum exists in the stonemason's mind[108] before he transfers it to the rock. The column drum can then be considered as matter relative to the form of the temple which exists in the builder's mind. In all cases a thing is produced when matter takes on a new form. Living beings were for Aristotle substances *par excellence*, constituted from the matter of their bodies, flesh, blood, bone, etc., and the form (soul) of their species, man, horse, dog, etc. A new individual living being is produced when the form, which existed previously in some other matter,[109] is transferred to matter which does not yet possess the form of the species.[110]

This theory does provide a structure for two different but complementary roles in generation, but it does not necessitate that Aristotle identify the form as the male's contribution and the matter as the female's. Nor can this identification stem solely from the observation that the mother contributes the material of menstrual blood during pregnancy. The matter of the father's semen could have received the form of the species directly from the mother while in her womb, and the menstrual fluid have acted simply as nourishment for an embryo so conceived. In fact, as we shall see, the material nature of semen caused Aristotle some embarrassment in explicating the finer details of his theory of reproduction—an embarrassment which could have

---

[108] The stonemason's mind is not itself matter, but the stonemason is, and neither his mind nor the form of the column drum it contains could exist without his material presence.

[109] Which, in the natural creation of new substances, has to be combined with the form in the same type of substance as the substance being created.

[110] *Metaph.* 1032[a]12–25.

been circumvented by having the female provide form for the male's matter.

The allocation of the different roles in conception was a direct consequence of Aristotle's unquestioned assumption of male superiority. His theory of substance had been developed in part to answer the conundrum of how, if knowledge was of the unchanging and the real (a hypothesis which no Greek philosopher except the Sceptics thought to challenge), it could also be anchored in this world. Plato had argued that the material objects in this world were in a constant state of flux and could not furnish the constancy, and therefore the reality, to be objects of knowledge. These objects (the Platonic Ideas) were situated in a transcendent, unchanging realm beyond this world, and their relationship to the particulars of sense perception is somewhat obscure. Aristotle's solution was to say that knowledge was indeed of the constant and real, the forms, but that these existed only in the things of this world. This gave form a privileged position over matter in that it was the ultimately real and knowable element in any individual substance. The form of an animal was identified with the soul of its *infima species* as this was the only unchanging element about it that could qualify as an object of knowledge: 'The ultimate species are "real things" while within them are individuals which do not differ in species (as e.g. Socrates and Coriscus).'[111] Forms are identical in so far as the substances possessing them perform the same function. Within a species the differences between individuals are a result of the matter in which the form has been substantiated and do not imply a difference of function; blue or brown eyes both exist for the purpose of seeing and a snub or a Roman nose for smelling: 'Some parts are specifically

---

[111] οὐσίαι μέν εἰσι τὰ ἔσχατα εἴδη, κατὰ δὲ ταῦτα τὰ τὸ εἶδος ἀδιάφορα (οἶον Σωκράτης, Κορίσκος), *PA* 644ª24–5. Cf. *An. Post.* 96ᵇ15, 97ª35–ᵇ6 *Metaph.* 1034ª7, where members of an ultimate species are only distinguishable by matter. *Eidos* does not always mean 'species' (see Balme 1962), and it has been argued that Arist. in fact believed that forms existed at the particular rather than the species level (e.g. Frede 1985, 18–19) because, while *eidos* as species is treated as a universal, the universal is said not to be a substance (*Metaph.* 1038ᵇ1–1039ª24) and is therefore not real and consequently not knowable. But what is knowable is *eidos* as form; therefore form cannot be a universal and therefore cannot be the species. I cannot deal at length with this complex issue here. In the biological works, Arist. makes no indication that forms are to be individuated below the species level until he comes to deal with the problem of family resemblance. The introduction of individual *eidē* at that point is very significant, and in the context of the rest of his biology reads a little *ad hoc*.

182   *The Female's Role in Reproduction*

identical, for example one man's nose and eye are identical with another's nose and eye.'[112] In *Metaph.* 1058ᵃ29–31 Aristotle asks how it is that women do not differ from men in species; later he states that the difference between the sexes was simply one of matter: 'And male and female are indeed modifications peculiar to animal, not however in virtue of its substance but in the matter, i.e. the body.'[113] The implication of this would be that women had exactly the same form as men. But difference in sex seems to be of a different order than other material differences. Being blue-eyed or brown-eyed does not necessitate a difference in function; to some extent being male or female does. This is shown at *GA* 716ᵃ18: 'Now, male and female differ in respect of their *logos*, in that the power or faculty possessed by the one differs from that possessed by the other.'[114] Differing in *logos* is, on occasion, tantamount to differing in *eidos*: 'At any rate, they must differ in kind, and in that the *logos* of each of them is distinct.'[115] Aristotle, however, could not allow the difference in sexual *logos* to set woman apart from man in a separate *eidos*, as it was only because of it that they could between them reproduce the human form, *eidos anthrōpos*. He resolved the impasse by saying that although woman did belong to the species *anthrōpos*, she did not achieve the perfect *eidos* as a man did; hence his famous definition of woman: 'For the female is as it were a deformed male' (τὸ γὰρ θῆλυ ὥσπερ ἄρρεν ἐστὶ πεπηρωμένον).[116] She could not herself possess the perfect form. She could not, therefore, pass on the form to her offspring.

While it is true that a difference in function for Aristotle normally

[112] ταῦτα δὲ τὰ μὲν εἴδει τῶν μορίων ἐστίν, οἷον ἀνθρώπου ῥὶς καὶ ὀφθαλμός, ἀνθρώπου ῥινὶ καὶ ὀφθαλμῷ, *HA* 486ᵃ16–18. These differences are 'idiosyncrasies' and should not be confused with 'individuation'. Matter individuates one instance of the human form from another in so far as it is a different spatio-temporal realization of the form. R. J. Hankinson has pointed out to me that it is not at all clear that Arist. would say that it is only matter which keeps two spatio-temporally distinct examples of the human form from being identical in every feature. While recognizing the force of this objection, I still believe that this is in fact what Arist. is inclined to say throughout most of his biology.
[113] τὸ δὲ ἄρρεν καὶ θῆλυ τοῦ ζῴου οἰκεῖα μὲν πάθη, ἀλλ' οὐ κατὰ τὴν οὐσίαν ἀλλ' ἐν τῇ ὕλῃ καὶ τῷ σώματι, *Metaph.* 1058ᵇ21–4.
[114] τὸ δ' ἄρρεν καὶ τὸ θῆλυ διαφέρει κατὰ μὲν τὸν λόγον τῷ δύνασθαι ἕτερον ἑκάτερον.
[115] τῷ γε εἴδει διαφέρειν καὶ τῷ τὸν λόγον αὐτῶν εἶναι ἕτερον, *GA* 729ᵃ26. In his Introduction to *Generation of Animals* Peck says that he transliterates rather than translates *logos* when it has the technical sense of 'the *defining formula*; the *definition* of a thing's *essence*, of its *essential being*' (p. xliv).
[116] Ibid. 737ᵃ28.

The Female's Role in Reproduction 183

implied a difference in form, it was open to him to say that it was the male who failed to reach the perfection of the *eidos* embodied in the female. In fact, because he defines the male as 'that which generates in another' (τὸ εἰς ἄλλο γεννῶν) and the female as 'that which generates in itself' (τὸ εἰς αὐτό),[117] he admits the possibility of a species which is entirely female and needs no male element to reproduce.[118] In this case the mother would have to provide both form and matter to her offspring, and the species form would have to be identified with the female. As the male needs 'another' in which to generate, no species could exist which was entirely male.

In the lower forms of life such as plants, testacea, some insects, and some fishes, the two generative principles of form and matter could coexist and such life-forms were classed as neither male nor female, or male and female only by analogy.[119] Life-forms further up the *scala naturae* held their position primarily because of their increased complexity and differentiation. As Aristotle puts it in a memorable passage, Nature does not like spit-and-lampstand (ὀβελισκολύχνιον) combinations,[120] and where it is possible to separate parts for specialized functions the separation will occur. So in the higher life-forms the generative principles of form and matter are separated. Form, being real and knowable, is superior and is therefore identified with the male. In species consisting of two sexes the female can provide only the material principle to generation. But it was not simply Aristotle's unquestioned belief in male superiority that led him to differentiate and rank the male and the female contributions to conception; his theory of substance in conjunction with his principle that Nature would separate whatever could be separated played an integral part. His primary aim was not to defraud women of their claims to parenthood. However, once the dichotomy of form and matter had been made and identified with the sexual dichotomy, in the fourth century BC it was inevitable that the menstrual fluid would be identified with the inferior principle.[121]

---

[117] *HA* 489ª9–12; *GA* 716ª14–15.
[118] The sea-perch (ἐρυθρῖνος), *GA* 741ª33–8.
[119] *HA* 537ᵇ22–538ª4; *GA* 715ª18–ᵇ 7. [120] *PA* 683ª23–6.
[121] *GA* 732ª4–10. It is simplistic to say, as does Horowitz 1976, 194, 'because Arist. associated females with material activities (providing food and clothes) and males with spiritual activities (scholarship and government) these distinctions became embodied in his embryology'.

THE PROCESS OF CONCEPTION ACCORDING TO
ARISTOTLE

As a naturalist, however, Aristotle had to explain not only the ontological status of a parent's contribution to its offspring but also the physical process whereby a new individual was created. Form and matter were not sufficient in themselves for the creation of any new substance. There also had to be a tool to transfer the form into the matter (the efficient cause) and an end which was served by the form being put into the matter (the final cause). So, bricks and mortar (material cause) are put into the shape of a house (formal cause) by the art of a builder (efficient cause)[122] in order to protect a man's possessions and provide him with shelter (final cause). Aristotle generally used artefacts to illustrate this theory, but thought it applied just as well, if not better, to natural objects. This is not to endow Nature with a deliberative faculty. Animal reproduction is purposive because it always follows a regular pattern and happens for some good, and nothing that follows a regular pattern happens by chance.[123] The final cause of such reproduction is to perpetuate the form of the species.[124] In the coming-to-be of natural objects, formal and final cause coalesce in a way that the form of a house and its purpose do not. The final as well as the formal cause is therefore identified with the male (as the more perfect representative of the species) and is transferred to the female matter during intercourse.

In living beings Aristotle identified the formal and final cause with the soul. This was not a spiritual entity separable from the body it inhabited, but all the functions that a body of any given species should be capable of performing. The number of functions a soul could perform increased as the vital heat of a body increased, and diminished as the vital heat dissipated until, at death, a corpse could perform no function at all. The same correlation between heat and soul-functions existed between species too. Plants have

[122] The builder's art (and the form of the male) are ultimate efficient causes because they are that from which the motion originates. The builder (and the father) are efficient causes because they are the agents possessing the form they transfer. The tools of the builder (and the semen of the father) are efficient causes because they are tools used by the agent. I am grateful to Mary Louise Gill for clarifying this point for me.

[123] Spontaneous generation is an exception to this rule, see Lennox 1982.

[124] For an excellent discussion on the teleological aspect of Arist.'s theory of reproduction, see Grene 1972.

very little heat and have only the nutritive faculty of soul allowing
them to grow and reproduce. Animals differ from plants in having
sensitive (and thus appetitive) soul, and the majority of them in also
having locomotive soul. Those that cannot change their position at
will 'dualize' between plant and animal. Humans are different from
all other animals in also possessing rational soul which allows
them to deliberate. In order to qualify as a member of the *eidos
anthrōpos* an individual of either sex must possess all the faculties
of the human soul, including the *bouleutikon* element.[125] Women,
however, are incapable of transferring all the human functions to a
new individual. Aristotle's theory of substance had led him to argue
that this must be so; he now had to explain how this incapacity came
about.

Aristotle argued that whatever was passed to the foetus originated
in the seminal residues.[126] In humans he identified the male contribution as semen and the female as menses. Both were residues of
nourishment which had been concocted in the stomach, liver, and
heart till the converted food had enough vital heat to carry nutritive
soul and could therefore be used in the growth of the individual
itself (see pp. 60–1 above). The concoction was caused by the vital
heat in the *pneuma*, the vehicle of all faculties of the soul which was
set in motion by the 'principle' (ἀρχή) of the soul located in the
heart, the hottest part of the body.[127] When, at puberty, this residue
ceased to be used by the adult to promote its own growth, part of it
continued to be used for replenishment of the adult's own body and
part of it was redirected and stored in the uterus or the passages
around the testes. Because he had a greater amount of vital heat, a
man was able to concoct the residue to an even higher degree, to the
point where it could carry the sentient soul as well.[128] Woman,

[125] *HA* 488b24; i.e. they must be able to deliberate and make choices, *EN*
IIIIb12, see Clark 1975, 21–2. Woman differs from man in that her *bouleutikon*
element is less authoritative, *Pol.* 1260a12.
[126] With the possible exception of *nous*, which comes from 'outside' (θύραθεν), *GA*
736b28, but cf. Charlton 1987.
[127] See Peck 1953; Solmsen 1957.
[128] *GA* 741a26–30. However, it generally could not be concocted to quite this
point until a man was 21 (*HA* 582a16–17), while young girls conceived easily
(582a19–20); but cf. 585a34–b1, where both semen and menses are said to be infertile at
their first appearance. Arist. may have been led to the belief that young women became fertile before young men by the fact that Athenian girls were married at a very
much younger age than men (see Pomeroy 1975, 64), so he could have seen several
young mothers but not so many young fathers (or at least none that admitted responsibility). The same observation might be made in our own society, though in fact

while endowed with enough vital heat in her principle to possess all the faculties of the human soul herself, did not have enough of it to concoct her nourishment to the state where it was hot enough to carry the sentient faculty, even after she had finished using it to build her own body. That she could concoct it enough to transfer nutritive soul to another entity was proved by the case of wind-eggs among birds which, while not developing into a mature animal, did go bad, proving that they contained some element of life, and were not totally inert.[129] This means that the menstrual fluid is indeed highly informed, but it does not add anything to the status of the mother's contribution to the embryo *vis-à-vis* the father's; it simply means she provides the matter in the right state to receive a higher form. An architect would not build a temple from unhewn rocks. The mother's matter has the same type of life as a plant and needs the father's contribution of sentient soul to upgrade the life to that of an animal.

Because menses do not require the same amount of heat as semen to be viable in generation, they can remain in a state of preparation in the woman's body. This means that unlike the Hippocratics, who recommended couples who wished to conceive to have intercourse just after menstruation when the womb and the passages of the body were empty, Aristotle believed coitus with a view to reproduction was best performed when 'a proper amount of menstrual liquid' was stored in the womb.[130] However, as this could be anything from the amount left behind after normal menstruation to the amount that had collected just before menstruation began, Aristotle was not committed to saying that one point in the cycle was categorically better than any other, though he did say that most women conceived best just after menstruation, as what was left behind after the discharge was the right volume for the foetus to begin to take shape.[131] He also believed there were some women who conceived best during their menstrual period[132] —a point of view which was reinforced by his confusion of the human menstrual cycle with the mammalian

modern research has shown that semen is generally fertile from its first ejaculation, while a young girl tends not to ovulate with every menstrual cycle for the first two years at least.

[129] *GA* 741ᵃ19–32.

[130] Ibid. 727ᵇ11. *GA* 777ᵇ20–31 shows that he also thought the moon's phases were in some way important for generation because of their association with heat and cold.

[131] *HA* 582ᵇ11–12; *GA* 727ᵇ12–18.   [132] *GA* 727ᵇ19.

oestrus cycle where a female 'in heat' bleeds as a signal that she is ready to conceive.[133] Semen, however, which has to be hot enough to carry the sentient soul, cannot be stored in a state of preparation. It has to be concocted at the very last minute before ejaculation, and even then the first semen to be discharged is not usually fertile as it has not been sufficiently concocted.[134] Before ejaculation there is no need for the male residue of nourishment to carry anything more than nutritive soul. Aristotle says that the two blood vessels leading to the head of each testicle from the kidneys are filled with blood, while two blood-vessel-like passages (φλεβικοὶ πόροι) leading to the head of each testicle from the aorta are not. When the passages from the kidneys double back at the head of the testicles and converge in the penis they contain white liquid.[135] At *GA* 717ᵇ23–6 Aristotle says it is the heating of the penis during intercourse which causes the semen to collect together. It seems as if this heat causes the *pneuma* to rush to the testicles through the *phlebikoi poroi* leading directly from the aorta and to heat the bloodlike residue in the passages leading from the kidneys to the degree where it can carry the sentient soul through the passages that double back to the penis.[136] Heat is of the essence, so men with long penises are infertile because the semen cools down before it reaches the female.[137]

Aristotle is adamant that the semen contributes no material to the 'fetation' (κύημα, the first mixture of male and female generative principles). It is merely the efficient cause which transfers the form from the father to the mother's matter and evaporates as soon as this has been achieved.[138] He says this because he wishes to keep the male and female contributions to conception distinct, so he cannot have the male element contaminated by any matter. This raises some very complex problems for Aristotle which could have been circum-

[133] *HA* 527ᵇ31–3. This misconception persisted until the early part of this century. Crawfurd 1915, 1335–6, says, 'The identity of oestrus or "heat" in animals and of menstruation in the human female admits of no doubt. ... We know that in most mammals non-satisfaction of sexual desire by intercourse tends to a quicker return to heat than normal; and it may be that the greater frequency of menstruation in the human female may in part be referable to the fact that civilisation has brought it about that in the human female sexual desire is often compelled to go unsatisfied.'
[134] *GA* 717ᵇ23–6, 739ᵃ10–13. This is only the case in animals with external testes.
[135] *HA* 510ᵃ13–29.
[136] *GA* 718ᵃ11–15. Arist. does not view the testes as an integral part of this system, but describes them as loom-weights which keep the passages from rising up into the body, ibid. 717ᵃ35–ᵇ1.
[137] Ibid. 718ᵃ23–6. [138] Ibid. 729ᵇ18–21.

vented if he had allowed that the material of the semen formed part of the fetation.[139] He could have admitted this possibility without detracting from the hierarchy of the male and female by claiming that it was necessary for the more refined matter of semen to be combined with the cruder menses in order for the embryo to have sentient soul. The fact that he refused to do so shows that the separation of form and matter was a very strong principle in his theory of reproduction, which he would have been unwilling to override in order to allow women to contribute form, even if he had thought it would facilitate his theory.

Aristotle's difficulties are shown in one of the analogies he used to illustrate the action of semen on menses: the curdling of milk into cheese by the action of rennet.[140] GA 739^{b}23 states that rennet is milk which contains vital heat and so is able to integrate the two substances to form one; but in order to make the analogy applicable to reproduction Aristotle should claim that the rennet does not remain in the curdled milk to become part of the cheese. Complete evaporation of the setting agent is more persuasive when fig-juice is used as the example. The fig-juice is squeezed on to a bit of wool which is then rinsed in a small quantity of milk which is in turn mixed with the rest of the milk to curdle it.[141] It is possible to imagine a sense in which the fig-juice would not retain a physical presence in the cheese through all these successive phases. Rennet, however, is itself analogous to the small quantity of milk that has had the wool soaked in fig-juice rinsed in it, and as Aristotle never claims that this evaporates on coming into contact with the larger amount, it would be hard for him to make a convincing argument that rennet does, especially since he has already explicitly said that it combines. Consequently, one of Aristotle's favourite metaphors for the action of semen on menses is in that respect misleading.

In further support of the contention that semen contributes only form and no matter to the embryo, Aristotle argues that some female insects have to insert part of their bodies into the male during

[139] The main problem is in determining in what sense semen can possess the human form since it is not, even potentially, a human itself, and the menses must come into contact with an actual form. The subject is treated by Preus 1975, 64–107. In such short compass as this, my aim is not to offer any new solution to the highly complex problem as it stands, but to indicate that Arist. would not have had such difficulties had he allowed the male to contribute matter to the embryo.

[140] GA 729^{a}12–14, 739^{b}21–34. This form of explanation is echoed by Pliny, NH 7. 66, and was the one accepted in some quarters down to Harvey in the 17th cent.

[141] HA 522^{b}3–5; GA 737^{a}14–16.

copulation; this is because insects have such a low vital heat that even the males are unable to concoct their seminal residue to a point where it can carry their *pneuma*, and so have to stay united with the female for a long time in order for the vital heat in the principle of the male to work directly on the material in the female. This process is like the potter working the clay directly with his hands.[142] Man and other animals are able to concoct semen to do the job for them, like artisans who work their material by means of a tool, and just as a tool or an artisan does not become part of the material being worked, so semen does not become part of the fetation: 'Necessity does not require that the tools should reside in the product that is being made, nor that the agent which uses them should do so.'[143] But an artisan does not make an artefact by placing his tool in his material and walking away; he has to stay in constant contact with the tool because the form that is being transferred to the matter resides in him. In the reproduction of natural products the male passes his form into the tool and so can leave it to do its work without his guidance.

Aristotle, however, argues that whatever fashions the developing embryo cannot be anything external to the foetus itself, since a tool or efficient cause always has to be in contact with the material it is working, and the growth and development of the embryo takes place internally;[144] the tool, therefore, has to be internal. Furthermore, it cannot be something which is not eventually part of the organism as there are no bits left over in the mature organism which are not functioning parts of it. In fact, at whatever point the development of a foetus is halted no such part can be found, nor is there any reason why something should begin developing the foetus and then disappear at some arbitrary point and leave the completion to something else.[145] The efficient cause at work in the actual development is therefore something internal to the embryo from the beginning and remains part of it when the development is complete. The semen

---

[142] Ibid. 730^{b}25–32.

[143] οὔτε γὰρ τὰ ὄργανα ἀνάγκη ἐνυπάρχειν ἐν τοῖς γιγνομένοις οὔτε τὸ ποιοῦν, *GA* 738^{b}25.

[144] At *GA* 740^{a}13–16 Arist. explicitly criticizes Democritus and others for claiming that the external parts of an animal became distinct first—as if they were fashioned from wood or stone, though this is the simile he had used himself when arguing that semen worked as a tool without becoming part of the child.

[145] *GA* 734^{a}2–16.

transfers the principle of the form into the matter so it can fashion this tool, and then evaporates.[146] Foetal development proceeds in a chain reaction guided by the principle transferred in this initial impetus. Aristotle ultimately develops an analogy for the role of the male semen as that which passes a movement from an agent to the first cog of an automaton. The initiating movement is external to the mechanism, but once the first cog is set in motion the source of movement can withdraw and leave all other movements to follow in a determined sequence.[147] The semen is needed to carry the impulse from the father to the matter presumably because the father himself never comes into direct contact with the menses in the womb during intercourse.

Semen, therefore, has only a temporary role as a tool. It is a conveyor of movements from the father to the menses, and once the menstrual fluid has taken on these movements and become 'ensouled' (ἔμψυχον), the tool can be discarded. Semen can be operative in transferring the movements from the father to the embryo because it is the sort of material the movements could work in. If it were not it could not work independently away from the father. The simile of a tool, which was developed to illustrate how semen worked as an efficient cause away from the father without contributing any matter to the process of conception, entails the corollary that the matter of the semen is the same sort of stuff as the matter of the substance from which it first received the form and of the substance into which it will pass the form, and this raises the same question as rennet and milk—Why should such matter not become part of the new substance? That it does not seems to be an unnecessary and counter-intuitive proposition, contrary to Aristotle's oft-stated precept that 'Like a good housekeeper, Nature is not accustomed to throw anything away if something useful can be made out of it.'[148] There are other indications that he is inclined to say that the semen does contribute matter to the embryo: for example, his remark at *GA* 726ᵃ33 that if a woman did emit semen the embryo would be a single mixture produced from two semens (ἕν μίγμα τὸ γινόμενον ἐκ δυοῖν σπερμάτοιν); his simile of rennet and milk becoming integrated into one and his claim that bigger

---

[146] Ibid. 737ᵃ8–16.   [147] Ibid. 734ᵇ10–18, 741ᵇ9.

[148] ὥσπερ γὰρ οἰκονόμος ἀγαθός, καὶ ἡ φύσις οὐθὲν ἀποβάλλειν εἴωθεν ἐξ ὧν ἔστι ποιῆσαί τι χρηστόν, *GA* 744ᵇ16–18.

animals have earthier semen and hairy animals sticky semen.[149] He tries to pre-empt criticism of such figures of speech at *GA* 767^{b}18–20 where he says, 'It comes to the same thing whether we say "the semen" or "the movement which makes each of the parts grow".'[150] But there is of course a great difference in that 'semen' implies the incorporation of some material and 'movement' simply the transfer of movement from one object to another, and it is difficult to imagine how a movement could be earthy or sticky.[151]

The tension over how semen fulfils its role is reflected in Aristotle's apparently conflicting statements over how long the process of conception takes. At *GA* 731^{a}19–21 he says that semen is produced so that, unlike insects, animals will not have to spend a long time in copulation because the semen will remain behind to 'set' the material 'over many days' (*ἐν ἡμέραις πλείοσιν*), probably seven since Aristotle concurs in his culture's perception that a miscarriage within the first seven days should be called an 'effluxion'.[152] This, however, seems to imply that the semen behaves exactly as Aristotle says a tool which forms the foetus cannot behave: 'To say that it fashions all the parts or some of the parts of the organism and then disappears is ridiculous.'[153] The image of the impetus passing to the automaton suggests rather that the semen passes the principle into the menses almost instantaneously. It may be that Aristotle is a little obscure about how long semen took to do its work because he was making an implicit differentiation between fertilization and conception. Perhaps, rather than thinking of the transfer of the movement as the movement that passes between two billiard balls when they collide, we should imagine the semen as

---

[149] Ibid. 736^{a}6–8; *HA* 523^{a}16. At *GA* 771^{a}31–2 he says that bigger animals also need more semen. This seems unnecessary if the job of the semen is merely to carry heat, but then a larger amount of fig-juice or rennet would be needed to set a larger amount of milk. The comment at *GA* 765^{b}2–4 that more compact semen is more fertile, and at 766^{b}32 that more fluid semen tends to produce girls, is merely a reflection of the amount of heat the semen contains and says nothing about the material of the semen itself.

[150] *τὸ γὰρ γονὴν λέγειν ἢ κίνησιν τὴν αὔξουσαν ἕκαστον τῶν μορίων οὐθὲν διαφέρει.*

[151] The lack of a specific subject for the verb 'master' (*κρατῆσαν*) at *GA* 766^{b}15 could be an illustration of Arist.'s begging the question of whether to say 'semen' or 'the principle in the semen'.

[152] *HA* 583^{a}25; *GA* 758^{b}2–6; see pp. 173–6 above.

[153] *ἀλλὰ μὴν καὶ τὸ φθείρεσθαί γε ποιῆσαν εἴτε πάντα τὰ μέρη εἴτε τινὰ ἄτοπον, GA* 734^{a}9–10.

acting on the fluid menses until they become solid enough to receive
the movement and only then passing on the movement and dis-
appearing. The semen would then remain over several days until the
fetation 'set', but still evaporate before any of the parts began to be
formed.

Aristotle believed that the sex of a future individual was determined at the end of conception and that this determination made the
fetation 'perfect' (*τέλειον*),[154] that is, the principle was finally
passed into the matter. If the *pneuma* had enough vital heat to master
the female material completely, it created a principle with none of
its original heat diminished, so the resultant individual had enough
vital heat in its principle to be able itself to concoct seminal residue
to its final form; that is to say, it would have the complete *eidos* and
be male.[155] If the *pneuma* from the semen of the father was over-
powered by the material of the mother, although it would be able to
generate the principle to allow an organism to develop towards its
own end (the female has her own *logos*),[156] it could not imbue this
principle with enough vital heat to be able itself to concoct semen,
so the organism would never attain the full form of the species but
would change over to its opposite, the female (because things do not
change over haphazardly, *GA* 768ª1):

When the 'principle' is failing to gain the mastery and is unable to effect
concoction owing to deficiency of heat, and does not succeed in reducing the
material into its own proper form, but instead is worsted in the attempt, then
of necessity the material must change over into its opposite condition. Now
the opposite of the male is the female, and it is opposite in respect of that
whereby one is male and the other female.[157]

The principle is not a part as such, and a perfect fetation is equivalent to an egg rather than an embryo.[158] It is from this point rather
than from fertilization, when the semen began to set the menses, but
had not passed over the principle, that a female is said to have

[154] Ibid. 737ᵇ11.   [155] Ibid. 766ª35–767ᵇ5.   [156] Ibid. 716ª18.

[157] ὅταν γὰρ μὴ κρατῇ ἡ ἀρχὴ μηδὲ δύνηται πέψαι δι' ἔνδειαν θερμότητος
μηδ' ἀγάγῃ εἰς τὸ ἴδιον εἶδος τὸ αὑτοῦ, ἀλλὰ ταύτῃ ἡττηθῇ, ἀνάγκη εἰς
τοὐναντίον μεταβάλλειν. ἐναντίον δὲ τῷ ἄρρενι τὸ θῆλυ (καὶ ταύτῃ τὸ μὲν
ἄρρεν τὸ δὲ θῆλυ), *GA* 766ª18–22. Cf. also ibid. 766ᵇ15–17: κρατήσαν μὲν οὖν εἰς
αὑτὸ ἄγει, κρατηθὲν δ' εἰς τοὐναντίον μεταβάλλει ἢ εἰς φθοράν. ἐναντίον δὲ
τῷ ἄρρενι τὸ θῆλυ. To beget a daughter was, therefore, a sign of a weak male
principle in comparison to the female's. Arist. remarks that Heracles produced only
one daughter in seventy-two children (*HA* 585ᵇ23–4).

[158] Ibid. 489ᵇ6–7.

conceived. Aristotle remarks that after copulation hinds conceive 'in only a few days'.[159]

Although it was not a part, the difference in principle affected the whole development of the foetus in so far as the body developed in the way needed to produce and store the seminal residue which it was capable of producing, i.e. the male developed testes (to keep the seminal vessels taut) and the system of blood vessels which allowed him to use them, the female the uterus with its attendant blood supply. Although it is the heat in the principle which determines the sex of the offspring, an animal is only truly male or female once these parts have developed.[160] A change in these parts, though small, can result in a change of principle.[161] A eunuch ceases to be fully male because the damage done to his testes means he can no longer produce semen. In this he is like a woman, but he cannot be classed as female as he does not have the specifically feminine parts of anatomy by which a female is a female. A female does not simply fail to produce semen from nourishment, she turns it into something else.

ARISTOTLE'S THEORY OF RESEMBLANCE

The process described so far has explained how a 'generic' individual of a species could be reproduced; what has passed from father to embryo via the semen has been the form of the species. This does not explain what makes each individual unique in features, or how parents pass on to their children their own idiosyncratic characteristics which are not contained in the species form. The explanation of how this does occur is one of the most tendentious parts of Aristotle's theory. It involves a differentiation in form at an individual level, and has generally had levelled against it the criticism that by denying *eidos* to the menses he made it unnecessarily difficult to account for a child's resemblance to its mother. In

---

[159] Ibid. 578ᵇ14–15. At *HA* 575ᵇ27–30 Arist. says that in horses impregnation can take up to three days. It is not clear here whether he thinks stallions and mares remained united for three days or whether he simply means it took three days for the semen to 'set' the menses and pass over the principle.

[160] *GA* 766ᵇ5–6. Though these parts are not brought into play until puberty, when the body does not need so much nourishment for growth and there is more left over to become seminal residue.

[161] *GA* 766ᵃ24–30.

the context of his whole philosophy, where idiosyncrasies of individuals of the same species are located in their matter,[162] it is in fact
more difficult to account for resemblance to the father, a difficulty
which could once again be resolved if Aristotle had been willing to
admit that the matter of the semen played a role in the generation of
a new individual.

The formidable arguments which Aristotle brought against pangenesis have already been documented. He reasoned persuasively
that the generative secretion did not have to originate from the nose
of a man to cause his child to resemble him in that feature; it was the
arrangement of the material which caused the resemblance. Semen
is able to transfer the organization of the material not because it is
drawn from a nose of a certain shape, but because it originates in a
body in which it would go towards a nose of such a shape: 'Our own
statement therefore must be the opposite of what the early people
said. They said the semen is that which was drawn from the whole of
the body; we are going to say the semen is that whose nature it is to be
distributed to the whole of the body.'[163] This places the ability of
semen to transmit idiosyncrasies of the father squarely in its material nature (i.e. the potential it has for taking on a certain shape)
which, since Aristotle generally insists that members of a species are
identical in form and differ in features only because of their matter,
would fall coherently within his theory of substance. Yet what he
terms his greatest argument against pangenesis is that most male
insects do not produce semen at all.[164] Now, even if it were possible
for the semen to transmit the species form without contributing any
matter, it could only be the matter of the semen which transmitted
the individuating characteristics of the father. If none of the matter in
the male semen is used by the embryo, the child, while taking its
species form from its father, will have to take from its mother all
individual differences marking it off from others of the same
species.[165]

To account for the fact that many children look like their fathers,

---

[162] But cf. n. 112 above.

[163] τοὐναντίον ἄρα ἢ οἱ ἀρχαῖοι ἔλεγον λεκτέον. οἱ μὲν γὰρ τὸ ἀπὸ παντὸς
ἀπιόν, ἡμεῖς δὲ τὸ πρὸς ἅπαν ἰέναι πεφυκὸς σπέρμα ἐροῦμεν, GA 725ᵃ21–4.

[164] Ibid. 723ᵇ19–24.

[165] At GA 738ᵇ34 Arist. says that if two different species mate, succeeding generations grow to resemble the female's 'outward appearance' (μορφή).

Aristotle has to depart from the theory upheld in the main body of his philosophy, and to assert that the form of an individual which is passed to the offspring from the father is not simply the species (e.g. human), or even the male soul (the perfect species form), but also the 'individual movements' that differentiate, for example, Coriscus from Socrates.[166] Moreover, the strongest movements in the semen are those of the most questionable entity, the individual: 'It is always the peculiar and individual characteristic that exerts the stronger influence.'[167] Ross's solution,[168] that individuals are not differentiated by simple matter, but by qualified matter, and that Socrates and Coriscus differ in the form of their matter, while probably true, is not helpful in explaining how this form can be substantiated in the differently qualified matter of the mother without some actual matter being transferred from the father.

Having located a man's individual characteristics in his individual form which can be passed to his offspring via his seminal residue, Aristotle cannot consistently locate those of the woman in her matter, but he also wants to avoid saying she passes on the human form in her seminal residue. He evolves the very weak *ad hoc* solution of saying that as the male principle in the form changes over to its opposite—the female—when mastered, so the individual father's principle changes over to its opposite—the individual mother's—when it is mastered:

Now everything, when it departs from type, passes not into any casual thing but into its own opposite; thus, applying this to the process of generation, the ⟨substance⟩ which does not get mastered must of necessity depart from type and become the opposite in respect of that 'faculty' wherein the generative and motive agent has failed to gain the mastery. Hence, if this is the 'faculty' in virtue of which the agent is male, then the offspring formed is female; if it is that in virtue of which the agent is Coriscus or Socrates, then the offspring formed does not take after its father but after is mother, since,

---

[166] Other sources for this interpretation, not common elsewhere in Arist., are *Metaph.* 1071ᵃ19–23, 27–9, 1038ᵇ14. For the purposes of my thesis I do not wish to enter into a lengthy discussion on the extent to which Arist. believed individual forms to exist; I merely intend to show that in his general discussion of conception he ignores such entities and only refers to them on an *ad hoc* basis when he has to explain resemblance to the father.

[167] ἀεὶ δ' ἰσχύει πρὸς τὴν γένεσιν μᾶλλον τὸ ἴδιον καὶ τὸ καθ' ἕκαστον, *GA* 767ᵇ30.

[168] Ross 1949, 170.

just as 'mother' is the opposite of 'father' as a general term, so also the individual mother is the opposite of the individual father.[169] Aristotle does *not* say that if the movements in the male semen fail to gain mastery the movements in the female residue will assert themselves. He says the movements *in the semen* change into their opposites. At *GA* 768ᵃ11–14 the father's form is said to contain the female's (i.e. mother's[170]) movements potentially. Now, a man could marry any woman; some marry several. For the mastery of his own individual movements to result in a resemblance to the particular woman he impregnated at any given time, the contribution of the female must be of some significance. Cooper explains how Aristotle can account for this without having to invoke movements in the menses by comparing it to the greater influence the nature of stone has on the finished statue of a less proficient sculptor.[171] This is an attractive suggestion but it still leaves us with the asymmetry of a father's idiosyncrasies lying in his form, a mother's in her matter. Aristotle could solve the impasse by admitting that woman contributed something from her individual form, even if she did not have the perfect species *eidos*, and the criticism most commonly brought against his theory is that he gets himself into such difficulties through his sexist refusal to grant woman any share in providing human form to the embryo. However, his theory of conception could stand, and would be much more consistent with the theory of substance enunciated elsewhere in his philosophy, if he would only grant men a share in providing matter, and therefore individuating characteristics, to the embryo. Placing the responsibility of passing on the form of the species squarely on the shoulders of the male would still be 'sexist', but it would work logically, just as does the present scientific theory which attributes equal amounts of genetic information to the contributions of both parents but maintains an asymmetry of roles in allocating the determination of the sex of a child solely to the father.

As it stands, Aristotle's theory of resemblance explains a son who

---

[169] ἐπεὶ δ' ἐξίσταται πᾶν οὐκ εἰς τὸ τυχὸν ἀλλ' εἰς τὸ ἀντικείμενον, καὶ τὸ ἐν τῇ γενέσει μὴ κρατούμενον ἀναγκαῖον ἐξίστασθαι καὶ γίνεσθαι τὸ ἀντικείμενον καθ' ἣν δύναμιν οὐκ ἐκράτησε τὸ γεννῶν καὶ κινοῦν. ἐὰν μὲν οὖν ᾖ ἄρρεν, θῆλυ γίνεται, ἐὰν δὲ ᾖ Κορίσκος ἢ Σωκράτης, οὐ τῷ πατρὶ ἐοικὸς ἀλλὰ τῇ μητρὶ γίνεται. ἀντίκειται γὰρ ὥσπερ τῷ ὅλως πατρὶ μήτηρ, καὶ τῷ καθ' ἕκαστον γεννῶντι ἡ καθ' ἕκαστον γεννῶσα, *GA* 768ᵃ7–9.
[170] See Cooper 1988, n. 9.   [171] Ibid. 32.

looks like his father as a straightforward case of the form completely mastering the mother's matter. A daughter who looked like
her mother resulted from the mother's matter (though not the *movements* in the matter) mastering both the individual and male movements of the father (*HA* 506^{a}5–6). Aristotle claimed that these were
the two most common outcomes. A son who resembled his mother
resulted from the father's individual movements being mastered,
but not those of his sex, and a daughter who resembled her father
from his male but not his individual movements being mastered.
All these cases involved the principles of 'mastery' (κρατέω) and
'reversion to opposite' (ἐξίστημι πρὸς τὰ ἀντικείμενα). Aristotle
also had to address those occasions when a child resembled a grand-
parent or some other ancestor. For this he introduced the theory of
'relapse' (λύομαι). He explains this as a process whereby the agent,
without being mastered by the material on which it is acting, has its
movement 'blunted' (ἀμβλύνομαι).[172] Although the movements of
the father may relapse, they can still master the material provided
by the woman. Similarly, once her matter has mastered the male's
movements, a relapse does not transfer the mastery back to the
father. The individual movements of the father could relapse into
those of his own father, or his father's father. Once the mother's
matter had mastered the father's movements, these movements too
could relapse into that of her mother or grandmother. Aristotle
does not say that it is the mother's movements which relapse.
Throughout, relapse is something that happens to the agent (the
movements in the semen) by virtue of the material it is working on.
Presumably, within her own body the movements of a woman's fore-
bears could affect the nature of the menstrual material which was
present for the male's movements to work on. In effect, then, relapse
on the mother's side would have taken place before the process of
conception.

Aristotle does not address the issue of how a child could resemble
his paternal grandmother or his maternal grandfather, but it must
involve a combination of relapse and mastery. In the former case,
the individual movements of the father relapse into those of his own
father, and these movements are in turn mastered by the opposite
female principle of this man's wife, the child's grandmother (a process best explained once again if the father's 'individual movements'
came from the matter he had received from both parents). In the case

[172] *GA.* 768^{b}15–23.

of resemblance to the maternal grandfather, the mother's matter has first to gain the mastery over the father's individual movements, to have already relapsed into those of her mother, and to have been mastered by the male principle opposite to those individual movements. This would explain the case of the woman at Elis who had intercourse with a black. The daughter of the union was white, showing that the woman's matter had mastered both the individual and male movements of the father. The daughter's son, however, was black. Her matter could not master the male principle of the boy's father, but her matter had caused a relapse of his individual movements in so far as her menstrual fluid had been shaped by the individual movements she had received from her father.[173]

Sometimes a child bears no resemblance to anybody in its family. In these cases Aristotle said that only the species aspect of the form had prevailed. Sometimes not even these are strong enough and the offspring that results cannot function as a human; then Aristotle says that the matter has fulfilled only its genus potentiality and the result can only be classed as animal. As the aim of reproduction is to produce an individual as like to the original form as possible, anything that is not an exact replica of the father can be said to be 'deformed'. Aristotle claims that these deformities are more often a case of excess rather than deficiency of matter because he believes they result (like the female) from the matter-to-form ratio being too high.[174] If there is too little matter, the form is simply substantiated on a smaller scale than usual. If there is too much, once the form has been substantiated it continues to try to inform whatever matter remains. Sometimes there is enough material for the form to be completely substantiated more than once. This does not happen so much in humans[175] and larger animals where the material was expended in the bulk of their bodies, though humans were recorded as having up to five children at one birth. In those animals in which multiple births were common, deformities of apparent excess could be caused by two individuals being crushed

---

[173] Ibid. 722ª10–11. An alternative possibility (which I will develop elsewhere) would be that while a woman did not have sufficient heat to concoct her seminal residue to the point of carrying sentient soul, once a man had implanted such a principle in her menses to create a new individual, the individual movements of her own form could work directly on the ensouled material in her body, just as the form of a male insect was thought to work directly on the material in a female insect's body without the medium of seminal fluid (see above, p. 189).

[174] Ibid. 771ᵇ28–772ᵇ25.

[175] In spite of the fact that they produced more seminal residue in comparison to their size than any other animal.

together through lack of space. The criterion by which to judge
whether the deformity arose in one individual through an excess of
matter, or in two through an insufficiency of space, was to investigate
how many principles there were in the body—for an individual was to
be identified not so much by the shape of its body as by the existence
of a principle. Animals which usually gave birth to only one offspring
at a time were therefore less likely to produce a monster (τέρας).

A female is the first deviation from the form, but because it is a
natural and necessary deviation Aristotle never labels it a *teras*,
under which heading he elsewhere lists everything that does not
happen regularly (ὡς ἐπὶ τὸ πολύ) and serves no purpose—from
a sixth toe to twins: 'Hence, also, such creatures seem rather to be
monstrosities because their formation is contrary to the general rule
and to what is usual.'[176] So, male monozygotic twins looking exactly like their father would be more of a monster than a single
daughter. The female is a regular and necessary 'deformity of
nature' (ἀναπηρίαν φυσικήν),[177] because without her nothing that
bore the complete form could ever be conceived.

Menstrual blood played a crucial role in Aristotle's theory of
conception, and while he did account the father's role superior, he
can hardly be said to have 'almost denied maternity'.[178] He could
have simplified his theory by allowing the male to duplicate some of
the female's role in contributing matter. That he did not, meant that
she played an essential part in conception as well as in nurturing the
foetus. The woman was not simply the earth in which the seed
planted by the male grew. Any seed which is planted is already a
mixture of male and female; the function of the earth is to provide
nourishment for its growth. Aristotle was not whole-heartedly
among those who believed that the woman provided only the place
for the foetus to develop, or even those who believed they provided
this plus the simple nourishment for its growth. However, the way in
which Aristotle thought the woman contributed something over and
above these two factors to conception only becomes clear when we
consider the development of the embryo inside the woman from its
conception to its birth.

[176] διὸ καὶ δοκεῖ τερατώδη τὰ τοιαῦτ' εἶναι μᾶλλον ὅτι γίνεται παρὰ τὸ ὡς
ἐπὶ τὸ πολὺ καὶ τὸ εἰωθός, GA 772ᵃ35–ᵇ1.
[177] GA 775ᵃ15.   [178] Horowitz 1976, 186.

UTILIZATION OF MENSTRUAL BLOOD DURING
PREGNANCY

During pregnancy a mother's monthly blood ceases to appear, but
the Greek theorists did not infer that it was no longer present in her
body; pregnancy did not change the nature of the digestive system
that produced menstrual blood. Pregnancy modified a woman's
body only in so far as the embryo absorbed the blood: 'Blood comes
down from all the body when a woman is pregnant and gradually
enters the womb, encircling that which is inside it; the blood makes it
grow.'[179] A continual supply of this blood was imperative. If a
pregnant woman menstruated her child could not be healthy,[180] and
if she was bled she miscarried.[181] A woman who was unnaturally
thin also tended to suffer miscarriages until she had put on some
weight.[182] All these statements may have been verified by observation, but they were also what the ancient authorities would expect
from the theory that the foetus was nourished by its mother's
menses—in each case nourishment was being diverted away from the
developing child.[183] Of course, in the Aristotelian theory, menstrual
blood was necessary for conception itself to take place. In the Hippocratic theories, while an absence of menstrual fluid promoted
rather than impeded conception, a continued absence made it impossible for a woman to bear a child because she provided insuffi-
cient nourishment. Even staunch believers in female seed viewed
menstrual blood as indispensable for the renewal of the human
race. Menses were considered so important for pregnancy that even

[179] κατέρχεται γάρ, ἐπὴν ἐν γαστρὶ ἔχῃ ἡ γυνή, ἀπὸ παντὸς τοῦ σώματος
αἷμα ἐπὶ τὰς μήτρας κατ᾽ ὀλίγον, καὶ περιιστάμενον κύκλῳ περὶ τὸ ἐν τῇσι
μήτρῃσιν ἐὸν αὔξει κεῖνο, *Mul.* i. 25 (viii. 64. 19–66. 1). Soranus goes so far as to say
that the menses derived their appellation of the 'monthly' (ἐπιμήνιον), from the fact
that they became the food for the embryo, and a sailor's monthly rations were called
ἐπιμήνια, *Gyn.* i. 19.
[180] *Aph.* 5. 60 (iv. 554. 7–8); *HA* 582ᵇ19–22. A little bleeding in the first month
was not thought to be dangerous, presumably because the foetus did not need as much
nourishment at that stage (*GA* 727ᵇ26–8).
[181] *Aph.* 5. 31 (iv. 542. 12–13).   [182] Ibid. 5. 44 (iv. 546. 8–9).
[183] The symbiosis could also work to the detriment of the mother. *Mul.* i. 32 (viii.
76. 4–6) says that if it is not getting enough fluid the embryo can set off to the liver and
hypochondria. *GA* 750ᵃ27–9 says that if fowls lay too often they die because all their
nourishment is being used up in producing eggs rather than in maintaining their own
bodies. Arist. believed that growth ceased in a woman after she had given birth to
three children and that one of the reasons women aged more quickly was because they
were worn out with childbearing (*HA* 582ᵃ22–5).

though the Hippocratics believed conception required the presence of female seed and the absence of menstrual fluid, *Mul.* 1. 6 (viii. 30. 21- 2) states that women who menstruate less than normal are 'not concerned about bearing children' (οὐ μνησίτοκοι), and do not become pregnant. In this condition, the affective deficiency in the woman is not a lack of desire for intercourse but of the nurturing disposition that leads a woman to want to be a mother.

The ancient theorists would have had no call to suspect the omnipresence of menstrual blood during pregnancy if there had not been several sustained periods when a woman was not pregnant and her blood could be seen to return at reasonably regular intervals. Of the 129 female case histories in the *Epid.*, 38 were in some stage of the procreative process. Although this is near 33%, it is not sufficient to sustain Rousselle's claim that women of childbearing age in Greece were usually either pregnant or nursing and therefore hardly saw their menstrual blood at all after marriage.[184] It is true that at *HA* 587^{b}2–5 Aristotle implies that one pregnancy was expected to follow hot on the heels of another when he says that if a woman has small purifications after parturition she is more ready for conception, and Greek women undoubtedly spent a greater part of their lives pregnant than do their modern counterparts, but this does not mean that one pregnancy followed another in succession to the extent of entirely suppressing the menstrual cycle. Contrary to Rousselle's claim, the Hippocratics do not cite the drying up of milk but the suppression of menses as the first sign of pregnancy (see n. 91 above), and they distinguish this from other occasions of suppression by noting that it was accompanied by feelings of nausea but no other pathological symptoms.[185]

It was important to know as soon as possible whether or not a woman was pregnant, because if her menses had been suppressed for any other reason prompt medical intervention was required; on the other hand, the doctor did not usually want to induce an abortion.[186] The methods used for ascertaining whether the non-appearance of the menses resulted from conception included rubbing a red stone on a woman's eyes; if the colour permeated it showed she was preg-

[184] Rousselle 1988, 37.

[185] *Aph.* 5. 61 (iv. 554. 9–11). Arist. says nausea occurs because in the early stages of pregnancy the child does not use up all the menses, so its mother has to void them by vomiting (*GA* 775^{b}10–14).

[186] But cf. pp. 174–5 n. 90 above on how women would be able to manipulate beliefs to procure an abortion if they wished.

202 *The Female's Role in Reproduction*

nant.[187] This method is predicated on the belief that there was a sympathy between the eyes and the reproductive system.[188] *Epid.* 2. 5. 8 (v. 130. 6–7) says that the eyes draw phlegm from the breasts. When all the extra nourishment in a woman's body was needed for the foetus the attraction worked in the opposite direction, thus drawing the colour from the stone into the eyes. Red would be the colour of choice as it corresponded to the blood that was draining from the area.[189]

Blood was the final form of food which enabled humans to grow and maintain their bodies. Nourishment was presented to the foetus already digested into this final form, so in its first day of life the new-born voided a bloody excrement from its digestive system.[190] There were, however, a number of different theories on the methods by which the developing foetus absorbed the blood into its body. According to Aristotle, some thought that the foetus suckled from a nipple or a lump of flesh in the womb in much the same way as it did from the breast once it was born.[191] In such cases the menstrual blood was believed either to have been converted to milk in the womb or to have solidified and replenished the lump of flesh. Both theories posited that the foetus took in food in a manner similar to that of a mature human. This requires either that the suckling as a form of nutrition took place only in the later stages of pregnancy, or that the body of the baby was more or less fully formed at conception, or at least that it developed its head almost immediately (as Hippon believed).[192]

Censorinus' list (6. 1–3), however, demonstrates that a belief in complete preformation was not widespread before Aristotle. Alcmaeon said that it was impossible to say what developed first in an embryo, Empedocles said it was the heart, Democritus the head and belly, and Anaxagoras the brain. In order to ascertain how a foetus develops, the author of *Nat. Puer.* recommends taking a batch of twenty hen's eggs and opening them on successive days. He speaks as if he had done it himself, and also describes in some detail an

[187] *Nat. Mul.* 99 (vii. 416. 1–3).
[188] *GA* 747ª10–18, where the same method is used as a test for infertility.
[189] The eyes could draw back some of this blood if it was suddenly no longer needed. *Epid.* 5. 53 (v. 238. 8) says that the whites of a woman's eyes turned red after an abortion.
[190] *HA* 587ª31. A mother's diet could show its effects on her foetus. *Superf.* 18 (viii. 486. 7–9) says that if a pregnant woman eats coal, there will be a birthmark on the head of the infant.
[191] *GA* 746ª20. Censorinus 6. 1 names Diogenes and Hippon.
[192] See Lonie, 1981, 185.

aborted foetus which he had seen.[193] He describes it as an egg which
had had its shell removed and in which could be seen lots of veins
and sinews but no distinct parts. Abortions and miscarriages were
too common in the ancient world[194] for many people to believe that
a foetus was an homunculus that grew uniformly. They knew that in
the first few weeks it was an amorphous mass which only gradually
became articulated, but they believed that each part to be articulated was already present in the undifferentiated mixture of the male
and female generative secretions: 'For that of which no part were
present would not grow at all, whether the nutriment that were
added were much or little, as having nothing to grow on to it. But,
having all, each grows in its own place.'[195] Even in theories of pangenesis such as that of Diogenes which claimed that semen contained
simply the material constituents of the body rather than the body
parts in miniature, all the different types of material were present at
the earliest stages of development. They were not the result of an
organizational principle working on completely unstructured
material.[196] In every case menstrual fluid was needed merely to
increase the bulk of each part already present in the seed when the
time came in the embryo's development for that part to be realized.
This is why Parmenides comments, 'Seed needs to preserve proportion for well-formed embryos.'[197]

The problem, then, was to explain how, until the digestive system
developed, the menstrual material was transformed into the
embryo's body. The author of *Nat. Puer.* says that the male and
female seed mingled together and heated up until the mixture was a
sphere filled with breath, which escaped by a passage it made for
itself through the middle of the seed and the membrane forming
around it (the 'fertilization' stage in which menstrual blood is not
used). Through this perforation (the umbilical cord) the seed drew in
fresh cold air from the mother. Menstrual fluid which surrounded
the membrane was drawn in along with the cold breath and

[193] *Nat. Puer.* 13 (vii. 490. 12–492. 2). He says it was an abortion after six days, but if
it was an aborted foetus it seems to have been considerably more advanced, at least
one month, Lonie 1981, 161; see pp. 173–6 and n. 95 above.
[194] Of the 38 pregnancies in the *Epid.*, 15 ended in abortion. *Septim./Oct.* 4 (vii. 442.
5–6) says that most abortions took place within the first forty days, i.e. before the
foetus was fully developed.
[195] οὗτινος γὰρ μὴ ἐνείη μοίρη ἐξ ἀρχῆς οὐκ ἂν αὐξηθείη οὔτε πολλῆς
ἐπιούσης τροφῆς οὔτε ὀλίγης, οὐ γὰρ ἔχει τὸ προσαυξόμενον· ἔχον δὲ
πάντα, αὔξεται ἐν χώρῃ τῇ ἑωυτοῦ ἕκαστον, *Vict.* 1. 7 (vi. 480. 12–14).
[196] Censorinus 6. 1.   [197] DK 28 B 18.

coagulated around the foetus to form the flesh of its body. [198] Once the heat inside the seed has solidified a hard envelope around itself, it is imprisoned and can no longer draw nourishment and expel breath from the whole of itself, so it begins to consume the moisture inside. The solid substances dry out into bones and sinews; the moister parts dry out, but not completely, so they remain soft and the fire can make a passage for itself through them. Once this passage is made, growth of the foetus proceeds from the inside out, that is to say it draws in the menstrual blood and converts it internally rather than having it coagulate around it. The menstrual fluid readily develops into the required body parts because, on the principle of like to like, the menstrual material from a certain part of the body is attracted to the seed which originated from the same part of the body. [199] The foetus eventually develops to the point where it can be said to possess its own blood and humours separately from its mother, though there might still be occasions when it could benefit from its mother's body fluids: 'Blood of another is useful, one's own blood is useful; blood of another is harmful, one's own blood is harmful; one's own humours are harmful, humours of another are harmful; humours of another are beneficial, one's own humours are beneficial.' [200]

Aristotle too performed the experiment with the hen's eggs suggested by the author of *Nat. Puer.*, and in the early stages he describes the developing embryo in much the same terms as the author of *Nat. Puer.* had done, full of bloody veins and white fibres enclosed in a membrane. [201] However, he did not believe that development progressed by parts in the seed becoming more distinct with the accumulation of menses, either through coagulation around the seed or an imbibing of blood resulting in swelling of the seed; the parts had to be developed successively in the menstrual material itself before they could begin to grow. [202] The heart was the

[198] *Nat. Puer.* 13–14 (vii. 488. 22–492. 18), cf. *Vict.* i. 9 (vi. 482. 13–484. 16). This theory of foetal development seems to be assumed in *Mul.* i. 25 (viii. 64. 19–66. 1). For a more detailed discussion of this material, see Lonie 1981, 176–90.

[199] *Nat. Puer.* 17 (vii. 496. 18).

[200] αἷμα ἀλλότριον ὠφέλιμον, αἷμα ἴδιον ὠφέλιμον. αἷμα ἀλλότριον βλαβερόν, αἷμα ἴδιον βλαβερόν, χυμοὶ ἴδιοι βλαβεροί, χυμοὶ ἀλλότριοι βλαβεροί, χυμοὶ ἀλλότριοι συμφέροντες, χυμοὶ ἴδιοι συμφέροντες, *Alim.* 40 (ix. 112. 4–7). As there were no blood transfusions in the ancient world and this passage occurs in an obstetric context, it seems as if the 'blood of another' (ἀλλότριον), must refer to the mother—though this text is so deliberately obscure that any interpretation is bound to remain controversial.

[201] *HA* 561ᵃ4–562ᵃ21.   [202] *GA* 734ᵃ16–26.

first thing to develop, and even this was not immediately recognizable but simply the part furthest on the road to realization: 'So too in the fetation, in a way all the parts are present potentially but the first principle has made the most headway, and on that account the first to become distinct in *actuality* is the heart.'[203]

The small red spot of the embryonic heart is the first distinct organ that can be detected with the naked eye (though the spinal cord and nervous system can be detected earlier with a microscope). Aristotle may have seen it in a developing embryo, but even if he had not he would have predicted that it would be the first organ to develop because it is the principle of maintaining life and growth in the fully developed animal. The *pneuma* which has come almost directly from the male heart via the semen has enough heat to carry this first principle of the soul into the female matter. The form now has its seat in the female matter, and from here it can direct operations so that the menstrual fluid, which is now an organism, develops towards its final form in a fixed sequence through its own power of nutritive soul. The organism passed through several stages of development before it looked anything like a human,[204] but because it contained the principle of nutritive soul it was always able to guide and convert the nourishment from the mother into the type of material that was needed for any particular part. This theory of embryological development (epigenesis), when compared to the preformationist theories which had a tenacious hold on scientific theory until the beginning of this century, was a profound insight on Aristotle's part.

Most ancient theorists believed that the foetus was fully formed fairly early in pregnancy[205] and that gestation was largely a time for the growth rather than the differentiation of parts. At *GA* 730[b]1–4 Aristotle says that the female contains both the material for the formation of the foetus and the further material which has to be added for its growth,[206] and at 766[a]10–11 that the material by which

---

[203] οὕτω καὶ ἐν τῷ κυήματι τρόπον τινὰ πάντων ἐνόντων τῶν μορίων δυνάμει ἡ ἀρχὴ πρὸ ὁδοῦ μάλιστα ἐνυπάρχει. διὸ ἀποκρίνεται πρῶτον ἡ καρδία ἐνεργείᾳ, *GA* 740[a]2–4.

[204] Ibid. 741[b]25–745[b]22.

[205] e.g. *Septim./Oct.* 9 (vii. 450. 1–4); *Nat. Puer.* 18 (vii. 498. 27); *HA* 583[b]3–7. Empedocles says, 'In seven times seven days [the unborn child is formed]', DK 31 B 153a. There is no general consensus on the period for articulation, see Lonie 1981, 194.

[206] Even mature animals need two types of nourishment, the nutritive (τὸ θρεπτικόν) and the growth-promoting (τὸ αὐξητικόν), *de An.* 416[b]12–20.

the foetus is increased is the same as that from which it came into being; but there are signs that he thought of the material which was informed by the male semen at conception as being of a higher quality than that which was utilized later simply as nourishment. In discussing the development of an egg he says that in two-coloured eggs the white is hotter and therefore nearer the actual form of the animal, and it is this that is used in the formation of the foetus:

That is why in the case of all double-coloured eggs the young animal gets its 'principle' of generation from the white, because hot substance is the place where the soul-principle is to be found, while it gets its nourishment from the yolk. With those animals, therefore, whose nature tends to be hotter than others we find there is a clear distinction between the part from which the 'principle' is formed and the part from which the nourishment is derived.[207]

The nutriment for the growth of an animal from an egg comes from the yolk, so it is different from and, in a sense, outside the organism, though at *GA* 733^{b}26–29 it is said that, like a scolex, an animal developing from an egg contains its primary matter within itself.[208] *GA* 751^b 21–8 says that even wind-eggs are differentiated into a nutritive and a higher grade material. In a wind-egg the white would not contain the 'principle', but it would be capable of receiving the principle where the yolk would not. If yolk contains nutritive soul and the white is yet further concocted, this would seem to suggest that female matter provides more than nutritive soul to the actual formation of the fetation.

When conception takes place within a woman, Aristotle says that the semen first sets the purest part of the menstrual blood, for the rest of it is too fluid to be of any use: 'In those species which emit semen, when the semen from the male has entered it causes the purest portion of the residue to "set"—I say "purest portion" because the most part of the menstrual discharge is useless, being fluid.'[209] The more fluid menses which are not set by the semen to

---

[207] διόπερ ὅσα δίχροά ἐστι τῶν ᾠῶν, τὴν μὲν ἀρχὴν τὸ ζῷον λαμβάνει ἐκ τοῦ λευκοῦ τῆς γενέσεως (ἐν γὰρ τῷ θερμῷ ἡ ψυχικὴ ἀρχή), τὴν δὲ τροφὴν ἐκ τοῦ ὠχροῦ. τοῖς μὲν οὖν τὴν φύσιν θερμοτέροις τῶν ζῴων διακέκριται χωρὶς ἐξ οὗ τε ἡ ἀρχὴ γίνεται καὶ ἐξ οὗ τρέφεται, *GA* 751^{b}5–9. Cf. *HA* 489^{b}7–9 and 560^{a}21–8 where the white of an egg is said to set under the influence of heat, and the yolk under cold.

[208] In fact the reproduction of a scolex seems to be the only type of which this is literally true, cf. *GA* 732^{a}32, 752^{a}27, 758^{b}10–15; *HA* 489^{b}7–9.

[209] ὅταν δ᾽ ἔλθῃ τὸ σπέρμα ἀπὸ τοῦ ἄρρενος τῶν σπέρμα προιεμένων, συνίστησι τὸ καθαρώτατον τοῦ περιττώματος—τὸ γὰρ πλεῖστον ἄχρηστον καὶ ἐν τοῖς καταμηνίοις ἐστὶν ὑγρόν, *GA* 739^{a}6–9.

form the embryo go to form the nourishment. *GA* 728ª26–31 says:

As we see, the menstrual fluid is semen, not indeed semen in a pure condition, but needing still to be acted upon. It is the same with fruit when it is forming. The nourishment is present right enough, even before it has been strained off, but it stands in need of being acted upon in order to purify it. That is why, when the former ['purer' menstrual fluid] is mixed with the semen and when the latter ['cruder' menstrual fluid] is mixed with pure nourishment, the one effects generation, and the other effects nutrition.[210]

Two different grades of material (generative and nutritive) are produced at the mingling of semen and menses (though here even the nutritive grade needs the male influence to become useful, perhaps an *ad hoc* solution to differentiating between two grades of seminal residue in the female without granting either of them a status above the lowest form of soul). The generative material is that which is set in the fetation and which, like the seed of a plant, has the principle of growth in it from the first.[211] The principle cannot begin to take in nourishment to form the body until the part of the body which conveys nourishment to the principle has been formed, so the nourishment which forms this part must already be present in the fetation, as the material for the first root is present in the seed:

Well, perhaps after all it is not true to say that all the nourishment comes from outside. In the seeds of plants there is some nutritive matter, which at first has a milky appearance; and it may be that in the same way, in the material of the animal, the residue left over from its construction is present as nourishment for it from the outset.[212]

The umbilical cord is like a root to the uterus.[213] At *GA* 740ª24–7 the embryo is said to draw nourishment from the uterus in the same way that a plant draws nutriments from the earth. These nutriments may have been the ultimate source of the female matter set by the male element in the seed of a plant, but they are in no way as

---

[210] ἔστι γὰρ τὰ καταμήνια σπέρμα οὐ καθαρὸς ἀλλὰ δεόμενον ἐργασίας, ὥσπερ ἐν τῇ περὶ τοὺς καρποὺς γενέσει, ὅταν ᾖ μήπω διηθημένη, ἔνεστι μὲν ἡ τροφή, δεῖται δ' ἐργασίας πρὸς τὴν κάθαρσιν. διὸ καὶ μιγνυμένη ἐκείνη μὲν τῇ γονῇ, αὕτη δὲ καθαρᾷ τροφῇ, ἡ μὲν γεννᾷ, ἡ δὲ τρέφει.

[211] *GA* 724ᵇ20, 739ᵇ35. There is an extended botanical analogy in *Nat. Puer.* 22–6 (vii. 514. 6–528. 16) with which Arist.'s simile should be compared.

[212] ἢ τοῦτ' οὐκ ἀληθές, ὡς πᾶσα θύραθεν, ἀλλ' εὐθύς, ὥσπερ ἐν τοῖς τῶν φυτῶν σπέρμασιν ἔνεστί τι τοιοῦτον τὸ φαινόμενον πρῶτον γαλακτῶδες, οὕτω καὶ ἐν τῇ ὕλῃ τῶν ζῴων τὸ περίττωμα τῆς συστάσεως τροφή ἐστιν, *GA* 740ᵇ5–9.

[213] Ibid. 745ᵇ23–6. Democritus (DK 68 B 148) says that the navel forms first in a foetus as an 'anchorage'.

informed as the female generative material; the female material in the seed of a plant is therefore something distinct from and superior to the nutriment in the earth that a plant uses in growth. Similarly, the principle of the chick is formed in the more concocted female seminal fluid (the white) than that which provides its nourishment during its development (the yolk), which is not to say that a chick is formed completely in the white of an egg before it starts to use the yolk. Aristotle says that the relationship between an oviparously born animal and its yolk mirrors that between the embryo of a viviparous animal and its mother, as long as it is in the mother,[214] so the material which a pregnant mother supplies to the embryo for nourishment is different from that which she supplied for its conception and for the formation of the principle and umbilical cord. The pre-eminence of the material used in the conception of a fetation is reflected when Aristotle remarks that the most honourable parts of the body are formed from the purest nourishment, and the necessary parts from the residue[215] —that is from the purest parts and the residue of the original menses. Parts such as nails and hair are formed from an even lower grade of material,[216] newly acquired nourishment and the growth-producing nourishment derived directly from the mother and outside: 'These are formed out of the supplementary and growth-promoting nourishment, this additional nourishment being obtained from the female and from outside.'[217] It is not clear whether the 'additional nourishment' refers just to the growth-producing nourishment or to the supplementary nourishment as well. If it refers to the growth-producing nourishment alone, it is making the point that this is not the same growth-producing nourishment which was present in the original fetation. If both types of nourishment function as antecedents, then the most natural way to read the phrase would be to take 'from the female' as describing the provenance of the newly acquired nourishment and 'from outside' that of the growth-producing nourishment. In either case, the remark seems to confirm that the nourishment which produces growth is different from and exterior to that which goes to

[214] *GA* 753ᵇ31–3.   [215] Ibid. 744ᵇ11–27.

[216] The worst time during pregnancy is when the baby's own hair begins to grow (*HA* 584ᵃ22–5); it now needs enough nourishment not only to build its own body but also to produce residues of its own.

[217] ἐκ τῆς ἐπικτήτου τροφῆς καὶ τῆς αὐξητικῆς, ἥν τε παρὰ τοῦ θήλεος ἐπικτᾶται καὶ θύραθεν, *GA* 745ᵃ2–4. Peck translates 'supplementary or growth-promoting nourishment', but I can see no reason to take the καί as disjunctive here.

form the foetus, perhaps because it is used as soon as it enters the womb (the hottest part of a woman's body) and does not have time to become as concocted as the original menses did while they were being stored there. Alternatively, the purer menstrual fluid could derive from the purer parts of a woman's food, which would mean that the superior form of nourishment would be available throughout pregnancy; and elsewhere Aristotle states explicitly that it is only the purest part which is used both for conception and for nourishment during pregnancy, while the less concocted part is directed to the breasts.[218] The theory of two grades of menstrual fluid, where one type is more concocted than that which provides simple nourishment, is not referred to clearly in any of Aristotle's general discussions on human generation because this would seem to imply that a woman could provide more than nutritive soul.

LENGTH OF GESTATION

Humans were thought to be unique among animals in not having a rigidly determined gestation period; it could be anything from seven to ten months: 'In men alone among the animals is the period of gestation of variable length: other animals have a single period, but with man there are several: children are born at seven months and ten months and at intermediate times.'[219]

Pregnancies which seem to have taken eleven months or longer were a result of miscalculating the time of conception.[220] A child born in the eighth month of pregnancy was thought to stand the least

---

[218] *GA* 776ᵃ25–ᵇ3.

[219] τοὺς τῆς κυήσεως χρόνους μόνῳ τῶν ζῴων ἀνωμάλους εἶναι συμβέβηκεν. τοῖς μὲν γὰρ ἄλλοις εἷς ἐστιν ὁ χρόνος, τοῖς δ' ἀνθρώποις πλείους· καὶ γὰρ ἑπτάμηνα καὶ δεκάμηνα γεννῶνται καὶ κατὰ τοὺς μεταξὺ χρόνους, *GA* 772ᵇ7–11. Cf. *Alim.* 42 (ix. 112. 12–116. 2); *Septim./Oct.* 4 (vii. 442. 3–4). In contrast, Arist. says that a calf born before ten months to the day is an abortion (ἐκβόλιον) and will not survive, *HA* 575ᵃ27–8.

[220] *Septim./Oct.* 13 (vii. 460. 7–9); *Nat. Puer.* 30 (vii. 532. 14–534. 10). Even this was not universally recognized as the extreme limit for gestation. Pliny (*NH* 7. 40) relates the story of a judge who awarded an inheritance to the child of a woman who gave birth thirteen months after her husband's death. The judge claimed that it could not be proven that the child was not the son of the deceased because the period of gestation for humans had never been satisfactorily settled. That Pliny tells the story shows that the judge's opinion was not generally shared, but that such a judgement could be given at all shows the uncertainty on the matter.

chance of survival.[221] This was because it was in the eighth month that the foetus began to descend in the uterus and became subject to a variety of diseases. A child born in the seventh month avoided these and only had the trauma of labour to contend with. A child born in the eighth had to contend with both, which made it impossible to survive.[222] Aristotle says, 'And indeed eight-month babies live, though less often than the others' (καὶ γὰρ τὰ ὀκτάμηνα ζῆ μέν, ἧττον δέ); but elsewhere he says that this is only in Egypt and other countries where the women are strong, and that generally in Greece if a child born in the eighth month survives it is thought that the mother must have been mistaken about the time of conception.[223] He gives no reason for the higher rate of survival among more premature babies, and although the Hippocratics do, this is manifestly an extreme example of folk belief influencing science in defiance of the observed phenomena.

Although, once out of the womb, women were believed to age much more quickly than men—because they were wetter or colder and therefore inferior—it took much longer for a female foetus to develop than a male[224]—because they were wetter or colder and therefore inferior. Aristotle thought the male was fully articulated (and about the size of a large ant) after 40 days, a girl after 90, and it was at these times too that they began to move.[225] *Nat. Puer.* 18 (vii. 500. 1-2) places the times at 30 and 42 days respectively. A pregnancy with a girl was therefore much more likely to be delayed till the tenth month and was generally harder in every way. The mother suffered more pain, more swollen legs, more strange desires, and

---

[221] *Septim./Oct.* 4 (vii. 442. 4). That this is a traditional belief is shown by Epicharmus (DK 23 B 59) and Empedocles (DK 31 B 69). *Alim.* 42 (ix. 114. 2-3) mentions the eighth-month birth after the seventh, ninth, and tenth, and remarks, 'it is not and it is' (οὐκ ἔστι καὶ ἔστι). This text is deliberately obscure and the exact meaning is not immediately clear, but it does emphasize the ambivalence felt about a foetus of eight months. See Hanson 1987b.

[222] *Septim./Oct.* 2, 10 (vii. 438. 8-11, 452. 4-8). *Epid.* 2. 3. 17 (v. 118. 8-9) says the pain felt in the womb in the eighth month of pregnancy is similar to that felt before menstruation.

[223] *GA* 772^{b}10-11; *HA* 584^{b}10-14.

[224] *GA* 775^{a}10-15; *Septim./Oct.* 9 (vii. 450. 4-10); *Steril.* 233 (viii. 446. 17). Though at *GA* 777^{a}31-^{b}16, in explaining why humans have a longer gestation period than other animals, Arist. says that it is because they are larger and longer-lived, and on these criteria males should have a longer gestation period than females.

[225] *HA* 583^{b}3-7. The passage adds that the male moves on the right and the female on the left, but then says that this is not always a basis for an accurate judgement. It is not clear if this refers to the time period or the position in the womb. If the foetus ceased to move after this time it was presumed to be dead (*Epid.* 7. 6 (v. 376. 20-1)).

had a worse colour when she was carrying a girl.[226] In the eight
birthings in which the sex of the child is mentioned in the *Epid.*, only
once is it said to be male.[227] None of the deliveries in the case
histories of the *Epid.* are normal; when the sex of the child was
female, it may have been mentioned as having some explanatory
value as to why the case was difficult. If the sex of the child was
male, it would not be considered to explain the complications in the
same way.

The baby is born when the supply of menstrual fluid finally ceases
to be sufficient and it fights its way out looking for food: 'When it is
time for the mother to give birth, what happens is that the child by
the spasmodic movements of its hands and feet breaks one of the
internal membranes. ... My assertion, then, is that what brings on
birth is a failure in food supply.'[228] There is a slight paradox here
because after birth the baby continues to derive all its nourishment
from the menstrual fluid in the form of milk, and it may be that one
of the reasons the supply inside the womb began to fail was that so
much was being diverted to the breasts. Aristotle thought that once
an embryo was perfected as a child, it made its way out because it
now required a different type of food.[229] The menstrual blood which
was coming through the umbilical cord is redirected to the breasts to
prepare this (an example of Nature's good timing), so the blood
vessels in the cord collapse and the child is born.[230]

The actual act of giving birth was always a dangerous time for
mother and child. In an epidemic at Thasos, the majority of women

[226] *HA* 583ᵇ12–21; *Aph.* 5. 42 (iv. 546. 4–5). Pica is also mentioned as a phenomenon of pregnancy at *Mul.* 1. 34 (viii. 78. 15).

[227] *Epid.* 3. 2. 12 (iii. 64. 1). The female births are *Epid.* 1. 13, cases iv, v, xi (ii. 690.
12, 694. 7, 708.7); 3. 3. 17, cases ii, xiv (iii. 110. 1, 140. 15); 4. 22 (v. 162. 5, 7). See
Hanson 1987a.

[228] ὁκόταν δὲ τῇ γυναικὶ ὁ τόκος παραγένηται, συμβαίνει τότε τῷ παιδίῳ
κινουμένῳ καὶ ἀσκαρίζοντι χερσί τε καὶ ποσὶ ῥῆξαί τινα τῶν ὑμένων τῶν
ἔνδον. ... τούτῳ δὲ τῷ λόγῳ ὅτι ἐπιλειπούσης τῆς τροφῆς, ἐξέρχεται τὸ
ἔμβρυον, *Nat. Puer.* 30 (vii. 530. 20, 536. 5–6). *HA* 10. 638ᵃ31–5 remarks that it is
because the *mylē* does not require a change of food that a woman could remain 'pregnant' with it all her life, cf. *GA* 775ᵇ25–35. The remark at *HA* 604ᵇ30–605ᵃ1 that
women sometimes give birth if they smell a lamp going out would seem to be a folk
element.

[229] *GA* 776ᵃ34–ᵇ4.

[230] Ibid. 777ᵃ21–8.

had difficult childbirth and this was the most likely time for them to sicken and die, though otherwise fewer women than men fell ill.[231] Of the 38 pregnancies in the *Epid.*, 15 are said to have died, and several of these deaths could have resulted from complications in the parturition, though there are only two explicit references to difficult childbirth among them.[232] Difficulties in childbirth could be caused if the child presented itself in any position other than head first, or if the child was dead and therefore incapable of initiating its passage through the birth canal.[233] Labour pains were generally thought to be caused by the baby struggling to get out. We are told that one of the women had the bed on which she was lying shaken repeatedly as an aid to the struggles of the foetus. She did not survive the ordeal.[234] Another method to promote easier labour was to deprive the foetus of nourishment, presumably to enhance its struggles. *Mul.* 1. 77 (viii. 172. 6–7) recommends bleeding at the ankle for difficult childbirth, and Aristotle says women were the only animals to have difficulty in giving birth, though the more active they were the more they used up the excess residue causing the problems, and they also learnt to hold their breath in exercise.[235] Needless to say, parturition with girls was more difficult than with boys because they were not as strong and took longer to fight their way out.[236] The consequence of this was that more boys than girls were born deformed because the male fought harder.[237] *Mul.* 1. 34 (viii. 80. 3–5) suggests, however, that at least one Hippocratic author was aware of birth contractions: 'Through the entire intervening time the woman has pains in her stomach from time to time inasmuch as her belly, especially her uterus, is contracting around the embryo.'[238]

All the birthing case histories described in the Corpus are abnormal in some way, but this does not mean that normal births were always left in the hands of midwives. *Mul.* 1. 34 (viii. 78. 17–80. 5)

---

[231] *Epid.* 1. 9 (ii. 646. 9–12).
[232] Ibid. 4. 24, 5. 103 (v. 164. 8, 258. 9–12).
[233] *Nat. Puer.* 30 (vii. 538. 8–11); *Mul.* 1. 33 (viii. 78. 1–10); 1. 47 (viii. 106. 16–17). Difficulties can also be caused in parturition by yawning which draws up the uterus (*GA* 719[a]19–21).
[234] *Epid.* 5. 103 (v. 258. 9–12). The procedure is described at *Mul.* 1. 68 (viii. 142. 20–144. 16). For a discussion of difficulties in childbirth see Hanson 1991, 87–95.
[235] *GA* 775[a]32–3.   [236] *HA* 584[a]26–30.   [237] *GA* 775[a]4–9.
[238] καρδιώσσει δὲ ἐν τῷ μεταξὺ ξύμπαντι χρόνῳ ἄλλοτε καὶ ἄλλοτε ἅτε τῆς κοιλίης περιστελλομένης ἀμφὶ τὸ ἔμβρυον, μάλιστα δὲ τῆς ὑστέρης, see Lonie 1981, 245.

and *Nat. Puer.* 30 (vii. 538. 17–27) describe what a normal birth would be like, and it may be that a normal birth was so routine that the Hippocratics did not bother recording those they attended. The fact that normal births were not solely the responsibility of midwives is suggested by Aristotle's comment that it was the *maia*'s (midwife's) job to cut the umbilical cord. This could be taken to imply that there was another person present doing everything else.[239] *Mul.* 1. 46 (viii. 106. 7–8) refers to an 'umbilical-cord-cutter' (ὀμφαλητόμος), suggesting that the traditional *maia*'s job had been curtailed to this one function when there was a Hippocratic doctor around.[240]

Mul. 1.72 (viii. 152. 7–12) says that lochia flow for 30 days after the birth of a boy and for 42 days after the birth of a girl, but that these are maximum amounts and that the flow can last for as little as 20 days after a boy and 25 days after a girl with safety.[241] The discharge after birth normally lasts from 21 to 28 days, and is usually only bona fide bleeding for the first ten days.[242] *HA* 587[b]4–6 suggests that 40 days was recognized as the absolute limit for lochial discharge, but that it was generally to the woman's advantage if they did not last this long: 'If the discharge takes place after birth in small quantity, and in cases where it only takes place at the beginning and does not continue till the fortieth day, then in such cases women make a better recovery and are the sooner ready to conceive again.'[243] The lochia accumulated because during the early days of pregnancy the foetus did not need all the mother's menstrual blood. The excess menses were stored in pockets in the chorion. As female foetuses took longer to develop, they under-utilized the menses for longer, so there was more to be stored. It was not used later in pregnancy and so was voided when the womb was open after parturition. The

[239] *HA* 587[a]9.
[240] On the other hand, midwives are seen in the Hippocratic Corpus performing complicated deliveries themselves, e.g. *Mul.* 1. 68 (viii. 144. 22–4), see Lonie 1981, 248.
[241] The same periods are given at *Nat. Puer.* 18 (vii. 502. 20–504. 2).
[242] Parker 1983, 55; Danforth 1982, 788. Lonie 1981, 193, argues that the author of *Nat. Puer.* posits periods of 30 and 42 days to buttress his theory on embryonic development of male and female foetuses, and wishes the periods to be measured in multiples of six to tie it into Pythagorean number theory. However, neither of the shortest healthy periods mentioned in the *Mul.* passage is a multiple of 6.
[243] ἐὰν δ' αἱ καθάρσεις μετὰ τὸν τόκον ἐλάττους γένωνται, καὶ ὅσων μόνον αἱ πρῶται, καὶ μὴ διατελέσωσιν εἰς τὰς τεττaράκοντα, ἰσχύουσί τε μᾶλλον αἱ γυναῖκες καὶ συλλαμβάνουσι θᾶττον.

first amount of lochia to flow was one and a half kotyls and from then it proceeded 'by proportion' (κατὰ λόγον) until it ceased.[244] This suggests that during the first month of pregnancy the foetus used up only one half kotyl on its development.

If the afterbirth does not come away naturally it has to be expelled by some artificial means.[245] Just like menstrual blood, lochia can move off to other parts of the body.[246] In a case where the afterbirth did not come away, the author of *Mul.* i. 38 (viii. 94. 17) recommends bleeding, and there is one case history where a woman was bled for this reason and survived.[247] The lochia did not flow simply from the womb; it was because they were drawn in all their abundance from all over the body that they eased subsequent menstruation by breaking down the passages of the body.[248] *Nat. Puer.* 21 (vii. 512. 14–16) mentions that, like other animals, women grow fatter when they are pregnant though they do not increase their intake of food and drink. This author thinks this results from the fatty part of a woman's food and drink being squeezed from her stomach into the surrounding flesh by the expanding uterus, but many ancient theorists would have explained it as the unused menstrual fluid backing up throughout a woman's body.

In contrast to normal menstruation, intercourse during a woman's lochial flow was avoided, not because of any harm or pollution which would accrue to the man, but because it could cause prolapse of the womb.[249] There is still no sign that men felt the blood to be taboo; in fact it was described with the same simile as that used for menarchal blood—like that of a sacrificial animal: 'The blood flows as from a sacrificial beast, if the woman is healthy and will remain healthy, and it coagulates quickly.'[250] Lochial, like menstrual blood, should flow quickly and easily from a woman

[244] *Nat. Puer.* 18 (vii. 502. 4–6).
[245] *Mul.* i. 37 (viii. 88. 18–90. 4). *Aph.* 5. 49 (iv. 550. 3–4) recommends sneezing to achieve this. A woman who has her lochia suppressed is one of the few women in the Hippocratic Corpus to be designated by her own name (Phrontis), *Mul.* i. 40 (viii. 96. 16).
[246] e.g. ibid. i. 41 (viii. 98. 6 & 100. 2–3).
[247] *Epid.* 2. 4. 5 (v. 126. 10–14).
[248] Cf. *Mul.* i. 1 (viii. 10. 1–12. 5).
[249] Ibid. 2. 143, 144 (viii. 316. 1–4, 13–18); *Nat. Mul.* 4, 5 (vii. 316. 9–11, 20–318. 3). Cf. Parker 1983, 65: 'In the case of birth, it is surely likely that the Greeks will have associated the impurity of mother and child during the first few days of life with their very real physical peril during that period.'
[250] χωρεῖ δὲ αἷμα οἷον ἀπὸ ἱερείου, ἢν ὑγιαίνῃ ἡ γυνὴ καὶ μέλλῃ ὑγιαίνειν, καὶ ταχὺ πήγνυται, *Nat. Puer.* 18 (vii. 502. 6–7).

without coagulating, so it cannot have been observation which led the Hippocratics to this opinion. They likened the blood of a woman after a healthy childbirth to that of a propitious sacrifice because, just as a woman's menarchal blood was an auspicious sign indicating she was ready to assume her allotted role in the service of the *oikos* and therefore of the *polis*,[251] so the wound of successful parturition was the culmination of this role and beneficial to society in general.

CONVERSION OF MENSTRUAL BLOOD TO MILK

A woman's blood, which was used to nurture the embryo in the womb, was converted finally into milk in the breasts to nourish the child once it was born: 'Periods generally harmonize for the embryo and its nutriment; and again nutriment tends upwards to milk and the nourishment of the baby.'[252] That menstrual blood which could not be evacuated from the womb would move off or be drawn to the breasts was readily accepted in antiquity. There was believed to be a general sympathy between the reproductive organs and the chest in every human body. In Hippocratic theory this sympathy could manifest itself in men when the genitals were affected secondarily by a chest complaint: for example, after a chronic cough the testicles could swell.[253] In women, on the other hand, where complaints more often were rooted in the reproductive system, the chest tended to show the secondary symptoms.[254] The breasts were the first line of defence against a woman's natural humidity, immediately prior to the evacuation of menses through the womb. *Gland.* 17 (viii. 574. 2–8) says that if a woman loses a breast, she dies because the moisture it would have received is directed to more vital parts of the body. The breasts were also instrumental in retaining enough moisture in a woman's body. If the periods were too heavy the Hippocratics advised placing a cup to the breasts, to draw the blood back upwards.[255]

---

[251] Cf. Clark 1975, 208: 'The female is not *per se* a citizen, but the male is so primarily as a householder.'

[252] περίοδοι ἐς πολλὰ σύμφωνοι, ἐς ἔμβρυον καὶ ἐς τὴν τούτου τροφήν. αὖτις δ' ἄνω ῥέπει ἐς γάλα καὶ ἐς τροφὴν βρέφεος, *Alim.* 37 (ix. 110. 16–18); cf. *HA* 583ᵃ31–3.

[253] *Epid.* 2. 1. 6 (v. 76. 13–16).   [254] *Mul.* 2. 133 (viii. 282. 10–12).

[255] *Aph.* 5. 50 (iv. 550. 5–6).

Aristotle believed the seminal secretion went through its final concoction in the chest before passing on to the generative organs in both sexes, thus establishing a connection between the two areas. The menstrual fluid which was not needed in the formation of the foetus and could not be voided through the closed uterus returned to this source:

> The milk collects in the upper part of the body, in the breasts, and this is accounted for by the original order of the body's construction. ... Thus when the embryo no longer absorbs this residual secretion but at the same time prevents it from making its way out, the whole of the residue is bound to collect in the empty spaces which are situated on the same passages.[256]

It is of course true that female breasts begin to develop around the same time as menarche and that during pregnancy, when menstruation has ceased, they swell—often considerably. It is therefore easy to understand how the ancient theories came to postulate that some of the menstrual material which was not being used up in the formation of the embryo went to the breasts. The method by which they thought it was converted into milk remains to be established.

The Hippocratics believed that suppressed menses could become milk even without the woman being pregnant.[257] The affinity between the two secretions was thought to be so close that *Epid.* 2. 3. 17 (v. 118. 10-11) calls milk 'sister of the menses' (*ἀδελφὰ τῶν ἐπιμηνίων*). There is, however, no indication of why the change of the locality of the residue should result in a change of nature. Aristotle says that the breasts were fleshy and placed on the chest to afford protection to the heart.[258] This meant they were near to the body's main source of heat; the swelling of the breasts was caused by *pneuma*, the vehicle of the soul's innate heat. Blood which remained for any length of time in the breasts was further concocted by this heat into milk, 'For milk is concocted, not decomposed, blood' (*τὸ γὰρ γάλα πεπεμμένον αἷμά ἐστιν ἀλλ' οὐ διεφθαρμένον*).[259] Aristotle believed that there was milk in the breasts of males,

---

[256] εἰς δὲ τὸν ἄνω τόπον καὶ τοὺς μαστοὺς συλλέγεται διὰ τὴν ἐξ ἀρχῆς τάξιν τῆς συστάσεως. ... ὅταν οὖν μὴ λαμβάνῃ μὲν τὸ ἔμβρυον τὴν τοιαύτην ἀπόκρισιν, κωλύῃ δὲ θύραζε βαδίζειν, ἀναγκαῖον εἰς τοὺς κενοὺς τόπους ἀθροίζεσθαι τὸ περίττωμα πᾶν, ὅσοιπερ ἂν ὦσιν ἐπὶ τῶν αὐτῶν πόρων, *GA* 776ᵇ4–5, 29–32.
[257] *Aph.* 5. 39 (iv. 544. 14–15).   [258] *PA* 688ᵃ17–22.   [259] *GA* 777ᵃ8.

though their flesh was too dense to allow it to pass through: 'Milk is found to occur in males as well as females; but in the male the flesh is firm, whereas in woman it is spongy and full of passages.'[260] At *HA* 522ᵃ11–21 he says that this does not happen frequently, just in certain individuals; he probably imagined it resulting from some seminal residue that had been left behind when most of it was drawn off to its proper place because the breasts of such individuals were a little spongier than normal male flesh. Because a woman was colder than a man, the small amount of seminal residue which regularly remained in her breasts was not in a concocted enough state to be further concocted into milk through proximity to the heart. Nevertheless, a few non-pregnant women could produce milk through eating certain foods, and the people round Mount Oeta could draw milk from nanny-goats which refused to submit to the male by rubbing their udders with nettles. To begin with only blood and putrid milk appeared, but eventually pure milk was obtained.[261] Because of the sympathy between the breasts and the womb, if blood is drawn from the breasts it draws on blood from the womb (the hottest part of a woman's body) to replenish itself. The menstrual material has been concocted in the womb to the point where it can take advantage of the extra heat from the heart when it returns to the breasts, and thus turn into milk. In animals which have many dugs, it is those nearest the heart which provide the most and best milk.[262] Generally speaking, once seminal residue had descended to the womb it did not return to the breasts for further concoction. In pregnant women, however, the menses that were not used for foetal development could not be evacuated because the stoma was closed, and after a certain point the accumulation began to be drawn off to the breasts where its second heating turned it into milk. Once the child was born its suckling continued to draw the menses back into the breasts from the womb even though the womb was no longer closed.

---

[260] ἐγγίγνεται δὲ καὶ ἐν τοῖς ἄρρεσι γάλα· ἀλλὰ πυκνὴ ἡ σὰρξ τοῖς ἄρρεσι, ταῖς δὲ γυναιξὶ σομφὴ καὶ πόρων μεστή, *HA* 493ᵃ14–15.

[261] Ibid. 522ᵃ6–11.

[262] *PA* 688ᵇ10–11: 'They [elephants' mammae] are high up, near the axillae, because that is the place of the foremost mammae in those that have many, and these are the ones that yield the most milk' (ὅτι πρῶτοι οὗτοι τῶν μαστῶν τοῖς πολλοὺς ἔχουσι μαστούς, καὶ ἱμῶνται γάλα πλεῖστον).

CONVERSION OF MOTHER'S NUTRIMENT TO MILK

There is another theory of milk production traceable in several
Hippocratic treatises and, to a lesser extent, in some of Aristotle's
writings which does not need to explain the conversion of menstrual
blood into milk. *Nat. Puer.* 21 (vii. 512. 3–7, 16–18) says:

The cause of lactation is as follows: when the womb becomes swollen
because of the child it presses against the woman's stomach and if this
pressure occurs while the stomach is full, the fatty parts of the food and
drink are squeezed out into the flesh. ... Now, from this fatty substance
which is warmed and white in colour, that portion which is made sweet by
the action of heat coming from the womb is squeezed into the breasts.[263]

There is, in this account, no need to explain how blood is converted because the sweetest part of a woman's nourishment is separated out into the breasts before it can ever become menstrual fluid. It
is an account shared by *Mul.* 1. 73 (viii. 154. 2–5) which says that the
sweetest part of the moisture from a woman's food and drink is
drawn into her breasts, and adds that this leaves the rest of the body
empty and less full of blood, not because the menstrual fluid has
been drawn on directly but because the material has been utilized in
a different way.[264] So the two secretions are still 'sisters', and in fact
the description is more appropriate in this theory, where they share
the same source, rather than where one is the progenitor of the
other. *Gland.* 16 (viii. 572. 3–7) shows a confusion of both theories, in
that it says that the breasts draw the nourishment to themselves from
the womb, but also that the omentum squeezes the nourishment into
the upper parts of the body on being compressed by the embryo.

As stated above, Aristotle also shows vestiges of this theory. In
PA 676ᵃ4–5 he remarks that the female jejunum can have its place

[263] δι᾽ ἀνάγκην δὲ τοιήνδε γίνεται τὸ γάλα· ὁκόταν αἱ μῆτραι ὀγκηραὶ
ἐοῦσαι ὑπὸ τοῦ παιδίου πιέζωσι τὴν κοιλίην τῆς γυναικός, τῆς δὲ κοιλίης
πλήρεος ἐούσης ὁ ἐκπιεσμὸς γένηται, ἀποπιδύει τὸ πιότατον ἀπό γε τῶν
βρωτῶν καὶ τῶν ποτῶν ἔξω ἐς τὸ ἐπίπλοον καὶ τὴν σάρκα. ... ἀπὸ τοῦ
πίονος διαθερμαινομένου καὶ λευκοῦ ἐόντος τὸ γλυκαινόμενον ἀπὸ τῆς
θέρμης τῆς ἀπὸ τῶν μητρῶν ἀποθλιβόμενον ἔρχεται ἐς τοὺς μαστούς.
[264] Lonie 1981, 204–5, believes that the passages of *Nat. Puer.* and *Mul.* 1. 73 are
both referring to menstrual blood *per se* when they talk of 'parts' of the mother's
nourishment. However, had the author wished to signify menstrual fluid it would
have been easier for him to say so, and given the affinity of menstrual blood for the
breasts, there would have been no need to develop the mechanics of squeezing.
Furthermore, *Nat. Puer.* 21 (vii. 512. 16) describes the nourishment as white before it
has entered the breasts.

anywhere in the upper intestine though the male's is always in the
lower gut. Ogle (ad loc.) comments, 'This strange statement has no
anatomical foundation.' The jejunum is the part of the digestive tract
where the food has been partially processed but is not yet excre-
mentitious matter. If, during pregnancy, the breasts were thought to
draw on food from this part of the digestive tract before it was digested
any further, Aristotle's anatomy would at least have a hypothetical
foundation in that he would want the jejunum in women to be further
up the body so that the food could be squeezed into the breasts. One
other small point tending to this conclusion is that at 688^{b}29–30 he
says that some animals have their breasts placed lower down their
abdomens because that is where food is set in motion.

Although the pressure pushing the nourishment into the breasts
ceases with the birth of the child, as with the alternative theory the
suckling continues to attract the milk, though in this case the breasts
are drawing material from the stomach rather than the womb. If a
woman's milk dries up too soon it is because the passages between
her breasts and stomach are blocked. This is not to deny the connection between breasts and womb completely of course. *Nat. Puer.*
maintained that there was a passage of material between the two, but
believed it went in the opposite direction to most opinions: in the
later stages of pregnancy the milk having been pressed into the
breasts from the stomach passed from the breasts to the womb for
the nourishment of the embryo: 'A small quantity goes to the womb
as well, through the same vessels; for the same vessels and others
similar to them extend alike to the breasts and the womb.'[265]

PRODUCTION OF MILK

The most often stated Hippocratic theory held that milk began to be
produced in the third (boy) or fourth (girl) month of pregnancy
when the child was fully articulated and began to move.[266] In the
early stages of pregnancy the menstrual material not needed to
build the body up from the seed is stored in the uterus and flows out
later as lochia. After the body is fully articulated and has grown to
the stage where it begins to move, it does not need so much nourish-

---

[265] καὶ ἐς τὰς μήτρας δὲ ὀλίγον ἔρχεται διὰ τῶν αὐτῶν φλεβῶν·
τείνουσι γὰρ ἐς τοὺς μαζοὺς καὶ ἐς τὰς μήτρας φλέβια ταὐτά τε καὶ παρα-
πλήσια ἄλλα, *Nat. Puer.* 21 (vii. 512. 18–20).
[266] *Epid.* 2. 6. 17 (v. 136. 8–9); *Nat. Puer.* 21 (vii. 510. 18–25); *Mul.* 1. 71 (viii.
150. 1–2, 9–10); *Steril.* 233 (viii. 446. 10–11, 17–18).

220 The Female's Role in Reproduction

ment and there is less room in the womb to store it. It is true that breasts can begin to swell early in pregnancy, and it may have been this fact which led the Hippocratics to argue that milk production began this early. But milk is not actually produced until just before parturition. *Epid.* 2. 3. 17 (v. 118. 9–11) and *Mul.* 1. 27 (viii. 70. 18–21) could both be interpreted as claiming that milk production occurred in the seventh or eighth month, as could Empedocles (DK 31 B 68), which would be more correct; but it is also possible that they are claiming that milk begins to go bad at this point.[267] If a child dies in the womb the breasts become thin and sag before the miscarriage, since the material there too will be evacuated; in a woman pregnant with twins the withering of the right breast signifies she will miscarry a boy, of the left a girl.[268] Milk flowing too copiously from the breasts of a pregnant woman also signified that the foetus could not be too healthy,[269] presumably because nourishment was being withdrawn from it before it was ready. As long as the child was in the womb it still needed to obtain some nourishment from the menses, so there could be only a gradual build up of milk in the breasts before parturition.

The deficiency of nourishment in the womb which instigated labour could have resulted not just from the growth of the foetus but also from a redirection of more material to the breasts to prepare for its birth. One obscure passage suggests that if parturition did not occur at this point the milk could begin to curdle in the breasts: '[As to] the milk of a primipara, at the completion of the eighth month, the nourishment changes; on which account the milk, sister of the menses, stretching into the tenth month, is a bad thing.'[270] As mentioned above, this passage could be indicating a different time-scale for the production of milk, but it could also be commenting on what happens to milk at the completion of its development if it is not made use of. Women having their first child were supposed to give

[267] See pp. 220–1 below.
[268] *Epid.* 2. 1. 6 (v. 76. 13–14); *Aph.* 5. 38 (iv. 544. 11–13).
[269] Ibid. 5. 52 (iv. 550. 9–11).
[270] πρωτοτόκων τὰ γάλακτα, τῆς μὲν ὀκταμήνου ἀπαρτιζούσης, τῆς δὲ τροφῆς μεταβαλλούσης· διὸ τὰ γάλακτα, ἀδελφὰ τῶν ἐπιμηνίων· πρὸς δεκά-μηνον τεινόντων γενόμενα, κακόν, *Epid.* 2. 3. 17 (v. 118. 9–11). The primary meaning of μεταβάλλω is 'to change', and here it could refer simply to a change of position (which is how Littré takes it). However, because the milk produced in the tenth month is described as 'a bad thing' (κακόν), it could also refer to a change in quality. An alternative reading for μεταβαλλούσης is ὑπερβαλλούσης, 'become excessive', again referring to a build up of milk which would be ready for use earlier in a primipara than in other pregnant women.

birth sooner than other pregnant women, so their milk was ready for utilization at the end of the eighth month. If it was not used at this point it began to turn. If, in a primipara, the pregnancy stretched into the tenth month the milk being produced could become bad, just as the menses could if trapped in a woman's body. Empedocles (DK 31 B 68) actually reads, 'On the tenth day of the eighth month, the milk becomes a white pus', but it has been emended to read 'blood' instead of 'milk'. If we allow the original reading to stand this passage too may have been referring specifically to the milk of a primipara.

Aristotle gives the two most extreme possibilities for the period of milk production. *HA* 522^{a}4 says that the milk starts to be formed as soon as the animal becomes pregnant, but *GA* 776^{a}15–16 that it does not appear until the mother is about to give birth. This is a reflection of Aristotle's belief that the menses contain two qualities of nourishment.[271] As the milk is derived from the menses, it too contains two types of nourishment: curds, the more concocted and therefore thicker and more nutritious part, and whey.[272] The lower-quality whey is not used as nourishment for the embryo at all, so it is diverted to the breasts from the very beginning of pregnancy; if it is not used up in this way the woman becomes ill.[273] The milk does not become useful until the seventh month of pregnancy (the earliest a human child can be born); before that all the nutritious part is used up for the embryo.[274] Towards the end of pregnancy the milk becomes better concocted and therefore useful, but Aristotle cannot make up his mind whether this is because the embryo is using less of the menses, since it grows less in the last few months and therefore the better concocted material goes to the breasts, or because the embryo is using more material in the womb, so that a smaller amount goes to the breasts and is therefore easier to concoct.[275] Sometimes so much material is diverted to the breasts after childbirth that it percolates through the flesh of the breast as well as

---

[271] i.e. that they always contain two grades, not that the menses can become more refined through concoction.

[272] *HA* 521^{b}26–522^{a}1.

[273] Ibid. 584^{a}6–9. *HA* 583^{a}31–4 seems to place this after the first month of pregnancy, during which time Arist. thinks it normal to discharge some menstrual material—presumably the 'whey' not being utilized in the initial formation of the embryo.

[274] In all other viviparous animals serviceable milk does not appear until just before parturition, but as the exact length of human gestation is not determined it has to be available at the earliest date (*GA* 776^{a}15–25).

[275] *GA* 777^{a}1–4.

the nipple.[276] Aristotle believes that the later milk (i.e. that produced after a woman has been nursing for a while) is useless.[277] This is probably because the later milk has too much curd, which is generally good, but bad for children.[278]

QUALITY OF MILK

Both the Hippocratics and Aristotle believed that a mother's milk was at its optimum around the time of parturition.[279] Soranus, however, claimed that a mother's milk was unwholesome for her baby during the first twenty days and that it was advisable to employ a wet-nurse for the first few weeks at least.[280] By this time the child's mother would have lost her own milk (it would be too painful to continue the flow by expression alone for twenty days), and it is possible that Soranus' advice reflects the practice of Roman senatorial women who for various reasons did not wish to breast feed. Greek women always had a less diversified life than Roman, so there was probably less occasion to employ wet-nurses. They had to be available, of course, because sometimes (for example if a woman died in childbirth) a baby would have to be nursed by someone other than its own mother. *Alim.* 40 (ix. 112. 7–9) indicates that the milk either of a mother or a wet-nurse could be thought superior depending on the circumstances: 'Another's milk is good, one's own milk is bad; another's milk is harmful, one's own milk is useful.'[281]

[276] *HA* 587^{b}19–21. There is no physiological foundation for this statement.

[277] Ibid. 522^{a}4.

[278] Ibid. 523^{a}3–12.

[279] *Steril.* 216 (viii. 416. 20–3) says the milk of a pregnant woman can indicate whether the foetus is a boy or a girl. The author advises making little cakes from the milk. If they burn the child will be a boy, if they collapse a girl. Similarly if the milk coagulates on exposure to flame the child will be a boy, if it liquifies a girl. This is obviously based on the hot/cold, firm/loose dichotomies.

[280] *Gyn.* 2. 87. That this was not a universally held belief is shown by Aul. Gell.'s story on Favorinus, where the woman he is castigating for not suckling her own child is avoiding it for reasons of her own health and would otherwise be nursing her own newborn (*Attic Nights* 12. 1).

[281] γάλα ἀλλότριον ἀστεῖον, γάλα ἴδιον φλαῦρον· γάλα ἀλλότριον βλαβερόν, γάλα ἴδιον ὠφέλιμον. The earlier part of the passage (see p. 204 and n. 200 above) talks in the same way about one's own and another's blood and humours, which in the context of embryonic development can refer only to the blood and humours of the foetus and the mother. The phraseology here makes it sound as if 'one's own' milk is that of the baby who is suckling rather than the nursing mother's; however, the variation of vocabulary in these phrases from the rest of the passage, and

The quality of a nurse's milk was obviously very important as it was so highly digested itself that a baby absorbed it almost unchanged; after the first day a baby's excrement became milky rather than bloody.[282] Livid milk was better than white in women, and dark women produced the best milk,[283] just as they had the most abundant menstruation. If the milk was warm, it could help in the cutting of teeth, but if it was putrid, it could cause flatworm in the child, and if phlegmatic, stone.[284] Nursing could cause some illnesses in the woman herself. Two case histories of nursing women are recorded in the *Epid.* One is a simple case of milk rash which disappeared when the woman stopped nursing, and the other a case of a woman who had a fever and a rough tongue while nursing and was only partially purged by vomiting worms.[285] Aristotle said that if a woman swallowed a hair while she was nursing it would cause her great pain until it either came out of its own accord or was sucked out through the nipple. The syndrome was even given a name, trichiasis.[286]

SUPPRESSION OF CONCEPTION

It was believed that it was impossible for a woman suckling one child to conceive another or to menstruate because, although the womb was open to receive the seed and release the blood, there was no excess menstrual material:

In the natural course of events, no menstrual evacuations take place during the suckling period, nor do women conceive then: and if they do conceive the milk dries up, because the nature of the milk is the same as that of the menstrual fluid and Nature cannot produce a plentiful enough supply to

the fact that they occur after a generalizing statement, suggests that they are an afterthought and 'one's own' milk is that of the mother and 'another's' that of a wet-nurse. A mother's milk can be called 'one's own' because it is the same material as the suckling child was nurtured on in the womb. However, this text is exceptionally obscure, perhaps deliberately so, and any attempt at elucidation is bound to be open to objections.

[282] *HA* 587^{a}32–3.   [283] Ibid. 523^{a}9–10.
[284] Ibid. 587^{b}15–17; *Morb.* 4. 55 (vii. 600. 3–21).
[285] *Epid.* 2. 2. 16, 4. 10 (v. 90. 5–6, 148. 24–150. 4).
[286] *HA* 587^{b}25–7. *Mul.* 2. 186 (viii. 366. 21–368. 5) discusses the treatment for trichiasis of the breast, but implies that it is a general inflammation rather than the removal of a hair. Erotian defines the disease as a cracking of the nipple into fine fissures. This may be an indication of Arist.'s lack of clinical experience.

provide both; so that if the secretion takes place in one direction it must fail in the other, unless some violence is done contrary to what is normal.[287] Nursing does tend to suppress ovulation, but a woman can become pregnant while nursing, and if she does it is not the case that her milk dries up.[288] It is true, however, that menstrual bleeding resumes as the flow of milk diminishes. Aristotle's theory suggests that he saw this occur more often than conception during lactation.[289] Nevertheless, Rousselle maintains that most Greek women became pregnant again while nursing, to the extent that if a woman saw her periods after weaning a child, and she was still of childbearing age, she would complain of amenorrhoea[290]—by which she seems to mean that it was thought that such a woman could not be menstruating properly, otherwise she would have conceived. In support of her thesis it is true that Aristotle says, 'Women continue to have milk until their next conception', but he immediately adds, 'and then the milk goes dry, alike in the human species and in quadrupedal Vivipara'.[291] As he has been talking of human lactation with no comparisons to other animals until this point, the reference to quadrupedal Vivipara suggests he is drawing more from his knowledge of animal husbandry than human physiology for this observation. Moreover, the number of non-pregnant and non-nursing female case histories in the *Epid.* suggests that young married women were not invariably with child.[292]

In ancient Greece, after a woman had conceived, borne, and nursed a child, she resumed periodical bleeding to renew her own morbid body before she undertook once again her vital task of renewing the human race.

[287] οὐ γίνονται δὲ οὔτε θηλαζομέναις αἱ καθάρσεις κατὰ φύσιν, οὔτε συλλαμβάνουσι θηλαζόμεναι· κἂν συλλάβωσιν, ἀποσβέννυται τὸ γάλα διὰ τὴν αὐτὴν εἶναι φύσιν τοῦ γάλακτος καὶ τῶν καταμηνίων· ἡ δὲ φύσις οὐ δύναται πολυχοεῖν οὕτως ὥστ᾽ ἐπαμφοτερίζειν. ἀλλ᾽ ἂν ἐπὶ θάτερα γένηται ἡ ἀπόκρισις, ἀναγκαῖον ἐπὶ θάτερα ἐκλείπειν, ἐὰν μὴ γίνηταί <τι> βίαιον καὶ παρὰ τὸ ὡς ἐπὶ τὸ πολύ, *GA* 777ᵃ13–19.

[288] Danforth 1982, 791.

[289] Soranus advises that the wet-nurse should be discouraged from indulging in coitus as this spoils and diminishes the milk or suppresses it entirely by stimulating menstruation (*Gyn.* 2. 88). He does not suggest that intercourse could divert the menstrual material immediately from lactation into pregnancy.

[290] Rousselle 1988, 37.

[291] τὸ δὲ γάλα ἔχουσιν ἕως ἂν πάλιν συλλάβωσιν τότε δὲ παύεται καὶ σβέννυται ὁμοίως ἐπ᾽ ἀνθρώπων καὶ τῶν ἄλλων ζῳοτόκων καὶ τετραπόδων, *HA* 587ᵇ27–32.

[292] Professor M. H. Jameson has remarked to me that there is a surprisingly high statistical likelihood of infertility among couples today, and with the greater disease and poorer diet in antiquity one would expect it to have been higher then. So a fair number of women would have menstruated without conception.

Conclusion

Inconsistencies are evident in each of the two major sources for scientific theories of women's bodies in the Classical era. In the Hippocratic Corpus these are due largely to its being compiled from the writings of many authors over an extended period of time, and in the Aristotelian to the fact that although Aristotle was a single author, the composition of the biological treatises spanned a large portion of his career during which he was continually adding to his knowledge and modifying his theories. The basic model of the female body differs so much between the two corpora, however, that the internal inconsistencies appear relatively minor. For the Hippocratics, woman is a radically different animal from man in structure and processes. For Aristotle she is a substandard man whose body only approximates to the ideal in human structure and processes.

Since in general during the Classical period women did not take part in battle or in dangerous sports, scientists of that time had even less opportunity to see inside women's bodies than inside men's, and so, even more than in the case of the human male body, theories on how the human female functioned were based to a great extent on the fluids women excreted. Menstrual blood is the linchpin of both the Hippocratic and the Aristotelian theories on how women differed from men. Whether a woman was healthy, diseased, pregnant, or nursing, in Classical Greece her body was defined scientifically in terms of blood-hydraulics. The ultimate difference between men and women, be it the nature of their flesh or the amount of their innate heat, manifested itself in the continuous accumulation and evacuation of blood which women—even healthy, active women—could not convert to their own use. For the Hippocratics, menstruation had no natural analogue in a man's body, and the process they adduced to account for it differentiated women from men in every aspect of health, disease, therapy, and reproduction. The excess of blood in their bodies led women to pass their lives teetering on the brink of ill health, but the regular periodic discharge of a major body fluid drained from their entire bodies prevented women from succumbing to serious illnesses as often as men did. In Aristotle's theory on the other hand, menses corresponded to semen in a man's body (albeit in substandard form), and was produced by the same processes. A woman differed from a man in having less innate heat, and menstruation was the major indicator and one of the most important consequences of this. But the production of menstrual blood was significant only in reproduction; it brought no benefit to the woman's body *per se*. These theories resulted from the different aims, methods, and philosophical systems of the Hippocratics and Aristotle. What they shared was the acknowledgement of menstruation as the chief phenomenon differentiating women from men, though for Aristotle its significance was less pervasive than for the Hippocratics. In both theories, however, even the bodies of men were originally constituted from menstrual blood, and in one form or another it nourished foetuses and infants of both sexes.

SILENCE ABOUT MENSTRUATION IN OTHER CLASSICAL
GREEK SOURCES

In spite of this importance of menstrual blood in the scientific definition of woman there is a dearth of menstrual allusion in the Greek classical canon, even in those texts which centre upon the difference between men and women. This is the more surprising as so much of the extant literature exploits the theme of the confrontation of the sexes in various arenas, particularly that of sexuality. Now, nobody would expect menstruation to be a leitmotif in Greek literature, but considering the emphasis placed on it in texts specifically explicating the female body, we might legitimately have expected one or two passing references. A subject which is in general deliberately avoided in the daily interchange of a society is, on occasion, deliberately exploited.[1] At Genesis 31: 35 Rachel excuses herself

---

[1] The following, somewhat eclectic, survey of the menstrual practices of various societies is meant only to illustrate societal attitudes documented as common and possible. I do not mean to imply on this criterion alone that ancient Greece had a

from rising, when she is sitting on the images she has stolen from her father because 'the custom of women' is upon her, assured that her father will press her no further and will not be in the least disposed to investigate her seat. The Talmud relates a story of a prison warder who poured the dregs of red wine on a betrothed female prisoner's clothes to ward off all the lustful, non-Jewish prisoners.[2] Anecdotes such as these would not have seemed out of place in, say, Herodotus. And even if he had no occasion to mention menstruation in connection with any of the many individual women who intrigue, act, and suffer in his *Histories*, his surveys of the sexual *mores* of different cultures could readily have encompassed descriptions of menstrual taboos and rituals. As Carolyn Dewald remarks, 'Ethnography is an ideal medium in which to convey the hidden fears and fantasies of one's own culture. In reports of exotic sexual customs, if anywhere, one would expect some of the darker aspects of Greek folk culture to assert themselves.'[3] At *Histories* 1. 198 Herodotus describes the extreme concern with purity shown by Babylonians and Arabians after intercourse. Husband and wife sit either side of a burnt offering of incense till dawn, at which time they both wash themselves; they touch no vessel until they have washed. At 2. 64 he claims that the Egyptians and Greeks are the only people to refrain both from lying with a woman in holy places, and from entering holy places after lying with a woman without first washing. He thus records the customs of those who are equal, or superior, to the Greeks in their fastidiousness on some sexual matters, and of others who are less particular. A comparison of menstrual practices would not have seemed out of place in such a context, no matter how taboo they were felt to be in Greece, but Herodotus gives no indication that he is interested in the subject.

Even the genres of Greek literature that deal quite openly with the most intimate areas of human experience are silent on the subject of menstruation. Defecation, urination, copulation; the anatomical general value system more like any one culture than another. Cf. Humphreys 1978, 12: 'If Bongo-Bongo rainmaking rites illuminate one aspect of Greek ritual, that does not imply any general affinity between the Bongo-Bongo and the Greeks'; and 29: 'the researcher [must] start with the assumption that the datum he is considering can only be defined and understood in terms of the relationships which link it to other data.'

[2] *Ta'an* 22. Cf. *Avod Zara* 18 for yet another story of a Jewish woman, forced into a brothel by the Romans, who kept herself unviolated by crying out, 'I am menstruating' when any prospective customers approached, see p. 249 below for a late Greek parallel to these stories.

[3] Dewald 1981, 102–3.

parts and physiological secretions involved in these processes: Aristophanes pokes fun at them all.[4] He makes, however, not a single reference to menstruation or menstrual blood. Jeffrey Henderson does not comment on this lacuna, and K. J. Dover dismisses it with the words, 'There are such things as "taboo" subjects which the comic poets did not try to exploit for humorous purposes: the plague of 430 BC is one, and menstruation is another.'[5] The plague had carried off a large portion of the friends and relatives of Aristophanes' audience with excrutiatingly painful symptoms, so we can readily understand why he did not attempt to raise a laugh from it. Other bodily emissions served as well-springs for so much of his humour precisely because they were ordinarily taboo; why was menstrual blood not exposed to the same end? Was there, as Dover suggests, so intense an anxiety about menstruation among males that it could not be mentioned even in the bawdiest context? If this were the case we would expect to be able to trace elsewhere in the culture explicit measures to minimize the threat posed by menstrual blood. In the words of Michel Foucault, the taboo would act as an 'incitement to discourse' rather than a blanket of silence.[6]

Although he was a great scientist, Aristotle was not above including folk elements in his biology, either to discount or to subscribe to them. He records as fact the bison's self-defence mechanism of propelling its excrement over a distance of eight yards and burning the hair off hunting dogs (*HA* 630ᵇ8–11); elsewhere he notes that honey does not come from flowers but from moisture in the air, especially when there is a rainbow (*HA* 553ᵇ27–31). Yet Aristotle consistently treats menstruation in a very matter-of-fact fashion without any indication that there were beliefs in its impurity that he had to take into consideration. Despite the large number of references he makes to menstruation, there are only two passages in the Aristotelian Corpus where a menstruating female could be interpreted as acting as a pollutant. The less well-known passage occurs at *HA* 578ᵃ1–4 where Aristotle says that among mules, contrary to all other animals, the male ages faster than the female. He says that some people attribute this to the fact that the female mule evacuates her menses with her urine and the male smells it.[7] It has been

[4] Henderson 1975 collects and organizes the references by topic. He comments, 55, that in comedy, 'the poets lose no opportunity to call attention to the female genitals in the most direct and arousing manner possible'.
[5] Dover 1982, 173.   [6] See Foucault 1978, 17–35.
[7] Saïd 1983, 109, incorrectly assigns this explanation to Arist. himself.

assumed that it was the menstrual blood which was supposed to act as the ageing agent.

body, nor does it cause anything other than the womb to swell. This, coupled with the inappropriate nature of the exemplum for the argument to hand, suggests that the passage is indeed a later interpolation, perhaps originally only a gloss in the margin but eventually ousting the original discussion on the instantaneous nature of reflections. Such marginalia would have been added to a papyrus no earlier than the Hellenistic period. Of the two possible Aristotelian references to menstrual pollution, therefore, one is concerned with the effect of urine rather than menses, and the other is the annotation of a later reader.

If a menstruating woman really was threatening as a pollutant it would seem that a work such as Hesiod's *Op.*, which gives advice to farmers on how best to cultivate their crops and organize their household, would have to address the threat explicitly and detail precautions to be taken against it. Robert Parker has stated that 'no other [Greek] texts show the same emphatic and explicit preoccupation' with rules of contamination as Hesiod,[11] but unlike later Greek and Roman handbooks on the same theme, such as Columella's *De Re Rustica*, Pliny's *Natural History*, or the tenth-century AD compilation *Geoponica*,[12] *Op.* never suggests that a menstruating woman walking through the fields or garden could adversely affect the crops. One passage in Hesiod which has been cited as showing fear of menstrual pollution among the Greeks is *Op.* 753–5: 'Nor should a man use water for his bath with which a woman bathed herself before; the punishment is awful, for a time.'[13] But this implies a repugnance over the female body generally, not at a specific period in the month. The adverbial phrase 'for a time' (ἐπὶ χρόνον) refers to the period of the worst punishment, not the period when bathing in the same water as a woman should be avoided. It is Proclus, the commentator of the Late Roman Empire, who associates it with menstruation.

It may be argued that the fact that a common term for menstruation in the scientific texts of Classical Greece was *katharsis* ('purification'), shows that in the culture in general menstrual fluid was regarded as impure and therefore as a pollutant. However, the term can refer to any sort of clearing or clarification which leaves an

---

[11] Parker 1983, 293.   [12] See below, p. 249.
[13] μηδὲ γυναικείῳ λουτρῷ χρόα φαιδρύνεσθαι | ἀνέρα· λευγαλέη γὰρ ἐπὶ χρόνον ἐστ᾽ ἐπὶ καὶ τῷ | ποινή.

entity in a less turgid state than previously.[14] It does not necessarily signify that the material which is discarded is viewed as defiling.

Since 'the concern for purity affected the individual in his everyday religious practice',[15] if Greek men were extremely anxious over menstrual blood, we might expect there to have been strong regulations against a menstruant entering sacred precincts, but there is no evidence that menstruation was subjected to such restrictions in the Classical period—though it is true that the paucity of epigraphical material from this period makes any generalization impossible. In the later period of antiquity, from which many more inscriptions survive in general, we do have some sacred laws pertaining to menstruation,[16] and the lack of such laws in the earlier period could result purely from the chance of survival. But there are some earlier epigraphical texts concerned with maintaining the purity of sacred precincts which limit the access of both men and women who have recently had intercourse[17] and bar parturients;[18] yet even in these contexts there is no attempt to control the movements of a menstruating woman.[19] From the dearth of such prohibitions, both Moulinier and Parker have argued for the opposite conclusion to that of Dover: the ancient Greeks had no particular anxiety about menstrual blood.[20]

No passing references, no jokes, no restrictions; we might begin to question whether male writers not explicitly concerned with the female body were aware of or concerned with the phenomenon at all. But it is only comparatively recently, with the advent of absorbent and disposable napkins and tampons, that a woman's blood has become completely invisible, and even now it would be a singularly inattentive husband or lover who did not know when a woman had entered her menstrual period. In the less avidly hygienic world of ancient Greece menstrual blood must have been much more

---

[14] Of an argument, Phld. *Lib.* 22 O; of pruning trees, Thphr. *CP* 3. 7. 12; of clearing land, *PS* 16. 577. 13.
[15] Parker 1983, 1.   [16] *LSCG* suppl. 54. 7–8, 91. 16, 119. 13; *LSCG* 55. 5.
[17] e.g. *LSCG* suppl. 115 A 11ff; *LSAM* 29.   [18] e.g. *LSCG* 68. 12–13.
[19] There are very few inscriptions dealing with birth and intercourse in the early period, but there are some, and they are much more common than inscriptions to do with menses in the later period. Moreover, the banning of intercourse and parturients from sanctuaries is also supported by literary evidence without any mention being made of menstruation, see Parker 1983, 74–103.
[20] Moulinier 1952, 70. Parker 1983, 100–3. Parker states that not only are the four sacred laws mentioned above in n. 16 late, but they also belong to non-Greek cults, 101–2.

conspicuous and, we might assume, have played a correspondingly more important role in the definition of womanhood for the layman as well as the scientific expert. Menstruation is one of the exclusively female bodily experiences, and unlike the others (defloration, parturition, lactation) happens to every woman whether she has any contact with a man or not. In addition, menses come in the form of blood, which when shed involuntarily usually signifies some injury or disease—often life-threatening; yet menstrual blood flows regularly from the woman's genitals (the source of life itself) without causing her any appreciable weakening. However close a man approaches to his society's idea of the feminine, he never discharges his vital fluid in this periodic manner. It is unlikely that scientific theorists were alone among Greek men in seeing significance in this fact.

LACK OF CULTURAL MYTH FOR MENSTRUATION IN GREECE

Yet prior to the development of natural philosophy, the Greeks do not appear to have had even a mythological *aition* to account for the fact that women menstruate and men do not.[21] It is true that the Greek myths that have reached us in various forms are notably deficient in female experience, but so are the mythological systems of most patriarchal cultures; yet they often include a myth explaining the origin of menstruation from a male point of view. The attitude evinced towards menstruation in these myths is overwhelmingly negative. This is, perhaps, hardly surprising in male-dominated societies where men, who had no part in the experience, were reluctant to vouchsafe women any sphere of superiority. In such cultures menstruation is often viewed as a punishment visited upon women for their inherent sinfulness. The Talmudic exegesis of God's curse upon Eve for tasting the fruit of the Tree of Knowledge

[21] Blum–Blum 1970, 298–9, claim that the myths of the blinding of men such as Teiresias and Erymanthus as punishment for watching a goddess bathe is a result of the destructive power of menstrual blood which was present because goddesses were performing 'purificatory ablutions', but the only evidence they put forward is to compare the cleansing of Artemis' image in the sea with the cleansing of women's genitals in the sea after menstruation in modern Greece. They also offer no evidence for the statement, 'it was after her first menstruation ... that a young girl would be led to the nearby spring for a ritual bath'. They are reading back into ancient material assumptions from modern practice.

in Genesis 3: 16, 'I will greatly multiply thy sorrow and thy conception', stated that the punishment encompassed menstruation.[22] Eve's punishment is greater than Adam's because it was her original sin which led to his. Sometimes woman suffers for the crime of a man. The Tukano Indians of the Amazon Basin have a myth that menstrual blood originated from the incest of the Sun with his daughter before she reached puberty. The Sinaugolo of New Guinea tell the story that the Moon, having come down to earth in the form of a man, made a woman pregnant. When her husband found out and killed him, the blood spurted up to the moon. In retribution the Moon said that all girls and young women (except pregnant women) would bleed whenever he appeared. There is also an Indian myth which tells of woman taking on a fourth part of Indra's guilt for killing the demigod Vivaspura in battle. Indra had already persuaded the earth, the streams, and the rocks to take three parts of his guilt, so he was free to live happily while for three days in every month woman is impure in all her actions. The Negritos of the Malay Peninsula do not believe that women menstruate because of any mythological crime; they believe that all humans were originally male and that woman came into being simultaneously with genital bleeding when a male was castrated by a great monitor lizard. This makes menstrual bleeding a physical rather than a spiritual deformity, but it has the same effect of displacing woman from the ideal form of humanity.[23]

Myths of this sort often explain and support strictures controlling the behaviour of a menstruating woman, and the fact that the Greeks had no menstrual myth must be viewed in tandem with the fact that the movements of a menstruating woman do not appear to have been any more inhibited than the movements of other women.

The reason for this apparent lack of attention to menstruation may lie in the mythical depiction of the origin of woman herself as a malicious afterthought of the gods. Helen King has shown in a structuralist analysis of the Hesiodic myths how woman can be seen to stand completely outside the 'gods/men/beasts matrix' in so far as she was a 'gift' of the gods to men, constructed with the express purpose of pushing the lot of man from the pole of the gods towards

[22] *Erubin* 100 b.
[23] These myths and others are collected in Weideger 1976, 95–109.

that of the beasts.[24] This description of the origin of woman makes her inherently 'other', inferior, and bad from her first appearance on the earth, without having to evoke any distinctively female physiology as evidence of a punishment inflicted on women for some crime in the mythological past. In Greek thought menstruation is the main evidence upon which the 'otherness' of women was ultimately predicated, rather than a separable phenomenon. In such a construct it is impossible to imagine women existing as women without menstruating, and it would be considered no more necessary to provide a mythological explanation for menstruation than for any other of the individual physical differences between men and women.

This model would suggest that the average Greek man did not regard women any differently during the period of their menstrual flow from the way he regarded them during the rest of the month. That is to say, that although menstruation may have been the most important sign of the radical difference between men and women, this was a steady and continual distinction in which the time of the month was an unimportant element in determining the parameters of behaviour and contact of one sex with the other.

ABSENCE OF CULTURAL TABOOS CONCERNING
MENSTRUATION IN CLASSICAL GREECE

Perhaps the most striking instance of the lack of taboo associated with a menstruating woman in ancient Greece is the positive encouragement both the Hippocratics and Aristotle give to a man to have intercourse with his wife while she is menstruating.[25] Of course, we do not know how often husbands complied with this advice, but the fact that the authors felt no need to preface their remarks with an argument to the effect that a fear of male genitals coming into direct contact with menstrual blood was irrational, strongly suggests that they did not expect such a fear to render their advice impracticable.

In many societies the separation of a menstruant to a greater or lesser extent makes this impossible. In some a woman is forbidden to

---

[24] King 1985, 26. See Loraux 1978; 1981, 75–117, for a more detailed exposition of the misogyny of Hes. and Semon. along these lines.

[25] e.g. *Mul.* 1. 17 (viii. 56. 15–17), *Nat. Mul.* 8 (vii. 324. 5–7); *GA* 727^{b}19–26, cf. p. 171 above.

address or even look at a man.[26] Among many present-day African, New Guinea, and Native American tribes menstruating women are isolated in huts built at some remove from the settlement. Even if a society has no other menstrual taboo, intercourse is very often forbidden or at least avoided during this period.[27] Among the Atuot of the South Sudan the women remain in the society while they are menstruating and men have to ask them a direct question to ascertain whether intercourse is allowed, since, apart from remaining celibate, women make no modification in their behaviour.[28] The Australian Walbiri seem almost unique in that they do not avoid menstrual blood and have no beliefs that contact with it brings danger.[29] The fact that Greek men did not hesitate to have their penises come into contact with menstrual blood is a strong argument against Dover's suggestion that they had a deep-rooted anxiety about menstruation.

Another widespread taboo placed on a menstruating woman is that she should not come into contact with any food that a man is going to eat, nor the vessels in which it is to be cooked.[30] Paula Weideger comments that it is in part this willingness to do without domestic service for a limited period each month which shows that the fear of menstruation is not trivial.[31] There is no trace of such a taboo in Greek society.[32]

The lack of menstrual references in the sacred laws is also especially telling because it is usually the holy places of a society that are strictly off limits to a menstruating woman. The prohibitions in Leviticus 15: 19–33 were promulgated primarily to ensure that the

[26] It should be noted that she is not necessarily considered threatening to other women, see n. 43 below.
[27] Paige–Paige 1981, 2. The societies with the least menstrual taboo according to Stephens 1961 are those that have only a taboo against sex, and even the Nuer, whom Douglas 1966, 144, cites as having 'no burdensome belief in sex pollution', avoid intercourse at this time. However, see Buxton 1973, 212–15, for the practices of the Mandari who advocate intercourse at this period yet do have other minor restrictions on the movements of menstruants.
[28] Burton 1981, 443.   [29] Douglas 1966, 142.
[30] Delaney–Lupton–Toth 1976, 14; Dalton 1979, 5–6. Paige–Paige 1981, 211, say this was the norm in the societies in their sample, but see Gottlieb 1988, 68–72.
[31] Weideger 1976, 92.
[32] Had there been one, it is unlikely that the Athenians would have left women behind at Plataea to do the cooking for the soldiers holding off the Theban siege in the Peloponnesian War, see Thuc. 2. 78. There were 110 women for 480 men. The number of women is due to the fact that cooking was very labour-intensive; making bread began with grinding corn. If they were unable to fulfil their allotted function at regular intervals they would have been more of a liability than a help to the garrison.

Temple was not polluted by a man who had come into contact with a menstruating woman on that day. A woman cannot enter the Temple until seven days after she has begun to menstruate or seven days after her menstrual flow has finished if it flows longer than usual. The same prohibition against entry into the Mosque operates in Muslim law, and in chapter 2 the Koran says, 'They will also question you as to the courses of women. Say, "They are a pollution. Separate yourselves therefore from women and approach them not until they be cleansed."' Zoroaster would not allow a menstruating woman to approach the sacred fire.[33] The Hindu lawgiver Manu decreed that a woman was impure during her menstrual period,[34] and while this may have had little significance for a Hindu woman (who played her part in the religion almost entirely through her husband), today in front of Hindu temples in India a request for menstruating women to remain outside is often posted in English. The Church Fathers of the West had varying opinions on a menstruating woman. Jerome thought there was nothing so unclean, while Augustine accepted it as a fact of nature which should not interfere with a woman's worship. With some exceptions, the Church in the West seems to have followed Augustine's teaching, though Sophronius said the Fathers of the Church forbade intercourse both during menstruation and for seven days after its conclusion on pain of leprosy, and in the seventh century Theodore, Archbishop of Canterbury, in his *Penitential* 14. 17, said that women who took communion while menstruating had to fast three weeks in penance. Even today women in the Orthodox Christian Church are not allowed to take communion if they are menstruating.[35]

FEAR AND ENVY OF FEMALE BLEEDING

The various forms of the separation of men and women during the menstrual period have generally been attributed to male fear of menstrual pollution,[36] but Marla N. Powers argues that this is a result of Western male bias, and in the case of the Native American tribe of the Oglala at least, she ties it instead to a celebration of the

---

[33] *Zend-Avesta* II, see Anquetil-Duperron iii. 1984, 562.

[34] Veda 5. 66, see Burnell 1971, 119.

[35] Jonkers 1943, 156–60; Morris 1973, 105–12; de Ste. Croix 1981, 109; Zias 1989, 29.

[36] See Buckley–Gottlieb 1988, 9–24.

woman's powers of reproduction—powers so different from a man's that she has to be kept away from him at this time.[37] Now, the female powers of reproduction are of course crucial to any society, and it may be that some earlier studies overemphasized the element of defilement at the expense of the latent power attributed to a menstruating woman in those societies which isolate her. Mary Douglas has shown,[38] however, that the two categories are by no means contradictory, and those cultures which would isolate menstruating women primarily because of their potency would do so because they considered these powers potentially harmful, i.e. a pollutant, to society. Despite Powers's denial at the end of her article ('Nowhere in the data is there evidence that practices associated with menstruation are in any way considered a sign of defilement or degradation toward the menstruating female'), she herself, in describing the ritual following a girl's first menstrual period, says that the shaman 'purifies' her, indicating that the liminal stage is passed and '*men* [my italics] need not fear contamination'. Powers also records the Oglala myth that menstruation began as the result of the adultery of the goddess Ite with the Sun, and that Ite was banished from the Sun as a punishment. She then explains that women are not allowed to cook their men's food when menstruating because this would necessitate their approaching the hearth at midday when the Sun was overhead, and symbolically having improper relations with him. This seems unnecessarily devious in the light of the terminology of contamination and purification which is used at the menarchal rite, especially when so many societies bar menstruating women from the preparation of food because of their fear of defilement.

Powers is correct in so far as so pervasive a fear of a menstruating woman shows that she was not simply an object of abject inferiority and disgust, but rather the locus of some power. This power can, occasionally, be harnessed to advantage, e.g. a menstruating woman was thought to be able to drive away hail and whirlwinds in ancient Rome,[39] but this normally occurs in contexts in which a menstruant's movements are otherwise circumscribed; she is not given licence to wander at will as a 'lucky charm'. Very often, even the positive uses to which menstruation can be put are deleterious to something. In those societies in which menstrual taboos operate

[37] Powers 1980. Though one could point out that it is at this time that she is at the nadir of these powers.
[38] Douglas 1966.   [39] Pliny, *NH* 28. 77; Plut. *Mor.* 700 E.

simply to separate a woman's menstrual power from other blood powers (e.g. among the Mandari the husband of a menstruating woman is forbidden to go hunting or fishing, and she herself is forbidden to touch any weapon)[40] or from other fertility powers (e.g. the women of the Beng are forbidden to enter the forest when menstruating),[41] it is feared that the menstrual blood will harm something important to society. While, therefore, it is too simplistic to interpret the almost universal menstrual taboo as signifying that the menstruant herself is 'dirty' or 'polluted', and while it is true that different cultures endow menstruation with 'meanings that are ambiguous and often multivalent',[42] the power of menstruation is thought to be, in the main, a destructive power. Those societies which elaborate menstrual restrictions do so because this power has to be contained, or entirely excluded from society. To a very large extent, as the foregoing survey of menstrual exclusion practices shows, this means male society. Other women do not seem to be so much at risk from a menstruant,[43] and in some cultures the menstrual huts can lie at the centre of an exclusively female subculture.

A separation with this social nature need not be unwelcome to the women involved. In a study on another Native American tribe, the Yurok, Thomas Buckley has shown that they may, in fact, view it as a positive period.[44] He goes so far as to argue that the custom was originally instituted by women and that the negative explanation of the removal of possible contamination was a subsequent compensatory development among men who were excluded from the retreat, rather than a positive interpretation elaborated by women as consolation for their banishment. It is impossible now to determine which sex initiated the tradition of menstrual seclusion, but it is worth remembering that the 50 per cent of adults who were thought of as 'different' from 'society' were those who bled once a month, rather than the other 50 per cent who did not do so. It is quite

---

[40] Buxton 1973, 215.   [41] Gottlieb 1988, 57.
[42] Buckley–Gottlieb 1988, 7.
[43] Eid. 1988, 11, say women themselves are often defined as vulnerable to menstrual pollution, even from their own blood, but the only example they give of the latter claim is in a note where they describe two cases in which menstrual blood on a tampon could be used in sorcery against a woman. In this context, women can also be in danger from their own hair, nail parings, etc., so in this case the woman would not seem to be threatened by her own menstrual blood *per se*. Women are usually threatened by menstruating women only during periods of pregnancy, parturition, and lactation.
[44] Buckley 1982.

possible that some of the Yurok women look forward to these days of retreat as a time of introspection or an opportunity of female bonding, and a ritual such as the *mikvah* (a ritual bath which Jewish women are required to take after menstruation before re-entering the synagogue) can be imbued with the positive symbolism of renewal. But the seclusion is often attended by physical, emotional, and spiritual deprivation in addition to any menstrual difficulties the woman might suffer. Female Christians in the West may have been praised for voluntarily refraining from attending church during their menstrual period, and they may have felt more virtuous for having done so, but this would stem from their internalization of the theory of pollution to such an extent that it was easier to go without the comfort of communion than to enter the presence of the divine while menstruating.[45] It does not show that such women felt they had better things to do than attend the patriarchal worship. Similarly, it may be true that women in societies which practise menstrual isolation look forward to their monthly seclusion as a break from routine, but the case of a New Guinea Mae Enga tribeswoman, whose husband axed her to death because she slept on his mattress while menstruating, suggests that it is not a break from routine which a woman can willingly forgo.[46] Buckley's young Yurok informant had revived the custom for herself and obviously felt free to come out and join her husband and him for dinner; her emotions and reactions cannot, therefore, be used to reconstruct those of women who are shunned by their menfolk and have no choice but to stay away from the social centre once a month.[47] Buckley, like Powers, is right to question the assumption that men shun menstruating women through simple fear and disgust, but, even if among the Yurok some women could view elaboration of menstrual taboos as celebrations

[45] Professor Shaye Cohen informs me that the reason women gave for their abstention from church attendance during menstruation was that they were possessed by a demon. He also tells me that it was not until the second century AD that Jewish women began to apply the strictures of Leviticus, which originally pertained only to the Temple in Jerusalem, to every synagogue and that the rabbis remark that this extension came entirely from the female side. Blum–Blum 1970, 188, remark that all the taboos on menstruation were collected from their female rather than their male informant, and that in explicating the taboos the informant had repeatedly emphasized the impurity of menses, e.g., pp. 20, 46, 48, 155.
[46] Delaney–Lupton–Toth 1976, 6.
[47] Douglas 1966, 151, records that amongst the Lele 'women found these rules [i.e. menstrual restrictions] extremely irksome'.

of a woman's reproductive powers, this does not prove that the
rituals did not also carry the meaning that she could pollute her
environment.

Because menstrual taboos are so widespread, various psychoanalytic theories have been propounded to explain their origins.
Most of these have hypothesized subconscious reactions of fear
and revulsion, focusing on women's unconscious aggressive
impulses or the male castration complex.[48] Bruno Bettelheim
suggested in a more positive vein that men were in fact envious of
a woman's power to bleed and so tried to debase menses: 'It
might be, then, that childbearing and menstruation were at one
time viewed as so elevating women that men sought revenge by
imposing unpleasant taboos on the menstruating women.'[49] The
strongest evidence for Bettelheim's claim is the subincision rites
among some Australian and New Guinea tribes in which the penis
is slit along the urethra, left to heal so that its underside resembles a vulva, and occasionally reopened to cause more bleeding
(the inhabitants of Wogeo, New Guinea actually refer to this process as 'men's menstruation').[50]

The ubiquity of menstrual taboos suggests that there is indeed
a fundamental psychological component, whether it be positive
or negative, in rituals which surround a menstruating woman;
but psychology alone cannot provide a sufficient explanation for
the disparity in the intensity of these rituals—from simple
avoidance of sex to complete seclusion of menstruants. Cultural
context must also influence the treatment of menstruating
women in any given society at any particular time, and it is in
the cultural context of Classical Greece that we must explain
the silence about menstruation in the more 'mainstream'
cultural texts when compared with the positive garrulousness of
the scientific texts.

---

[48] Summarized in Paige–Paige 1981, 18–20 & 26–8.

[49] Bettelheim 1954, 122. Ashley-Montagu 1937 had originally hazarded the same
suggestion, but commented that his own hypothesis (that subincision was meant to
imitate menstruation and feminize the penis) 'must appear somewhat fantastic', 302.
See Bettelheim 1954, 63, for a subtle analysis of the preconceptions of male anthro-
pologists which could explain why Ashley-Montagu was so diffident in putting
forward this theory.

[50] Ashley-Montagu 1937, 206, but cf. Lewis 1980, 2, on the Gnau who explicitly
deny that they equate subincision with menstruation.

MENSTRUAL BLEEDING AS A FACTOR IN SOCIAL
STRUCTURE

Douglas suggests that social structure determines whether or not
menstruation is a problem for a society.[51] She argues that if domi-
nation of the wife by the husband is accepted as the central principle
of social organization, if the full weight of any political/legal system generally sides with a man against his wife, and if the right to
any marriage that secures considerable wealth and/or power for the
husband is strictly dictated along genealogical lines, there are unlikely to be highly developed ideas of female pollution; in these
circumstances a man does not feel threatened by the women he lives
with and so feels less need for periodic assertion of his power.[52] If, on
the other hand, women can play off one man against another (e.g.
husband against brother or suitor against suitor), if there are legal or
social sanctions against a man's complete power over his wife, or if
the produce of her labour significantly affects the social standing of
her husband, ideas of female pollution are more likely to flourish;
these act as a periodic reassertion of the husband's supremacy. It
should be noted that the nature of a culture's menstrual taboos
cannot be taken as a measure of women's 'status' in that culture.

Douglas's theory has since been supported by a more rigorous
examination of the data available,[53] but Karen and Jeffery Paige
wish to subsume the theory of husband dominance under their
theory that rituals surrounding all reproductive events in the life
cycle are politically motivated attempts to resolve conflict rather
than simply indicators of tension.[54] They argue that in stable societies with strong fraternal interest groups[55] men can rely on supporters in the community to protect their interests and need only

[51] Douglas 1966, 140–58.
[52] Though it may be that women were originally subjected to such dominance
because they were felt to be threatening.
[53] Paige–Paige 1981, 33. An unpublished paper by Raymond Kelly on differences
in menstrual practices among New Guinea tribes, referred to in Ortner–Whitehead
1981, 20, conforms to this hypothesis. His findings were that in those tribes where
male prestige depended on hunting, etc., and was little influenced by women, there
was less elaboration of menstrual taboo than in those tribes where a woman contributed to her husband's prestige by, for example, raising pigs.
[54] Though a strong case could be made that acknowledging tension is one way to
defuse it.
[55] A fraternal interest group is a male 'consanguineal kin group [which] act[s] as a
corporate unit, using force if necessary, to defend their interests and resolve disputes',
Paige–Paige 1981, 53.

'ritual surveillance' to ensure that the parties involved maintain an agreement. On the other hand, men in unstable societies with weak fraternal interest groups need more elaborate reproductive rituals to act as occasions on which to gauge their support and standing in the community. Paige and Paige's arguments are more persuasive when applied to puberty and birth than to menstrual rituals. The political repercussions of puberty (which usually herald a marriage and the possibility of a new alignment within a community) and parturition (which, if successful, consolidates an alignment and strengthens a particular group within the community as well as the community as a whole) are plain to see and in these cases their theory appears to be viable and to have strong support in the data. However, in accounting for the elaboration of menstrual ritual in societies characterized by weak fraternal interest groups (as opposed to Douglas's theory which explains rather why societies organized on lines of complete husband dominance should minimize this almost universal taboo), the political explanation seems woefully inadequate. Paige and Paige can only suggest that by isolating his menstruating wife at the edge of the village a man is demonstrating his loyalty to the community and testing his political support by showing that he is 'disinterested in exploiting her fertility . . . [and] in protecting it from the claims of adulterers'.[56] That is, he is demonstrating that he is not solely concerned with the growth of his own conjugal unit—a too powerful one being a possible threat to the rest of the community—and simultaneously testing whether any man would undermine the integrity of his conjugal unit given the chance. This theory ignores the fact (which Paige and Paige themselves acknowledge) that among even primitive tribes menstruation is not usually considered a fertile period, so avoiding intercourse at this time to show lack of concern in the growth of one's own family would be rather like one country showing goodwill to another by interrupting arms production whenever its factories broke down. As for showing disinterest in protecting a wife from adultery, threatening any man who violates the taboo with disease, death, or insanity and/or his tribe with a typhoon and a withering of produce hardly smacks of nonchalance. It would seem, then, that while the correlations of Paige and Paige (between elaborate menstrual taboo and unstable societies with weak fraternal interest groups) and Douglas (between lack of menstrual taboo and societies with

[56] Ibid. 229.

uninhibited husband dominance) can both be supported by some data, Douglas's explanation of the correlation is more satisfactory. Paige and Paige's theory, however, may be helpful in understanding some aspects of rites surrounding menarchal and lochial bleeding. Whatever the psychological underpinnings of a society's attitude towards menstruation, the extent and nature of any rituals that centre on a menstruant seem to correlate with the community's social structure and, possibly, in rituals surrounding the unique or less frequent occasions of a woman's bleeding at puberty and parturition, with its political needs.[57] Most of the societies in Douglas's sample, and all of Paige and Paige's, were very simple societies, and we should be careful in applying their findings to more complex societies, such as those of ancient Greece. But in so far as relatively little cross-cultural study of the menstrual practices of, for example, Western industrialized nations has yet been attempted, we have no closer anthropological paradigms against which to compare individual complex societies.[58]

MENSTRUAL BLEEDING IN THE SOCIAL STRUCTURE OF
CLASSICAL GREECE

The almost complete lack of menstrual taboo in ancient Greece should be examined in the context of a social structure exhibiting Douglas's three criteria. The social structures of all Greek *poleis* were different, but in so far as most of the texts whose silence about menstruation suggests the lack of taboo were produced in Athens, and since Athens is the *polis* about whose social structure we are best informed anyway, it seems legitimate to take it as an example of how Douglas's theory might be applied.

Athenian culture strongly emphasized the dominance of a husband over his wife by making him her *kyrios* upon marriage. Though a woman did retain strong ties with her family of origin, she was generally much younger than her husband, and this by itself would go a long way to neutralizing any challenge to a husband's authority at an individual level. It is true that the man who had given the woman in marriage had the authority to dissolve the union

[57] At this point I do not wish to argue for the priority of cultural conceptions or of social structure.
[58] But see now Olesen–Woods 1986; Buckley–Gottlieb 1988.

when he wished,[59] but in the Classical period there are only three
cases known where divorce did proceed from the woman's side, and
if a woman herself attempted to end a marriage without a male
champion society tended to allow a husband complete authority
over her, even to the point of open coercion as in the case of Al-
cibiades and Hipparete.[60]

Athenian society also rigidly separated the female from the male
sphere so that a wife had very little opportunity to affect the social
standing of her husband positively or negatively. At 2. 46 Thucydides has Pericles say, 'The greatest glory of a woman is to be
least talked about by men, whether they are praising you or
criticizing you', and if the paucity of references to specific contemporary women in extant sources is a reliable guide, most Athenian
women of the Classical period took this advice to heart.

In Athens of the Classical period also, the institution of the epiklerate dictated, along strict genealogical lines, which man was eligible to marry a woman who brought with her not just a dowry but
also her father's entire property because he had had no sons.

Ancient Athens, therefore, came close to filling the paradigm of a
society which Douglas predicts would have little or no menstrual
taboo. Women operated under such controls that they had no
opportunity to threaten the male sphere; the demarcation of the
roles of men and women was not 'precarious', so no rituals had to be
elaborated to force the poles apart.[61]

In the same vein, ancient Greek medical theory corroborated
male physical and mental dominance by explaining menstruation
as the end result of a month-round physical debility of the female
body. Outside a medical context there was no need to refer to the
actual period of menstrual bleeding to buttress the male contention
that women were weaker; it was understood to be encompassed in
more general allusions to female physiology.

When portraying the differences between male and female, therefore, the literary texts would have had no call to focus on menstrual
bleeding as in itself setting women apart. This explanation goes
some way towards accounting for the conspicuous absence of menstrual jokes in Old Comedy. In terms of Aristophanes' scatological
humour, menstruation, unlike defecation, was a bodily process that

[59] Harrison 1968, 30–2, see Dem. 41. 4.   [60] Pomeroy 1975, 64–5.
[61] Blok 1987, 40–1, comments that in Classical Greece instances when woman is
not the opposite of man tend to 'disappear from view'.

he and the majority of his audience would neither have experienced personally nor been encouraged to conceal from public view, so presenting it to the whole *polis* on stage would not bring the same sense of release.[62] Henderson suggests that from the relatively infrequent references to urination in Aristophanes, 'one can probably conclude that the Greeks were more casual than we about urination'.[63] A bodily process's potential for arousing laughter decreases in direct relation to the effort which is normally expended on concealing it.[64] When urination is exploited for its humorous potential in ancient comedy, it is mainly to poke fun at incontinent old men;[65] menstruation could not be used to denote lack of control in the same way. If, in addition, the appearance of the menstrual flow did not affect relations between men and women, Aristophanes could make no particular sexual comic point with it.[66]

Just as in comedy a great deal was made of the physical differences between men and women without reference being made to menstruation, so a woman's body led to her having limitations placed on her access to some religious sanctuaries without these sanctions being restricted to or intensified at one period of the month. Women were banned altogether from some sanctuaries (e.g. of Heracles) and sacrifices (e.g. of Zeus Apotropaia, Zeus Amalos, Poseidon Phykion), and those who had just given birth, or were about to do so, were forbidden to enter some sanctuaries, even that of Demeter at Lykosoura. Childbirth also seems to have been forbidden within the

---

[62] Henderson 1975, 54: 'By talking openly of (or acting out) farting, shitting and pissing, a comic hero breaks free from and violates social inhibitions and the natural inhibitions of the adult.'

[63] Ibid. 35.

[64] This does not mean that menstruation or urination was deliberately displayed or a common topic of conversation, just that it was accepted when it appeared.

[65] Henderson 1975, 194.

[66] It could, perhaps, have been exploited to some effect in scenes of transvestism. One possible menstrual joke occurs at *Lys.* 1073 when Spartan envoys are said to approach 'as if they have pig-pens (χοιροκομεῖον) around their thighs'. The rest of the scene's humour depends on their having very obvious erections. Hesych. remarks that a certain female garment was known as a 'pig-pen'. Henderson 1975, 194, having noted Hesych.'s explanation, goes on to say that the word 'might possibly carry an obscene meaning . . . although the joke . . . is very obscure'. Since the Greek slang for vagina was χοῖρος ('piggie'), King suggests that the garment referred to was the menstrual cloth (King 1985, n. 139). The joke would then be that the bulge made by the penis at its most masculine is likened to the bulge made around the vagina at its most feminine. If this is the case it is even more surprising that Ar. did not utilize the possibilities of the concealment or exposure of menstrual blood in his scenes of cross-dressing.

sanctuaries of Asclepius, although women went there who were desirous of conceiving or bringing forth a child.[67] Moulinier argues that it is not the baby so much as the afterbirth and bloody matter which were considered to be the primary pollutants.[68] However, many patients in the Asclepiadic sanctuaries at least could be expected to have been oozing some secretion and they were allowed in, though they were expected to have the decency not to die there—which would have entailed pollution.

It was probably this desire to prevent a death in the sanctuary which caused the restriction on parturition. Throughout the ancient world both mother and child ran a great risk of death during and immediately after parturition. Euripides makes Iphigeneia say of Artemis: 'She who forbids approach by any man whose hand is stained with bloodshed or with touch of childbirth or of burial, finds him unclean and bans him.'[69] Here it is not just the parturient or corpse itself which is barred from Artemis' altar, but anyone who has touched either. It is difficult to prove that the contagion does not emanate from some physical emission of the body, but as death is not necessarily accompanied by any such emission it is more likely that it was the liminal aspect of birth and death which was thought to present the danger. Women were obviously more often involved in the first of these and so would more often be a source of pollution. It would seem from Euripides' *Electra* 654, 1131–3 that a woman was thought to be past the liminal stage if she were healthy ten days after birth, at least it was at this point that she was ritually 'purified'. The lochia, on the other hand, were believed to flow for a further ten to thirty days, so a woman was not viewed as a source of pollution throughout the time of her discharge, which argues against Moulinier's conclusion.

A possible indication that a woman was most threatening in her reproductive years generally is that many priestesshoods seem to have been reserved for older women past menopause.[70] Plutarch says that the Pythia was the only woman allowed in the temple at Delphi, and as a condition of her office she had to be past 50.[71] When performing her sacred office, the Pythia was dressed as a young

[67] See Cole 1992, 109–10; Phillips 1973, 199. [68] Moulinier 1952, 68.
[69] ἣ καὶ λοχείας ἢ νεκροῦ θίγῃ χεροῖν | βωμῶν ἀπείργει, μυσαρὸν ὡς ἡγουμένη, *IT* 382–3.
[70] See Drew–Bear–Lebeck 1973, 70–1. [71] *De Pyth. or.* 22. 405 c–d.

virgin,[72] thus combining the two poles of a woman's life when her body was not producing excess blood and she was therefore assimilated to the body of a male. The body of a woman was thought to be more dangerous for a particular period of her life cycle—menarche to menopause—not for a particular period of her menstrual cycle.

WOMEN'S VIEWS OF THEIR BODIES IN CLASSICAL GREECE

It seems extremely doubtful that Greek women supplied the terms 'frivolous' or 'inactive' for male authors to use to describe their way of life. Not only female slaves but citizen women probably had as little time for rest and recreation as most ordinary men in ancient Greece. The women in each household had to prepare food for the *oikos* (and in the case of bread, for example, this meant beginning from grinding the corn), to provide clothing, keep house, and minister to the sick and young children.[73] It is true that for most of these tasks women would not have needed the strength that men considered the virtue of the male body, but would women have accepted that their bodies were inferior for being weaker? The sorts of tasks their culture-determined body-type disqualified them from performing (fighting in battle and labouring outside the house) were not inherently any more attractive than those which most women were doing. While they may have been more valued in our extant sources because they were more socially visible, women may not have valued them above the tasks done in the home, and to the extent that male tasks were performed to support and defend the home, women may have seen them as subordinate. Men may have felt women were too weak to protect and provide for themselves, but women may have viewed the same breakdown of tasks as evidence that they were the valued members of society, their body-type so superior in its necessity to the state that male bodies were sacrificed for their sake. I would take issue with those who would claim that such a construction would have been self-delusion on the women's part. It is true that men would not necessarily have subscribed to it even if it had been articulated, and that they could have pointed to the glory won by men in myth and history simply for being great warriors—but it would have been male values of society which said

---

[72] Diod. 16. 26. 6.   [73] Pomeroy 1975, 71–4.

such things were important. Incipient Joans of Arc may have felt their bodies to be inferior, but most women would have agreed with men about the nature of the difference between men and women without necessarily agreeing that they were inherently inferior. They could have allowed men their martial glory and shrugged off devaluation of their work as long as female society concurred in allowing women domestic glory and devalued the male contribution to a gender-dichotomized society. Again, this is not to claim that in the long run the male sphere was not empowered by its greater articulation, but it is an attempt to explain how the muted group in society may have interpreted a shared model without defining themselves as inferior or persevering for centuries in mute anger and hatred.

DEVELOPMENT OF MENSTRUAL TABOOS DURING ANTIQUITY

As the social forms of any community are dynamic, not fossilized, so should we expect menstrual taboos to evolve or diminish over time rather than remain static throughout a culture's history. Douglas argues that an order is created in a society by exaggerating differences between within and without, above and below, male and female, etc.[74] When any of these antitheses threaten to coalesce some principle must be elaborated to force them apart again.

Once women began to challenge complete male dominance more seriously and show that they were capable of taking a more active role in society, menstruation *per se* became more important in establishing the male's natural supremacy in Greek culture. In the Hellenistic period, although the social roles of men and women remained strongly gender-based, the range of activities in which women could be autonomous agents gradually widened.[75] As the control of women became less complete, sacred laws appeared prohibiting the entry of a menstruant into some sacred precincts, and marginalia about the effect menstruating women have on mirrors were added to an Aristotelian treatise. In ancient Rome the institution of *patria potestas* might seem to indicate complete male dominance, but Roman women were always *de facto* freer than their

---

[74] Douglas 1966, 4.   [75] See Pomeroy 1975, 120–48; 1984.

Greek counterparts.[76] This could explain, at least in part, the
extreme anxiety over a menstruating woman displayed by Pliny in
his *Natural History*. At one point he says, 'nothing could easily be
found that is more remarkable than the monthly flux of woman',
and he believed its proximity could dim mirrors, blunt knives, turn
new wine sour, wither crops, dry up seeds, drive dogs mad, etc.[77]
These beliefs are echoed in such works as Columella's *De Re Rustica* and Plutarch's *Moralia*.[78] In his novel of the second century AD,
Leucippe and Cleitiphon, Achilles Tatius has one of his characters
employ the same stratagem to keep a man from a woman as the
gaoler had in the Talmud story (see p. 227 above). He tells him
Leucippe is menstruating and it would not be right to have intercourse at that time (iv. 7. 7). After receiving this information the man
agrees to wait three or four days before consummating the union.

While the cultural concern over menstruation as a sign of the
threat women could pose was heightening, medical interest in the
phenomenon as a mark of sexual difference was waning. We can see
this to some extent in the development of Hippocratic to
Aristotelian theories. In Hippocratic theory, menses have no real
analogue in the male body; in Aristotle's theory, they are the female
equivalent of semen. Aristotle's death occurred in the year following that of Alexander the Great (323 BC), the traditional terminus
of the Classical period and the beginning of the Hellenistic. His
theories were developed fifty to seventy-five years later than the
Hippocratic treatises were written, so although the two systems are
in one sense contemporary rivals within the same culture,
Aristotle's belongs to a slightly later chronological period during
which attitudes regarding the competence of women outside the
home may already have begun to change. Whether or not this had
any influence in limiting the physiological role of menstrual blood
in Aristotle's theory of women's bodies, by arguing that women were
indeed much more like men than had previously been thought, his
theory would have facilitated the entry of women into traditional
male spheres while still placing heavy emphasis on their subordin-

---

[76] See Gardner 1986, 263–4.
[77] *Nihil facile reperiatur mulierum profluvio magis monstrificum*, Pliny *NH* 7. 64–5;
17. 266; 28. 77–86. Pliny's claims about the powers of a menstruating woman were
recorded by the Inquisition in their handbook for identifying witches, *Malleus Malefi-
carum*.
[78] Colum. *RR* 10. 357–63, II. 3. 38, 50, 64; Plut. *Mor.* 700E. Cf. Ael. 6. 36; Tac.
Hist. 5. 6. 5.

ation to men. Aristotle's theory of female physiology, if not partly the result of, was at least better adapted to the changing social relationships between men and women in antiquity, and this, added to the general respect in which the Peripatos was held in Alexandria, may explain why even doctors working in the Hippocratic tradition adopted a more Aristotelian account of sexual differentiation.

In later medicine, menstrual blood had a less pervasive role in female physiology than Aristotle had given it. It may have been that Herophilus' particular interest in anatomy began the move away from concern with the female process of menstruation to the configuration of female reproductive organs, with the consequence that any gynaecological theories which Erasistratus did develop with a physiological emphasis seemed outdated and were not referred to so often in later literature. Or, Herophilus may have been more attracted to gynaecology than Erasistratus precisely because it was becoming more a concern of anatomy than physiology. In either case, Herophilus had the greater influence on later gynaecological theory. For Herophilus, the fundamental difference between male and female bodies was now located in the fact that the male has his genitals outside his body and the female has hers within.[79] A woman does not need to menstruate to reveal this fact. Menstrual blood is still necessary for conception and pregnancy, but the physiological processes that produce it are no longer of importance in differentiating male and female bodies, and for certain women menstruation itself can be harmful.[80] By the Roman period menstruation was considered harmful to all women, though some could sustain it better than others.[81] In Graeco-Roman science, therefore, the definition of a woman's body developed from that of a body so different from a man's that it had to menstruate to stay alive to one that was so similar that it would have been better for it to cease this process altogether. As the process of menstruation began to lose its place as a fundamental physiological divide between man and woman, menstrual blood itself started to play a new role in segregating women from men at certain times and places within the culture. In the Classical period this had not been necessary.

[79] See von Staden 1989, 165–9, 296–9. In fact, in T 193, 365, Herophilus lists the affections common to women as conceiving, nourishing the embryo, parturition, and lactation. He makes no mention of menstruation.
[80] See von Staden 1989, 299–300.   [81] Soranus, *Gyn.* I. 29.

A MODERN PARALLEL

A suggestive parallel to the ancient material is provided by developing attitudes towards menstruation in modern Britain and America. These societies seem relatively free of an irrational fear of menstrual contamination; they place few, if any, restrictions on a menstruant, and where these appear they are generally not too burdensome. However, when permanent waves were first introduced it was believed that they would not take if the woman was menstruating,[82] and in my teens there were those who discouraged me from attending the public swimming-pool during this period. Moreover, although various surveys indicate that many couples abstain from sex during a woman's menstrual period,[83] the reason given for avoiding intercourse during menstruation is usually one of aesthetics rather than of fear of contamination of any sort.

It may be argued that husband dominance in Britain and America, while it undoubtedly exists, is not of the uninhibited type described by Douglas but is constantly checked by the wife's family, rival suitors, the law, etc. On Douglas's theory, then, menstrual taboos should be more developed than these comparatively slight restrictions imply. However, the male fear of menstrual blood has to a large extent been disguised rather than eliminated from contemporary society by modern medical explanations of the natural processes which cause it.[84] In the earlier decades of this century, the process of the blood draining from a woman's body into her womb was thought to be physically debilitating, validating for women the title of the weaker sex and thereby supporting male dominance without having to focus on the period of external bleeding as such.

[82] Delaney–Lupton–Toth 1976, 8. In 1987 a graduate student assured me that this was true. She had had a perm which had failed to take, and on returning to the hairdresser to complain was asked whether she had been menstruating at the time. When she replied in the affirmative the hairdresser said that that was the reason, though she also volunteered the information that other hairdressers thought the scalp was affected by menstrual hormones some time after menstruation itself! No doubt there are some who think that the pre-menstrual period is also a risky time to have a perm, the point being that although a perm can fail at any time, it is still possible for our society to give and accept as an explanation that the failure is caused by something integral to the femaleness of a body.

[83] Delaney–Lupton–Toth 1976, 14; Asso 1983, 59.

[84] A menstruating woman in our society is disguised rather than displayed, cf. Parker 1983, 59. For purposes of daily intercourse, men do not expect or desire to be told when a woman is menstruating, though they may consider that they can tell from her behaviour when she is, e.g. 'She's on the rag'.

More recently, in 1970, Edgar Berman, a Democratic party functionary, declared that he would not like to see a woman as President of the United States because of her 'raging hormonal imbalances', and it was to these female hormones that Gen. Galtieri attributed Mrs Thatcher's reaction to the invasion of the Falklands in 1982. These condemnations of the female make no explicit reference to menstruation, and base the belief that women are fundamentally unsuited to govern on the action of substances which are in their bodies all month round. Hormones are an integral and continuous part of being a woman. A culture which had no conception of hormonal activity, or did not associate it with menstruation, might not immediately recognize that there was a menstrual allusion here.

Until recently, menstruation itself was rarely if ever mentioned outside a medical context. As with the early religious codes which used menstruation as a divine sign to validate women's inferior status, once the social restrictions had been laid down there was no need to refer continually to the reasons for them as long as nobody tried to overstep them. It was only when women began to challenge the definition of their sex and the parameters of their existence that references to the reasons for the definition and parameters began to appear outside the canon in which they were inscribed.

The constraints placed upon women in our own society have been steadily diminishing, and the social norm of male dominance is coming to be challenged more directly. It no longer suffices to claim that women are a priori weaker or less intelligent than men. Correspondingly, menstruation is coming to be articulated as a problem more explicitly.[85] The fact that it occurs only in women and that some of them do experience difficulties with it has enabled men—encouraged until very recently by many gynaecologists in the medical community, over 95 per cent of whom are male—to define it reassuringly as a bodily infirmity which, even if it only occurs periodically, makes a woman unfit for certain tasks.[86] Premenstrual syndrome (PMS) and dysmenorrhoea previously served no purpose in society; woman was already defined as physically and mentally incapacitated to challenge men, so specific problems around the menstrual period itself would have been over-

[85] Note especially Douglas 1966, 139: 'wherever the lines [governing behaviour between people] are precarious we find pollution ideas come to their support.' In this connection it is interesting to note that even Freud was never concerned to develop a theory of psychological reactions (male or female) to menstruation.

[86] Delaney–Lupton–Toth 1976, 49–58; Asso 1983 pp. xiii–xiv.

determination. There was no particular medical concern for those women who did suffer. Now that women have shown themselves (for the purposes of our society at least) the intellectual and physical equals of men, some medical opinion has backed the belief that menstrual difficulties are debilitating and widespread.[87] One of the arguments used to keep women from the workplace in our society has been that they lose too many workdays through dysmenorrhoea, though this is disproved by the US Department of Labor statistics. In 1980, for example, men who had never been married lost 3% of their weekly working hours and women who had never married 3.4%. Illness was cited as the reason for 1.4% of men's absences and 1.5% of women's.[88] These figures show that women are not notably more inclined to absenteeism than men and that absences are more often attributed to familial obligations, etc., than to incapacity through illness. PMS has been accepted as a defence for a woman's illegal actions, even murder, and is often proffered by a woman herself in excuse for socially unacceptable behaviour without considering what other factors may, for example, have caused her to lose her temper or burst into tears. It is possible under these circumstances to imagine a scenario in which women were eventually allowed equality with men in the workplace during most of the month, provided they agreed to withdraw from society either just before or during their menstrual period.[89]

[87] The theory of PMS was first developed by a female gynaecologist, Kathleen Dalton, see Dalton 1979. That some women do in fact suffer from the syndrome need not be a political issue. Modern medicine has been able to control diabetes, a much more serious hormonal disease, and President Kennedy suffered from Addison's disease, a debilitating hormonal complaint if not kept under control by drugs. Steinem 1985 offers a humorous look at the possible positive interpretations that could be placed on menstruation by men if they themselves menstruated and women did not.

[88] Leon 1981; Taylor 1981.

[89] Ardener 1975, 48, comments *re* Douglas's remark that sex pollution is not highly developed where male dominance is accepted as a central principle of organization, 'It is tempting to follow this by arguing that it was the weakening of the authority of the American male which led to the sudden discovery of the need for vaginal deodorants.'

References

Abse 1950   D. W. Abse, *The Diagnosis of Hysteria* (London, 1950).

Allan 1952   D. J. Allan, *The Philosophy of Aristotle* (London, 1952).

Amundsen–Diers 1969   D. W. Amundsen and C. J. Diers, 'The Age of Menarche in Classical Greece and Rome', *Human Biology* (USA), 41. 1 (1969), 125–32.

—— 1970   eid., 'The Age of Menopause in Classical Greece and Rome', *Human Biology* (USA), 42. 1 (1970), 79–86.

Anquetil-Duperron A. H Anquetil-Duperron, *Zend-Avesta*, 3 vols.
1984   (Paris, 1771; repr. New Yoik, 1984)

Ardener 1975   Edwin Ardener, 'Belief and the Problem of Women', in S. Ardener (ed.), *Perceiving Women* (London, 1975), 1–17.

Arendt 1959   Hannah Arendt, *The Human Condition* (Garden City, NY, 1958).

Arthur 1973   Marilyn B. Arthur, 'Early Greece: The Origins of the Western Attitude toward Women', *Arethusa*, 6 (1973), 7–58.

—— 1982   ead., 'Cultural Strategies in Hesiod's *Theogony*: Law, Family and Society', *Arethusa*, 15 (1982), 63–82.

Ashley-Montagu 1937   M. F. Ashley-Montagu, *Coming into Being among the Australian Aborigines* (London, 1937).

Asso 1983   Doreen Asso, *The Real Menstrual Cycle* (Chichester, 1983).

Bailey 1963   D. Sherwin Bailey, *Sexual Ethics: A Christian View* (New York, 1963).

Bailey 1989   Robert C. Bailey, 'The Efe: Archers of the African Rain Forest', *National Geographic*, 176 (1989), 664–86.

Balme 1961   D. M. Balme, 'Aristotle's Use of Differentiae in Biology', in S. Mansion (ed.), *Aristote et les problèmes de méthode* (Louvain, 1961), 195–212.

—— 1962   id., 'γένος and εἶδος in Aristotle's Biology', *CQ*² 12 (1962), 81–98.

—— 1965   id., 'Aristotle's Use of the Teleological Explanation', Inaugural Lecture, Queen Mary College, London, 1965.

—— 1980   id., 'Aristotle's Biology Was Not Essentialist', *Archiv für Geschichte der Philosophie*, 62 (1980), 1–12.

—— 1985   id., 'Aristotle *Historia Animalium* Book Ten', in Jürgen Wiesner (ed.), *Aristoteles und seine Schule* (Berlin, 1985).

Balss 1923   H. Balss, 'Präformation und Epigenese in der griechischen Philosophie', *Archivio di storia della scienza*, 4 (1923), 319–25.

—— 1936   id., 'Die Zeugungslehre und Embryologie in der Antike', *Quellen und Studien zur Geschichte der Naturwissenschaft und der Medizin*, 5 (1936), 193–274.

Barb 1953   A. A. Barb, 'Diva Matrix', *JWCI* 16 (1953), 193–238.

Barrett 1964   W. S. Barrett, *Euripides: Hippolytos* (Oxford, 1964).

Beattie 1984   J. H. M. Beattie, 'Objectivity and Social Anthropology', in S. C. Brown (ed.), *Objectivity and Cultural Divergence* (Cambridge, 1984).

Bettelheim 1954   Bruno Bettelheim, *Symbolic Wounds: Puberty Rites and the Envious Male* (New York, 1954).

Betz 1986   Hans Dieter Betz, *The Greek Medical Papyri in Translation, Including the Demotic Texts* (Chicago, 1986).

Blayney 1986   Jan Blayney, 'Theories of Conception in the Ancient Roman World', in Beryl Rawson (ed.), *The Family in Ancient Rome: New Perspectives* (London, 1986), 230–6.

Blok 1987   Josine Blok, 'Sexual Asymmetry: A Historiographical Essay', in Josine Blok and Peter Mason (eds.), *Sexual Asymmetry: Studies in Ancient Society* (Amsterdam, 1987), 1–57.

Blüh 1949   O. Blüh, 'Did the Greeks Perform Experiments?', *American Journal of Physics*, 17 (1949), 384–8.

Blum–Blum 1970   Richard Blum and Eva Blum, *The Dangerous Hour: The Lore of Crisis and Mystery in Rural Greece* (New York, 1970).

Blundell 1985   Susan Blundell, *Theories of Evolution in Antiquity* (Beckenham, 1985).

Bonner 1920   C. Bonner, 'The Trial of St. Eugenia', *AJP* 41 (1920), 253–64.

—— 1950   id., *Studies in Magical Amulets, Chiefly Graeco-Roman* (Ann Arbor, Mich., 1950).

Boorse 1977   Christopher Boorse, 'Health as a Theoretical Concept', *Philosophy of Science*, 44 (1977), 542–73.

—— 1981   id., 'On the Distinction between Disease and Illness', in M. Cohen, T. Nagel, and T. Scanlon (eds.), *Medicine and Moral Philosophy* (Princeton, NJ, 1981), 3–22.

Bouché-Leclercq 1882   A. Bouché-Leclercq, *Histoire de la divination dans l'antiquité* (Paris, 1879–82).

Bourgey 1953   L. Bourgey, *Observation et expérience chez les médecins de la collection hippocratique* (Paris, 1953).

—— 1980   id., 'Hippocrate et Aristote: L'origine, chez le philosophe, de la doctrine concernant la nature', in M. Grmek (ed.), *Hippocratica* (Paris, 1980), 59–64.

Bowen 1959   E. Bowen, 'The Virgin and the Empress', *Harper's Magazine*, 219 (Nov. 1959), 50–5.

Boylan 1983   Michael Boylan, *Method and Practice in Aristotle's Biology* (Washington, DC, 1983).

Brain 1986   Peter Brain, *Galen on Bloodletting* (Cambridge, 1986).

Buckley 1982   Thomas Buckley, 'Menstruation and the Power of Yurok Women: Methods in Cultural Reconstruction', *American Ethnologist*, 9 (1982), 47–60.

Buckley–Gottlieb 1988   Thomas Buckley and Alma Gottlieb (eds.), *Blood Magic* (Berkeley, 1988).

Burguière–Gourevitch–Malinas 1988   Paul Burguière, Danielle Gourevitch, and Yves Malinas (eds.), *Soranos d'Éphèse, Maladies des Femmes*, i (Paris, 1988).

Burkert 1985   Walter Burkert, *Greek Religion* (Cambridge, Mass., 1985).

Burnell 1971   Arthur C. Burnell, *The Ordinances of Manu* (London, 1884; repr. New Delhi, 1971).

Burton 1981   J. W. Burton, '"The Moon is a Sheep"': A Feminine Principle in Atuot Cosmology', *Man*, 16 (1981), 441–50.

Buxton 1973   J. Buxton, *Religion and Healing in Mandari* (Oxford, 1973).

Byl 1980   S. Byl, *Recherches sur les grands traités biologiques d'Aristote: sources écrites et préjugés* (Brussels, 1980).

Campese 1983   Silvia Campese, 'Madre materia: donna, casa, città nell'antropologia di Aristotele', in Campese–Manuli–Sissa (1983), 15–79.

Campese–Manuli–   Silvia Campese, Paola Manuli, and Giulia Sissa
Sissa 1983   (eds.), *Madre Materia* (Turin, 1983).

Casabona 1966   Jean Casabona, *Recherches sur le vocabulaire des sacrifices en grec, des origines à la fin de l'époque classique* (Aix-en-Provence, 1966).

Charlton 1987   William Charlton, 'Aristotle on the Place of Mind in Nature', in Gotthelf–Lennox (1987), 408–23.

Clark 1975   Stephen R. L. Clark, *Aristotle's Man* (Oxford, 1975).

—— 1982   id., 'Aristotle's Woman', *HPT* 3 (1982), 177–91.

Cohn-Haft 1956   Louis Cohn-Haft, *The Public Physicians of Ancient Greece* (Northampton, Mass., 1956).

Cole 1992   Susan G. Cole, 'γυναιξὶ οὐ θέμις: Gender Difference in the Greek *Leges Sacrae*', *Helios*, 19 (1992), 104–22.

Cooper 1988   John M. Cooper, 'Metaphysics in Aristotle's Embryology', *PCPS* 214 (1988), 14–41.

Crawfurd 1915   Raymond Crawfurd, 'Superstitions of Menstruation', *The Lancet*, 18 Dec. 1915, 1331–6.

Culham 1987   Phyllis Culham, 'Ten Years After Pomeroy: Studies of the Image and Reality of Women in Antiquity', *Helios*, 13 (1987), 9–30.

Cutler 1980   W. B. Cutler, 'Lunar and Menstrual Phase Locking', *AJOG* 137 (1980), 834–9.

Dalton 1979   Katharina Dalton, *Once a Month* (Pomona, 1979).

Daly 1943   C. D. Daly, 'The Role of Menstruation in Human Phylogeny and Ontogeny', *IJP* 24: 151 (1943), 169.

Danforth 1982   David N. Danforth (ed.), *Obstetrics and Gynecology* (Philadelphia, 1982).

Dean-Jones 1991   Lesley Dean-Jones, 'The Cultural Construct of the Female Body in Classical Greek Science', in Sarah B. Pomeroy (ed.), *Women's History and Ancient History* (Chapel Hill, NC, 1991) 111–37.

—— 1992   ead., 'The Politics of Pleasure: Female Sexual Appetite in the Hippocratic Corpus', *Helios*, 19 (1992), 72–91.

Delaney–Lupton–Toth 1976   Janice Delaney, Mary Jane Lupton, and Emily Toth (eds.), *The Curse* (New York, 1976).

Delcourt 1957   Marie Delcourt, *Héphaistos ou la légende du magicien* (Paris, 1957).

—— 1961   ead., *Hermaphrodite Myths and Rites of the Bisexual Figure in Classical Antiquity*, trans. Jennifer Nicholson (London, 1961).

del Guerra 1953   G. del Guerra, *Il libro di Metrodora sulle malattie delle donne e il recettario di cosmetica et terapia* (Milan, 1953).

de Ley 1981   H. de Ley, 'Beware of Blue Eyes: A Note on Hippocratic Pangenesis', *AC* 50 (1981), 192–7.

den Boer 1979   W. den Boer, *Private Morality in Greece and Rome: Some Historical Aspects, Mnem.* Suppl. 57 (Leiden, 1979).

de Ste. Croix 1981   G. E. M. de Ste. Croix, *The Class Struggle in the Ancient Greek World* (London, 1981).

Detienne 1977   Marcel Detienne, 'Potagerie des femmes ou comment engendrer seule', *Culture*, 1 (1977/8), 2–8.

—— 1979   id., *La Cuisine du sacrifice en pays grec* (Paris, 1979).

Devereux 1967   G. Devereux, 'Greek Pseudo-Homosexuality and the Greek Miracle', *Sym. Oslo.* 42 (1967), 69–92.

Dewald 1981   Carolyn Dewald, 'Women and Culture in Herodotus' Histories', in Foley (1981), 91–125.

Dickison 1973   Sheila K. Dickison, 'Abortion in Antiquity', *Arethusa*, 6 (1973), 159–66.

Diels 1906   H. Diels, *Die Handschriften der antiken Ärzte*, ii (Berlin, 1906).

Diller 1959   H. Diller, 'Stand und Aufgaben der Hippokratesforschung', *Jahrbuch der Akademie der Wissenschaften und der Literatur* (Mainz, 1959), 271–87.

Dobson 1925   J. F. Dobson, 'Herophilus of Alexandria', *Pro-
                   ceedings of the Royal Society of Medicine* (1925),
                   19–32.

Dodds 1973   E. R. Dodds, 'The Religion of the Ordinary Man
                   in Classical Greece', *The Ancient Concept of Pro-
                   gress and Other Essays on Greek Literature* (Ox-
                   ford, 1973), 140–55.

Douglas 1966   Mary Douglas, *Purity and Danger* (London,
                   1966).

—— 1975   ead., 'Couvade and Menstruation: The Rele-
                   vance of Tribal Studies', *Implicit Meanings,
                   Essays in Anthropology* (London, 1975).

Dover 1964   K. J. Dover, 'Eros and Nomos', *BICS* 11 (1964),
                   31–42.

—— 1966   id., 'Aristophanes' Speech in Plato's *Sym-
                   posium*', *JHS* 86 (1966), 41–50.

—— 1973   id., 'Classical Greek Attitudes to Sexual
                   Behaviour', *Arethusa*, 6 (1973), 59–73.

—— 1982   id., *Greek Homosexuality* (Cambridge, Mass.,
                   1982).

Draper 1985   Patricia Draper, 'Two Views of Sex Differences
                   in Socialization', in Roberta L. Hall (ed.),
                   *Male–Female Differences: a Bio-Cultural Per-
                   spective* (New York, 1985), 5–25.

Drew-Bear–   T. Drew-Bear and W. D. Lebeck, 'An Oracle of
Lebeck 1973   Apollo at Miletus', *GRBS* 14 (1973), 65–73.

Duke 1955   T. T. Duke, 'Women and Pygmies in the Roman
                   Arena', *CJ* 50 (1955), 223–4.

Dunn 1972   J. Dunn, 'Vicarious Menstruation', *AJOG* 114
                   (1972), 568–9.

Düring 1961   I. Düring, '... *De Part. An.* I. 1, 639^{b}30–640^{a}2', in
                   S. Mansion (ed.), *Aristote et les problèmes de
                   méthode* (Louvain, 1961), 213–21.

—— 1969   id., *Naturphilosophie bei Aristoteles und Theo-
                   phrast: Verhandlungen des 4. Symposium
                   Aristotelicum* (Heidelberg, 1969).

Edelstein 1967   Ludwig Edelstein, *Ancient Medicine* (Baltimore,
                   1967).

Eliade 1963   Mircea Eliade, *Patterns in Comparative Religion*
                   (Cleveland, 1963).

Erbse 1969   Hartmut Erbse, *Scholia Graeca in Homeri
                   Iliadem*, 6 vols. (Berlin, 1969–83).

Ewart 1964   Andrew Ewart, *The World's Wickedest Women: Intriguing Studies of Eve and Evil through the Ages* (New York, 1964).

Faraone 1989   Christopher A. Faraone, 'Clay Hardens and Wax Melts: Magical Role-Reversal in Vergil's Eighth *Eclogue*', *CP* 84 (1989), 294–300.

Farnell 1904   L. R. Farnell, 'Sociological Hypotheses concerning the Position of Women in Ancient Religion', *ARW* 7 (1904), 70–94.

Fausto-Sterling 1985   Anne Fausto-Sterling, *Myths of Gender* (New York, 1985).

Fehrle 1920   E. Fehrle, *Studien zu den griechischen Geoponika* (Leipzig, 1920).

Flint 1982   Marcha Flint, 'Male and Female Menopause: A Cultural Put On', in Ann M. Voda, Myra Dinnerstein, and Sheryl R. O'Donnell (eds.), *Changing Perspectives on Menopause* (Austin, Tex., 1982).

Foley 1981   Helene Foley (ed.), *Reflections of Women in Antiquity* (New York, 1981).

Foucault 1978   Michel Foucault, *The History of Sexuality*, i. *An Introduction*, trans. Robert Hurley (New York, 1978).

—— 1985   id., *The Use of Pleasure*, trans. Robert Hurley (New York, 1985).

Frede 1982   Michael Frede, 'The Method of the So-called Methodical School of Medicine', in J. Barnes, J. Brunschwig, M. Burnyeat, and M. Schofield (eds.), *Science and Speculation* (Cambridge, 1982).

—— 1985   id., 'Substance in Aristotle's *Metaphysics*', in Gotthelf (1985), 17–26.

Fredrich 1899   C. Fredrich, *Hippokratische Untersuchungen* (Berlin, 1899).

Friedrich 1979   Paul Friedrich, *The Meaning of Aphrodite* (Chicago, 1979).

Gardner 1986   Jane F. Gardner, *Women in Roman Law and Society* (London, 1986).

George 1982   Sarah George, 'Human Conception and Fetal Growth: A Study in the Development of Greek Thought from the Presocratics through Aristotle', diss. (U. of Penn., 1982).

262 *References*

Gerber 1978 — Douglas E. Gerber, 'The Female Breast in Greek Erotic Literature', *Arethusa*, 11 (1978), 203–12.

Giallongo 1981 — Angela Giallongo, *L'Immagine della donna nella cultura greca* (Rimini, 1981).

Gifford-Jones 1971 — W. Gifford-Jones, *On Being a Woman: The Modern Woman's Guide to Gynecology* (New York, 1971).

Girard 1977 — René Girard, *Violence and the Sacred* (Baltimore, 1977).

—— 1978 — id., *De choses cachées depuis la fondation du monde* (Paris, 1978).

Gohari–Berkowitz–Hobbins 1977 — Parviz Gohari, Richard L. Berkowitz, and John C. Hobbins, 'Prediction of intra-uterine growth retardation by determination of total intra-uterine volume', *AJOG* 127. 3 (1977), 255–60.

Gold 1988 — Barbara Gold, 'Dionysus, Greek Festivals and the Treatment of Hysteria', *Laetaberis*, 6 (1988), 16–28.

Golden 1990 — Mark Golden, *Children and Childhood in Classical Athens* (Baltimore, 1990).

Goldhill 1984 — Simon Goldhill, *Language, Sexuality, Narrative, the Oresteia* (Cambridge, 1984).

Goldin 1955 — Judah Goldin (trans.), *The Fathers According to Rabbi Nathan* (New Haven, Conn., 1955).

Golub 1983 — S. Golub (ed.), *Menarche: The Transition from Girl to Woman* (Lexington, Mass., 1983).

Gotthelf 1985 — Allan Gotthelf (ed.), *Aristotle on Nature and Living Things: Philosophical and Historical Studies Presented to David M. Balme on his Seventieth Birthday* (Bristol, 1985).

Gotthelf–Lennox 1987 — Allan Gotthelf and J. G. Lennox (eds.), *Philosophical Issues in Aristotle's Biology* (Cambridge, 1987).

Gottlieb 1988 — Alma Gottlieb, 'Menstrual Cosmology among the Beng of the Ivory Coast', in Buckley–Gottlieb (1988), 55–74.

Gould 1981 — Stephen Jay Gould, *The Mismeasure of Man* (London, 1981).

—— 1982 — id., 'Women's Brains', *The Panda's Thumb: More Reflections in Natural History* (New York, 1982), 152–9.

References 263

Gourevitch 1984 — Danielle Gourevitch, *Le Mal d'être femme: la femme et la médicine dans la Rome antique* (Paris, 1984).

Gracia 1978 — Diego Gracia, 'The Structure of Medical Knowledge in Aristotle's Philosophy', *Sudhoff's Archiv*, 62 (1978), 1–36.

Grene 1963 — Marjorie Grene, *A Portrait of Aristotle* (London, 1963).

—— 1972 — ed., 'Aristotle and Modern Biology', *JHI* 33 (1972), 395–424.

—— 1978 — ed., 'Individuals and their Kinds: Aristotelian Foundations of Biology', in Stuart F. Spicker (ed.), *Organism, Medicine and Metaphysics: Essays in Honor of H. Jonas* (Boston, 1978), 121–36.

Grensemann 1968 — Hermann Grensemann, *Hippokrates über Achtmonatskinder. Über das Siebenmonatskind, CMG* I 2, 1 (Berlin, 1968).

—— 1975 — id., *Knidische Medizin*, pt. i (Berlin, 1975).

—— 1982 — id., *Hippokratische Gynäkologie* (Wiesbaden, 1982).

—— 1987 — id., *Knidische Medizin*, pt. ii (Stuttgart, 1987).

Grimal 1967 — P. Grimal, *Love in Ancient Rome*, trans. Arthur Train (New York, 1967).

Grmek 1989 — Mirko D. Grmek, *Diseases in the Ancient Greek World* (Baltimore, 1989).

Gross 1980 — Rita M. Gross, 'Menstruation and Childbirth as Ritual and Religious Experience among Native Australians', in Nancy A. Falk and Rita M. Gross (eds.), *Unspoken Worlds: Women's Religious Lives in Non-Western Cultures* (New York, 1980), 277–92.

Guralnick 1981 — Eleanor Guralnick, 'Proportions of Korai', *AJA* 85 (1981), 269–80.

Guthrie 1962 — W. K. C. Guthrie, *A History of Greek Philosophy*, i. *The Earlier Presocratics and the Pythagoreans* (Cambridge, 1962).

—— 1965 — id., *A History of Greek Philosophy*, ii. *The Presocratic Tradition from Parmenides to Democritus* (Cambridge, 1965).

—— 1981 — id., *A History of Greek Philosophy*, vi. *Aristotle: An Encounter* (Cambridge, 1981).

Haggard 1929   Howard W. Haggard, *Devils, Drugs and Doctors* *(London,* 1929).

Hanson 1970   Ann Ellis Hanson, 'P. Antinoopolis 184: Hippocrates' *Diseases of Women',* *Proceedings of the* *XIIth International Congress of Papyrology* (Amsterdam, 1970), 213–22.

—— 1971   ead., 'Studies in the Textual Tradition and Transmission of the Gynecological Treatises of the Hippocratic Corpus', diss. (U. of Penn., 1971).

—— 1975   ead., 'Hippocrates: *Diseases of Women* I', *Signs,* 1 (1975), 567–84.

—— 1984   ead., review of *Hippokratische Gynäkologie,* ed. Hermann Grensemann, *CW* 78 (1984/5), 62–3.

—— 1987*a*   ead., 'Diseases of Women in the *Epidemics',* in Gerhard Baader and Franz Steiner (eds.), *Actes* *du colloque hippocratique 1984* (Stuttgart, 1987), 29–41.

—— 1987*b*   ead., 'The Eighth Month Child: Obsit Omen', *BHM* 61 (1987), 589–602.

—— 1989   ead., 'Greco-Roman Gynecology', *SAMPh* *Newsletter,* 17 (1989), 83–92.

—— 1990   ead., 'The Medical Writer's Woman', in David Halperin, John Winkler, and Froma Zeitlin (eds.), *Before Sexuality* (Princeton, NJ, 1990), 309–38.

—— 1991   ead., 'Continuity and Change: Three Case Studies in Hippocratic Gynecological Therapy and Theory', in Sarah B. Pomeroy (ed.), *Women's History and Ancient History* (Chapel Hill, NC, 1991), 73–110.

—— 1992   ead., 'Conception, Gestation and the Origin of Female Nature in the *Corpus Hippocraticum',* *Helios,* 19 (1992) 31–71.

Harding 1955   Esther Harding, *Women's Mysteries* (New York, 1955).

Hare 1979   J. E. Hare, 'Aristotle and the Definition of Natural Things', *Phronesis,* 24 (1979), 168–79.

Harlap 1979   Susan Harlap, 'Gender of Infants Conceived on Different Days in the Menstrual Cycle', *New England Journal of Medicine,* 300 (1979), 1445–8.

Harris 1973   C. R. S. Harris, *The Heart and the Vascular System in Ancient Greek Medicine* (Oxford, 1973).

Harrison 1968   A. R. W. Harrison, *The Law of Athens,* 2 vols. (Oxford, 1968–71).

Hartog 1980	François Hartog, *Le Miroir d'Hérodote* (Paris, 1980).
Hays 1964	H. R. Hays, *The Dangerous Sex: The Myth of Feminine Evil* (New York, 1964).
Heidel 1941	W. A. Heidel, *Hippocratic Medicine, its Spirit and Method* (New York, 1941).
Henderson 1975	Jeffrey Henderson, *The Maculate Muse* (New Haven, Conn., 1975).
—— 1987	id., 'Older Women in Attic Old Comedy', *TAPA* 117 (1987), 105–29.
Hogbin 1970	Iain Hogbin, *The Island of Menstruating Men: Religion in Wogeo, New Guinea* (Scranton, 1970).
Holderman 1913	E. S. Holderman, *A Study of the Greek Priestess* (Chicago, 1913).
Hopfner 1938	Theodor Hopfner, *Das Sexualleben der Griechen und Römer* (Prague, 1938).
Horowitz 1976	Maryanne Cline Horowitz, 'Aristotle and Woman', *JHB* 9 (1976), 183–213.
Humphreys 1978	S. C. Humphreys, *Anthropology and the Greeks* (London, 1978).
Hussey 1972	Edward Hussey, *The Presocratics* (London, 1972).
Jackson 1988	Ralph Jackson, *Doctors and Diseases in the Roman Empire* (London, 1988).
Jaeger 1938	Werner Jaeger, *Diokles von Karystos* (Berlin, 1938).
Johns 1982	Catherine Johns, *Sex or Symbol: Erotic Images of Greece and Rome* (Austin, Tex., 1982).
Joly 1966	Robert Joly, *Le Niveau de la science hippocratique* (Paris, 1966).
—— 1976	id., 'La structure du "Fœtus de huit mois"', *AC* 45 (1976), 173–80.
—— 1983	id., 'Hippocrates and the School of Cos', in Michael Ruse (ed.), *Nature Animated* (Dordrecht, 1983), 29–47.
Jones 1989	Lesley Ann Jones, review of *Knidische Medizin*, pt. ii, by Hermann Grensemann, *AJP* 110 (1989), 164–6.
Jones 1946	W. H. S. Jones, *Philosophy and Medicine in Ancient Greece* (Baltimore, 1946).
Jones–Wentz–Burnett 1988	Howard W. Jones, Anne Colston Wentz, and Lonnie S. Burnett, *Novak's Textbook of Gynecology*, 11th edn. (Baltimore, 1988).

Jonkers 1943

E. J. Jonkers, 'Einige Bemerkungen über kirchliche und heidnische Reinheitsvorschriften in den ersten sechs nachchristlichen Jahrhunderten', *Mnem.*[3] II (1943), 156–60.

Jordanova 1980

L. J. Jordanova, 'Natural Facts: A Historical Perspective on Science and Sexuality', in C. P. MacCormack and M. Strathern (eds.), *Nature, Culture and Gender* (Cambridge, 1980), 42–69.

Jouanna 1974

J. Jouanna, *Hippocrate, pour une archéologie de l'école de Cnide* (Paris, 1974).

——— 1983

id., *Hippocrate, Maladies II* (Paris, 1983).

Just 1975

R. Just, 'Conceptions of Women in Classical Athens', *JASO* 6. 3 (1975), 153–70.

Katz 1976

Phyllis B. Katz, 'The Myth of Psyche: a Definition of the Nature of the Feminine?', *Arethusa*, 9 (1976), III–18.

Katzeff 1981

Paul Katzeff, *Full Moons* (Secaucus, NJ, 1981).

Kember 1971

O. Kember, 'Right and Left in the Sexual Theories of Parmenides', *JHS* 91 (1971), 70–9.

Kerényi 1972

K. Kerényi, *Zeus und Hera* (Leiden, 1972).

Keuls 1985

Eva C. Keuls, *The Reign of the Phallus: Sexual Politics in Ancient Athens* (New York, 1985).

Kiefer 1934

Otto Kiefer, *Sexual Life in Ancient Rome* (London, 1934).

King 1983

Helen King, 'Bound to Bleed: Artemis and Greek Women', in Averil Cameron and Amelia Kuhrt (eds.), *Images of Women in Antiquity* (Beckenham, 1983), 109–27.

——— 1985

ead., *From Parthenos to Gyne: The Dynamics of Category*, Ph.D thesis (London, 1985).

——— 1986

ead., 'Agnodike and the Profession of Medicine', *Proc. Camb. Phil. Soc.*, NS 32 (1986), 53–75.

——— 1987

ead., 'Sacrificial Blood: The Role of the *Amnion* in Ancient Gynecology', *Helios*, 13 (1987), II7–26.

——— 1989

ead., 'The Daughter of Leonides: Reading the Hippocratic Corpus', in Averil Cameron (ed.), *History as Text* (London, 1989), 13–32.

——— (forthcoming)

ead., 'Once upon a Text: The Hippocratic Origins of Hysteria', in G. S. Rousseau and R. Porter (eds.), *Hysteria in Western Civilization* (Berkeley, forthcoming).

Kirk–Raven–
Schofield 1983

Koelbing 1980

Kreuzer 1969

Kudlien 1965

——— 1968

Kühn 1956

Kullmann 1979

Kung 1980

Lacey 1968

Laín 1970

Lang 1983

Laser 1983

Leach 1966

Le Blond 1935

Lefkowitz 1981

Lennox 1977

——— 1980

——— 1982

G. S. Kirk, J. E. Raven, and M. Schofield, *The Presocratic Philosophers* (Cambridge, 1983).
H. M. Koelbing, 'Le médicin hippocratique au lit du malade', in M. D. Grmek (ed.), *Hippocratica* (Paris, 1980), 321–32.
Helmut Kreuzer, *Literarische und naturwissenschaftliche Intelligenz: Dialog über die 'zwei Kulturen'* (Stuttgart, 1969).
F. Kudlien, 'Seven Cells of the Uterus: The Doctrine and its Roots', *BHM* 39 (1965), 415–23.
id., 'Early Greek Primitive Medicine', *Clio Medica*, 3 (1968), 305–36.
J.-H. Kühn, *System- und Methodeprobleme im Corpus Hippocraticum* (Wiesbaden, 1956).
Wolfgang Kullmann, *Die Teleologie in der aristotelischen Biologie*, Sitzungsberichte der Heidelberger Akademie der Wissenschaften, 1979. 2.
Joan Kung, 'Some Aspects of Form in Aristotle's Biology', *Nature and System*, 2 (1980), 67–92.
W. K. Lacey, *The Family in Classical Greece* (Ithaca, NY, 1968).
Entralgo P. Laín, *The Therapy of the Word in Classical Antiquity*, trans. L. J. Rather and J. M. Sharp (New Haven, Conn., 1970).
H. S. Lang, 'Aristotle and Darwin: The Problem of Species', *IPQ* 23 (1983), 141–53.
Siegfried Laser, *Medizin und Korperflege* (Göttingen, 1983).
Edmund Leach, 'Virgin Birth', *PRAI* (1966), 39–49.
Jean-Marie Le Blond, 'The Biological Bias of Aristotle', *The Modern Schoolman*, 12 (1935), 82–4.
Mary R. Lefkowitz, 'The Wandering Womb', *Heroines and Hysterics* (New York, 1981), 12–25.
J. G. Lennox, 'A Study of the Interaction between Aristotle's Metaphysics and his Biological Works', diss. (U. of Toronto, 1977).
id., 'Aristotle on Genera, Species and "the More and the Less"', *JHB* 13 (1980), 321–46.
id., 'Teleology, Chance and Spontaneous Generation', *JHP* 21 (1982), 219–38.

268　　　*References*

Leon 1981　　Carol Boyd Leon, 'Employed but Not at Work: A Review of Unpaid Absences', *MLR* 104 (Nov. 1981), 18–22.

Lesky 1951　　E. Lesky, *Die Zeugungs- und Vererbungslehren der Antike und ihr Nachwirken* (Akademie der Wissenschaften und der Literatur, Mainz, Abhandlungen der geistes- und sozialwissenschaftlichen Klasse, 1950, 19, Wiesbaden).

Levine 1971　　Edwin Burton Levine, *Hippocrates* (New York, 1971).

Lévi-Strauss 1976　　Claude Lévi-Strauss, *Structural Anthropology*, ii, trans. Monique Layton (New York, 1976).

Lewis 1980　　Gilbert Lewis, *Day of Shining Red* (Cambridge, 1980).

Licht 1932　　Hans Licht, *Sexual Life in Ancient Greece* (London, 1932).

Lind 1978　　Levi Robert Lind, 'Popular Knowledge of Anatomy and Medicine in Greece before Hippocrates', *Arch. ital. anat. e embriol.* 83 (1978), 33–52.

Linders 1972　　T. Linders, *Studies in the Treasury Records of Artemis Brauronia found in Athens* (Stockholm, 1972) .

Lloyd 1961　　G. E. R. Lloyd, 'The Development of Aristotle's Theory of the Classification of Animals', *Phronesis*, 6 (1961), 59–81.

——— 1968　　id., *Aristotle, the Growth and Structure of his Thought* (Cambridge, 1968).

——— 1970　　id., *Early Greek Science: Thales to Aristotle* (London, 1970).

——— 1978　　id., 'The Empirical Basis of the Physiology of the *Parva Naturalia*', in G. E. R. Lloyd and G. E. L. Owen (eds.), *Aristotle on the Mind and the Senses*, (Cambridge, 1978), 215–39.

——— 1979　　id., *Magic, Reason and Experience* (Cambridge, 1979).

——— 1983　　id., *Science, Folklore and Ideology* (Cambridge, 1983).

——— 1987　　id., *The Revolutions of Wisdom* (Berkeley, 1987).

Longrigg 1989　　James Longrigg, 'Presocratic Philosophy and Hippocratic Medicine', *History of Science*, 27 (1989), 1–39.

Lonie 1978   Iain M. Lonie, 'Cos vs. Cnidus and the His-
                          torians', pts. I–II, *History of Science*, 16 (1978),
                          42–75, 77–92.

—— 1981   id., *The Hippocratic Treatises 'On Generation';
                          'On the Nature of the Child'; 'Diseases 4'* (Berlin,
                          1981).

Loraux 1978   Nicole Loraux, 'Sur la race des femmes et quel-
                          ques-unes de ses tribus', *Arethusa*, 11 (1978),
                          43–87.

—— 1981   ead., *Les Enfants d'Athéna: idées athéniennes sur
                          la citoyenneté et la division des sexes* (Paris, 1981).

—— 1987   ead., *Tragic Ways of Killing a Woman* (Cam-
                          bridge, Mass., 1987).

Louis 1964–9   Pierre Louis, *Aristote: Histoire des animaux*, 3
                          vols. (Paris, 1964–9).

—— 1975   id., 'Monstres et monstrosités dans la biologie
                          d'Aristote', in J. Bingen, G. Cambier, and G.
                          Nachtergael (eds.), *Le monde grec. Pensée, lit-
                          térature, histoire, documents. Hommages à C.
                          Préaux* (Brussels 1975), 277–84.

Luria 1927   S. Luria, 'Studien zur Geschichte der antiken
                          Traumdeutung', *Bull. de l'Acad. des Sciences de
                          l'URSS*, 21 (1927), 441–66, 1041–72.

McClees 1920   Helen McClees, *A Study of Women in Attic In-
                          scriptions* (New York, 1920).

McClintock 1971   Martha K. McClintock, 'Menstrual Synchrony
                          and Suppression', *Nature*, 229 (1971), 244–5.

—— 1981   ead., 'Social Control of the Ovarian Cycle and
                          the Function of Estrous Synchrony', *American
                          Zoologist*, 21 (1981), 243–56.

MacCormack 1980   Carol P. MacCormack, 'Nature, Culture and
                          Gender: A Critique', in C. P. MacCormack and
                          M. Strathern (eds.), *Nature, Culture and Gender*
                          (Cambridge, 1980), 1–24.

McDaniel 1948   Walton Brooks McDaniel, *Conception, Birth
                          and Infancy in Ancient Rome and Modern Italy*
                          (Gainesville, Fla., 1948).

MacDowell 1978   Douglas M. MacDowell, *The Law in Classical
                          Athens* (Ithaca, NY, 1978).

Mackay *et al.* 1983   Eric V. Mackay, Norman A. Beischer, Lloyd W.
                          Cox, and Carl Wood, *Illustrated Textbook of
                          Gynaecology* (Sydney, 1983).

Majno 1975   Guido Majno, *The Healing Hand* (Cambridge, Mass., 1975).

Malinowski 1929   Bronislaw Malinowski, *Sexual Life of Savages in North-Western Melanesia* (New York, 1929).

Mansfeld 1980   Jaap Mansfeld, 'Plato and the Method of Hippocrates', *GRBS* 21 (1980), 341–62.

—— 1983   id., 'The Historical Hippocrates and the Origins of Scientific Medicine', in Michael Ruse (ed.), *Nature Animated* (Dordrecht, 1983), 49–76.

Manuli 1980   Paula Manuli, 'Fisiologia e patologia del femminile negli scritti ippocratici dell'antica ginecologia greca', in M. D. Grmek (ed.), *Hippocratica* (Paris, 1980), 393–408.

—— 1983   ead., 'Donne mascoline, femmine sterili, vergini perpetue: La ginecologia greca tra Ippocrate e Sorano', Campese–Manuli–Sissa (1983), 149–204.

Meyer 1939   A. W. Meyer, *The Rise of Embryology* (Stanford, 1939).

Micale 1989   Mark Micale, 'Hysteria and its Historiography', pt. i, *History of Science*, 27 (1989), 223–61.

Micalella 1977   D. Micalella, 'Vino e amore: Ippocrate, *Antica medicina* 20', *QUCC* 24 (1977), 151–5.

Miller 1944   Harold W. Miller, 'Medical Terminology in Tragedy', *TAPA* 75 (1944), 156–67.

Millet 1970   Kate Millet, *Sexual Politics* (New York, 1970).

Milne 1976   John Stewart Milne, *Surgical Instruments in Greek and Roman Times* (Oxford, 1907; repr. Chicago, 1976).

Morris 1973   Joan Morris, *The Lady was a Bishop* (New York, 1973).

Morsink 1979   Johannes Morsink, 'Was Aristotle's Biology Sexist?', *JHB* 12 (1979), 83–112.

—— 1982   id., *Aristotle on the Generation of Animals: A Philosophical Study* (Washington, DC, 1982).

Most 1981   G. Most, 'Callimachus and Herophilus', *Hermes*, 109 (1981), 188–96.

Moulinier 1952   L. Moulinier, *Le Pur et l'impur dans la pensée des Grecs* (Paris, 1952).

Müller 1868   Carl Müller, *Fragmenta historicorum graecorum*, 5 vols. (Paris, 1868–84).

Nardi 1971   E. Nardi, *Procurato aborto nel mondo greco-romano* (Milan, 1971).

Ogle 1882	William Ogle, *On the Parts of Animals* (London, 1882).
Olesen– Woods 1986	Virginia L. Olesen and Nancy Fugate Woods (eds.), *Culture, Society and Menstruation* (Healthcare for Women International, 7; Washington, DC, 1986).
Ortner– Whitehead 1981	Sherry B. Ortner and Harriet Whitehead (eds.), *Sexual Meanings: The Cultural Construction of Gender and Sexuality* (Cambridge, 1981).
Owen 1967	G. E. L. Owen, 'τιθέναι τὰ φαινόμενα', in J. M. E. Moravcsik (ed.), *Aristotle, A Collection of Critical Essays* (Garden City, NY, 1967), 167–90.
Padel 1983	Ruth Padel, 'Women: Model for Possession by Greek Daemons', in Averil Cameron and Amelia Kuhrt (eds.), *Images of Women in Antiquity* (Beckenham, 1983), 3–19.
Paige–Paige 1981	Karen Erickson Paige and Jeffery M. Paige, *The Politics of Reproductive Ritual* (Berkeley, 1981).
Parker 1983	Robert Parker, *Miasma: Pollution and Purification in Early Greek Religion* (Oxford, 1983).
Patterson 1985	Cynthia Patterson, ' "Not Worth the Rearing": The Causes of Infant Exposure in Ancient Greece', *TAPA* 115 (1985), 103–23.
Peck 1953	A. L. Peck, 'The Connate Pneuma: An Essential Factor in Aristotle's Solution to the Problem of Reproduction and Sensation', in E. A. Underwood (ed.), *Science, Medicine and History: Essays in Honour of Charles Singer* (London, 1953), 111–21.
Pellegrin 1986	Pierre Pellegrin, *Aristotle's Classification of Animals*, trans. Anthony Preus (Berkeley, 1986).
Phillips 1973	E. D. Phillips, *Aspects of Greek Medicine* (London, 1973).
Pigeaud 1981	J. Pigeaud, *La Maladie de l'âme: Étude sur la relation de l'âme et du corps dans la tradition médico-philosophique antique* (Paris, 1981).
Podolsky 1934	Edward Podolsky, *Young Women Past Forty* (New York, 1934).
Pohlenz 1938	M. Pohlenz, *Hippokrates und die Begründung der wissenschaftlichen Medizin* (Berlin, 1938).
Pomeroy 1975	Sarah B. Pomeroy, *Goddesses, Whores, Wives and Slaves* (New York, 1975).

—— 1977   ead., 'Technikai kai Mousikai', *AJAH* 2 (1977), 51–68.

—— 1978   ead., 'Plato and the Female Physician (*Rep.* 454D2)', *AJP* 99 (1978), 496–500.

—— 1984   ead., *Women in Hellenistic Egypt. From Alexander to Cleopatra* (New York, 1984).

Potter 1922   Irving W. Potter, *The Place of Version in Obstetrics* (St. Louis, Mo., 1922).

Powers 1980   Marla N. Powers, 'Menstruation and Reproduction: An Oglala Case', in C. R. Simpson and E. S. Person (eds.), *Women, Sex and Sexuality* (Chicago, 1980), 117–28.

Préaux 1973   Claire Préaux, *La Lune dans le pensée grecque* (Brussels, 1973).

Presser 1974   H. B. Presser, 'Temporal Data Relating to the Human Menstrual Cycle', in M. Fenn, F. Halberg, R. M. Richart, and R. L. Vande Wiele (eds.), *Biorhythms and Human Reproduction* (New York, 1974), 145–60.

Preus 1975   A. Preus, *Science and Philosophy in Aristotle's Biological Works* (New York, 1975).

—— 1979   id., '*Eidos* as Norm in Aristotle's Biology', *Nature and System*, 1 (1979), 79–101.

Price 1989   A. W. Price, *Love and Friendship in Plato and Aristotle* (Oxford, 1989).

Pritchett 1979   W. Kendrick Pritchett, *The Greek State at War*, iii (Berkeley, 1979).

Randall 1960   J. H. Randall, *Aristotle* (New York, 1960).

Redfield 1977   James Redfield, 'The Women of Sparta', *CJ* 73 (1977/8), 146–61.

Reiche 1960   H. A. T. Reiche, *Empedocles' Mixture, Eudoxan Astronomy and Aristotle's Connate Pneuma* (Amsterdam, 1960).

Richlin 1983   Amy Richlin, *The Garden of Priapus: Sexuality and Aggression in Roman Humor* (New Haven, Conn., 1983).

—— 1984   ead., 'Invective against Women', *Arethusa*, 17 (1984), 67–80.

Richter 1971   D. C. Richter, 'The Position of Women in Classical Athens', *CJ* 67 (1971), 1–8.

Riddle 1985   John Riddle, *Dioscorides on Pharmacy and Medicine* (Austin, Tex., 1985).

References 273

1987   id., 'Folk Tradition and Folk Medicine: Recognition of Drugs in Classical Antiquity', in John Scarborough (ed.), *Folklore and Folk Medicine* (Madison, Wisc., 1987), 33–61.

Riele 1978   G. J. M. J. te Riele, 'Une nouvelle loi sacrée en Arcadie', *BCH* 102 (1978), 325–31.

Robinson 1917   William J. Robinson, *Woman: Her Sex and Love Life* (New York, 1917).

Ross 1949   David Ross, *Aristotle* (London, 1949).

1955   id., *Parva Naturalia* (Oxford, 1955).

Rostand 1960   Jean Rostand, *Error and Deception in Science*, trans. A. J. Pomerans (London, 1960).

Rousselle 1980   Aline Rousselle, 'Observation féminine et idéologie masculine: le corps de la femme d'après les médecins grecs', *Annales ESC* 35 (1980), 1089–115.

1988   ead., *Porneia. On Desire and the Body in Antiquity*, trans. Felicia Pheasant (Oxford, 1988).

Rush 1976   A. K. Rush, *Moon, Moon* (New York, 1976).

Russell 1950   Bertrand Russell, *Unpopular Essays* (London, 1950).

Saïd 1983   Suzanne Saïd, 'Féminin, femme et femelle dans les grands traités biologiques d'Aristote', in Edmond Lévy (ed.), *La Femme dans les sociétés antiques. Actes des colloques de Strasbourg (mai 1980 et mars 1981)* (Strasburg 1983), 93–123.

Savalli 1983   I. Savalli, *La donna nella società della Grecia antica* (Bologna, 1983).

Scarborough 1983   John Scarborough, 'Theoretical Assumptions in Hippocratic Pharmacology', in F. Laserre and P. Mudry (eds.), *Formes de pensée dans la collection hippocratique* (Geneva 1983), 307–25.

1989   id., 'Contraception in Antiquity: The Case of Pennyroyal', *Wisconsin Academy Review*, 35 (1989), 19–25.

Schaps 1979   D. M. Schaps, *Economic Rights of Women in Ancient Greece* (Edinburgh, 1979).

Schilling 1961   R. Schilling, 'Vestales et vierges chrétiennes dans la Rome antique', *Revue des sciences religieux*, 35 (1961), 113–17.

Schumacher 1963   J. Schumacher, *Antike Medizin* (Berlin, 1963).

Sealey 1990   R. Sealey, *Women and Law in Classical Greece* (Chapel Hill, NC, 1990).

Segal 1978   Charles Segal, 'The Menace of Dionysus: Sex Roles and Reversals in Euripides' *Bacchae*', *Arethusa*, 11 (1978), 185–202.

Seltman 1956   Charles Seltman, *Women in Antiquity* (New York, 1956).

Shaw 1975   Michael Shaw, 'The Female Intruder: Women in Fifth-Century Drama', *CP* 70 (1975), 255–66.

Simon 1978   Bennet Simon, *Mind and Madness in Ancient Greece* (Ithaca, NY, 1978).

Simpson 1872   James Y. Simpson, *Clinical Lectures on the Diseases of Women* (New York, 1872).

Singer 1957   C. Singer, *A Short History of Anatomy and Physiology from the Greeks to Harvey* (New York, 1957).

Sissa 1983   Giulia Sissa, 'Il corpo della donna: Lineamenti di una ginecologia filosofica', in Campese–Manuli–Sissa (1983), 84–145.

—— 1984   ead., 'Une virginité sans hymen: le corps féminin en Grèce ancienne', *Annales ESC* 39 (1984), 1119–39.

Skinner 1970   Henry Alan Skinner, *The Origin of Medical Terms* (New York, 1970).

Slater 1971   P. E. Slater, *The Glory of Hera* (Boston, Mass., 1971).

Smith 1979   Wesley D. Smith, *The Hippocratic Tradition* (Ithaca, NY, 1979).

Solmsen 1957   Friedrich Solmsen, 'The Vital Heat, the Inborn Pneuma and the Aether', *JHS* 77 (1957), 119–23.

Spiro 1968   Melford E. Spiro, 'Virgin Birth, Parthenogenesis and Physiological Paternity: An Essay in Cultural Interpretation', *Man,* 3 (1968), 242–51.

Steinem 1985   Gloria Steinem, 'If Men Could Menstruate', *Outrageous Acts and Everyday Rebellions* (New York, 1985), 337–40.

Stephens 1961   William Stephens, 'A Cross-Cultural Study of Menstrual Taboos', *Genetic Psychology Monographs*, 64 (Nov. 1961), 385–416.

Sussman 1978   Linda S. Sussman, 'Workers and Drones; Labor, Idleness and Gender Definition in Hesiod's Beehive', *Arethusa*, 11 (1978), 27–41.

Tage 1952   V. H. Ellinger Tage, *Hippocrates on Intercourse and Pregnancy* (New York, 1952).

Taylor 1981	Daniel E. Taylor, 'Absences from Work among Full-Time Employees', *MLR* 104 (Mar. 1981), 68–70.
Thivel 1981	A. Thivel, *Cnide et Cos? Essai sur les doctrines medicales dans la collection hippocratique* (Paris, 1981).
Thompson 1913	D'Arcy W. Thompson, *On Aristotle as a Biologist* (Oxford, 1913).
Thompson 1955–8	Stith Thompson, *Motif-Index of Folk-Literature*, 6 vols. (Bloomington, Ind., 1955–8).
Thompson 1972	Wesley E. Thompson, 'Athenian Marriage Patterns: Remarriage', *CSCA* 5 (1972), 211–22.
Tolson 1977	Andrew Tolson, *The Limits of Masculinity* (London, 1977).
Toynbee 1929	J. Toynbee, 'The Villa Item and a Bride's Ordeal', *JRS* 19 (1929), 67–88.
Trall 1873	R. T. Trall, *The Health and Diseases of Women* (Battle Creek, Mich., 1873).
Turner 1968	V. Turner, *The Drums of Affliction* (Oxford, 1968).
Tyrrell 1984	William Blake Tyrrell, *Amazons: A Study in Athenian Mythmaking* (Baltimore, 1984).
Untermann 1972	Isser Yehuda Untermann, 'Family Purity: Its Wide Implications', *Israel Magazine*, 4 (Jan. 1972), 68–74.
Utian 1980	W. H. Utian, *Menopause in Modern Perspective: A Guide to Clinical Practice* (New York, 1980).
van der Waerden 1960	B. L. van der Waerden, 'Greek Astronomical Calendars and their Relation to the Athenian Civil Calendar', *JHS* 80 (1960), 168–80.
Vatin 1970	C. Vatin, *Recherches sur le marriage et la condition de la femme mariée à l'époque hellénistique* (Paris, 1970).
Vernant 1983	J.-P. Vernant, 'Hestia-Hermes: The Religious Expression of Space and Movement in Ancient Greece', *Myth and Thought among the Greeks* (London, 1983), 127–75.
Vidal-Naquet 1981	Pierre Vidal-Naquet, *Le Chasseur noir: formes de pensée et formes de société dans le monde grec* (Paris, 1981).
von Staden 1975	H. von Staden, 'Experiment and Experience in Hellenistic Medicine', *BICS* 22 (1975), 178–99.

—— 1989   id., *Herophilus: The Art of Medicine in Early Alexandria* (Cambridge, 1989).

—— 1992   id., 'Women and Dirt', *Helios*, 19 (1992), 7–30.

Wächter 1910   Theodor Wächter, 'Reinheitsvorschriften im griechischen Kult', *Religionsgeschichtliche Versuche und Vorarbeiten*, 9 (1910–11), 1–144.

Wagenvoort 1947   H. Wagenvoort, *Roman Dynamism* (Oxford, 1947).

Walcot 1978   Peter Walcot, 'Herodotus on Rape', *Arethusa*, 11 (1978), 137–47.

Weideger 1976   Paula Weideger, *Menstruation and Menopause* (New York, 1976).

Weisstein 1971   N. Weisstein, 'Psychology Constructs the Female', *Social Education*, 35 (1971), 362–73.

Wellmann 1901   M. Wellmann, *Die Fragmente der sikelischen Ärzte Akron, Philistion und des Diokles von Karystos* (Berlin, 1901).

Wender 1973   Dorothea Wender, 'Plato: Misogynist, Paedophile, and Feminist', *Arethusa*, 6 (1973), 75–90.

West 1978   M. L. West, *Hesiod: Works and Days* (Oxford, 1978).

Winkler 1981   Jack Winkler, 'Gardens of Nymphs: Public and Private in Sappho's Lyrics', in Foley (1981), 63–89.

Withington 1928   E. T. Withington, *Hippocrates*, iii (Cambridge, Mass., 1928).

Wood 1981   C. T. Wood, 'The Doctor's Dilemma: Sin, Salvation, and the Menstrual Cycle in Medieval Thought', *Speculum*, 56 (1981), 710–27.

Wycherley 1969   R. E. Wycherley, *How the Greeks Built Cities* (Garden City, NY, 1969).

Zeitlin 1978   Froma Zeitlin, 'The Dynamics of Misogyny: Myth and Mythmaking in the *Oresteia*', *Arethusa*, 11 (1978), 149–84.

Zias 1989   Joseph Zias, 'Lust and Leprosy: Confusion or Correlation', *BASOR* 275 (1989), 27–31.

Zinserling 1973   Verena Zinserling, *Women in Greece and Rome* (New York, 1973).

GENERAL INDEX

abortion 30, 95, 118, 173–6, 202 n.189,
  203, 209 n.219
  see also miscarriages
Acron 13
afterbirth, *see* lochia
age at death 106
ageing 103–8
Alcmaeon 149, 202
Alexandrian medicine, *see* Herophilus,
  Erasistratus
Anaxagoras 149, 164, 202
'andrology' 110, 112–19
Apollo 111, 149
Archagathus 22 n.75
archē, see principle
Archigenes 25 n.78
Ares 111 n.2
Aretaeus 25
Aristophanes 228, 244–5
Aristotelian errors 16 n.51, 18, 92, 228
Artemis 29, 52 n.32, 111, 232 n.21, 246
Asclepius 34 n.103, 35, 246
  see also sacred laws
Aspasia, *see* physicians, female
Athena 149, 151
audience 26–7, 37, 40
automaton 190, 191

barrenness, *see* fertility
births, multiple 67, 165–6, 198
  see also twins
bladder 66
bleeding 142–4, 145, 147, 200, 214
brain 41 n.2, 75, 84
breasts 57–8, 61, 87, 92
  bleeding from 142
  cancer of 134 n.76, 136 n.82
  connection to eyes 202
  men's 216–17
  in miscarriage 167 n.64
  tenderness in 125 n.39
  see also lactation

causes, Aristotelian 179–80, 184
  efficient 187, 189–92
  formal and material 180–99
Celsus 23
cervix 65, 69, 79, 121, 128–9
  see also stoma
childbirth 34–5, 71, 135 n.79, 142,
  211–15, 242, 245–6
children 46, 118, 140, 148, 155
Cleopatra, *see* physicians, female
clitoris 78–80, 158
clyster 66, 90–1, 124 n.33, 142
Cnidos 12 n.39
  see also 'schools' of medicine
compendia, medical 25–6, 33
complexion 123
conception 62, 99, 100, 116
  duration of 172–6, 191–3
  early theories of 148–53
  female seed in 153–60
  male contribution to according to
    Hippocratics 160–2
  process of according to Aristotle
    184–93
  sexual hierarchy in according to
    Aristotle 176–83
  suppression of 223–4
  time of 170–2, 175, 186
  see also pangenesis, resemblance, sex
    determination, fertility
concoction 60, 185–7, 192, 216–17, 221
contagion 137
contraceptive 152, 157 n.33, 172–3, 175
Corpus, Aristotelian:
  composition of 13–15, 112
  relationship to Hippocratic Corpus
    19–20
Corpus, Hippocratic:
  composition of 5–6
  gynaecological treatises 10–12
  relationship to Aristotelian Corpus
    19–20

cultural relativism 1-4, 25, 86, 103, 226
  n.1
  in amount of bleeding 89 n.154, 92
  in categorization of disease 112, 137
  in determining prematurity 210
  in menopause 106 n.21, 108
  in role of moon 97-101
  social importance of father 148
  see also gender roles, traditional
    medicines, Aristotelian errors
cupping-glass 64, 66
defloration 50, 54, 102, 103
  see also menarche

deformity 182, 198-9, 212
Demeter 245
Democritus 149, 166, 167, 189 n.144,
  202
Diocles of Carystus 13, 19, 97
Diogenes of Apollonia 8 n.29, 149, 202
  n.191, 203
Dionysus 75, 149, 151
dissection 8, 16-17, 22, 25 n.78
divorce 148, 152 n.18, 244
Dogmatists 9
dropsy 119, 135, 144
dualizers 185

'effluxion' 173-6, 191
eggs 202-3, 204, 206-8
Egypt 150, 210, 227
eidos 17 n.56
  see also form, species, causes, soul
ejaculation 155-9, 162, 169, 187
emetic 124, 125 n.36, 132, 141, 142, 144
emmenagogue 132-3
Empedocles 13, 44-5, 97, 149, 163, 167,
  202
empiricism:
  Hippocratic 7-8, 202-3
  Aristotelian 15-19, 82, 204
  see also examination
Empiricists 9
endoxa 16, 29, 31
enema 124, 132, 141
Epidemics 12-13
epigenesis 205
epikleros 148, 244
epilepsy 2-3, 29
epistaxis 118, 125 n.36, 138, 139-40,
  143-4, 145
Erasistratus 22, 250
eunuchs 61, 193

examination 35-6, 83
exercise 56, 89, 116, 247
  see also inactivity, female

Fallopian tubes 66-7, 68, 91, 172
fertility 118, 121, 134, 224 n.292
  recipes for 152, 171
  of semen 187, 191 n.149
  tests for 17, 73, 77, 202 n.188
  see also conception, menarche,
    menopause
fetation 187-9, 192
flesh 55-9, 63, 84, 121, 147 n.117, 164
flux 129-30, 134, 141, 142-3, 146
foetus 202-9, 213-14
  see also fetation, gestation
form, individual 195-9
  see also causes, soul, species

Galen 24, 66, 133, 152 n.19
gender:
  categories of disease 110-19
  differentiation by biology 41-4, 134
  roles 38-40, 147 n.117, 247, 248-53
genos 17 n.56
gestation 209-11, 221 n.274
  see also fetation, foetus
girls, unmarried 27 n.80, 29, 52, 103,
  138-9, 140
  see also puberty
glands 55-6, 57
Great Vein 142-3

haemorrhoids 92, 118, 131, 132, 139, 144
Hagnodike, *see* physicians, female
hair 84-5, 134, 208
halitosis 73
heart 205, 216
  see also principle
hellebore 123, 132
Hera 151
Heracles 192 n.157, 245
Heraclitus 8 n.29
hermaphrodites 169
Herodotus 227
Herophilus 22, 32, 66, 250
Hesiod 230, 233-4
Hippon 149, 202 n.191
'horns' of the womb 66-7
hot, and cold:
  causing hair growth 84-5
  differentiating men and women 44-6,
    60-1

effect of moon on 97–8
effect of summer on 96 n.180
role in ageing 104–5, 107–8, 164
role in conception 161, 167, 169–70,
  184–93, 206
role in lactation 216–17
humidity 46, 49, 215
and conception 161, 167–8, 169–70
and hair growth 84–5
increased with waning moon 97, 98
and menstruation 55–60, 87
and old age 104–8
reduced in summer 96 n.180
regimen for 115, 120–1
humours 10, 48, 120–3, 135, 141, 147,
  165, 168
hymen, *see* defloration

inactivity, female 48, 58, 95, 104
insects 188–9
intercourse:
avoidance of during menstruation
  234–6, 249, 251
during menstruation 171, 234
in maintaining health 126–9
see also sexuality
irrationality 57, 74–6, 133, 139, 144

jejunum 218–19

katharsis 230–1
kuēma, see fetation

labia 78, 132 n.66
labour pains 212
see also childbirth
lactation 211
from menstrual blood 215–17
from mother's nutriment 218–19
time of 219–22
quality of milk 222–3
in suppression of conception 223–4
see also breasts
leucorrhoea 124, 155
lochia 63, 101, 142, 213–15, 243, 246
logos 182

marriage:
age of girls at 27 n.80, 47–8, 50
age of men at 54, 105
of half-siblings 153
purpose of 152
relations within 243–4

masturbation 54, 80
materia medica 30 n.90
menarche 47–55, 138–9, 143, 243
see also puberty
menopause 105–8, 134, 138, 177, 246–7
menstrual cloths 52 n.32, 152, 245
  n.66
menstrual huts 235, 238–40, 242
see also seclusion of women
menstruation, *passim*:
abundance of 134–5
accumulation in body 55–65
amount of 86–94
as a cure 136–47
frequency of 94–101
lack of reference to 114, 226–32, 234,
  243–7, 250 n.79
as pollutant 236–40, 249
retention of 125–34
synchronization of 97–101
vicarious 140, 143
Methodism, *see* Soranus
Metrodora, *see* physicians, female
midwives 32, 34–5, 36, 212–13
see also traditional medicine
mikvah 239
milk, *see* lactation
mirror 229–30
miscarriages 167 n.64, 173, 175, 200,
  220
see also abortion
misogyny 21, 37–40, 150–1, 178–9, 183,
  196, 234 n.24
see also gender
modesty, female 33–4, 35
moistness, *see* humidity
'moles' 136 n.82, 142, 161–2, 211 n.228
monster, *see* deformity
moon 94, 96, 97–101, 186 n.130, 233
mule 228–9
mythology 42–3, 148–9, 151–2, 232–4

night emissions 155
nose bleeds, *see* epistaxis
nourishment, two types of 205–9, 221–2
nous 185
nursing 223

observations, *see* empiricism
odour therapy 73–4, 131 n.55
oestrous 91–2, 171, 187, 229
ovaries 67–8
ovulation 95 n.173, 172, 224

Pandora 42-3, 101, 233-4
pangenesis 162-6, 168, 203
Parmenides 44-5
parthenogenesis 150-1, 161-2, 163, 183
parthenos 52
    see also girls, unmarried
parturition, *see* childbirth
passages in body 56-7, 66, 72, 77, 171
    widening of 48-9, 54, 62-3, 126, 154-5
penis 61, 78, 79-80, 154, 157-8, 187, 245
    n.66
pessaries 80, 88, 132, 133, 141, 174
phainomena 16, 17
Philistion 10 n.32, 13
physicians, female 31-3
physis 45-7, 59, 104, 115, 120-3, 140
plants 207-8
Plato 31, 75, 181
Pliny 23
PMS 125-6, 210 n.222, 252-3
pneuma 60, 61, 64, 185, 187, 189, 192, 216
pockets of womb, *see* horns
pollution, female 241, 246
    see also taboo
Poseidon 2, 245
pregnancy 144, 200-11
    frequency of 201, 213, 224
    pains of 210-11
    signs of 175, 201
    tests for 201-2
Presocratics 5, 43-5, 112, 149
principle 184, 189-93, 195, 199, 205, 208
prolapse, of womb 71, 76-7, 136 n.82,
    214
prostitutes 175 n.90
psychē 75
psychoanalytic theories of fear of
    menstruation 240
puberty 83, 103, 134, 143, 193 n.160, 242
    male 61, 154-5
Pythagoreans 13, 44, 149, 213 n.242
Pythia 246-7

quickening 210

rennet 188, 190
resemblance 160-1, 162, 168, 178-9,
    193-9
    see also pangenesis
rhoos, *see* flux
right, and left 28, 44, 167, 210 n.225, 220
ritual 101, 152, 237, 241-3, 246
    see also sacrifice

Rufus of Ephesus 25
Roman period 21, 25, 227 n.2, 230, 237
    medicine of 22-3, 250
    status of women in 108 n.226, 152
    n.18, 222, 248-50

sacred laws 231, 235-6, 245-7, 248
sacrifice 101-3, 214-15
scala naturae 17, 82, 183
scolex 206
Scythians 59
seasons 96 nn.180, 181
seclusion, of women 27 n.80, 97, 101,
    108, 114-15, 137, 244
seed, female 49, 53, 68, 78-9, 155
    see also conception, pangenesis, semen
semen 49, 53, 59, 60-1, 83-5, 87
    see also conception, pangenesis, seed,
    female
sex determination 28, 45, 46-7, 166-70,
    182-3, 185, 192-3
sexism, *see* misogyny
sexuality 155, 157-60, 177-8, 187 n.133,
    226
    female desire in 75-6, 80 n.126, 96
    n.180, 134
    'schools' of medicine 9-10
    see also Sicilian school
Sicilian school 13, 19, 25 n.78, 64 n.74
    see also 'schools' of medicine
social structure 241-53
Soranus 23-4
soul 184-6, 187, 190, 195, 205
    see also form, species
species 181-3, 193, 195
    see also form, soul
spleen 63
spontaneous generation 184 n.123
stoma 51, 62, 90, 92-4, 128-9
    in Aristotle 54, 130
    interior 67
    of vagina 78
    see also cervix, womb
stone, in the bladder 80-1
subincision 240
substance, Aristotelian 179-81, 190
suicide 29, 50
survival rates 144-6
sutures 81, 84

taboo 228, 234-43, 248-50
Talmud 227, 232-3

teeth 81-2
testicles 28, 116, 142, 167, 215
  parallel to female reproductive
    organs 67-8
  role in concocting semen 61, 187, 193
testimony, women's 27-31, 75 n.109,
  157-60, 174-5, 177, 247-8
  men's erroneous 28, 30-1
theories:
  Hippocratic 7-8
  Aristotelian 15-19
Thesmophoria 101
traditional medicine 29-31, 136, 153,
  157, 211 n.228
in *materia medica* 133, 152
in 'wandering womb' 74
  see also midwives, Asclepius
tragedy 26, 103, 111 n.2, 149, 246
twins 67, 167 n.64, 168-9, 220
  see also births, multiple

umbilicus 203, 207, 211, 213

uniform and non-uniform parts 164
urethra 66, 80-3

vagina, anatomy of 77-9, 80-3, 166, 245
  n.66
  lubrication of 155-7
  pathology of 114, 128, 136 n.82
virgin, *see* girls, unmarried

wet-nurse 222, 224 n.289
'whites', *see* leucorrhoea
wind-egg 161, 186, 206
womb, anatomy of 65-9, 142, 193, 217,
  219
  in conception 155-60, 166, 207, 209
  in menstruation 62-5
  pathology of 69-77, 106, 116, 128-9,
    135-6, 142
  in sex determination 167, 169-70
  volume of 90-4

Zeus 111 n.2, 149, 151, 245

INDEX LOCORUM

ACHILLES TATIUS
Leucippe and Cleitophon iv. 7.7: 249

ACTA SANCTORUM
Oct. III, 162: 134 n.76

AELIAN
Nat. An. 6. 36: 249 n.78

AESCHYLUS
Eum. 658–66: 149
736–8: 149

ALCMAEON
DK 24 B 3: 5 n.13

ANONYMUS LONDINENSIS
20. 25: 10 n.32

ANTIOCHINUS
fr. 135: 150 n.9

ANTIPHON
DK 87 B 36: 176 n.96

ARISTOPHANES
Eccl. 526–50: 28 n.85
Lys. 163–6: 76 n.112
1073: 245 n.66
fr. 504: 66 n.82

ARETAEUS
CD 2. II: 74 n.108
SA 2.I: 102 n.198

ARISTOTLE
An. Post. 96ᵇ15: 181 n.III
97ᵃ35–ᵇ6: 181 n.III
de. An. 416ᵃ12–20: 205 n.206
EN IIIIᵇ12: 185 n.125
1134ᵇ10, 1161ᵇ27: 148
1172ᵇ36: 29 n.88
GA 715ᵃ18–ᵇ7: 183 n.119
716ᵃ14–15: 183 n.117
716ᵃ18: 182 and n.114, 192 n.156
716ᵃ27–31: 46
716ᵇ5–12: 61 n.63

716ᵇ32–3: 67 n.85
717ᵃ35–ᵇ1: 187 n.136
717ᵇ23–718ᵃ15: 61 n.64
717ᵇ23–6: 187 and n.134
718ᵃ11–15: 61, 187 n.136
718ᵃ23–6: 187 n.137
719ᵃ19–21: 212 n.233
719ᵃ21–2: 76 n.116
719ᵇ29–34: 82 n.137
720ᵃ7–10: 82 n.137
720ᵃ12–14: 76 n.115
720ᵇ33–5: 31 n.94
721ᵇII: 165 n.59
721ᵇ30–4: 164 n.57
722ᵃ3–8: 164 n.56
722ᵃ10–11: 198 n.173
722ᵃ16–ᵇ4: 164 n.55
722ᵇ4–5: 163 n.52
722ᵇ7–30: 163 n.51
722ᵇ22–4: 163 n.53
723ᵃ2–23: 164 n.55
723ᵇ19–24: 194 n.164
723ᵇ33–724ᵃ4: 162 n.48
724ᵃ4–8: 164 n.57
724ᵃ10: 165 n.59
724ᵇ20: 207 n.211
725ᵃ11–22: 60 n.57
725ᵃ21–4: 194 n.163
726ᵃ33: 190
726ᵇ3–13: 60 n.57
726ᵇ31–727ᵃ1: 61 n.59
727ᵃ5–9: 177 n.98
727ᵃ5–7: 61 n.60
727ᵃ9–20: 104 n.208
727ᵃ9–10: 104 n.208, 177 n.100
727ᵃ12–16: 92 n.165, 140 n.91
727ᵃ16–19: 60 n.56
727ᵃ22–5: 65 n.76, 91
727ᵃ26–30: 53 n.37, 177 n.99
727ᵇ7–12: 178 n.103
727ᵇ7–11: 80 n.125
727ᵇ8: 159 n.36

727^{b}10–14, 99 n.190
727^{b}11: 186 n.130
727^{b}12–18: 186 n.131
727^{b}19–26: 234 n.25
727^{b}19: 186 n.132
727^{b}23–5: 99 n.190
727^{b}26–8: 200 n.180
727^{b}33–728^{a}2: 79
728^{a}17: 1 n.61, 46 n.15
728^{a}21–5: 130 n.51
728^{a}26–31: 207 and n.210
728^{a}31–4: 177 n.102
728^{a}32–4: 31 n.95, 79 and n.124
728^{b}15: 91
728^{b}19–23: 84 n.142
728^{b}22–32: 47
728^{b}26–7: 84 n.144
728^{b}27–31: 61 n.65
728^{b}28–31: 61 n.62
729^{a}12–14: 188 n.140
729^{a}26: 182 n.115
729^{b}18–21: 187 n.138
730^{b}1–4: 205
730^{b}2–4: 61 n.58
730^{b}25–32: 189 n.142
731^{a}19–21: 191
731^{b}18–732^{a}12: 60 n.53
732^{a}4–10: 183 n.121
732^{a}32: 206 n.208
733^{a}29: 159 n.36
733^{b}26–29: 206
734^{a}2–16: 189 n.145
734^{a}9–10: 191 n.153
734^{a}16–26: 204 n.202
734^{b}10–18: 190 n.147
736^{a}6–8: 191 n.149
736^{b}2–5: 17 n.56
736^{b}28: 185 n.126
737^{a}8–16: 190 n.146
737^{a}14–16: 188 n.141
737^{a}28: 182 n.116
737^{b}11: 46, 192 n.154
737^{b}28–34: 64 and n.74
738^{a}17–21: 98 n.185
738^{a}26–33: 124 n.32
738^{b}25: 189 n.143
738^{b}34: 194 n.165
739^{a}6–9: 206 n.209
739^{a}10–13: 187 n.134
739^{a}32–7: 79, 80 n.126
739^{b}17–20: 156 and n.28
739^{b}21–34: 188 n.140
739^{b}23: 188

739^{b}35: 207 n.211
740^{a}2–4: 205 n.203
740^{a}13–16: 189 n.144
740^{a}24–7: 207
740^{b}5–9: 207 n.212
741^{a}5–9: 150 n.9
741^{a}6–33: 179 n.106
741^{a}15–32: 162 n.44
741^{a}19–32: 186 n.129
741^{a}26–30: 185 n.128
741^{a}33–8: 183 n.118
741^{b}9: 190 n.147
741^{b}25–745^{b}22: 205 n.204
744^{b}11–27: 208 n.215
744^{b}16–18: 190 n.148
745^{a}2–4: 208 n.217
745^{b}23–6: 207 n.213
746^{a}20: 202 n.191
746^{b}27–9: 134 n.75
746^{b}31–5: 17 and n.58
747^{a}1–3: 134 n.75
747^{a}4–23: 17
747^{a}7–23: 77 n.119
747^{a}10–18: 202 n.188
748^{b}20–9: 229
750^{a}27–9: 200 n.183
751^{b}5–9: 206 n.207
751^{b}21–8: 206
752^{a}27: 206 n.208
753^{b}31–3: 208 n.214
758^{b}2–6: 176 and n.94, 191 n.152
758^{b}10–15: 206 n.208
759^{a}25–^{b}1: 31 n.94
760^{b}30–3: 18 and n.59
763^{b}33: 167 n.64
764^{a}12–20: 61, 167
764^{a}33–7: 44 n.9
764^{b}20–8: 166 n.63
765^{a}23–5: 167 n.65
765^{b}2–4: 191 n.149
765^{b}35–766^{b}10: 47
766^{a}10–11: 205
766^{a}18–22: 192 n.157
766^{a}24–30: 193 n.161
766^{a}35–767^{b}5: 192 n.155
766^{b}5–6: 193 n.160
766^{b}15–17: 192 n.157
766^{b}15: 191 n.151
766^{b}32: 191 n.149
767^{a}2–6: 95 n.175, 97 n.184
767^{b}18–20: 191 and n.150
767^{b}30: 195 n.167
768^{a}1: 192

Aristotle (*cont.*):
GA (*cont.*):
768ᵃ7–9: 196 n.169
768ᵃ11–14: 196
768ᵇ15–23: 197 n.172
771ᵃ31: 191 n.149
771ᵇ28–772ᵇ25: 198 n.174
772ᵃ35–ᵇ1: 199 n.176
772ᵇ7–11: 209 n.219
772ᵇ10–11: 210 n.223
773ᵃ14: 104 n.205
773ᵃ15–29: 54
773ᵃ16–20: 130
774ᵃ5–6: 135 n.79
775ᵃ4–9: 212 n.237
775ᵃ10–15: 210 n.224
775ᵃ15: 199 n.177
775ᵃ20–2: 104 n.206
775ᵃ32–3: 212 n.235
775ᵇ10–14: 201 n.185
775ᵇ25–35: 211 n.228
776ᵃ9–15: 136 n.81
776ᵃ15–25: 221 n.274
776ᵃ15–16: 221
776ᵃ25–ᵇ3: 209 n.218
776ᵃ34–ᵇ4: 211 n.229
776ᵇ4–5: 216 n.256
776ᵇ19–22: 61 n.66
776ᵇ29–32: 216 n.256
777ᵃ1–4: 221 n.275
777ᵃ8: 216 n.259
777ᵃ13–19: 224 n.287
777ᵃ21–8: 211 n.230
777ᵃ31–ᵇ16: 210 n.224
777ᵇ17–30: 96 n.181
777ᵇ20–31: 186 n.130
782ᵇ18: 84
783ᵃ23–7: 84 n.145
783ᵇ9–784ᵃ12: 85 n.147
HA 486ᵃ16–18: 182 n.112
488ᵇ24: 185 n.125
489ᵃ9–12: 178 n.103, 183 n.117
489ᵇ6–7: 192 n.158
489ᵇ7–9: 206 nn.207 and 208
491ᵃ34: 19 n.65
491ᵇ3–5: 81
493ᵃ14–15: 217 n.260
493ᵃ24–ᵇ6: 82 n.137
493ᵇ4–7: 82–3, 83 n.140
494ᵇ20–5: 17 n.56
494ᵇ33: 19 n.65
497ᵃ24–35: 82 n.137
501ᵇ20–4: 81 n.133

506ᵃ5–6: 197
510ᵃ13–29: 61 n.64, 187 n.135
512ᵇ1–5: 142
518ᵃ33–5: 134 n.76
521ᵃ24–25: 85 n.146
521ᵃ27: 129
521ᵇ26–522ᵃ1: 221 n.272
522ᵃ4: 221, 222 n.277
522ᵃ6–11: 217 n.261
522ᵃ11–21: 217
522ᵃ19–20: 28 n.84
522ᵇ3–5: 188 n.141
523ᵃ3–12: 222 n.278
523ᵃ9–10: 223 n.283
523ᵃ16: 191 n.149
524ᵃ3–9: 31 n.94
527ᵇ31–3: 187 n.133
537ᵇ22–538ᵃ4: 183 n.119
538ᵇ10: 82 n.136
539ᵃ30–ᵇ5: 150 n.9
541ᵇ1–12: 31 n.94
542ᵃ32: 96 n.180
543ᵇ26–31: 104 n.208
544ᵃ12–15: 31 n.94
545ᵇ26–31: 106, 177 n.101
553ᵇ27–31: 228
557ᵃ8–10: 147 n.116
560ᵃ21–8: 206 n.207
561ᵃ4–562ᵃ21: 204 n.201
573ᵃ7: 91
575ᵃ27–8: 209 n.219
575ᵇ27–30: 193 n.159
578ᵃ1–4: 228
578ᵇ14–15: 193 n.159
581ᵇ1–2: 102
581ᵇ19: 54 n.41
582ᵃ16–29: 53 n.38
582ᵃ16–17: 185 n.128
582ᵃ19–20: 185 n.128
582ᵃ21–4: 104 n.105
582ᵃ22–5: 200 n.183
582ᵃ34: 100
582ᵃ34–ᵇ3: 29 n.89
582ᵇ3–4: 96 n.181
582ᵇ5–6: 88 n.152
582ᵇ7–9: 125
582ᵇ7–8: 92 n.164
582ᵇ11–19: 171 n.75
582ᵇ11–12: 99 n.190, 186 n.131
582ᵇ19–22: 200 n.180
582ᵇ22–6: 76
582ᵇ25: 94 n.172
583ᵃ12: 123 n.30

Index Locorum

583^a15: 160 n.40
583^a25: 173 and n.85, 191 n.152
583^a31-3: 221 n.273
583^a31-3: 215 n.252
583^b3-7: 205 n.206, 210 n.225
583^b12-21: 211 n.226
583^b23-8: 104 n.205, 105 n.214
584^a3^b19: 126 n.41
584^a6-9: 221 n.273
584^a22-5: 208 n.216
584^a26-30: 212 n.236
584^b10-14: 210 n.223
585^a34-^b1: 185 n.128
585^b23-4: 192 n.157
587^a9: 213 n.239
587^a31: 202 n.190
587^a32-3: 223 n.282
587^b2-5: 201
587^b4-6: 213 and n.243
587^b15-17: 223 n.284
587^b19-21: 222 n.276
587^b25-7: 223 n.286
587^b27-32: 224 n.291
$604^b30-605^a1$: 211 n.228
$608^a11-609^a18$: 57
630^b8-11: 228
632^a22-30: 67
HA 10: 15 and n.46
634^a35-40: 125 n.38
634^b36-9: 156 n.29
635^b19: 157 and n.30
635^b29-31: 157 n.31
636^b12-24: 156, 159 n.37
636^b35-40: 159 n.37
637^a1-4: 160
637^a3-15: 162
637^a11-15: 166 n.61
637^a23-8: 158 and n.34
637^b10: 162
637^b16-18: 161
637^b17-20: 150 n.9
637^b18-19: 165 n.60
637^b22-4: 162 n.45
638^a22-5: 161 n.43
638^a31-5: 211 n.228
IA 707^b5-28: 18 n.62
Insomn. $459^b24-460^a23$: 229 and n.8
Long. 466^b14-16: 104 n.207
Metaph. 986^a23-^b5: 44
1032^a12-25: 180 n.110
1034^a7: 181 n.111
$1038^b1-1039^a2$: 181 n.111
1038^b14: 195 n.166

1058^a29-31: 182
1058^b21-4: 182 n.113
1071^a19-23: 195 n.166
1071^a27-9: 195 n.166
PA 644^a24-5: 181 n.111
648^a29-30: 44
648^a34: 44 and n.10
650^a3-32: 60 n.54
653^a27-9: 81 n.131
653^b1-3: 81 n.131
656^a2-7: 82 n.138
656^b13: 19 and n.65
658^b2-6: 84 n.143
661^b34-6: 81 n.134
666^b21-4: 18 n.60
670^b17-22: 44
676^a4-5: 218
683^a23-6: 183 n.120
688^a17-22: 216 n.258
688^b20-11: 217 n.262
688^b29-30: 219
689^a4-17: 82 n.137
689^a6-9: 82 and n.139
689^a11-12: 14 n.45
Pol. 1260^a12: 185 n.125
1335^a28-32: 105 n.215

ARISTOTLE, PSEUDO-
Prob. 879^a26-35: 96 n.180
880^a11-22: 96 n.180
893^b10-17: 84 n.141

ARRIAN
Epict. 2. 18. 13: 96 n.181

CENSORINUS
De die natalis 6. 1-3: 202 and n.191
6. 1: 203 n.196

CHARITON
Chaereas and Callirrhoe 2. 8. 4-11: 28 n.85

COLUMELLA
RR 10. 357-63: 249 n.78
11. 338: 249 n.78

DEMOSTHENES
40. 12-13: 54 n.40
40. 56: 54 n.40
57. 20: 153 n.20

DEMOCRITUS
DK 68 B 122a: 5 n.13
148: 5 n.13, 207 n.213

DIODORUS SICULUS
Bibl. Hist. 1. 80. 4: 150 n.10
16. 26. 6: 247 n.72

DIOGENES
DK 64 B 6. 9: 5 n.13

EMPEDOCLES
DK 31 B 57–67: 5 n.13
68: 220, 221
69: 210 n.221
153a: 173 n.84, 205 n.205
DK 62 B 65: 44
67: 44

EPICHARMUS
DK 23 B 59: 5 n.13, 210 n.221

EURIPIDES
Andr. 930–53: 28 n.85
El. 527–9: 58 n.49
654, 1131–3: 246
Hipp. 293–6: 34 n.102
IT 382–3: 246 n.69

GALEN
Anatom. Admin. 2. 1: 8 n.27
Dieb. Dec. 3. 2: 97 n.182
Ut. Diss. 4: 74 n.108
10: 67 n.84

GELLIUS, AULUS
Attic Nights 12. 1: 222 n. 280

GENESIS
3: 16: 232
31: 35: 226

GEOPONICA
1. 6: 100 n. 192
5. 10: 100 n. 192

HERODOTUS
Histories 1. 5: 175 n.90
1. 198: 227
2. 64: 227

HESIOD
Op. 60–95: 42
63: 43
102–4: 111 n.2
176: 43 n.6
582–9: 96 n.180
753–5: 230 and n.13
Th. 513: 43 n.6
570–616: 42

57²: 43
592–9: 58 n.49
927–8: 151 n.15

Hesychius
s.v. στέφανον ἐκφέρειν 55 n.43

HIPPOCRATES
Acut. 7 (ii. 268. 9–11): 66 n.82
34 (ii. 296. 1–6): 120
Acut. App. 9 (ii. 442. 2): 145 n.114
10 (ii. 450. 4): 145 n.114
Aër. 1 (ii. 12. 9–14): 2 n.5
2 (ii. 14. 1–19): 8 n.28
3–4 (ii. 14. 20–22. 14): 113 n.7
3 (ii. 14. 19–18. 17): 118
(ii. 18. 2–5): 119
4 (ii. 18. 18–22. 14): 118
(ii. 18. 23): 120
(ii. 20. 13–14): 143 n.106
(ii. 22. 1–3): 119
8 (ii. 36. 9–16): 7 n.23
9 (ii. 38. 23–5): 80 n.128
(ii. 40. 7–42. 5): 80 n.129
10 (ii. 46. 3–4): 119
(ii. 46. 5–7): 121
(ii. 50. 6–9): 121 n.23
14 (ii. 60. 1–2): 162 n.46
(ii. 60. 2): 164
20–2 (ii. 72. 22–82. 5): 59
21 (ii. 76. 4–5): 87
22 (ii. 78. 10–11): 163
Aff. 20 (vi. 228. 20–230. 22): 63 n.73
Alim. 17 (ix. 104. 5): 114
37 (ix. 110. 16–18): 215 n.252
40 (ix. 112. 4–7): 204 n.200
(ix. 112. 7–9): 222 and n.281
42 (ix. 112. 12–116. 2): 209 n.219
(ix. 114. 2–3): 210 n.221
Aph. 1. 21. 5 (iv. 468. 11–470. 7): 143 n.103
3. 11 (iv. 490. 4–5): 121
3. 14 (iv. 492. 3–4): 121 n.23
3. 27 (iv. 500. 1–3): 143–4
3. 28 (iv. 500. 4–8): 143 n.104
5. 28 (iv. 542. 5–6): 132 n.68
5. 31 (iv. 542. 12–13): 200 n.181
5. 32 (iv. 542. 14): 92 n.165, 139 n.90
5. 33 (iv. 544. 1–2): 92 n.165, 139 n.90
5. 36 (iv. 544. 7–8): 141 and n.96
5. 38 (iv. 544. 11–13): 167 n.64, 220 n.268
5. 39 (iv. 544. 14–15): 216 n.257
5. 42 (iv. 546. 4–5): 211 n.226

5. 44 (iv. 546. 8–9): 200 n.182
5. 49 (iv. 550. 3–4): 214 n.245
5. 50 (iv. 550. 5–6): 58 n.50, 92 n.165,
  142 n.100, 215 n.255
5. 52 (iv. 550. 9–11): 220 n.269
5. 57 (iv. 552. 11): 88, 134 n.77
5. 59 (iv. 554. 3–6): 73 n.104
5. 60 (iv. 554. 7–8): 200 n.180
5. 61 (iv. 554. 9–11): 175 n.91, 201
  n.185
6. 12 (iv. 566. 7–8): 144 n.108
6. 21 (iv. 568. 7–8): 144
6. 29 (iv. 570. 6): 131 n.57
Art. 42–4 (iv. 182. 13–188. 16): 71 n.98
57 (iv. 246. 9): 70 n.90
Carn. 19 (viii. 608. 22–610. 10): 174
Coac. 2. 304 (v. 650. 15–17): 132 n.67
406 (v. 676. 9): 145 n.114
513 (v. 702. 18–19): 145 n.114
520 (v. 704. 9–10): 139
537 (v. 706. 15–16): 125 n.39
541 (v. 708. 2–3): 125 n.39
de Arte 5 (vi. 8. 3–6): 7 n.20
11 (vi. 20. 7–9): 30–1, 31 n.93
Decent. 12 (ix. 238. 19–240. 4): 34
Epid. 1. 8 (ii. 642. 4–8): 143 n.105
  (ii. 646 9–648, 5): 138 and n.86
1. 9 (ii. 646. 9–12): 212 n.231
  (ii. 656. 2–6): 117
  (ii. 658. 6–10): 138 n.86
  (ii. 658. 10–12): 140 n.93
1. 13 case i (ii. 682. 14–15): 145 n.112
case iv (ii. 690. 12): 211 n.227
case v (ii. 694. 7): 211 n.227
case xi (ii. 708. 7): 211 n.227
case xiv (ii. 716. 5–14): 144 n.110
2. 1. 6 (v. 76. 13–16): 215 n.253
  (v. 76. 13–14): 220 n.268
2. 2. 8 (v. 88. 7–8): 52 n.34
2. 2. 16 (v. 90. 5–6): 223 n.285
2. 3. 1 (v. 102. 20–104. 3): 114 n.8
2. 3. 17 (v. 118. 2–3): 175 n.91, 176
  (v. 118. 8–9): 210 n.222
  (v. 118. 9–11): 220 and n.270
  (v. 118. 10–11): 216
2. 4. 5 (v. 126. 10–14): 214 n.247
2. 5. 1 (v. 128. 3–5): 28 n.82
2. 5. 5 (v. 130. 2): 142 n.100
2. 5. 6 (v. 130. 2–5): 171 n.78
  (v. 130. 3): 142
2. 5. 8 (v. 130. 6–7): 202
2. 6. 17 (v. 136. 8–9): 219 n.266
2. 6. 19 (v. 136. 11–12): 57 and n.47

3. 1 (v. 104. 1): 52 n.34
case vi (iii. 50. 1–52. 9): 139 n.87
case vii (iii. 52. 11–54. 7): 144 n.110
case ix (iii. 58. 1–7): 144 n.110
3. 2. 12 (iii. 64. 1): 211 n.227
3. 3. 17 case ii (iii. 110. 1): 211 n.227
case xiv (iii. 140. 15): 211 n.227
3. 12 (iii. 136. 9–10): 52
3. 14 (iii. 96. 4–98. 1): 117
3. 17 case i (iii. 104. 5): 145 n.112
case vii (iii. 122. 1–17): 139 n.87
case viii (iii. 124. 7): 145 n.111
case xi (iii. 134. 1–14): 139
case xii (iii. 136. 1–12): 139 n.87
case xv (iii. 142. 6–146. 6): 139
4. 10 (v. 148. 24–150. 4): 223 n.285
4. 19 (v. 156. 4–15): 46 n.14
4. 21 (v. 160. 13–162. 3): 175 n.91
  (v. 160. 15–162. 1): 96 n.179
4. 22 (v. 162. 5): 211 n.227
  (v. 162. 7): 211 n.227
4. 24 (v. 164. 8): 212 n.232
  (v. 164. 9–10): 131 n.59
4. 25 (v. 168. 15–17): 139 and n.88
4. 26 (v. 170. 8–17): 27 n.80
4. 38 (v. 180. 5–14): 131 n.60
5. 12 (v. 212. 5–10): 139
  (v. 212. 9 10): 106 n.41
5. 14 (v. 212. 20–214. 6): 145 n.115
5. 39 (v. 230. 21–33): 46 n.14
5. 42 (v. 232. 9–16): 171 n.78
5. 50 (v. 236. 11–20): 27 n.80
5. 53 (v. 238. 8): 202 n.189
5. 63 (v. 242. 8): 142 n.101
5. 80 (v. 250. 8): 145 n.113
5. 91 (v. 254. 7–10): 131 n.60
5. 93 (v. 254. 13–14): 46 n.14
5. 97 (v. 256. 9–12): 46 n.14
5. 103 (v. 258. 9–12): 212 nn.232, 234
6. 1. 4 (v. 268. 1–2): 143 n.104
6. 2. 25 (v. 290. 7–12): 167 n.64
6. 3. 1 (v. 334. 13): 106 n.220
6. 3. 14 (v. 300. 1–2): 53, 54
6. 4. 21 (v. 312. 10–11): 28 n.83, 167
6. 5. 1 (v. 314. 5–13): 138 n.85
6. 5. 11 (v. 318. 14–15): 65
6. 7. 1 (v. 334. 13): 147 n.117
  (v. 334. 14–18): 137 n.83
  (v. 334. 14–15): 138
6. 8. 10 (v. 348. 3–5): 30
6. 32 (v. 356. 4–15): 134 n.74
7. 6 (v. 376. 20–1): 210 n.225
7. 8 (v. 378. 19): 106 n.220

HIPPOCRATES *(cont.)*
Epid. *(cont.)*
7. 52 (v. 420. 14): 46 n.14
7. 101 (v. 454. 4): 106 n.220
7. 106 (v. 456. 14–17): 46 n.14
7. 123 (v. 468. 4–6): 140 n.94
Genit. 1 (vii. 470. 1–21): 162 n.47
2 (vii. 472. 16–474. 4): 46, 48
3 (vii. 474. 11–13): 155 and n.25
4 (vii. 474. 14–18): 78–9, 79 n.122
  (vii. 474. 14): 155
  (vii. 474. 14–476. 8): 157
  (vii. 474. 16–18): 155 n.27
  (vii. 476. 8–12): 127 n.43
  (vii. 476. 12–14): 127 n.44
  (vii. 476. 14–15): 125 n.37
  (vii. 476. 16): 11
5 (vii. 476. 17–20): 28
  (vii. 476. 17–19): 172
7 (vii. 478. 16–24): 168 n.67
8 (vii. 480. 8–9): 168 n.68
  (vii. 480. 13–14): 162
9 (vii. 482. 9–22): 65 n.78
11 (vii. 484. 15–16): 165
  (vii. 484. 18–19): 165 n.58
Gland. 1 (viii. 556. 1–7): 56 and n.44
  (viii. 556. 4): 87 n.148
3 (viii. 556. 18–558. 7): 87 n.149
16 (viii. 572. 1): 57
  (viii. 572. 2–3): 56
  (viii. 572. 3–7): 218
  (viii. 572. 13): 58 n.49
17 (viii. 574. 2–8): 215
Haem. (vi. 426. 9–442. 25): 132
9 (vi. 444. 1–5): 132 n.66
Hebd. 5 (viii. 636. 21–2): 46 n.14
51 (viii. 669. 16): 116 n.14
Hum. 5 (v. 482. 14): 114
Int. 10–13 (vii. 188. 26–200. 23): 132
13 (vii. 200. 3): 132
30–4 (vii. 244. 6–252. 16): 63 n.73
Jusj. (iv. 628. 6–630. 2): 32 and n.97
  (iv. 630. 9–10): 174
  (iv. 630. 11–12): 8
  (iv. 630. 14–15): 33 and n.100
Lex 2–3 (iv. 638. 11–640. 12): 32 n.97
Loc. Hom. 40 (vi. 330. 16–19): 132
47 (vi. 344. 3–4): 135
  (vi. 344. 7): 78
Medic. 1 (ix. 206. 4–10): 33
Morb. 1. 7 (vi. 152. 21–2): 139 n.90
  (vi. 152. 20–1): 92 n.165, 139 n.90
2. 8 (vii. 16. 11–12): 19 and n.64

2. 12 (vii. 20. 11–15): 132
2. 36 (vii. 52. 15–21): 8 n.25
2. 47 (vii. 70. 4–72): 8 n.25
4. 32 (vii. 542. 6–7): 121 n.21
  (vii. 542. 9): 120
4. 38 (vii. 556. 3–6): 144 and n.107
4. 41 (vii. 562. 8–10): 114
4. 45 (vii. 568. 13–16): 87 n.149
  (vii. 568. 14–16): 58
4. 55 (vii. 600. 3–21): 223 n.284
  (vii. 604. 6): 116 n.14
4. 57 (vii. 610. 3): 116 n.14
  (vii. 612. 19–21): 119 and n.19, 121, 135
Morb. Sacr. 2 (vi. 364. 19–20): 162 n.46
5 (vi. 368. 10–11): 120
7 (vi. 372. 4–374. 2): 2 n.3
11 (vi. 380. 20–382. 1): 2 n.4
  (vi. 382. 6–11): 8 n.27
13 (vi. 384. 22–386. 4): 3 n.6
Mul. 1. 1: 11
  (viii. 10. 1–2): 126
  (viii. 10. 1–9): 63 and n.72
  (viii. 10. 1–12. 5): 214 n.248
  (viii. 10. 7–8): 12
  (viii. 10. 11–12. 5): 126 n.40
  (viii. 10. 13–15): 129 n.50
  (viii. 10. 16–19): 72 n.102
  (viii. 12. 2–4): 90
  (viii. 12. 2): 56
  (viii. 12. 6–21): 55
  (viii. 12. 19–21): 129
  (viii. 12. 21): 45
  (viii. 14. 2–3): 95 n.175
  (viii. 14. 5–7): 48, 58 n.49
1. 2 (viii. 14, 16, 18, 19): 70 n.91
  (viii. 14. 8–24. 19): 127 n.42
  (viii. 14. 8–9): 125 n.37
  (viii. 14. 9–10): 127
  (viii. 14. 10): 65
  (viii. 14. 12–14): 128
  (viii. 14. 14–19): 128 n.48
  (viii. 14. 16–17): 127 n.43
  (viii. 14. 17–16. 1): 72 n.101
  (viii. 16. 1–2): 51 n.30, 127 n. 45
  (viii. 16. 2–18. 14): 133 n.73
  (viii. 16. 3–4): 62
  (viii. 16. 3): 96 n.181
  (viii. 18. 16–18): 131 n.61
  (viii. 18. 21–20. 25): 132 n.64
  (viii. 20. 25–22. 1): 92 n.165, 139 n.90
  (viii. 22. 1–2): 12

(viii. 22. 3–4): 139 n.89
I. 3 (viii. 22. 9–10): 132 n.69
(viii. 22. 12–13): 130 n.53
(viii. 22. 12): 130
(viii. 26. 10–12): 131 n.58
I. 4 (viii. 26. 5): 96 n.178
I. 5 (viii. 28. 10–11): 134 n.78
(viii. 28. 11): 128 n.47
(viii. 28. 12, 15): 58 n.50
(viii. 28. 13): 62
I. 6 (viii. 30. 6–11): 87, 88 n.150, 89
(viii. 30. 11–13): 113
(viii. 30. 16–17): 101 and n.195
(viii. 30. 17–19): 134
(viii. 30. 20): 58
(viii. 30. 21–2): 201
I. 7 (viii. 32. 1–7): 106
(viii. 32. 2): 71 n.96
(viii. 32. 4–7): 72 n.101
(viii. 32. 7–8): 70 n.95
(viii. 32. 7–8): 70 n.93
(viii. 32. 8): 70 n.94
(viii. 34. 1–2): 70 n.93
I. 8 (viii. 34. 9–10): 153–4
(viii. 36. 9–10, 14–15): 141 n.98
(viii. 36. 10): 130 n.52
(viii. 38. 1–2): 141 n.99
I. 8–12 (viii. 34. 6–56. 12): 122
I. 9 (viii. 38. 10–12): 141 n.98
(viii. 40. 1): 130 n.52
(viii. 40. 5–6): 141 n.99
I. 10 (vii. 42. 1): 128 n.46
(viii. 40. 12–42. 8): 173
(viii. 40. 13–14): 160 n.40
I. 11 (viii. 42. 9–18): 152
(viii. 42. 9–16): 30 n.90
(viii. 44. 3–8): 141 and n.97
(viii. 44. 3): 123
(viii. 44. 20): 58 n.50, 116
(viii. 44. 22–4): 141
(viii. 46. 14): 173
(viii. 46. 19–24): 174
(viii. 46. 20–1): 154 n.22
(viii. 46. 22–4): 116
I. 12 (viii. 48. 19): 174 n.86
(viii. 50. 9): 116
I. 13 (viii. 50. 19–52. 8): 74 n.106
(viii. 51. 1): 36 n.107
I. 16 (viii. 54. 1): 154 n.22, 174 n.86
I. 17 (viii. 56. 15–19): 171 and n.75
(viii. 56. 15–17): 234 n.25
(viii. 56. 16–17): 99 n.190
(viii. 56. 17–22): 62 n.68

(viii. 56. 19–21): 158
(viii. 56. 20–2): 79 n.123
I. 19 (viii. 58. 10): 88 n.151
(viii. 58. 11): 36 n.107, 80 n.27
(viii. 58. 13): 80 n.27
I. 20 (viii. 58. 15–60. 3): 51 n.29
I. 21 (viii. 60. 16–17): 36
I. 23 (viii. 62. 12–18): 30 n.90
I. 24 (viii. 62. 20–1): 62 n.68, 154, 171
   n.75
(viii. 64. 1): 163 n.50
(viii. 64. 3–5): 62 and n.69, 100
   n.193
(viii. 64. 4–5): 171 n.76
(viii. 64. 5–6): 155 n.26
(viii. 64. 9–11): 130 n.52
I. 25 (viii. 64. 19–66. 1): 200 n.179, 204
   n.198
(viii. 66. 1–3): 95 n.175
I. 27 (viii. 70. 18–22): 220
I. 30 (viii. 74. 11): 101 n.196
I. 32 (viii. 76. 4–6): 200 n.183
I. 33 (viii. 78. 1–10): 212 n.223
I. 34 (viii. 78. 15): 211 n.226
(viii. 78. 16–80. 5): 34
(viii. 78. 17–80. 5): 212 and n.238
(viii. 80. 3–5): 212
I. 37 (viii. 88, 18–90. 4): 214 n.245
(viii. 90. 9–10): 80 n.127
(viii. 92. 2–3): 88
I. 38 (viii. 94. 5–10): 136 n.82
(viii. 94. 9–10): 75 n.111
(viii. 94. 17): 142, 214
I. 40 (viii. 96. 10): 78
(viii. 96. 16): 214 n.245
(viii. 98. 1): 36 n.107
I. 41 (viii. 98. 6): 214 n.246
(viii. 98. 10–11): 48 n.19
(viii. 100. 2–3): 214 n.246
I. 44 (viii. 102. 5–6): 12
I. 46 (viii. 106. 7–8): 213
(viii. 106. 7): 35 n.105
I. 47 (viii. 106. 16–17): 212 n.233
I. 53–4 (viii. 112. 6–20): 123 n.29
I. 57–8 (viii. 114. 8–116. 19): 123 n.29
I. 57 (viii. 114. 8–13): 94 n.172
I. 59 (viii. 118. 3): 36 n.107
(viii. 118. 10): 80 n.127
I. 59–61 (viii. 120–126. 3): 135 n.80
I. 60 (viii. 120. 8–9): 36 n.107
I. 61 (viii. 124. 7): 101 n.196
(viii. 124. 15–21): 65
I. 62 (viii. 126, 4–19): 30

HIPPOCRATES (*cont.*)
Mul. (*cont.*)
(viii. 126. 7): 113
(viii. 126. 8): 125 n. 37
(viii. 126. 14–19): 112 and n. 4
1. 64 (viii. 132. 11–13): 36 n. 107
1. 68 (viii. 142. 20–144. 16): 212 n. 234
(viii. 144. 22–4): 35 n. 105, 213 n. 240
1. 71 (viii. 148. 24–150. 22): 136 n. 82,
161 n. 43
(viii. 150. 1–2, 9–10): 219 n. 266
(viii. 150. 19–22): 142
1. 72 (viii. 152. 7–12): 213
(viii. 152. 7): 101
1. 73 (viii. 152. 22–154. 1): 12
(viii. 154. 2–5): 218
1. 74 (viii. 154. 12–13): 98 n. 186
1. 76 (viii. 170. 7–8): 173 n. 82
1. 77 (viii. 172. 6–7): 142, 212
1. 78 (viii. 190. 3–4): 90 n. 159
(viii. 194. 13–15): 90 n. 159
1. 80 (viii. 200. 18–21): 90 n. 159
2. 110 (viii. 234. 3–5): 130 n. 52
(viii. 236. 20–238. 1): 142
2. 111 (viii. 238. 16–240. 4): 123 n. 31
(viii. 238. 16–17): 122
(viii. 238. 22–240. 1): 105 n. 210, 106
2. 113 (viii. 242. 9–10): 102, 130 n. 52
2. 114 (viii. 246. 6–9): 130 n. 52
2. 119 (viii. 260. 21): 106 n. 220
2. 120 (viii. 262. 10): 147 n. 117
2. 121 (viii. 264. 18–19):
106 n. 220, 126 n. 41
(viii. 264. 19–20): 147 n. 117
2. 123 (viii. 266. 11): 70 n. 89, 73 n. 103
2. 124 (viii. 266. 20): 70 nn. 89, 95, 72
n. 103
2. 126 (viii. 270. 20–272. 1): 74 n. 106
2. 127 (viii. 272. 9): 70 nn. 89, 92
2. 128 (viii. 274. 10): 70 n. 95
(viii. 274. 17): 96 n. 178
(viii. 276. 8): 126 n. 41
2. 133 (viii. 280. 7–282): 175 n. 91
(viii. 282. 10–284. 1): 136 n. 82
(viii. 282. 10–12): 215 n. 254
(viii. 298. 3–4): 96 n. 178
(viii. 302. 11): 126 n. 41
2. 134 (viii. 302. 13): 70 n. 95
2. 137 (viii. 310. 6–7): 70 n. 89
(viii. 310. 10–12): 147 n. 117
(viii. 310. 10–11): 71 n. 97, 106
2. 138 (viii. 310. 23–4): 70 n. 94
(viii. 312. 1–2): 116

2. 142 (viii. 314. 22–4): 74 n. 106
2. 143 (viii. 316. 1–4): 214 n. 249
(viii. 316. 1–3): 71 n. 98
2. 144 (viii. 316. 13–18): 214 n. 249
(viii. 316. 13): 136 n. 82
(viii. 318. 21): 71 n. 98
2. 145 (viii. 320. 11–12): 123 n. 31
2. 146 (viii. 322. 3): 67
(viii. 322. 8–14): 73 n. 104
2. 149 (viii. 326. 1): 77 n. 118
2. 150 (viii. 326. 8): 70 n. 92
2. 153 (viii. 328. 1–3): 116
(viii. 328. 3–5): 71 n. 98
2. 162 (viii. 338. 14): 67
162 (viii. 338. 15–16): 160 n. 40, 173
(viii. 340. 3): 125 n. 36
2. 166 (viii. 344. 12–13): 92–3, 93 n. 167
2. 167 (viii. 344. 22–4): 92–3, 93 n. 167
2. 168 (viii. 346. 19–20): 160 n. 40
2. 169 (viii. 350. 9–10): 126 n. 41
2. 170 (viii. 350. 16–17): 65
2. 182 (viii. 364. 14–15): 133 n. 72
(viii. 364. 15): 122 n. 28
2. 185 (viii. 366. 6–20): 73 n. 105
2. 186 (viii. 366. 21–386. 5): 223 n. 286
2. 188 (viii. 368. 19–22): 108 n. 225
2. 201 (viii. 384. 1): 70 n. 94
2. 209 (viii. 404. 21–406. 1): 91 n. 160
2. 212 (viii. 406. 16): 136 n. 82
Nat. Hom. 4 (vi. 38. 19–40. 1): 120
5 (vi. 42. 20–44. 2): 121 n. 21
9 (vi. 52. 14–54. 1): 113 n. 7
11 (vi. 58. 1–60. 19): 7 n. 19
(vi. 58. 13): 142
12 (vi. 60. 20–64. 14): 147 n. 117
(vi. 64. 3–10): 105 n. 209
Nat. Mul. 1 (vii. 312. 1–8): 123 n. 31
(vii. 312. 3, 9–10): 122
(vii. 312. 6–7): 105 n. 210, 106
(vii. 312. 12–13): 123
2 (vii. 314. 13): 126 n. 41
3 (vii. 314. 16–18): 71 n. 96
(vii. 314. 16–17): 53 n. 36
(vii. 314. 21): 74 n. 106
(vii. 316. 5): 126 n. 41
4–5 (vii. 316. 9–318. 23): 71 n. 98
4 (vii. 316. 9–11): 214 n. 249
5 (vii. 20–318. 3): 214 n. 249?
6 (vii. 320. 1): 36
8 (vii. 324. 5–7): 234 n. 25
(vii. 324. 9): 126 n. 41
13 (vii. 330. 12–13): 88
14 (vii. 332. 6–7): 74 n. 106

16 (vii. 336. 1–5): 94 n.172
18 (vii. 338. 3–22): 131 n.55
(vii. 338. 5–6): 131 n.62
(vii. 338. 7): 131 n.56
(vii. 338. 8–9): 132 n.70
22 (vii. 340. 15–20): 152
32 (vii. 346. 14–18): 133 n.71
33 (vii. 370. 11–12): 91 n.161
35 (vii. 378. 18–20): 126 n.41
44 (vii. 388. 6–8): 116
53 (vii. 394. 13): 88
59 (vii. 398. 7): 96 n.178, 98 n.186
67 (vii. 402. 6–12): 51 n.29
96 (vii. 412. 19–414. 3): 73 n.104
98 (vii. 414. 20): 173 n.82
99 (vii. 416. 1–3): 77 n.120, 202 n.187
Nat. Puer. 12 (vii. 486. 2): 173
13–14 (vii. 488. 22–492. 18): 204 n.198
13 (vii. 488. 22): 174 n.87
(vii. 490. 2–3): 174 n.87
(vii. 490. 5–7): 28 and n.86
(vii. 490. 12–492. 2): 203 n.193
(vii. 490. 13–14): 176 and n.95
(vii. 492. 2): 174 n.87
14 (vii. 492. 7–15): 176 n.96
15 (vii 494. 18–20): 99 n.190
(vii. 492. 21–494. 5): 126
(vii. 492. 21–494. 2): 62
(vii. 494. 4): 63
(vii. 494. 10–13): 98 and n.187
(vii. 494. 10–15): 63
(vii. 494. 11–15): 49 n.20
(vii. 494. 13–15): 49 and n.21
(vii. 494. 18–20): 62 n.68, 171 n.75
(vii. 494. 22–3): 45
(vii. 496. 9–10): 11
17 (vii. 496. 18): 204 n.199
(vii. 496. 19–20): 164 n.54
(vii. 498. 14–15): 66
(vii. 498. 15–25): 164 n.54
18 (vii. 498. 27): 205 n.206
(vii. 500. 1–2): 210
(vii. 502. 4–6): 214 n.244
(vii. 502. 6–7): 101, 214 n.250
(vii. 502. 20–504. 2): 213 n.241
20 (vii. 506. 23–510. 17): 83
(vii. 508. 6–7): 49, 155
21: 12
(vii. 510. 18–25): 219 n.266
(vii. 512. 2–3): 55
(vii. 512. 3–7): 218 and n.263
(vii. 512. 14–16): 214
(vii. 512. 16–18): 218 and n.263

(vii. 512. 16): 218 n.264
(vii. 512. 18–20): 219 n.265
22–6 (vii. 514. 6–528. 16): 207 n.211
26 (vii. 526. 19–528. 2): 150 n.10
30: 12
(vii. 530. 20): 211 n.228
(vii. 532. 6): 65
(vii. 532. 14–534. 10): 209 n.220
(vii. 532. 14–15): 175 n.92
(vii. 532. 16–18): 65 n.78
(vii. 532. 17–19): 175
(vii. 532. 18–534. 10): 175 n.91
(vii. 536. 5–6): 211 n.228
(vii. 538. 8–11): 212 n.233
(vii. 538. 17–27): 213
31 (vii. 540. 1–16): 67
(vii. 540. 16–542. 2): 169
Praec. 2 (ix. 254. 4–5): 29
Prog. 1 (ii. 110. 1–8): 7 n.20
7 (ii. 126. 13–128. 1): 143
(ii. 128. 3–4): 143 n.106
9 (ii. 134. 3–4): 116 n.14
12 (ii. 142. 1–3): 118 n.17
21 (ii. 172. 12–14): 143 n.106
24 (ii. 184. 8–12): 118 n.17
Prorrh. 1. 123 (v. 552. 5–554. 1): 133
1. 132 (v. 558. 1): 145 n.114
1. 141 (v. 562. 5): 145 n.114
1. 142–3 (v. 562. 6–10): 125 n.39
2. 8 (ix. 28. 2–6): 132 and n.65
2. 24 (ix. 54. 11): 57 n.46
(ix. 54. 14–15): 96
Salubr. 2 (vi. 74. 4–76. 5): 120
(vi. 74. 14–16): 120
(vi. 74. 21–76. 1): 105 n.209
5 (vi. 78. 3–80. 17): 87 n.149, 124
n.33
6 (vi. 82. 2–6): 120–1, 121 n.22
Septim./Oct. 2 (vii. 438. 8–11): 210 n.222
4 (vii. 440. 13–442. 1): 175 n.92
(vii. 440. 14–442. 1): 30 and n.91
(vii. 442. 3–4): 209 n.219
(vii. 442. 4): 210 n.221
(vii. 442. 5–6): 203 n.194
9 (vii. 446. 19–448. 1): 173 n.83
(vii. 448. 2): 173 n.84
(vii. 448. 5–7): 95–6, 96 n.177
(vii. 448. 19–21): 173 n.84
(vii. 450. 1–4): 205 n.205
(vii. 450. 4–10): 210 n.224
(vii. 450. 9): 104 n.205
(vii. 450. 10): 104, 124 n.35
10 (vii. 452. 4–8): 210 n.222

HIPPOCRATES (*cont.*)
Septim./Oct. (*cont.*)
13 (vii. 458. 11–460. 9): 98, 172 and
   n. 80
(vii. 458. 11–460. 1): 175 n. 92
(vii. 458. 16–17): 88
(vii. 460. 7–9): 209 n. 220
Steril. 213 (viii. 408. 15–16): 92
(viii. 408. 16–17): 36
(viii. 412. 1–3): 58 n. 50
(viii. 412. 1): 92
(viii. 412. 5–6): 176 n. 96
(viii. 412. 24–414. 3): 88
214 (viii. 414. 17–19): 30 n. 90
215 (viii. 416. 8–11): 175
216: 46 n. 13
(viii. 416. 20–3): 45, 222 n. 279
219 (viii. 424. 1–13): 73 n. 104
220 (viii. 424. 16–21): 160 n. 40, 173
222 (viii. 428. 15–18): 160 n. 40
(viii. 430. 8–9): 66 n. 82
(viii. 430. 15–16): 91
230 (viii. 438. 15): 122
(viii. 442. 27–444. 9): 121–2, 122
   n. 25
(viii. 444. 8–10): 142
(viii. 444. 10–11): 122
232 (viii. 446. 2): 142
233 (viii. 446. 10–11, 17–18): 219
   n. 266
(viii. 446. 17): 210 n. 224
241 (viii. 454. 8–10): 154 n. 24
246 (viii. 458. 24–460. 2): 52 n. 33
Superf. 1 (viii. 476. 3): 66–7
18 (viii. 486. 7–9): 202 n. 190
31 (viii. 500. 5–10): 167–8, 171 n. 77
34 (viii. 504. 20–506. 7): 51
Vict. 1. 2 (vi. 470. 6–10): 115
(vi. 470. 8–13): 8 n. 28
(vi. 470. 19–20): 115 n. 10
1. 7 (vi. 480. 11): 162 n. 46
(vi. 480. 12–14): 203 n. 195
1. 9 (vi. 482. 13–484. 16): 204 n. 198
1. 24 (vi. 500. 10–22): 161
1. 26–8 (vi. 498. 13–502. 93): 169 n. 70
1. 26 (vi. 498. 13–14): 153 n. 21
(vi. 498. 17–21): 174 n. 88
1. 27 (vi. 500. 14–19): 169
(vi. 500. 19–20): 170
1. 28 (vi. 502. 13–14): 168 n. 69
1. 30 (vi. 504. 14–22): 166 n. 62
1. 33 (vi. 512. 11–12): 105 n. 209
1. 34: 170 n. 73

(vi. 512. 13–19): 45, 167 n. 66
(vi. 512. 14, 17–18): 58
(vi. 512. 17–19): 95 n. 174
(vi. 512. 17–18): 115
1. 35 (vi. 512. 20–522. 16): 120, 123
(vi. 516, 7–9): 169, n. 72
1. 36 (vi. 552. 17–524. 10): 56
2. 60 (vi. 574. 4): 115
2. 64 (vi. 680. 9–16): 115 n. 12
3. 68 (vi. 594. 3–604. 19): 115 n. 11, 120
3. 85 (vi. 636. 11–12): 115 n. 13
4. 90 (vi. 654. 10–11): 115–16
Virg. (viii. 466. 11): 48
(viii. 466. 16): 48
(viii. 468. 8–17): 131 n. 63
(viii. 468. 23–470. 1): 48
VM 1 (i. 572. 5–8): 7 n. 20
2 (i. 572. 21–574. 2): 30 and n. 92
12 (i. 396. 1–5): 124 n. 34
14 (i. 602. 9–11): 120
20 (i. 620. 14–622. 3): 8
22: 64 n. 74
(i. 626. 17–18): 65
(i. 626. 18–628. 4): 66 and n. 81
(i. 628. 3–5): 63
(i. 628. 3–4): 117 n. 15

HOMER
h. Ap. 307–52: 151 n. 15
Il. 2. 266: 65 n. 79
6. 428: III n. 2
12. 205: 65 n. 79
13. 618: 65 n. 79
18. 483: 150 n. 9
19. 59: III n. 2
21. 484–3: III n. 3
24. 605–6: III
   758–9: III n. 2
Od. 8. 375: 65 n. 79
11. 324: III n. 2
15. 478: III n. 2
18. 202: III n. 2
20. 61: III n. 2

HYGINUS
Fab. 274. 10–13: 32 n. 98

KORAN
2: 236

LEVITICUS
15: 19–33: 235

LUCIAN
True Histories 1. 22: 149 n. 5

PARMENIDES
DK 28 B 16: 203 n.197
    17: 5 n.13, 44, 167 n.64
    18: 5 n.13

PHILODEMUS
Lib. 220: 230. n. 14

PHILOGELOS
235: 73 n.105

PINDAR
Pythian 3. 32–4: III

PLATO
Rep. 454 D 2: 31
Tht. 149 B: 35 n.104
Ti. 91 B–D: 70

PLINY
NH 7. 40: 209 n.220
    64–5: 249 n.77
    66: 97 n.181, 188 n.140
    17. 266: 249 n.77
    28. 44: 138 n.85
    77–86: 249 n.77
    77: 237 n.39
    79: 52 n.32

PLUTARCH
Lyc. 14: 47 n.18
Them. 32. 1–2: 152 n.20
Mor. 245 F: 134 n.76
    405 C–D: 246 n. 71
    650 F–651 F: 45 n.11
    700 E: 237 n.39, 249 n.76

SEMONIDES
Iamb. 7. 2–6, 24, 46–7, 58–62: 58 n.49
    90–1: 28 n.85

SOPHOCLES
OT 190–202: III n.2

SORANUS
Gyn. 1. 8: 74 n.108
    1. 16–17: 50

1. 19: 94, 200 n.179
1. 20: 89 n.155
1. 21: 89
1. 22–3: 59 n.51
1. 24: 126 n.39
1. 26: 108 n.226
1. 27: 159
1. 28: 131 n.54
1. 29: 250 n.81
1. 31: 127 n.45
1. 33: 52 n.32
1. 34: 152 n.18
2. 87: 222 n.280
2. 88: 224 n.289
3. 1–5: 110 and n.1
3. 7: 140 n.91
3. 26: 108 n.226
3. 29: 74 n.107

TACITUS
Hist. 5. 6. 5: 249 n.78

TALMUD
Avod Zara 18: 227 n.2
Erubin 100: 232 n.22
Ta'an 22: 227 n.2

THEODORE
Penitential 14. 17: 236

THEOPHRASTUS
CP 3. 7. 12: 231 n.14

THUCYDIDES
Histories 2. 46: 244
    2. 78: 235 n.32

XENOPHON
Const. Lac. 1. 3: 47 n.18
Mem. 2. 2. 4: 152 n.17
Oec. 7. 23: 58 n.49

ZEND-AVESTA
II: 236 n.33